ACTA UNIVERSITATIS STOCKHOLMIENSIS
Stockholm Studies in Social Anthropology N.S. 8

Watermarks

Urban Flooding and Memoryscape in Argentina

Susann Ullberg

For the *inundados* of Santa Fe

List of contents

Acknowledgements i

Chapter 1 | Introduction 1
   Disaster and memory 1
      Marta and *la Inundación* 2
   The relevance of the study: Disasters in focus 4
   Disasters and the study thereof 5
      Conceptualising disaster 6
      The concept of vulnerability 8
      Coping with disaster: Vulnerability and resilience 8
      The problem: Resilience and memory 11
   Further theorising memory 13
      From collective memory to memoryscape 13
      Modes of remembering 15
      Temporalities of remembering 16
      Forms of remembering 18
      Memory and oblivion 19
   Exploring the traces of disaster: Methodological concerns 21
      Composing a field 22
      Translocality 23
      Transtemporality 23
      Mapping the Santafesinian flood memoryscape 24
      Memory and methodology 25
   Reflexion and roadmap 27
      Organisation of the chapters 29

Chapter 2 | Context 33
   Urban life and vulnerability in Argentina 33
   Argentinian politics of regret 33
      Democracy, human rights and the explosion of memory in Argentina 36
      Argentina, the barn of the world, through breakdown and recovery 38
      The Argentinian political map of the 21st century 41
   Santa Fe, generous province and the barn of Argentina 42
      The Santafesinos and their city 45
      A *barrio* in Santa Fe City 51
      Middle- and low-income economies in Santa Fe 54

- Migration, industrialisation and urbanisation 57
- Social stratification and urbanisation 59
- Poverty and social assistance 62
- Among *changarines, cirujas* and *piqueteros* 63
- The urban outskirts and notions of perilous places.. 65
  - The Coastside: The harbour and Alto Verde 67
  - Life on the islands 68
- Urban and suburban vulnerabilities in the past and in the present.. 70

PART ONE 73

Chapter 3 | *La Inundación* and the making of an accidental community of memory 75

- The post-disaster 75
- Narrating *la Inundación* 76
  - Withering weather 76
  - The canonisation of *la Inundación* 77
- Placing memory 81
  - A driveabout in the flood memoryscape 81
    - City of comrades in the Cordial City 82
    - Perilous people and places 83
  - Walking the embankment 84
    - Place and inscription of disaster memories 86
- Writing and performing disaster memories: Testimonials.. 88
  - Telling *la Inundación*.. 88
    - Launching books, making memory 89
    - Writing and performing flood memories from Santa Rosa de Lima.................... 91
- The sounds of disaster 93
  - Charity concerts 94
  - Voices from a tragedy 95
- Visualising *la Inundación*: The documentaries 96
  - *Inundaciones*: Recording and recalling evacuation 97
  - *Inundados* in an ethno-biographical gaze 99
  - *La Inundación* visualised: Photography in private and public 102
- Materialising and placing disaster memories 104
  - Forgotten monuments? 105
  - The Flooded Mothers and the Plaza 29 de Abril square 106
- The making of an accidental community of memory 110

Chapter 4 | Post-disaster protests and the making of a polity of remembering 111

- Disaster politics and politics of memory 111
- Narrating inundation and indignation.. 111
- Victims as activists 116
  - The *inundados* protest movement in the national context 116

- From disaster solidarity to accountability 117
- Morality, memory and mobilisation 119
- Work of memory, work of protest 120
  - Anniversaries: The 29th 121
  - Making memorable places 122
    - Making memory in memorable places 124
  - Inscriptions of blame: Four examples 127
    - I: *Escraches* and street graffiti 127
    - II: Juxtaposed artefacts of memory 131
    - III: Pamphlets and books 133
    - IV: *Documentos* and reports 134
      - Assembling *documentos* 134
      - Presenting results 137
  - Voicing blame 141
  - Visualising blame 142
- On the making of a polity of remembering 145

Chapter 5 | Flood management and the logic of omission 147
- Politics of memory / oblivion in politics 147
  - The official memorial of *la Inundación*? 147
    - Unveiling hidden transcripts 151
  - Bureaucratic practices and cycles of exclusion 154
  - Archives and the materialisation of selective remembering 156
    - Santafesinian archives 157
  - Public infrastructure of memory and oblivion 160
    - Works of development, works of risk 161
    - Works of defence 163
  - Law and memory 168
    - Risk reduction and regulation in Argentina 169
    - Legislation regarding flood management in Santa Fe 170
    - Governmental amnesia and judicial amnesty during *la Inundación* 171
  - The Contingency Plan: Launching a new disaster management policy 174
    - Plans as social artefacts 175
    - The 2005 contingency plan for Santa Fe: Remembering risk 176
      - A plan, form or content? 177
      - Planning for disaster risk reduction 178
    - Flood management and shelved plans 180
- On the political and bureaucratic logic of omission 183

PART TWO 185

Chapter 6 | Urban flooding as mythico-history 187
- Floods in the past 187
  - Commemorating origins 188
  - Myths and legends 190

  The legend of the angry Paraná River 191
  The Catholic and the Atlantis 193
  Flooding and myth 194
 The Great Flood 194
  The quest for artefacts of disaster memory 195
  Disaster on display 196
Los inundados in Santafesinian literature and art 199
 The social category of *inundados* 201
  Los Inundados – the novella 202
  Los Inundados – the movie 205
  Los Inundados – the song 209
  Narrating *los inundados* in images, texts and songs 210
On the mythico-history of flooding in Santa Fe 212

Chapter 7 | Flooding and embedded remembrance in the urban outskirts 213

Remembering recurrent flooding 213
Historicising floods through media reports 214
 Forgetting flooding? 216
Disaster memories in the everyday suburban economy 218
 On the top of the flood embankment 219
  Between *trámites* and *planes* 221
  The extraordinary repair of *la Inundación* 223
 Trading memories at the *Trueque* 225
 Notions of the economy of solidarity 228
Landscape, task and small talk on the Coastside 231
 The rowabout 232
 Absent places 235
 Intergenerational place-making through conversation 237
Safety buildings, risk reminders 240
Commemoration in Alto Verde: Foundation, *fiesta* and flooding 242
On embedded remembrance 245

Chapter 8 | Conclusion 247

Watermarks 247
The Santafesinian flood memoryscape 247
Normalisation of disaster: Adaptation or vulnerability? 251
In sum 255

Sammanfattning på svenska 257

Reference list 259

List of figures 302

Index 303

Acknowledgements

This study has taken more time to complete than I would care to admit. The good thing about this is that along the way I have enjoyed the support of a lot of people. While I carry the sole responsibility for its final result, I am indebted to all of them for their invaluable help.

Many a Santafesino is present in this book. The number of people engaging in my work and supporting me in innumerable ways are simply too many to list here. I am grateful to each and every one of them for sharing their lives and memories with me.

In Sweden, I want to thank everybody at the Department of Social Anthropology at Stockholm University for providing me with various kinds of much-needed support and input at different stages of my work. My supervisor Gudrun Dahl deserves a very special mention. She supported me in getting into graduate school in the first place and has since then sustained me through thick and thin to the end. Her careful reading of my many scattered texts has been invaluable in helping me to pull it all together. Different people have read and commented on the entire manuscript: Annika Rabo helped me to sort things out and shorten down the version that was too long. Helena Wulff was generous enough to take her time to read on very short notice. Her insightful remarks on both major and minor points have improved this study. Johanna Gullberg, Anette Nyqvist, Renita Thedvall, Lotta Björklund-Larsen, Hans Tunestad, Gladis Aguirre, Philip Malmgren, Shahram Khosravi, Hannah Pollack Sarnecki, Johan Lindqvist, Mattias Viktorin and Karin Norman have read and commented on larger or smaller pieces of this study at different crucial points in time. I am grateful to them for their suggestions, encouragement and for being around. I am indebted to the administrative staff at the department who has been helpful to me in many ways. I am deeply thankful to Lina Lorentz, who undertook a meticulous final proofreading of the manuscript before sending it to print.

I am grateful to friends and colleagues at CRISMART and the Department of Security, Strategy and Leadership at the Swedish National Defence College for their support of my anthropological endeavour and approach to the study of crisis. I owe special thanks to Eric Stern and Bengt Sundelius for giving me the opportunity as an undergraduate student to join the research environment at CRISMART many years ago. I am also grateful to Anna Fornstedt Hellberg for keeping me on board as an overdue graduate student and to Fredrik Bynander for sparing me from work this last year. My thanks to all other CRISMARTers, former and present, for having read my work and given me food for thought, other than anthropological. Huge thanks to Stephanie Young for her unfailing belief in my work and for helping me out with the copyediting of the final manuscript. In the context of CRISMART, I want to mention Paul 't Hart at the Utrecht School of Governance and the Australian National University, who read several chapters of the final draft and gave me important feedback. His support throughout the years has meant more to me than he probably realises.

I am indebted to Aud Talle, who unfortunately is no longer with us, for getting this project started in the first place. Åsa Boholm at the School of Global Studies at the University of Gothenburg read an unfinished version of the entire manuscript. Her comments and questions greatly improved the study. Paul Mitchell was kind enough to proofread the entire manuscript. At another crucial point in time, Aisha Renée Malmgren made an excellent translation of one of my articles from Spanish to English, which ended up being one of the chapters. As an affiliate student with the Latin American Institute at Stockholm University I have greatly enjoyed discussions with many a colleague at different seminars and I have received many useful comments from them on my work throughout the years. I am particularly thankful to Mona Rosendahl for her encouragement and support.

In Argentina, I have been sustained by discussions at the Centro de Antropología Social at the Instituto de Desarrollo Económico y Social with many people. Rosana Guber has been a source of inspiration and comfort since my years as an undergraduate and has helped me with this research project from beginning to end. Sergio Visacovsky has been encouraging and generous in his support. Germán Soprano, Graciela Rodríguez and Sabina Frédéric have in different ways supported my work. Within the Santafesinian academic realm I have enjoyed the help from Silvia Montenegro, Gabriel Cocco, Rosario Feuillet, Adriana Collado, Julio Arroyo, Silvia Wolansky, Luís Escobar, Hugo Arrillaga, Teresa Suarez, Carlos Ceruti, Carolina Bravi, Nancy Balza, Pilar Guala, Mariana Rabaini, Alejandro Ramirez and Carlos Paoli. I am particularly grateful to Eugenia Martínez Greco and Alicia Serafino who took time from their own research to assist me in fieldwork. Their contribution and friendship was much more than I could ever have asked for! At the Instituto de Geografía at the Universidad de Buenos Aires, I am particularly indebted to Claudia Natenzon, Ani Murgida and Jesica Viand for their interest in my work.

In June 2004, I spent two weeks as a guest graduate student at the research centre Disaster Studies at Wageningen Universiteit. I am grateful to Thea Hilhorst for having me and to the Swedish Research Council for Environment, Agricultural Sciences and Spatial Planning for funding this stay. In August that same year, I attended the EASA Summer School in Vienna. There I enjoyed fruitful conversations with fellow graduate students and with senior scholars on contemporary anthropology and on my own initial ideas. My thanks to Helena Wulff, Thomas Filitz, Nicolas Argenti and in particular to Eduardo Archetti, who left us much too soon, but who is vividly remembered. In 2008, I spent four months at the University of Florida as a guest scholar at the Department of Anthropology and the Center for Latin American Studies. I am indebted to Tony Oliver-Smith for inviting me. He and his family made the time in Gainesville a particularly pleasant stay for me and my family. Wilma Hagan and her family were outstandingly generous to us during and after our stay. I am grateful also to Ana Margheritis, Scott Catey and Wanda Carter. I thank the Swedish Foundation for International Cooperation in Research and Higher Education for funding this stimulating exchange. Throughout these years, I have been sustained by multidisciplinary conversations within the Disaster, Conflict and Social Crisis Research Network of the European Sociological Association and more recently in the environment of the Centre for Natural Disaster Science in Sweden.

I am indebted to Chachi Bildt for connecting me with María Rosa Genevois who opened her home and heart to me and to Maria Belén Alvarez Rivera for unfailing friendship and many a *mate*. In regards to this book, I am grateful to Barbara Beattie for correcting the entire manuscript and enhancing the text, to Christer Engström for taking time to make the cover design and to Roberto Robuffo for drawing the maps.

The research has generously been funded by Sarec at the Swedish International Development Cooperation Agency and the Swedish Emergency Management Agency, later the Swedish Civil Contingencies Agency. It has also been supported by research and travel grants from the Department of Social Anthropology and the Institute for Latin American Studies at Stockholm University; the Emil and Lydia Kinander Foundation; the Helge Ax:son Johnsson Foundation; and the Swedish Society for Geography and Anthropology. The completion of the thesis was made possible by way of support from the strategic research area Security and Emergency Management in the Swedish Government Bill 2008/09:50.

Last but not least, my deepest gratitude goes to family and friends in Sweden, Argentina and elsewhere for always supporting my choices and being there for me. To Jazbel and Mateo for being the centre of my universe. To Javier *por el aguante* and for walking this road with me.

Stockholm, April 2013
Susann Ullberg

Chapter 1 | Introduction

Disaster and memory

On April 29th, 2003, a disastrous flood occurred in the Argentinian city of Santa Fe. It came to be called simply "*la Inundación*" (the Flood) by the city's inhabitants. Twenty-three people perished during the emergency. Another hundred people died due to indirect consequences of the disaster in the following months and years. Around 130 000 inhabitants had to evacuate for weeks and months, some even for years. Hundreds of these families had no home at all to return to. The disaster management capacities of local authorities were largely surpassed. In general, the Santafesinos were shocked by this unexpected catastrophe. Judging from the reactions, the flood was like a bolt from the blue. However, this was far from the first flood to strike the city. Because it is situated between the Paraná and Salado rivers, flooding has in fact been part of the city's local history since the time of the settlement of the place by Spanish conquerors in the 16th century. Since the mid-17th century, at least 30 extraordinary floods have affected Santa Fe.

As events, disasters are extraordinary and totalising, "[s]weeping across every aspect of human life" (Oliver-Smith 2002:24). Because of this, one would expect such events to be memorable and shape ideas and practices on how to deal with them successfully. In light of the case of Santa Fe, the empirical question arises whether this is always the case. In the multidisciplinary field of disaster studies, the relation between social experience and action in the context of recurrent disasters is often thought of in terms of adaptation. The overall purpose of the present investigation is to problematise this theoretical assumption from an anthropological perspective. In order to achieve this, the aim of the study is to understand the role of memory in disaster preparedness. Taking Santa Fe City as a case in point, this study explores ethnographically how people in different urban settings engaged with their flooding past through processes of remembering and forgetting, constituting what I call an urban flood memoryscape. Based on translocal and transtemporal ethnographic fieldwork in this city in the years 2004-2011 and drawing on anthropological and sociological theories of memory, the study enables an understanding of how this memoryscape is configured in time and space. The ethnography at hand is a contribution to the anthropology of memory as much as to disaster anthropology, and engages in multidisciplinary discussions about disaster vulnerability and resilience.

Marta and *la Inundación*

Marta was a woman in her fifties who lived in the same *barrio* (neighbourhood) in Santa Fe as I did during my fieldwork in the city in 2005. This neighbourhood, Barrio Roma,[1] was located on the Westside of the city. Marta was born there in the early 1950s and she had lived there her entire life, also after she got married. Prior to the 2003 disaster, she had never been affected by flooding despite living next to the flood-prone neighbourhoods in the outskirts on the Westside. Barrio Roma, was located on higher ground and was protected by the railway embankment. She told me that as a girl she used to go to the railway embankment to watch the Salado River flood the poor on the other side of the railway.

When I first met her in 2004 she was trying to get back on her feet after the 2003 disaster. She had been divorced for many years, living with her two teenage sons and working as a secretary at a law firm. *La Inundación*, as this particular disaster was remembered and referred to by most people in Santa Fe, had been the worst experience of her life, she said. On April 29th, when the family realised that the water was going to invade their home, they first put a few things on the table, then placed them on the top of the wardrobes and finally had to evacuate to the roof of the house. Finally, they evacuated to an aunt's home in the city centre. After two weeks, Marta returned to the house. She could not believe what she saw! The entire *barrio* was in ruins and her home was unrecognisable. The furniture, the books, the photos; it was all ruined, she told me. What had been left inside the house had been submerged in the floodwater, while the things stored on the roof were soaked by rain. Even before the flooding, the house lacked maintenance and had been in a bad shape. After her divorce, Marta had never been able to pay for having work done on the house. Due to the flooding, the house was at that point completely ruined. Martha knew it was going to take years of work to fix the house and replace the furniture. Being a single mother with a secretary's salary and two nearly grown-up children to support, the outlook was devastating, even with the economic compensation that the provincial government granted to the victims of the disaster. It was simply too little money, according to Marta. To make matters worse, she had no home insurance for several years, having been forced to cut her expenses to the bone. The experience of *la Inundación* in those conditions pushed her into deep depression for several months. For several years she had not been able to pay for her health insurance which would have allowed her to pay for therapy. Because of this, Marta ended up seeking help from one of the psychologists appointed by the provincial government, who attended flood victims for free. Marta did not feel this was of much help to her though.

When I met her again in the years to follow, she told me she was feeling better. She had been able to pay for the repair of parts of the house, which made her feel happy and sad at the same time because it reminded her of everything she had lost. The memories of the flooding could not be erased with paint or a pair of new chairs. She had also engaged in the protest movement that was

---

[1] The formal name of this neighbourhood was "Roma" but people generally called it "Barrio Roma." This was common also when referring to other neighbourhoods.

active in the city streets and squares, claiming that the government officials should be tried in court for their responsibility in the disaster, and demanding major economic compensation. This engagement, she told me, was painful because neither the government, nor the judges had responded to any of their demands. Yet the protests she participated in were at the same time rewarding because she had met so many other people with whom she shared the experience of being flood victims; of being *inundados*.

When I first arrived in the city in July 2004, and for the rest of my fieldwork, I was told countless stories similar to Marta's. *La Inundación* was on everybody's lips, conveyed in narratives, images, practices and monuments. The process of remembering, or memory-work (Irwin-Zarecka 1994; Ingold et al. 1996:226), of this particular disaster was unprecedented in Santa Fe City, casting a shadow of oblivion over most other past floods in the city. While Marta's memories of *la Inundación* and those of the other *inundados* in 2003 were omnipresent in Santa Fe in the 2000s, other flood victims' memories of other disastrous past floods were largely absent in what I call the urban flood memoryscape. As I ethnographically explored social remembering around flooding in many different social and institutional contexts in the city throughout my fieldwork, I came to realise that memory was heterogeneous and unevenly distributed in this urban community. The concept of memoryscape, which I shall define and discuss in the following pages, conveys this particular configuration of selective and stratified remembering and forgetting in Santa Fe.

How can we understand this phenomenon and what are the effects of such a selective process? How does memory mediate past disaster experiences and shape notions of disaster preparedness? These are the questions that this study sets out to answer by exploring how past floods have been socially remembered and forgotten in different urban contexts in Santa Fe. The present inquiry is an ethnography of how the recurrent problem of flooding in this city is remembered and forgotten in different social and institutional settings at the turn of the 21st century. The investigation is at the same time a social history of flooding in Santa Fe, even if I have no claims of being exhaustive in this sense. *La Inundación* of 2003 plays a key role in this account, as we shall see particularly in Part One of the book, yet it is not the only flood remembered as will become clear particularly in Part Two. The conspicuousness of memories of *la Inundación* in this study is not a construction by the hand of the ethnographer, but a consequence of its salience in the memoryscape explored. In Santa Fe, when people talked about "*la Inundación*," they referred to the 2003 flood, not just any of the many past floods. Not knowing the history of the city, one could easily get the impression that that there had only been one flood in the past, when it was in fact the last flood of many to strike Santa Fe. Given this salience, I use the event narratively as a looking glass, through which I explore the processes of remembering and forgetting. This was also the disaster through which many people in Santa Fe remembered their flooding past. For the rest of this introductory chapter, I shall outline the theoretical and methodological framework that guides my analysis.

The relevance of the study: Disasters in focus

Risk reduction and disaster management are increasingly on governmental agendas worldwide. Global changes in environmental patterns have large ecological and social effects, and present a major challenge to humanity at large, but in particular to political decision makers at macro and micro levels. In an international perspective, the number of natural disasters, and especially weather-related catastrophes, has more than doubled since the 1980s (Munich Re 2012). Extreme events related to processes of climate change not only occur more frequently nowadays, but have in some cases also intensified (Intergovernmental Panel on Climate Change 2012). Their impact is increasingly severe, due to processes of societal vulnerability. Global statistics show that while mortality rates due to disasters have decreased worldwide, the economic losses, as direct consequence of disasters, have increased at large, affecting both national budgets and low-income households (United Nations International Strategy for Disaster Reduction 2012; Munich Re 2012). Despite regional variations, the shadows of catastrophe loom large on the recovery of local economies, politics and social life, sometimes for years.

Recent major catastrophes such as the earthquake in Haiti and the floods in Pakistan (both 2010), the Horn of Africa Crisis (2011-2012), the typhoons in China and the Philippines (2012), the floods in India, Sudan and North Korea (all 2012) and the earthquakes in Iran (2012) show how disaster risk and poverty are closely interlinked. Many of the so-called natural disasters that occur are, rather than natural, related to conditions of vulnerability as the result of poverty, social inequality, political instability, and environmental degradation found in many low-income countries (Maskrey 1989; Oliver-Smith 1994; Wisner et al. 2004; Jones and Murphy 2009; Wisner, Gaillard, and Kelman 2011a). Disasters occur in response to skewed development and contribute to jeopardising development gains. Disaster events and development processes are therefore closely interrelated (M. B. Anderson 1994). Repeated exposure to disasters may lead to a spiral of degradation of the social, economic and political conditions for people who already struggle with poverty-related problems (Beckman 2006; Segnestam 2009). Paradoxically, paths of development can produce unintended consequences (Ferguson 1990; Escobar 1994; Heijmans 2004; Tsing 2011). Recent disasters in high-income countries such as the earthquake, tsunami and nuclear disaster in Japan in 2011 reflect this situation (cf. Numazaki 2012:35). Macro-economic growth and the development of complex systems of interdependency at global level can also produce risk and vulnerability (Beck 1992; Giddens 2003; Wisner et al. 2004; Wisner, Gaillard, and Kelman 2011a). While on the one hand, climate change, environmental degradation and market competition endanger rural livelihoods (Beckman, ibid.; Christoplos et al. 2010), on the other hand, increasing urbanisation, prompted by economic factors, also promotes vulnerability. Urban so-called informal settlements and inner city slums with unstable living conditions flourish in ravines, on steep slopes, along flood plains or adjacent to noxious industrial areas or dangerous high traffic areas. Concentration of people in risk areas and unsafe buildings, reduction in the capacity of households to recover economically from the impact of a misfortune, and continued environmental degradation are only a few examples of how development, or the lack thereof, can lead to disaster. Given the impact of disasters on people's lives, and the societal losses resulting from such events, there is a need to expand the knowledge about their causes and effects in order to enhance mitigation.

Disasters and the study thereof

In popular views, disasters are often considered to be the work of nature or the result of unfortunate coincidences. Many languages have variations of the words crisis, catastrophe and disaster. Within the social sciences, the terms crisis, disaster, emergency, contingency, calamity and catastrophe are sometimes used synonymously, which makes it a challenge to come up with a concept that can be productively used in analysis. This lack of common terms and definitions of terms has long preoccupied scholars in these fields (Quarantelli 1998; Perry 2007; Quarantelli, Lagadec, and Boin 2007; Boin and 't Hart 2007). In this work, my starting point is the common denominator of all the above-quoted terms, namely that they convey a sense of emergency and a rupture of continuity in social life. Rather than entering the above-mentioned discussion, my quest is to understand how people engage with and make sense of such moments, regardless of the type of disruptive event. For the sake of coherence, I shall nevertheless apply the term disaster to analyse the ethnographic case at hand.

Within the social sciences, disasters and crises have been the topics of research most prominently by sociology, geography and political science.[2] Social anthropology in general has historically been rather modest in focusing analytically on crises and disasters as social phenomena, in spite of the subject's holistic embrace of society. As has been pointed out (Torry et al. 1979; Oliver-Smith and Hoffman 2002), there are references to calamities and crises in classical ethnographic literature, but they tend to be scattered and undeveloped, only because the anthropologist was researching other issues among the people who were hit by the crisis. A possible reason for the historical scarcity of ethnography of crises and disasters is the traditional focus of the discipline on "states of equilibrium" or "everyday life." For a long time, this focus precluded more elaborated interest in the disruptions of the "normal" flow of social life.[3] The anthropological interest in disasters continued to be rather marginal, with the exception of the work by Oliver-Smith (1977a; 1977b; 1979a; 1979b; 1986) and Torry (1973; 1978; 1978). In the 21st century, the field of disaster anthropology has been grow-

---

[2] Over time, certain lines of division have emerged between "disaster studies" and "crisis studies," even if they have sometimes overlapped. The first field has referred to studies in geography and sociology, while the latter has referred to political science and the study of international relations and public administration. Crises and disasters have been analysed also within the disciplines of psychology, social psychology, history and economics.
[3] In the classical anthropological literature, crises and disasters are rather mentioned in passing (cf. Firth 1936; Evans-Pritchard 1956; V. W. Turner 1967, 1972, 1975, 1995; Bohannan och Bohannan 1968).

ing quickly however. Visacovsky (2011) has argued that this has to do with the proper empirical expansion of the discipline and increased transdisciplinary communication, as much as with the understanding that classical anthropological problems can be found in contemporary societies. I suggest that other contributing factors are the increasing instant media attention to disasters worldwide and the political urge to find solutions to such costly events. In addition, it seems that many anthropologists become acutely aware of disasters as fields of study and action when a major catastrophe strikes their own country or city.[4] Whatever the reasons are, at the turn of the 21st century, disaster anthropology is growing fast.[5]

Conceptualising disaster

Disasters put societies to the test. Material resources, organisational capacities, social and cultural capital are forced to limits in unexpected or unbearable ways. A notion of untenability is inherent in any available definition of the concept of disaster. Throughout the years the concept has earned numerous definitions, which all share a focus on the extraordinary character of a disaster; a temporally circumscribed disruption of an established social order (Vigh 2008). In this study I draw on the definition by Oliver-Smith and Hoffman who state that a disaster is "a process/event combining a potentially destructive agent/force from the natural, modified or built environment and a population in a socially and economically produced condition of vulnerability, resulting in a perceived disruption of the customary relative satisfactions of individual and social needs for physical survival, social order, and meaning" (2002:4).

It might seem contradictory to define disaster both as a process and an event. I nevertheless agree with Oliver-Smith and Hoffman (ibid.) that both these aspects must be included in the definition. When we conceptualise disasters as extraordinary and disruptive events, there is an underlying and unexamined structural-functionalist assumption that generally society and social life are well-functioning systems of normality (Hewitt 1998). This assumption of social equilibrium has been questioned for being misleading. Drawing on political ecological perspectives, the critics argue that it is precisely the "normal" historical processes that cause risk and exposure to hazards. Disasters are then the result of unequal social, economic and political conditions, rather than extraordinary and unexpected bolts from the blue (Hewitt 1983; Wisner et al. 2004; Bankoff,

---

[4] This became clear for example in the wake of the Katrina hurricane in the USA in 2005 and after the East Japan Disaster in 2011, when numerous anthropology (and other social science) conference sessions were organised, special issues in anthropological journals and research web sites published (see for example "Understanding Katrina: Perspectives from the Social Sciences" 2013; "An STS Forum on Fukushima" 2013; "American Anthropological Association Katrina Resources — SSRC" 2013).

[5] For interesting work in this vein see for example (Das 1996. 2001; Oliver-Smith and Hoffman 1999; Fortun 2001; Petryna 2002; Hoffman and Oliver-Smith 2002; Fassin and Vasquez 2005; Barrios 2005; Ruano Gómez 2005; Revet 2007, 2013; Ivarsson 2007; Langumier 2008; Camargo da Silva 2009; Le Menestrel and Henry 2010; Lovell, Bordreuil, and Adams 2010; Button 2010; Lovell 2011; F. Hastrup 2011; Sather-Wagstaff 2011; S. Visacovsky 2011; Zenobi 2011; Benadusi et al. 2011; Harms 2012).

Frerks, and Hilhorst 2004; Wisner, Gaillard, and Kelman 2011a). A processual understanding of disasters and crises can also be found in the aforementioned theories of risk and uncertainty (Beck 1992; Giddens 2003; Z. Bauman 2005). While the political ecological approach emphasises the unequal production and distribution of risk within and between societies and communities, risk theories tend to neglect aspects of social stratification and relations of power. In my view, this makes risk theories flawed and not applicable to grasp fundamental questions of cause and effect when a disaster occurs. As this study will show, we are indeed not all in the same boat when the worst happens.

Now, even if disasters can be seen as the outcomes of a process, they can simultaneously be conceptualised as events. They are situations that reconfigure on-going processes and thus change the course of things in one way or another after they have occurred. Veena Das labels such temporal and spatial moments as "critical events," by which she refers to situations that produce new modes of action and redefine existing social categories (Das 1996). The lived experience of a disaster is often that of an "event" rather than a "process." People involved in and affected by a disaster interpret it as a liminal moment of stress and loss that disrupts everyday life. While plenty of ethnographic research has shown that uncertainty and insecurity can be the normal state of things, such as in so-called high reliability organisations[6] (Gusterson 1998; Perin 2004) and certainly often in everyday life under poverty and armed conflict (Scheper-Hughes 1993; Scheper-Hughes 2008; Vigh 2008; Finnström 2008; Höjdestrand 2009; Gren 2009), things can always become worse. When people living in poverty experience an earthquake, like that in Haiti in 2010, or an industrial disaster, like that in Bhopal in 1984 or in Chernobyl in 1986, this adds yet another burden to their already strained lives. In many cases, we need to see the crisis **as** the context rather than **in** the context (Vigh 2008). Yet disaster victims, no matter where they are (Hoffman 1999) experience disasters as "a temporary abnormality linked to a particular event," to borrow the words from Scheper Hughes (2008:36). No matter if the misfortune is small or big, individual or collective, people who experience them tend to single out and identify the harsh events that compose their lives, when they think and talk about it. The difference resides in where the baseline is. What constitutes a disaster or a crisis in one cultural context may not be the case in another. The degree of vulnerability also varies with the particular context, which determines the impact of a particular hazard. Hence, in this study, I analyse disaster both as an event that disrupts everyday life and as a historically embedded process that has a before and an afterlife. Such an understanding makes it relevant to look into the social processes of remembering and forgetting, which are constitutive to both process and event.

---

[6] So-called high reliability organisations refer to organisations that successfully avoid catastrophes in an environment where accidents would be expected due to risk factors and complexity, such as nuclear power plants for example.

The concept of vulnerability

Another concept that is central to the understanding of disaster as a process/event is that of "vulnerability." This concept too has multiple uses in the field of disaster studies (Weichselgartner 2001; Jacobs 2005; Manyena 2006; Oliver-Smith 2009). Basically it refers to those conditions that expose a local population to a given hazard. Wisner et al. (2004) have developed what they call the "pressure and release model" to analyse how societal vulnerability is produced. This model holds that vulnerability is produced through a causal chain of root causes, dynamic pressures and unsafe conditions, which, combined with a hazard, generate a disaster. Wilches-Chaux (1989) has differentiated between 11 types of vulnerability, namely physical, economic, social, political, technical, ideological, cultural, educational, ecological, institutional and natural. To pinpoint which factors determine the type and degree of vulnerability is at once simple and complex, however. In the words of Bankoff and Hilhorst: "At one level, the answer [to this question] is a straightforward one about poverty, resource depletion and marginalisation; at another level, it is about the diversity of risks generated by the interplay between local and global processes and coping with them on a daily basis" (2004:1). Hence, some countries in the world are more vulnerable than others. In the same way, within countries, some regions or populations are more vulnerable than others. Beckman (2006) has shown that while governmental institutions may be resilient to disaster, local communities can at the same time find themselves in conditions of vulnerability. Heterogeneity is valid also for a local community in which some neighbourhoods, households and individuals may be more vulnerable than others. Anthropologists have emphasised through ethnographic research (Oliver-Smith 1996) that social stratification within a local community promotes unequal distribution of risk and allocation of resources between the community members. Yet, vulnerability is not a fixed feature of social groups or categories, but rather given by the existing life conditions in a particular context. Such conditions vary, not only between members in a community, but also over time (Wisner et al. 2004:15).

For the case of recurrent disastrous flooding in Santa Fe City and how people have coped with it, varying levels of vulnerability are a vital part of the explanation, as has been shown by Argentinian scholars (Gentile 1994; Natenzon 1998; Herzer et al. 2000; Herzer et al. 2002; Celis and Herzer 2003; Natenzon 2003; Viand 2009; Herzer and Arrillaga 2009). This was confirmed to me in the course of my fieldwork in the different urban contexts where I carried out my fieldwork, as will be outlined in Chapter Two.

Coping with disaster: Vulnerability and resilience

The concept of vulnerability is today well established at the centre stage in understanding why and how so-called natural disasters occur. The question of how people and institutions cope and survive such events has not until recently received as much attention in the field of disaster studies. The concept of "resilience" changed this trend. "*Resilio*" is originally a Latin verb which means to leap or spring back, recoil, and rebound or shrink back again. A well-established concept in psychiatry, physics and ecological sciences respectively,[7] it has also become a leading concept in the academic field of disaster studies and in the policy world of risk reduction and disaster and crisis management (Pelling 2003; United Nations International Strategy for Disaster Reduction 2005; Ronan and Johnston 2005; Vale and Campanella 2005; Paton and Johnston 2006; Comfort, Boin, and Demchak 2010; Rajib Shaw and Sharma 2011; Chandra 2011; Aldrich 2012). According to some scholars, a discursive shift took place in the wake of the Hurricane Katrina in 2005. The goal of securing "disaster resistant communities" by reducing vulnerability and risk, was changed to a striving for creating "resilient communities," able to deal with disasters that would inevitably occur (McEntire et al. 2002; de Bruijne, Boin, and van Eeten 2010:28).

In the multidisciplinary field of disaster studies, much of the current use of the resilience concept stems from the ecological sciences. Ecological resilience theory builds on the conceptualisation of society and environment as "social-ecological" and "complex adaptive systems" (Folke 2010). Resilience theory articulates with theories on collective and organisational learning in the wake of crises[8] as both apply the notion of adaptation to explain how communities cope with such events (Berkes and Folke 2000; Folke et al. 2005; Brower et al. 2009; Barthel, Sörlin, and Ljungqvist 2010; Barthel, Folke, and Colding 2010; Cundill 2010; March 2010; Gerlak and Heikkila 2011). Both resilience theory and theories of collective and organisational learning resonate in this sense with earlier anthropological theories of adaptation, as propounded by cultural ecologists (Steward 1955; White 2007), ecological anthropologists (R. Rappaport 1971, 1984) and cultural materialists (M. Harris 1979). These approaches to the study of societies under stress were however harshly criticised within anthropology for reducing human life to calories, for focusing too much on systemic equilibrium (Vayda and McCay 1975) and for being homeostatic and unable to explain social change (Torry et al. 1979). As a result, environmental anthropology in the 1990s went "from pigs to policies" (Townsend 2009) and to a more political-ecological take on the relation between culture and nature. Contemporary resilience theory has been criticised for not being able to account for the social, political and economic inequalities found within any social-ecological system (Nadasdy 2007; Hornborg 2009).

Returning to the realm of disaster studies, similar critique can be addressed to how the resilience concept is used in this field. In this context, resilience is conceptualised broadly as the capacity to adjust to and to recover from a crisis. Most definitions include the notion of "adaptability" (Comfort 1994; Handmer and Dovers 1996; Klein, Nicholls, and Thomalla 2003; Kendra and Wachtendorf 2003). Adaptability is defined as "the capacity to adapt existing resources and skills to new situations and operating conditions" (L. Comfort

---

[7] A valuable overview and genealogy of the resilience concept in the field of disaster studies has been written by Manyena (2006).
[8] One of the main tenets of ecological resilience theory is that social-ecological systems in stress develop "communities-of-practice," which enhance resilience to pressure and uncertainty through processes of adaptive management (Barthel, Folke and Colding 2010:256).

1999: 21) or "the ability to adjust to 'normal' or anticipated stresses and to adapt to sudden shocks and extraordinary demands" (Tierney 2003:2). Bankoff, in his study of disaster history in the Philippines (Bankoff 2002), argues for the notion of "cultures of disaster" to convey how this society has "come to terms with hazard in such a way that disasters are not regarded as abnormal situations but as quite the reverse, as a constant feature of life. This [is] cultural adaptation whereby threat has become an integral part of the daily human experience, [and] where it has become so 'normalised' in a sense" (ibid.: 153). This latter stance rings anthropologically familiar to the thesis of the "culture of poverty" (O. Lewis 1959, 1966), harshly criticised for being both reductionist and ethnocentric.[9]

Hence, the current use of the concept "adaptability" and "adaptation" in disaster studies needs to be problematised because of their inherent notion of recovery which "unintentionally imply a return to normalcy after disaster – instead of a reduction of future vulnerability" (McEntire et al. 2002:270). Put otherwise: "[R]eferences to restoration of normality or normality may be of little use if 'normal' was the situation of vulnerability for some of the population now affected" (Wisner, Gaillard, and Kelman 2011b:31).

Critique has been raised against resilience theory for being "curiously devoid of people" (F. Hastrup 2009:115). This critique, with which I agree, refers to the way an abstract entity such as "a system" or "a community" is ascribed agency in terms of coping capacity, instead of conceiving of such capacities to be produced by way of social, economic and political relations. In the field of disaster scholarship and policymaking,[10] there is a current advocacy for "local participation" in order to achieve resilient communities (cf. Revet 2013). This echoes the "reconstruction from below" paradigm emerging within parts of the post-conflict development interventions in the 21st century (Hilhorst, Christoplos, and Van Der Harr 2010). In these fields of policy and research, a rather axiomatic understanding of what a community is prevails. The notion of community is rarely problematised, but often based on "overly simplistic ideas of communities as homogeneous, ignoring processes of inequality and exclusion within communities" (ibid.: 1109). It is presumed to stand for a small-scale close-knit social body, more often than not thought of as something inherently good, especially in relation to larger scales of social organisations such as the region or the nation. This is a view that can be traced to early sociological theories about so-called traditional and modern societies (Tönnies 1887; Durkheim 2001 [1912]). Amit (2002) has pointed out that this concept is so over-used, both in academic and everyday language, that it can easily be dismissed as a truism. According to Brint (2001), the community concept has in fact increasingly been abandoned and alternative concepts such as "social network" or "social capital" have instead been proposed. However, I do not think we solve the problem of definitions or lack of

---

[9] For an excellent overview and analysis of Lewis's work on the culture of poverty, its background and theoretical as well as policy implications, see Bourgois (2001).
[10] It is perhaps noteworthy that in the policy field of risk reduction and disaster management, the concept of resilient communities is currently, if not a buzzword (Dahl 2001), a dominant paradigm. Established in one of the global key policy documents, the so-called Hyogo Framework for Action (United Nations International Strategy for Disaster Reduction 2005), it is perhaps not surprising to find 5,370,000 hits on "community resilience" by a quick Google search in September 2012.

explanatory power by changing one problematic concept for another equally ambiguous. In fact, as we shall see, I use the concept myself in this study (in particular in Chapter Three). My critique is that a community should not be presumed to be a homogeneous phenomenon, nor should it be normatively used. If we are to have any analytical use of the concept, we need to unpack it empirically, taking into critical account the social, cultural, political and economic aspects that shape, make possible and limit people's sharing and sense of belonging. I thus think of "community" following Amit (2002, 2012) as a "modality of sociation." This refers to a dynamic social process that takes place in daily and localised face-to-face relations and in symbolic interaction on different social scales. This approach enables us to explore how resilience is fundamentally a human agentive capacity rather than a systemic property (Scheper-Hughes 2008; Gren 2009; F. Hastrup 2011).

The problem: Resilience and memory

Returning now to the research problem at hand; how is experience from critical events transformed to cultural meanings of recurrent disaster? In order to grasp this we need to look into the processes that mediate such experiences, that is, remembering and forgetting. In the multidisciplinary field of disaster studies, the role of memory has been studied mainly from a psychological perspective (Wright 1993; Christianson and Engelberg 1999; Enander 2006). This research in general lacks theorising around the social aspects of memory although an exception can be found in resilience theory, which takes a systemic approach to memory. Scholars working in this vein have argued that collective memory is of fundamental importance in social-ecological systems for learning from stress and adapting to strain (Berkes, Colding, and Folke 2002; Barthel, Folke, and Colding 2010; Barthel, Sörlin, and Ljungqvist 2010). From this point of view, resilience in post-disaster social-ecological systems are fostered through "social-ecological memory" (Barthel, Sörlin, and Ljungqvist 2010:364-70) or the "memorialisation mechanism" (Tidball et al. 2010:594).

In line with other scholars (Harms 2012) I find the "social-ecological memory model" problematic from a social theory perspective. For one, it conceives of collective memory as a cognitive faculty of communities. This in itself is a contradiction in terms since it is people who have cognition and not communities. Yet even from the point of view of psychology, some scholars would categorise such an understanding as naïve (Kirmayer 1996). While the general and specific knowledge that we use to navigate in the world includes both cognitive and embodied memory, Freudian insights have served to underscore the fragility and the relative endurance of [individual] cognitive memory (ibid.). While the social-ecological memory model recognises the selective nature of memory, this feature is seen as distortions (Barthel, Folke, and Colding 2010:256) or maladaptations (Barthel, Sörlin, and Ljungqvist 2010:396). According to this view, such flaws are due to emotional processes, while it is held that traumatic memories from events such as environmental crises and natural disasters are nevertheless likely to be remembered correctly (Barthel, Folke, and Colding 2010). This stance reflects not only a deterministic functionalist understanding of memory, but also one that has been questioned in the field of trauma studies for ignoring the very context of remembering (Kirmayer 1996). Furthermore, such reasoning implies that there are true and false memories, an analytical dichotomy that from the view of social memory has been defined as a sterile debate in the first place. In the words of Fentress and Wickham, "The issue of whether or not a given memory is true is interesting only in so far as it sheds light on how memory itself works" (1992:xi). Another problem with this model is that memory is merely seen as a function serving the reproduction of the system. For resilience theorists, memory merely reproduces knowledge. This functionalist understanding stems from the early thinkers in the sociology of memory, most notably that of the French sociologist, Maurice Halbwachs (1941, 1980). In contemporary resilience theory, the functionalist stance is reflected in the choice of metaphors, likening memory to a library for instance (Barthel, Folke, and Colding 2010). This trope is based on an understanding of memory as an archive, a repository of experience, which is then transferrable to and between people and organisations. Such a storage model of memory has however been questioned in anthropology for ignoring social agency and the political struggles involved in (re)constructing the experience of the past (Trouillot 1995:14-16). Much of what we remember from the past is in fact a product of present concerns as much as preoccupations with the future, rather than merely being shaped by the past (Halbwachs ibid.).

As we shall see in what follows, the anthropology and sociology of memory is well established within the multidisciplinary field of memory studies. Yet its impact on the fields of disaster and environmental studies has overall been rather limited. A recent exception to this is the anthropological research, which has begun to explore the intersection between disaster and memory (Revet 2007, 2011; Langumier 2008; Camargo da Silva 2009; Sather-Wagstaff 2011; F. Hastrup 2011; Zenobi 2011; Harms 2012). There are several points of connection between these ethnographic studies and the one at hand, yet there are also a number of important differences. Most of the studies referred to above focus on the process of reconstruction from singular disasters, while this study deals with a history of many recurrent disasters. One can assume that the extraordinariness and singularity of a disaster shapes the ways in which such events are ascribed meaning in particular manner – there is no prior experience or memory to articulate new experiences and memories. Consequently, these studies approach disaster memory mainly in terms of commemoration of those singular disasters as one of the many ways in which people recover and make meaning of tragedy through narration, ritual, and monuments. My study, in contrast, explores a social world in which disasters are recurrent. This is thus a distinct analytical point of departure, similar to the research carried out by Harms (ibid.) in the Ganges delta between India and Bangladesh. Also, most of these studies focus on one or a few modes and forms of disaster memory. In this inquiry I propose a comprehensive analytical framework to scrutinise the heterogeneity and multiple scales involved in remembering and forgetting recurrent disastrous flooding. This framework includes multiple and interactive modes, temporalities and forms of remembering. The present ethnography thus contributes to an incipient line of research, making it theoretically relevant to scholars from many disciplines, ranging from the anthropology of memory to the multidisciplinary field of disaster studies.

Further theorising memory

The capability to remember and forget is a human feature that has long puzzled thinkers. While memory has been a topic for thinkers since the time of the Greek philosophers, it is nevertheless often alleged that a "memory turn" from the 1960s onwards has taken place on a global scale through an unprecedented societal engagement with the past of collective experiences (Connerton 1989, 2009; Huyssen 2003). This memory turn involves both a discourse on memory in society (Antze and Lambek 1996; Hodgkin and Radstone 2003a) and numerous social practices by which people engage more actively than ever with their past. Among the latter are practices ranging from family genealogy and nostalgic home décor, to spontaneous commemorations and truth commissions in the wake of violent pasts. As we shall see in the next chapter, Argentina is indeed a case in point in this latter sense.

In this study I analyse processes of urban disaster memory in several different ethnographic contexts. Each context has its particular dynamics and therefore constitutes a particular case of remembering and forgetting, even if they are interrelated and part of a larger whole. It is this larger whole that I call a memoryscape. In what follows I shall develop the theoretical underpinnings of this concept which encompasses all cases in the study.

From collective memory to memoryscape

"The past is foreign country: they do things differently there" is an often quoted line in the study of memory.[11] The line refers essentially to the idea that the past is different from the present, yet the two are intrinsically connected in one way or another (cf. Lowenthal 1985; Ingold et al. 1996). The past is mediated by memory. In common talk this is mostly thought of as an individual, personal and mental feature (cf. Fentress and Wickham 1992:8-16) and the object of study for psychologists, psychoanalysts and neuroscientists. Yet it is by now well established that memory is also a social phenomenon. What the past means to people and the making of society has long been an anthropological concern (Munn 1992; Ingold et al. 1996). Maurice Halbwachs (1941, 1980) is generally credited with coining the concept of "collective memory." Although many scholars still use this same term, several other terms have been developed throughout the years to better conceptualise this phenomenon.[12] Some scholars have opted for the term "social memory" to underscore that memory is made in social interaction (Fen-

---

[11] The original quote is the opening line in the novel *The Go-Between* (Hartley 1953).
[12] For a comprehensive overview of the anthropological and sociological study of memory, see (Climo and Cattell 2002; Olick, Vinitzky-Seroussi, and Levy 2011).

tress and Wickham 1992) while others have preferred "cultural memory" to underscore how memory is imbued with cultural meaning (Sturken 1997, 2007; Assmann 2011b). The term social or collective "remembering" has also been used in order to emphasise the processual and non-fixed character of this phenomenon (Middleton and Edwards 1990; Cole 2001; Argenti 2007; Argenti and Schramm 2012). "Memory-work" as a term also underscores that remembering is a social process (Küchler 1993; Irwin-Zarecka 1994; Ingold et al. 1996; Fabian 2007). Historians, on their part, use the term "oral history" to denote non-documenting practices of remembering the past (Vansina 1965).[13]

In this study I draw upon many of these theoretical insights. I have nevertheless chosen to conceptualise social memory as "memoryscape" because I consider that it offers a more comprehensive understanding of the different aspects of social memory. It is a concept increasingly used in the field of memory studies to analyse processes of collective memory, which is indicative of its usefulness (Nuttall 1992; Edensor 1997; Yoneyama 1999; Akiko 2002; Shaw 2002; Argenti and Röschenthaler 2007; Butler 2007; Basu 2007; Sather-Wagstaff 2011; McAllister 2010; McAllister 2011). The memoryscape concept draws upon the spatiality of memory and the notion of landscape. Several of the above-mentioned scholars in fact use it literally to describe how people remember through their physical and material environment. Tim Edensor, for example, defines it as "the organisation of specific objects in space, resulting from often successive projects which attempt to materialise memory by assembling iconographic forms" (Edensor 1997). Other scholars have rather drawn on Appadurai's work on globalisation (1996)[14] and developed the idea of "global memoryscapes" to convey transnational movements of memories (Ebron 1999; K. R. Phillips and Reyes 2011).

The study at hand does not focus of global connections, yet I suggest that the concept memoryscape can be useful to convey and analyse the movement of memory also on smaller scales, in this case on the local, regional and national scales. Hence, I too use the concept primarily metaphorically, even if the material landscape also forms part of the Santafesinian flood memoryscape. I draw in particular on the work by Jennifer Cole (2001), whose ideas I shall develop more closely in what follows. I am also inspired by Margaret Paxson's work on social memory in a Russian rural village (Paxson 2005). She does not use the term memoryscape herself but she does liken social memory to a metaphorical landscape, more of a conceptual terrain. This is similar to the way I define the memoryscape concept, namely as the situated and dynamic configuration of different memories in a particular social setting. These memories, which are

---

[13] In addition to these more generic terms, several more specific terms have been developed to denote who is remembering and in relation to whom or what. There is the dichotomy of "public and vernacular memory" (Bodnar 1992) and that of "dominant and counter memory" (Foucault 1977). Finally there are numerous specific terms used such as "postmemory" (Hirsch 1997, 2012) and "intergenerational memory" (Argenti and Schramm 2012) to denote remembering over and between generations.
[14] In his analysis of the cultural processes that constitute globalisation, Appadurai (1991) refers to the movement of people, resources and ideas as "ethnoscapes," "mediascapes," "technoscapes," "financescapes" and "ideoscapes".

recounted in narratives, materialised in artefacts, spatialised in places and embodied in rituals and in everyday social practices, are the path-dependent result of selective remembering, forgetting and transformation over time in response to the vicissitudes of social life in particular settings and at particular points of time. The memories are furthermore differently distributed over the various sections of society and scale of public life, which are linked to historical processes of social geography.

Jennifer Cole (2001) has used the concept of memoryscape in her research on how people in Madagascar remember and forget their colonial past. Her point of departure is the metaphorical notion of "landscape of memory," drawing on Kirmayer's analysis of the differences in (individual) remembering in the context of trauma (1996). This comes close to Paxson's ideas of memory as a conceptual terrain (ibid.). Kirmayer compares how survivors from the Holocaust and adults who have suffered sexual abuse in their childhood remember and forget their respective traumatic experiences. In his research, Kirmayer shows that while the Holocaust survivors cannot forget their trauma, those exposed to sexual abuse tend to suffer from amnesia. Hence, Kirmayer concludes that the differences in these "symptoms" of trauma are not psychological but instead contingent upon the social context in which the remembering actually takes place (ibid.: 175). Following this line of thinking, Cole suggests that "it is the social practices, the larger social context of meaning, and the way that these converge to create a virtual space of recounting that constitute [a] metaphorical terrain" (ibid.: 289) that which she calls a memoryscape. In her analysis, this is constituted "by the diachronic tendencies that enable continuity of historical consciousness over time, as well as the way these diachronic tendencies intersect with synchronic heterogeneity…" (ibid.: 290). Cole underscores that memory is temporally constituted by social practices which are at the same time traditional practices and memories shaped by present concerns. I too understand the memoryscape to be constituted in time as much as in space. In her research, Cole focuses on the interrelationship between individual and social remembering. I agree that memory is an intersubjective phenomenon. My study will display plenty of examples of how individual and group memories are entwined shaping each other through social relations. Yet, the urban memoryscape is also constituted by the coexistence and interrelation of the different group memories. Taking this into account does not contradict the stance that remembering is intersubjective. Rather it reveals that the memoryscape is made in a dynamic process of remembering and forgetting, taking place at multiple interconnected scales. In what follows I shall further develop the theoretical underpinnings of the concept memoryscape, delineating the modes, temporalities and forms that constitute it.

Modes of remembering

Many thinkers differentiate between different ways or modes of remembering. One is simple evocation (Ricoeur 2004), as conveyed by Marcel Proust in his widely cited book *Remembrance from things past* (2006) when the main character eats a Madeleine cake and this sensory experience evokes all kinds of memories from his childhood. This is what Aristotle called "*mneme.*" In contrast, he called the act of recalling something "*anamnesis*" (Ricoeur ibid.). The latter is related to the word amnesia because without the effort and will to remember, the object is likely to be forgotten. In this sense, the work of the French historian Pierre Nora has been influential through his concept "*lieux de mémoire*" (Nora 1989, 2001). This concept, sometimes translated as "sites of memory" or "realms of memory,"[15] refers to places of commemoration such as museums, cemeteries, and archives; to commemorative objects such as monuments, texts and symbols; and to ritual practices of commemoration like anniversaries, festivals, eulogies. In a similar vein, Connerton has instead suggested the concept "memorial," even if this concept specifically refers to how remembering can be related to particular places (Connerton 2009). Both these concepts are useful in conveying the act and place of recalling, yet it seems to me that they do not clearly enough state what mode of remembering they refer to. After all, there is a qualitative difference between trying to retrieve something during small talk conversation and participating in a public anniversary act. When analysing the act of recalling (or *anamnesis*), I think we need a conceptual differentiation in the sense. Hence I suggest the concepts of "commemoration" and "reminiscence" for this purpose. By commemoration I refer to a regular pattern of remembrance; a ritual recall often but not always carried out in public settings. In contrast, reminiscence refers to the simple effort to recall something from the past, as during a conversation or in an interview.

In this study, I differentiate between "evocative," "reminiscent" and "commemorative" modes of remembering.[16] As we shall see in the ethnographic chapters, these three modes co-exist and intersect, yet sometimes one mode is dominant over another in a memoryscape. The conspicuousness of one mode of remembering or another is forged by the socio-spatial differentiation of urbanity, that is, where the remembering subject is positioned in the urban context.

Temporalities of remembering

By using the concept memoryscape I want to emphasise the spatial dimensions of remembering, yet memory is essentially linked to temporality. Two distinct positions can be discerned in how time and memory is generally understood. On the one hand there is the approach which holds that memory is accumulated knowledge that evolves from the past into the present. This is a diachronic take on memory which has been called "the dynamics of memory approach" (Misztal 2003:67-74). It underscores the historical continuity of things remembered and stresses the presence of the past in the present through psychological and social processes alike. This approach does not represent an essentialist view of tradition

---

[15] The concept *lieux de mémoire* is used in its original French in Nora´s well cited article and is generally not translated when discussed in other works. Nora himself offers the translation of "sites of memory" (1989:7).

[16] Fentress and Wickham make a similar categorisation of remembering calling them "recognition," "recall" and "articulation" respectively (1992:26).

or a view of society as unchangeable, but rather a perspective of memory as a historical process that shapes the present as a result of the past. Historical sociologists and economic historians refer to this as "path dependence" (Mahoney 2000). This negotiation between historical facts and present concerns is culturally shaped on the basis of certain norms and beliefs and therefore in itself a historical product (Appadurai 1981).

On the other hand there is the synchronic understanding of memory. This holds that the memory of the past is forged in the present and is therefore often referred to as a "presentist" model of memory.[17] This stance is most notably represented by Halbwachs himself who was the first to underscore that what people remember from the past is conditioned by the needs and interests of a community in the present (1980:43). Fentress and Wickham follow Halbwachs's understanding of memory as a synchronic process that "tells us who we are, embedding our present selves in our pasts[by] inventing the past to fit the present, or, equally, the present to fit the past" (1992:201).

This brings us to the relation of memory and history, which generally have been juxtaposed in the above mentioned strands of time. The epistemological relation between "history" (referring both to things past and historiography) and "memory" has been somewhat strained over time, especially in academia (Hodgkin and Radstone 2003b:2-3). History has been seen as structured by a chronological periodisation of time and generally taken to represent objective facts and what really happened, hence calling for "critical distance and documented explanation" (Misztal 2003:99). Memory, on the opposite end, has been understood as subjective, emotional and empathetic, and to be based on selectivity and on people's experiences to the point of mythologising the past in a non-linear fashion (Misztal ibid.; Radstone 2000:9-13). History was seen as coming from and about the past, while memory was the past made in the present. Antze and Lambek have argued that the memory turn in the 1980s contributed to blur these conceptual boundaries between history and memory (1996).

In the present study I conceive of history and memory as representing different temporalities and different modes of engaging with the past, yet I see them as entangled processes that make the memoryscape. If we are to keep up with these distinct categories of engaging with the past, perhaps it is more constructive to see them as forming part of a continuum on which "the constructs of public-collective memory find their place at one pole, and the 'dispassionate' historical inquiries at the opposite pole. The closer one moves to the middle ground, that is, to an attempt at general interpretations of the group's past, the more the two areas – distinct in their extreme forms – become intertwined and interrelated" (Friedländer 1993:vii). In line with other scholars who conceptualise history and memory as processes that mediate one another (Boholm 1997; Basu 2007; Wulff 2007), I see the Santafesinian flood memoryscape as constituted by

---

[17] The so-called presentist approach is found in many studies such as those analysing how tradition has been invented (Said 1979; Hobsbawm and Ranger 1992) and those studying the politics of memory (Passerini 1992; J. Rappaport 1990; Radstone and Hodgkin 2003; Johnson 2007), as well as in more phenomenologically oriented memory studies (Feld and Basso 1996; Basso 1996).

path-dependent processes and shaped by processes of social remembering that is subject to people's positions, interests and values in the present.

Forms of remembering

Memories can be mediated and socialised through many different forms, such as narration, spatialisation, materialisation, visualisation and embodiment in any of the different modes of remembering that I have outlined above. In my fieldwork in Santa Fe City, I observed and participated in several of these forms of remembering.

Telling stories about the past is a social practice that is crucial for human action because it structures "temporally distributed events into interpretable wholes" (Wertsch 2002:57). Narratives can thus be defined as a temporal way of ordering (Rapport and Overing 2000:283) which makes them a central feature of socialisation and crucial in and for remembering (Fentress and Wickham 1992:49-51). In turn, remembering through informal conversation and telling stories are key in constituting subjectivity, identity and place (Borgström 1997), because memory is essentially a communicative practice (Fabian 2007:80). Malkki (1995), in her study on Hutu refugees in Tanzania in the mid-1980s, analyses how their different narratives constitute what she calls a "mythico-history," a narrative representation of the past that was a combination of myth and history (p.54). As we shall see in the following pages, in Santa Fe City, narratives about the city's flood past were produced orally, textually and visually in everyday conversations, stories, texts, myths and films.

The importance of space for memory was already underscored by Halbwachs (1980). It has been argued that every memory is related to a place (Gordillo 2004). Even if this is perhaps an overstatement, ethnographic research has indeed showed how memories are spatially embedded in landscapes and how places serve as cues to memory (Nuttall 1992; Ingold and Bradley 1993; Küchler 1993; Feld and Basso 1996; Basso 1996; Hayden 1997; Boholm 1997; Shaw 2002). Plenty of ethnographic studies have also shown that localities are produced through processes of remembering (Bohlin 2001; L. Lewis 2001; Regis 2001; Orta 2002; Gordillo 2004; Paxson 2005; Riaño-Alcalá 2006; Weszkalnys 2010). Connerton has suggested that his concept of "memorial" mentioned earlier can be paired with the concept "locus" to think about different types of place memory (2009:7-39). He exemplifies the memorial concept with commemorative place names and pilgrimages. By the locus concept he refers to the evocative remembering produced in environments such as in one's home or in the street.

Memory is embedded in space also in a materialised or objectified sense. Kontopodis (2009) has argued that temporality is impossible without materiality because it requires its own substance of expression. Hence, as Kontopodis reminds us, remembering and forgetting is therefore also mattering because things operate as links to the past (ibid.). Human memory is often supported by mnemonic tools, technologies and databases (Middleton and Edwards 1990;

Brown and Middleton 2005). Archaeology as a science is based on material premises and analogous to historiography in that it constitutes a practice of memory in itself. Objects are historical subjects in themselves, being crafted or produced at some point (Appadurai 1988). Things work symbolically as mnemonic cues that remind us of events, places and people past (Kwint, Breward, and Aynsley 1999; Forty and Küchler 2001). This is what Nora (ibid.) refers to when he speaks about *lieux de mémoire*, that is, material artefacts such as monuments, archives and flags that shape particular memories of the past in the present.[18] Memory similarly mediates what has been called the "paradox of the presence of absence" (Bille, Hastrup, and Sørensen 2010) referring to the ambiguous interrelation between what is there and what is not.

When it comes to embodied memory, Connerton (2009) differentiates between "incorporating" and "inscribing" practices to denote how this takes place. He exemplifies inscribing practices with the example of writing (ibid.: 72-79) while by incorporating practices he refers to culturally normative bodily postures and gestures. In his view the latter are "'forgotten' as maxims only when they have been well remembered as habits" (ibid.: 83). This view draws upon ideas of the civilising process (Elias 1978) and comes close to Bourdieu's concept of "habitus," that is, "embodied history, internalized as a second nature and so forgotten as history" (1990:56) By focusing on performative rituals as well as everyday life, several scholars have recently shown ethnographically how the past is re-enacted through the body and becomes lived past, challenging the notion of memory as merely a representation of the past (Cole 2001; Shaw 2002; Wulff 2007; Argenti 2007; Argenti and Schramm 2012).

The memoryscape is made through many different social practices such as those mentioned above. Some of these are inherent in daily life in neighbourhoods and institutions; others are enacted in ritual or political spheres of action, as this study shall illustrate. As all cultural forms they can be said to not only be **of** memory but **for** memory (cf. Geertz 1973; Cole 2001:190; Wulff 2007; Sather-Wagstaff 2011:47). The memoryscape is not only made through practices of remembering, however. Forgetting also plays a vital role in this process.

Memory and oblivion

Forgetting is often seen as the opposite of remembering. In the context of psychology and psychiatry it is sometimes even pathologised (Hacking 1996). Most scholars today however would say that memory and oblivion work in tandem, interacting dialectically (Fabian 2007:78). Several scholars would have it that the

---

[18] In relation to this is also the diachronic notion of "heritage," referring to something that is passed on from preceding generations. In a global context, the UNESCO differentiates between tangible and intangible heritage which has resulted in the inclusion of cultural practices and skills as identified legacies to be protected. Objects, places and monuments are still the main sites of public heritage however (Rowlands and Jong 2008:17), not seldom giving rise to a politics of heritage, that is, processes of contestation around the authenticity, representativity and legitimacy of such sites of memory (Schramm 2010; Volk 2010; Sather-Wagstaff 2011).

contemporary world is obsessed with memory and that this in itself is an expression of cultural amnesia (Nora 1989; Forty 2001; Huyssen 2003). Connerton (2009) speaks of oblivion as an inherent feature of modernity as materialised in capitalist production. The connection between oblivion and modernity is made also by Paul de Man (1970) who argues that forgetting is what makes modernity possible because it allows for a fresh start over. Forty likewise reminds us that "[t]he very word 'amnesty' speaks of a public forgetting, and most of the social contract theories of the state upon which modern democracies are founded assume their members are prepared to forget the more divisive differences existing between them" (2001:7). This is what Connerton (2008:61-62) has called "prescriptive forgetting" which is similar to the notion of "structural amnesia" (Barnes 2006) referring to the selective remembering only of the issues that are socially important.[19] The ambiguity in different forms of memory, by which certain things are forgotten so that others can be remembered, can be seen as part of a violent past and has been observed also in other postcolonial contexts (Ferme 2001; Shaw 2002; Argenti 2007). Yet oblivion is not always easily accomplished. De Man argues that the more effort one makes to forget the past, the more dependent one becomes on it (ibid.: 400). In Ireland, the Great Famine and the Troubles resist forgetting because memories are embodied (Wulff 2007). In Argentina, the atrocities occurred during the last military regime continue to haunt Argentinian social and political life (Robben 2007). As we shall see in this study, in Santa Fe there are disastrous floods that are forgotten at a public or an aggregated level, but that are remembered locally.

      Other scholars have pointed to the dangers of forgetting because history (and in particular atrocities) risks repeating itself. When oblivion is a threat to existence in the present and the future, remembering becomes a duty, as has been the case with the Holocaust (Augé 2004:87-89; Margalit 2011). Such stances turn memory into a moral and a political concern, which is also the case in post-dictatorship Argentina (Jelin 2002; Catela da Silva and Jelin 2002; Jelin and Kaufman 2006; Jelin 2007). Some authors talk about forgetting as a matter of neglect or repression rather than a cognitive loss of memory. The Czech writer Milan Kundera's oft-quoted words ring true here: "The struggle of man against power is the struggle of memory against forgetting" (Kundera 1999:4). Forgetting as "repressive erasure" (Connerton 2008:60) appears in its most brutal form in the history of totalitarian regimes. Argentina is certainly a case in point, not least through the applied systematic enforced "disappearances" of thousands of people; a euphemism for the clandestine political crime of kidnapping, torturing and killing carried out by the last military regime in the years 1976-83 (Crenzel 2011b:8). In a less violent form, forgetting can be inherent to organisational structures and practices in the form of omitting past events and decisions from the records.

---

[19] Classical anthropological examples of structural amnesia are the genealogies in which the names of ancestors who do not give their names to units within the lineage structure tend to be forgotten (Fortes and Evans-Pritchard 1940).

This connects to the research which focuses on the relationship between material objects and forgetting (Forty 2001). The point of departure of the Western tradition of memory has been that material objects are analogous to human memory, that is, things represent memory, whereby the disappearance of a thing would thus lead to forgetting. This assumption is challenged by recent studies on ephemeral monuments, that is, objects that are produced in order to commemorate by abandoning them and letting them decay (Argenti 2001; Küchler 2001). These studies show that the forgetting entailed by the abandonment or destruction of monuments in fact led to remembering through its absence (Forty 2001).

In sum, I suggest that memoryscape is a useful concept for the purposes of the study at hand because it encompasses key aspects of the phenomenon. The concept offers a model to grasp the different temporalities, modes and forms of memory. It embraces remembering and forgetting as interactive configurative forces of memory-work, and includes both time and space as mutually constitutive in this process. Memories are the products of social relations that unfold both in time and in space. Different memories are related and interact with each other through articulation or contestation. This is not necessarily an interaction between equals however. What is being remembered in different settings and levels in a society is also a consequence of who remembers and from which position in the social space this remembering takes place at a given point in time. The spatiotemporal qualities of the concept memoryscape thus enable us to think about the asymmetries of social memory. Not all memories are equally remembered in society and oblivion also lingers in the memoryscape. The concept, it seems to me, enables a deeper understanding of how memories are shared.

Exploring the traces of disaster: Methodological concerns

Disasters are critical and often unexpected events that produce intense processes of meaning-making in society. How and why did the worst happen? Who was affected? Who was responsible? These are questions that are prone to arise sooner or later in the affected community. Disasters as disruptive events bring existing social and material relations to the fore. They forge cultural and economic processes of continuity as much as change. This makes disasters good to think for social scientists, yet also difficult to think because of their multidimensionality (Oliver-Smith 2002). How then do we go about studying them in contexts of upheaval and loss? The translocal and transtemporal models of ethnographic fieldwork seem particularly apt to explore people's memories of disaster. This is because they can capture the diverse processes in a heterogeneous social environment, but also because the post-disaster context tends to be fraught with multiple public and private efforts to make meaning out of the unthinkable, a liminal process that is bound to change over time. I shall, in what follows, outline the process of my fieldwork, which can be described as being both translocal and transtemporal, carried out between the years 2004 and 2011.[20]

Composing a field

Already at the planning stage for this research project, I identified many possible locations to explore processes of remembering and forgetting recurrent disasters. Argentina was at the outset the country of my choice because I had personal as well as ethnographic experience from living and working there for many years. There were also family reasons that made me want to undertake my field study in this country. I considered several possible field sites at first: a village in the northeast Littoral region, a small town on the Argentinian prairie, the *pampa*, or an urban neighbourhood in a city – any place where flooding has been a recurrent problem (Natenzon 1998; Natenzon 2003; Herzer et al. 2000; Herzer et al. 2002; Celis and Herzer 2003; Hardoy, Pandiella, and Barrero 2011). Eventually I came to choose Santa Fe City for my fieldwork. This choice was initially not motivated by a particular interest in urban disasters, but rather by the historical conditions of this particular community with so many disastrous floods throughout time.

My initial idea was that of a yearlong fieldwork somewhere in this city, along the lines of the "classical" or "Malinowskian" ethnographic endeavour, generally characterised by a long-term stay in one place, be it a village or the neighbourhood in a city. Yet I ended up undertaking an urban translocal fieldwork instead. There is no doubt that fieldwork in which several fields in one (Hannerz 2001, 2003a) are explored is common nowadays. Perhaps it was already more common in earlier periods than is generally thought. Even Malinowski, who is credited with founding the ethnographic method, in fact carried out a fieldwork in many different locations and not only in one single place, especially when he followed the Kula ring of the Trobriands. This casts some doubts on the innovativeness of contemporary fieldworks (Björklund 2001; Hannerz 2003b). Even if it is based more on a legend than on facts (Mitchell 2010) and even though the notions of both "holism" and "[ethnographic] field" have been subject to thorough critique since the reflexive turn in anthropology (Clifford and Marcus 1986; A. Gupta and Ferguson 1997; Marcus 1998; Amit 1999) it seems to stand strong in the imaginary of contemporary students in social anthropology, at least judging by my own reasoning. What is nevertheless new is at least the label for this type of fieldwork, namely "multisited" or "multilocal" (Marcus 1998; Hannerz 2003b) or translocal (Lindqvist 1996; Hannerz 2003a; Garsten 2010; Röschenthaler 2010).

---

[20] In 2012 and 2013, as I wrote the dissertation, I carried out some follow-up research through the internet and virtual communication, which added relevant ethnography.

Translocality

In contrast to multisitedness or multilocality, the principal feature of the concept translocality is relationality or interaction across localities (Lindqvist 1996; Hannerz 2003a). The translocal field has often been associated with global phenomena that take place in multiple locations within a world system (Marcus 1995; Garsten 2010). Yet, I argue that this concept can be adapted also to less globalised ethnographic fields, that is, to fields less contingent upon global processes. This is perhaps particularly the case with local phenomena in urban contexts because such contexts tend to be heterogeneous and complex yet interconnected. The Swedish anthropologist Karin Norman (2001) describes how her ethnographic field in the small Swedish town of Smedjebacken consisted of many different locales that had no clear or directly visible link, but which nevertheless were associated in that they together constituted that particular urban whole. She tells how she carried out fieldwork all these different locales, simultaneously or in parallel. Norman's fieldwork may be considered a borderline case among translocal fieldworks (Hannerz 2001:17) because her field by and large consisted of one and the same locality (that is, the small town of Smedjebacken). Likewise, my field in Santa Fe City could be considered this way. The many different settings that I included in my fieldwork were after all located in the same city. But then the question arises on how a locality is defined and where the spatial boundaries to other localities are drawn, as discussed by Gupta and Ferguson (1997). This seems particularly relevant to bear in mind for studies in urban contexts characterised by diversity, complexity and scale, which blur the analytical borders between different social spaces and locales. Narratives, practices and identities show that urban space is constituted of separate yet interconnected localities that people inhabit as much as transit.

Transtemporality

The long term inquiry has been one of the hallmarks of anthropological research. Time is seen as key to enabling the ethnographer to grasp the complexities of social life in a particular field and achieve an understanding of the "native's point of view." The "classical" fieldwork model referred to above has generally implied a period of one to two years of sustained and intensive empirical work, most notably connected to doctoral studies (Howell and Talle 2011:7). Firth distinguished between the "dual-synchronic study," by which he means a comparative study of two ethnographic presents, and the "diachronic study," which is the continuous study of events over time (1936). The first refers to so-called "restudies" that a number of anthropologists have subsequently undertaken by returning many years later to their earlier field sites. The latter is what Howell and Talle call "multitemporal fieldwork," defining this as the "many returns to the same place across the years, but not necessarily in a systematic chronological pattern" (ibid.: 3). The ethnographer's return to the field over a long period of time enables not only the development of profound ethnographic knowledge, but a different understanding of continuity and change. However, the multitemporal fieldwork, in contrast to the re-study, "gives rise to a more processual understanding – a description *through* time – in which one [the ethnographer] is enabled to witness the many events that provoke change or resistance to change (ibid.: 12. Italics in original).

I argue that my repeated returns to Santa Fe City over the years constitute such a description through time, even if the period of time in which I have undertaken this fieldwork is far from the decades of long-term research that contributors to Howell and Talle's volume have been able to accrue.[21] In line with the reasoning around multisitedness, multilocality and translocality, I shall nevertheless use the term transtemporal fieldwork instead, because I consider that it better conveys the interrelatedness of different events across the passing of time, and especially because it deals with remembering.

Mapping the Santafesinian flood memoryscape

The starting point of my fieldwork was a reconnaissance trip to Santa Fe in July 2004. My long-time friend Maria, who is a sociologist, accompanied me on this first visit. In February 2005 I returned to carry out what Wulff (2002) has called "yoyo-fieldwork," commuting weekly between Santa Fe City and my home in the province of San Luis some 700 kilometres from there. In the midst of the fieldwork in 2005, I got unexpected help from two young doctoral students in social anthropology at the National University of Rosario. Eugenia and Alicia were both native Santafesinos. They offered to assist me not only for the purpose of gaining fieldwork experience but also to achieve a deeper understanding of *la Inundación* themselves. While this disaster had not affected them directly, it had dismayed them as much as so many other people in the city. I returned to the city several times during the period 2008-2009. I then again travelled back and forth between the field and the home, spending in total three months in the city.

During the entire period of fieldwork (2004-2011) I regularly followed events and debates concerning flooding in Santa Fe through different sources on the internet and in virtual communication with certain interlocutors (through e-mail and increasingly through social media). The virtual dimension of this urban universe was thus the parallel and the in-between-physical-stays locale in which I carried out my inquiry. The virtual connections made possible my continuous follow-up on things, almost to the last minute of finishing this manuscript. As we shall see in some of the chapters, there is ethnography that dates from 2012 which I have included when relevant to the analysis. I argue that this "polymorphous engagement" (Gusterson 1997), the mobility between many fields in the field and the work of time contributed in making my fieldwork in Santa Fe eminently translocal and transtemporal, enabling my understanding of how the urban memoryscape was configured.

---

[21] The chapter *Forty-five years with the Kapayo* by Terence Turner (2011) in this book is particularly telling in this regard.

Halbwachs' observation about the heterogeneity inherent in social memory (1980) was indeed applicable also to my field. Heterogeneity is after all one of the key features of urbanity. In Santa Fe City, relations of social, economic and political inequality shaped not only social and spatial organisation, but also my fieldwork in this particular setting. The starting site for my fieldwork was the neighbourhood I had ended up living in during 2005, Barrio Roma. This neighbourhood had been flooded for the first time in 2003. This was also one of the neighbourhoods in which the protest movement of the flood victims was initially formed, which I shall analyse in Chapter Four. I could have chosen to limit my study to this neighbourhood, or to only follow the protest work of the activists. I could also have decided to carry out participant observation within the local bureaucracy in order to explore further the processes of organisational memory. Yet instead of selecting one of these sites I selected them all. As new doors of ethnographic opportunity opened in the field in the course of fieldwork, I chose to follow new threads in this urban web of memory-making in order to include other urban and suburban neighbourhoods, other NGOs, and other governmental agencies. This implied that I moved between many different locations and urban contexts within the same ethnographic field, sometimes within the same day. This mode of "methodological improvisation" (Cerwonka and Malkki 2007) is probably a rule more than an exception in all ethnographic fieldwork but perhaps even more so in urban translocal fieldwork (Hannerz 2001; Henning 2001).

Memory and methodology

Participant observation was the technique that I mostly applied in this fieldwork as I shared the flood memories of and with my interlocutors listening to their stories, participating in their daily and ritual practices and visiting particular places. The residents in Barrio Roma, where I lived myself, were among my first interlocutors. Marta, mentioned at the beginning of this introductory chapter, was one of them. This neighbourhood, and many others in the western districts of the city, were seriously flooded in *la Inundación* in 2003 for the first time in history. At a later stage, I expanded the field to include three other low-income neighbourhoods, namely Santa Rosa de Lima and Villa del Parque on the Westside and Alto Verde on the eastern Coastside. In contrast to Barrio Roma, these three latter neighbourhoods had been flooded on many occasions throughout history.

Apart from listening to numerous stories I participated in many rituals of commemoration of the 2003 disaster, which were ubiquitous in the city in 2005 but also upon my return in 2008, 2009 and 2011. I participated intensively in the activities carried out by the protest movement claiming justice and compensation for the damages from the 2003 flood. This protest movement consisted of a cluster of protesting disaster victims and established NGOs which together formed what I shall call a "polity of remembering." Their activities consisted of meetings, press conferences, public demonstrations and commemorations in public spaces. The fact that they were acting in public made my access to them fairly uncomplicated. I was allowed to join some of their meetings. Several of the members of the movement were my neighbours in Barrio Roma. They took this into consideration as well as the fact that I was a scholar from abroad, which could eventually contribute to their cause, at least at a symbolical level.

With the help of my research assistants, I carried out 20 semi-structured interviews with public officials in the municipal and provincial administration, and 32 open interviews with interlocutors in different urban contexts. Apart from interviewing people as residents or flood victims, I interviewed several junior and senior officials within municipal and provincial public administration, more specifically in those institutions that were responsible for the flood and disaster management of the city. I also talked to people in different NGOs active in the city with different social issues, particularly organisations involved in different ways in the response to and in the reconstruction work after the 2003 flood.

In addition, I engaged in hundreds of informal conversations with interlocutors from various social categories of class, gender, age and profession. I accompanied many of them in "walk-, drive- and rowabouts" (cf. Riaño-Alcalá 2006), that is, walking, driving and rowing with them as they went about their daily activities around the city, while encouraging them to tell me the stories about the different places. I also followed the municipal inspectors of flood embankments and water pumps on their inspection rounds, and the district health assistant on his round in the neighbourhood. I mapped the places that throughout the fieldwork proved to shape and be shaped by people's flood memories. In order to do this I walked the city a lot, both with interlocutors guiding me as well as on my own observing and talking to new people I met. Overall I was very mobile and moved frequently from one urban location to another, either walking or by some means of transport. I was as much translocal as the field was itself. I undertook fair amount of "hanging out" in the neighbourhoods mentioned when possible, especially in the afternoon, in the evenings and the weekends when people were actually at home. It was not difficult to get into conversations with people spontaneously in the street, local stores, markets and squares, or getting to talk to people during local events such as neighbourhood feasts, anniversary ceremonies, and exhibition openings. Yet in order to access new field sites, I also drew upon my growing urban network. I contacted and visited local institutions such as schools, primary care health centres and social services, FM radio stations, NGOs and neighbourhood associations. Approximately halfway through fieldwork in 2005 the field was expanded to include other neighbourhoods around the city, namely La Nueva Tablada, Barranquitas Oeste and Centenario. These neighbourhoods ranged from low-income to middle-income residential categories.

I undertook archival work in local public archives, more specifically, in three historical archives and one newspaper archive.[22] The archival work was later facilitated as these archives were increasingly digitalised and published on line.[23] Similarly, I collected newspaper accounts and governmental documents and policy statements through the internet. Books, movies, artwork, recorded music and other artefacts that constitute the local flood memoryscape were also part of my collection.

When possible, I used different devices to document my observations. I sometimes used an mp3-recorder to record the interviews but most of the times I took notes. I have not transcribed entire interviews but only the parts that I have found most relevant as I have listened through them. In contrast, I used my digital camera a lot both to take still pictures and to make videos. Certainly, these records have sustained my memories from the field.

Reflexion and roadmap

I conclude this introductory chapter with a short reflexion on the ethnographic study of memory and a description of the organisation of the book. The practice of ethnographic fieldwork has been compared to that of making jazz music in that both are improvisatory yet based on exhaustive preparation and practice (Cerwonka and Malkki 2007:182-3). The nature of this reflexive methodology is what makes anthropology (and other sciences applying ethnography) particularly prone to serendipity and theoretical insights. The way my fieldwork took shape in a translocal and transtemporal mode brought me crucial empirical and analytical insights.

The order of the chapters to some extent follows my ethnographic endeavour in discovering and making visible the different glares and shades characterising this particular memoryscape. This organisation roughly corresponds with the temporal and spatial order in which I, in the first part of my fieldwork (2004-2005), came to participate in the making of these many memories. This began in the local *barrio* and within the protest movement, after which I moved on to the bureaucracy, the archives and ended up in the poverty-stricken urban outskirts. During the years that followed (2006-2011), I undertook research in all these ethnographic settings more or less in a parallel manner. Hence, even if the chapters are organised temporally following my fieldwork endeavour, they do not follow a strict chronological order. In each and every one of them, there are observations from different moments of fieldwork. The organisation of the chapters is also analytical. Each chapter can be said to represent a particular dimension of the urban flood memoryscape. It can perhaps be useful to think of

---

[22] These were all provincial archives: the General Archive of the Province of Santa Fe, the Newspaper Archive (Hemeroteca) and the Historical Archive. Another newspaper archive was that of the local newspaper *El Litoral*.
[23] These archives could be accessed from one single web portal (Gobierno de la Provincia de Santa Fe 2006a).

them as different sides the same phenomenon or as different pieces of a multidimensional puzzle. It goes without saying that I cannot account for every side in such a large urban complex, hence; the selection of field sites has been contingent on an explicit relation to past flooding.

The different chapters also convey how this research process took place as a reflexive journey through a memoryscape. A meta-narrative frames the ethnography by way of certain detailed descriptions on how I, the ethnographer, without having experienced flooding in Santa Fe myself, came to know and thereby share the memoryscape. Before initiating my fieldwork I had lived in Argentina for more than 15 years. In many ways I passed as an Argentinian woman, not only by the looks but also because I speak the language fluently with an Argentinian accent. After so many years in the country (almost half my life) I shared many cultural practices and historical references. I also had emotional engagements with people and places. Yet, in all those years I had never set foot in Santa Fe City and prior to undertaking this study, I knew very little of the city. I was thus an "insider" and "outsider" at the same time (cf. Narayan 1992). Hence, the purpose of the meta-narrative is to illustrate reflexively how the dynamics of social remembering that mediate past social experiences takes place by way of constructing situated knowledge. I thereby hope to achieve what Narayan has called the "enactment of hybridity" in ethnographic writing, that is, "mix[ing] lively narrative and rigorous analysis . . . regardless of our origins" (ibid.: 682).

Throughout the study I use the term "interlocutor" instead of the ethnographically more established term "informant." The term interlocutor has not been much used in contemporary anthropology despite a tendency to do so in the 1980s, which emerged as a response to the crisis of ethnographic representation after the postcolonial and postmodern critique (Asad 1973; Clifford and Marcus 1986; Marcus and Fischer 1986). The critique included the "anthropology . . . still based on raw materials delivered by 'informants' . . . processed into 'cultural' identities that [could] be sold on Western academic markets" (Pels and Salemink 1994:2-3). The term interlocutor, brought in to anthropology from literary theory, became equally criticised however by postcolonial scholars (i.e. Said 1989) for being only seemingly dialogic and democratic (Pels and Salemink 1994). This might have prevented the spread of the term to mainstream anthropology (and to other disciplines using ethnographic methods) or perhaps it was not deep enough a critique. My choice of the term is to denote a methodological and an epistemological stance of reflexivity. It seems appropriate to use the term interlocutor instead of informant because the shared experience of remembering past flooding together with the Santafesinos forged the process of remembering and forgetting in particular ways. I did not only observe and listen to what people remembered, but I inquired and asked about what was seemingly forgotten, making people recall by reminiscence. My presence after a while even evoked memories of flooding to people, since I (reluctantly) became the "scholar of *la Inundación*" in the urban contexts where I carried out fieldwork. My subject position made many people in the public administration conveniently forget past events for fear of issues of accountability. My participation as a foreign anthropologist in politicised rituals of commemoration several times pushed me into situations of acting as an interlocutor with public officials or even before the Swedish mass media and authorities[24] on behalf of the activists. In addition, my understanding of many of the stories and social practices were anchored by my own memories of experiencing life in Argentina as a long-time resident myself. Hence, anthropological knowledge was produced through these ethnographic encounters between the Santafesinos and me. In order to acknowledge such collaboration involved in the production of anthropological knowledge, Holmes and Marcus (2010) have suggested the concept "epistemic partners." I choose the term interlocutor, but I side with these scholars and others (K. Hastrup and Hervik 1994) in the understanding that anthropological knowledge is fundamentally the result of ethnographic interaction.

Organisation of the chapters

Chapter Two aims at situating the reader ethnographically, geographically and temporally in Argentina and in Santa Fe City of the 21st century, which is where this study takes place. An overview of Argentinian contemporary politics is offered to enable the understanding of the modes and forms of remembering *la Inundación* taking place in Santa Fe City. Delving into national, regional and local economy provides the reader with necessary knowledge about the constitution of social vulnerabilities in Santa Fe in the face of disasters, which have developed over time through processes of immigration, agriculturalisation, urbanisation, political violence and economic hardship. Finally, the chapter acquaints the reader with Santafesinian social life and urban landscape of the past and the present through life histories and social history.

Parts I and II consist of three and two chapters respectively. The two parts highlight their respective ethnographic focus. The first part describes the tension between the intense memory-work sparked in the wake of *la Inundación* undertaken by the 2003 victims and the official oblivion about flooding. The second part shifts focus to other less conspicuous parts of the flood memoryscape. Here I analyse the history of flooding in Santa Fe and the memories of the people in the poor urban outskirts. As will become clear, the social category of flood victims, *inundados*, is central in the ethnography because it is an important emic category in the Santafesinian flood memoryscape. In order to grasp its heterogeneity and turn it into an object of inquiry in itself, I differentiate between three subcategories, namely the flood victims of 2003 as "*inundados/victims*," the activists in the protest movement that formed in the wake of this disaster as "*inundados/activists*," and finally the dwellers in the poor lowland districts who have recurrently been flooded subjects throughout history as "*floodprone/inundados*." Some people actually overlap and belong to two or even all three subcategories, yet the differentiation runs along these lines.

---

[24] On two occasions in 2005, two different *inundados-activists* handed over to me large cases with documents and photographs documenting *la Inundación*. Both of them asked me to take the documentation back with me to Sweden to make the case there in mass media and to try to get support from Swedish public and private organisations.

Part I begins with Chapter Three, depicting how *la Inundación* was remembered at large in Santa Fe City. The focus is on the victims of this disaster, the *inundados/victims*. I argue that they constituted an "accidental community of memory" (Malkki 1995) in the wake of this disaster. This particular subcategory of flood victims included people living in the low and middle-income neighbourhoods on the Westside. Many of the *inundados/victims* lived in middle-income neighbourhoods and were flooded for the first time in their lives in 2003. This category nevertheless also included people from the working classes and the large sector of the urban poor that live in the Westside shantytowns. Many of these people had been flooded before, even if the 2003 flood was said to have been the worst of them all. During my fieldwork, memories of *la Inundación* loomed large in the everyday lives of the *inundados/victims* through absences, smells and small talk. Parallel to this evocative and reminiscent remembering, they created memory of *la Inundación* through practices, places and artefacts of commemoration. This chapter analyses the constitution of this accidental community of memory and its place in the Santafesinian flood memoryscape.

Chapter Four deals with the politicisation of *la Inundación*. Here the focus is on the *inundados/activists* that constituted what I call a "polity of remembering" because of their use of memory as a key tactic of mobilisation. The polity consisted of a protest movement that was formed in the post-disaster context of *la Inundación*. It comprised a loose cluster of *inundados/victims*, NGOs, and other Santafesinos who mobilised in different public venues to demand political accountability of the disaster, and for economic compensation for their losses. I analyse the memory-work carried out by the *inundados/activists* as a moral quest and a political tool for the acknowledgement of their claims.

Chapter Five turns to the realm of flood management politics and bureaucracy in Santa Fe. It addresses how the problem of flooding in general and with *la Inundación* in particular has been dealt with in the politics and within public administration of Santa Fe. Hence, the chapter analyses how the problem of flooding has been managed by politicians and public officials following what I call a "logic of omission." This refers to the selective remembering and forgetting undertaken through everyday bureaucratic practices, objects, legislation and contingency plans, as well as to different public works, both infrastructure and monumental decorative works.

Part II begins with Chapter Six, which describes how flooding in Santa Fe has also been remembered as part of history ever since the foundation of the city in colonial times. It was depicted both as a recurrent and singular phenomenon on the continuum of myth and history. I analyse the different practices, places, monuments, myths, visual and literary narratives that turned flooding into an urban "mythico-history" (Malkki 1995) that reified the emic social category of "*inundados*."

Chapter Seven turns to the people who historically have embodied this social category of *inundados*. They are the poor people living on the urban Westside and the suburban Coastside that I call the *flood-prone/inundados*, because they were recurrently flooded due to conditions of social vulnerability and geographical exposure. This chapter analyses what I call "embedded remembrance" of past flooding takes place in the flood-prone urban outskirts. What at first seemed to be forgetting was rather another way of remembering. This notion of embedded remembrance refers to the ways in which their flood memories and forms of remembering are embedded in everyday practices, places and objects.

In the concluding Chapter Eight, I summarise the findings from the analysis and discuss the implications for current debates on vulnerability, resilience and adaptation to environmental disasters.

Chapter 2 | Context

Urban life and vulnerability in Argentina

Flooding has been a recurrent problem in Santa Fe City throughout history. As I have argued in the previous chapter, vulnerability is a central concept to understanding why and how disasters occur in the first place, but also to understand how they unfold and are remembered. In Oliver-Smith's words: "[a] disaster is a historical event - and the aftermath of disaster is process coming to grips with history" (1979b:96). Hence, this chapter has a twofold aim. One is to sketch the social and economic history of Argentina and of Santa Fe City. This way I want to provide the reader with an understanding of those historical processes that have forged vulnerable life conditions in Santa Fe and put people living in this city at risk in the first place. By providing a number of life stories of different interlocutors living in some of the districts I hope not only to illustrate the historical processes I describe, but also to introduce the reader to some of my field sites in Santa Fe City. The second aim of the chapter is to describe more contemporary social and political processes that have taken place in Argentina of recent decades, because I argue that these processes have contributed to shaping the urban flood memoryscape in Santa Fe. From the end of the last dictatorship (1976-1983)[25] onwards, the human rights movement and the democratisation processes at the national level have largely shaped political and social life, not least when it comes to the topic of memory. In order to understand how the Santafesinian flood memoryscape is configured, it is therefore necessary to learn about the "politics of regret" (Olick 2007) and the importance of making memory in contemporary Argentina. What follows is thus an itinerary that takes the reader from the capital city of Buenos Aires and political and economic matters on a national scale that are relevant to the case, to regional aspects of the province of Santa Fe and urban life by the rivers in some of the districts in Santa Fe City.

Argentinian politics of regret

In the neighbourhood of Núñez in the northern part of the City of Buenos Aires, close to the La Plata River and past the city's elegant racecourse and parks, reminiscent of London or Paris, are the premises of what in Argentina is commonly known as the ESMA. It is a beautiful complex of colonnaded whitewashed build-

---

[25] During the years of this military dictatorship, there were four military juntas in government led by different *de facto* presidents: Jorge Videla, Roberto Viola, Leopoldo Galtieri and Reynaldo Bignone.

ings with red-tiled roofs surrounded by lush trees located along the fashionable Liberty Avenue. The acronym ESMA stands for the *Escuela de Suboficiales de Mecánica de la Armada* which is the Argentinian Navy Petty-Officers School of Mechanics. During the dictatorial rule of the country between 1976 and 1983, the ESMA became the largest of the many illegal detention centres used. The military government in power called this regime the "National Reorganisation Process" referred to in State discourse by its Spanish acronym PRN.[26] This was the last in a series of military dictatorships in Argentina in the 20th century,[27] unquestionably the most violent. The PRN later became known as the Dirty War (*Guerra Sucia*) due to the atrocities committed by the military government against thousands of Argentinian and foreign citizens. At the ESMA, and in the other detention centres, military task units were in charge of forced disappearances, torture, illegal execution, and appropriation of children born to mothers imprisoned there, who were then subjected to identity forgery and illegal adoption. These practices of State terrorism can be seen as macabre examples of Foucauldian biopower and of how the Argentinian State in those years exercised a systematic obliteration of the social body by erasing citizen subjects who threatened their social and political order (Guber 1999a:71).[28]

In Buenos Aires, during the dictatorship, the ESMA then became a place of horror. In 2000, the Legislature of the City of Buenos Aires passed a bill enabling the withdrawal of the concession of the premises where the school was located, in order to create a museum of the Dirty War. In 2002, the National Congress and the Senate passed a bill to establish March 24th as the "National Day of Memory for Truth and Justice"[29], to "consolidate the collective memory of [that period in] society, generate feelings opposed to any kind of authoritarianism and sponsor the permanent defence of the rule of law and full respect for human rights" (Honorable Congreso de la Nación Argentina 2002. My translation).[30]

On that day in 2004, exactly 28 years after the military takeover in 1976, the sitting president Néstor Kirchner formalised the creation of the "Realm for the Memory and the Promotion and Defence of Human Rights"[31] at the former ESMA premises through an inaugural ceremony. President Kirchner was accompanied by his wife, Cristina Fernández (who was at the time a national senator), his cabinet and by representatives of most, if not all, human rights organisations. The most emblematic of these NGOs were the Mothers of the Plaza

---

[26] The acronym stood for its name in Spanish: *Proceso de Reorganización Nacional*
[27] Democratically elected governments were overthrown by the Argentinian military on six occasions during the 20th century: 1930, 1943, 1955, 1962, 1966 and 1976.
[28] Such practices are not exclusive to Argentina, however, but have been carried out in many other countries, for example in Guatemala (Sanford 2003), Nicaragua (Lundgren 2000), and Cambodia (Hinton 2005) throughout history. It is still occurring in countries such as Colombia (Rozema 2011) just to mention a few.
[29] In Spanish: *Día Nacional de la Memoria por la Verdad y la Justicia*
[30] Throughout this study, all translations of quotations from Spanish to English are mine unless otherwise stated.
[31] In Spanish: *Espacio para la Memoria y para la Promoción y Defensa de los Derechos Humanos*

de Mayo, the Grandmothers of the Plaza de Mayo[32] and the Sons and Daughters for Identity and Justice Against Oblivion and Silence, more known by their acronym H.I.J.O.S.[33] Tens of thousands of people attended the inauguration, carrying the light blue and white national flag. National mass media cabled out the event live to the other 38 million of Argentinian inhabitants. In a passionate inaugural speech, President Kirchner exorcised the macabre atrocities committed by "the murderers," referring to the military, and urged everybody to "never again allow obscurity to reign in the motherland." On behalf of the Argentinian state, the president asked for forgiveness for having been shamefully silent on these matters during those twenty years of democracy and declared that justice must replace impunity. He was referring to the fact that after the initial judicial trial and sentencing of the members of the military junta in 1985,[34] the leaders and all other people accused of torturing and murdering thousands of people had been granted amnesty by two controversial laws[35] and by presidential pardon only a couple of years later.[36] Only in 2003, by initiative of the Kirchner government, were these two laws annulled by the National Congress and in 2005 definitely voided as unconstitutional by the Supreme Court of Justice. This allowed for the re-opening of cases that involve crimes against humanity beginning in 2006 and being carried out in the years to follow. In this context, one of the imprisoned dictators, Jorge Videla, who made the infamous declarations at a press conference in 1979[37] that the military government ignored the fate of and the responsi-

---

[32] What began as a desperate search by mothers and grandmothers for their missing sons and daughters and grandchildren during the Dirty War, was with time transformed into several human rights organisations, most notably the Madres de Plaza de Mayo and the Abuelas de Plaza de Mayo. These organisations and the women that integrate them are colloquially referred to as *las Madres* and *las Abuelas*. In protests they typically wear white head scarves with their children's names embroidered, to symbolise the blankets of the lost children. The name of the organisation comes from the square Plaza de Mayo in central Buenos Aires, where they enacted their protest every week. In 1986 the association split into two groups. The Asociación Madres de Plaza de Mayo emphasised the ideological legacy of their disappeared children and focused on social work, while the Madres de la Plaza de Mayo-Línea Fundadora focused on legislation to help in recovering the remains of the disappeared, tracing and getting back the sons and daughters of the disappeared (many times illegally adopted to other families), and bringing ex-officials to justice

[33] The acronym stands for the Spanish name *Hijos por la Identidad y la Justicia contra el Olvido y el Silencio*. *Hijos* is the generic word for children (as in sons and daughters) in Spanish. It is an organisation founded in Argentina in 1995 by the children of the people disappeared and killed during the Dirty War. Many of its members were born in captivity as their mothers had been illegally imprisoned. When these mothers were killed, many of the children were adopted out to other families, often to military families themselves who brought up these children under a different identity.

[34] These trials, in Argentina called the *Juicio a los Comandantes*, were the civil lawsuit of the members of the *de facto* military government of the *PRN*. The trials were carried out in 1985 in which five out of nine accused commanders were sentenced to prison.

[35] The *Ley de Punto Final* (Full Stop Law) in 1986 dictated the end of investigation and prosecution against people accused of political violence during the dictatorship and the *Ley de Obediencia Debida* (Law of Due Obedience) in 1987 exempted subordinates from accusation when they were carrying out orders.

[36] In 1989 and 1990, the sitting President Carlos Menem issued several decrees that granted amnesty to all convicted militaries.

[37] Videos from this press conference are available on line (see for example *Videla Habla Sobre Los Desaparecidos 1979* 2012).

bility for the thousands of missing people referred to as the *desaparecidos*[38] (and who later denied any responsibility in the trials), recently admitted the killings of seven to eight thousands of them (Reato 2012).

Democracy, human rights and the explosion of memory in Argentina

Argentinian society as a whole was far from oblivious about its violent past. At the time of transition to democracy, different groups in society immediately engaged in a contest over the meaning of past events as a means of coming to terms with the cultural trauma of political violence, creating a polyphonic social memory of the Dirty War (Robben 2005, 2007). The Argentinian State established a truth commission[39] to determine what had happened and who was responsible. After the amnesty laws in 1986-87, the human rights organisations above-mentioned have incessantly struggled to bring the military (back) to court and to find out the fate of the disappeared people. Post-dictatorship Argentina, similar to other countries on the Southern Cone such as Chile and Uruguay that have suffered political violence, has experienced an "explosion of memory" (Crenzel 2011a). This situation can be compared to experiences on the African continent, where a similar phenomenon has occurred in the wake of post-colonialism (Werbner 1998). The work carried out in Argentina particularly in matters of human rights has in fact established a global model for dealing with violent pasts (Sikkink 2008). In addition, there is a huge literature on human rights in Argentina, including both scholarly works and first-person accounts (ibid.: 2). Around 200 documentary films and motion pictures have been produced about the Dirty War throughout the years.[40] Official memorials other than the ESMA museum are abundant, in particular in the city of Buenos Aires, but also in other cities around the country such as the Museo de la Memoria (Memory Museum) and the Bosque de la Memoria (Memory Forest) in Rosario. In the city capital of Buenos Aires there are close to twenty memorials to the Dirty War such as the monument to the *desaparecidos* in the park Parque de la Memoria (cf. Huyssen 2003). There is also the area in the emblematic square Plaza de Mayo that is called Pañuelos de la Pirámide de Mayo (Scarves of the Mayo Pyramid). It was here that the protesting *Madres* and *Abuelas* dressed in

---

[38] The *desaparecidos*, literally the "disappeared [people]," refers in Argentina to the thousands of people who suffered forced disappearance during the Dirty War. According to international law, forced dissappearance is when a person is secretly abducted or imprisoned by a state or political organisation or by a third party with the authorisation, support, or acquiescence of a state or political organisation, followed by a refusal to acknowledge the person's fate and whereabouts, with the intent of placing the victim outside the protection of the law. In Argentina, the majority of *desaparecidos* were murdered and most of these bodies have never been found.

[39] The National Commission on the Disappearance of Persons was created in 1982 by the newly elected President Raúl Alfonsín to investigate the fate of the *desaparecidos* and other crimes during the Dirty War. The result of their inquiry was presented in a 50,000 page-long report *Nunca Más* (Never Again), a bestseller in Argentina (Sikkink 2008:25n5; Crenzel 2011b).

[40] An overview of these films is found on line (Memoria Abierta 2012).

their characteristic white head scarves before walking around the Plaza de Mayo square in protest for their missing children and grandchildren.[41]

Another important part of this Dirty War memoryscape is the Falklands War. This was the war fought between England and Argentina during 74 days in 1982 over the control of the Falkland Islands, or the Islas Malvinas as they are called in Spanish. Argentina lost that war and the country's longstanding claim to sovereignty over the islands continued. The government has tried to rally regional and international support for this in later years (*La Nación* 2012; Usborne 2012). This claim is recalled on numerous memory sites throughout the entire country. Even in the most remote places of the huge but sparsely populated country[42] stand large signboards stating that "The Falklands are Argentinian [territory]!"[43] Monuments to the more than six hundred fallen soldiers of the war are found all over the country. Plenty of war veteran foundations have worked hard to keep alive the memory of the war, in tribute to their fallen comrades but also as a way of gaining attention to their own situation as veterans (Guber 1996, 1999a).

At the turn of the 21st century, Argentinian society is deeply involved in what Olick (2007) calls the politics of regret, referring to the process by which societies deal with past atrocities in order to settle future societal relations and achieve political legitimacy. The politics of regret consist of truth commissions, public apologies, and economic reparations that are situated at the heart of modernity (Olick 2007:130-38; Trouillot 2000). In contrast to the ideas of the universality of human rights and of transitional justice, which largely disregard the historically situated aspect of this phenomenon, the politics of regret is intimately connected to the phenomenon of social memory. It is fair to say that in Argentina, the violent years through the 1960s, 1970s and 1980s are recalled mainly through the trope of the Dirty War and that this has taken precedence over other memories in the Argentinian memoryscape at the turn of the 21st century. Yet, Argentina has long been a society in which remembering is a central political and social practice. Performances, narratives and artefacts for creating nationness (B. Anderson 1991) and historical knowledge about the colonial past and emancipation pervade social and institutional life. Guber has observed that "[i]n Argentina the importance of memory is outstanding" (Guber 1999a:4). Although Argentinians quite often disagree on the meanings of the past, "no one doubts whether the past is relevant to the present; nor would anyone debate about the criteria of what is and what is not 'historically plausible' in the Argentine past" (ibid.: 65). The bicentenary of the independence from Spain celebrated in 2010 was consequently a huge act of commemoration, although not only of the past but also oriented to the present and the future. The celebrations that displayed the

---

[41] Other memorials are squares and schools. Most schools in Argentinian are named after an emblematic person. In this case several schools have the names of disappeared persons (Instituto Espacio para la Memoria 2012).
[42] Argentina is the eighth largest country in the world with a territory of approximately 2,7 million km² but with only 14,4 inhabitants per km² in 2010 (Instituto Nacional de Estadísticas y Censos 2010a).
[43] In Spanish: *Las Malvinas son Argentinas*

cultural and geographical diversity in the country included concerts, performances, conferences, exhibitions, and music festivals. At the official webpage of the commemoration, people were encouraged to vote for the two hundred symbols that best represented them as Argentinians. Different people, places, artefacts, food and other things from the past and the present were suggested (Presidencia de la Nación Argentina 2010a). The future was envisioned by encouraging public debate on numerous social and political issues ranging from cultural diversity, identity and immigration to regional economy, environment, education and public health, just to mention a few topics.[44] Symbolically at least, these celebrations seemed to offer an optimistic, democratic and encouraging image of the nation's past, present and future, in contrast to the often gloomy images conveyed by the Argentinians themselves who often claim to live in the worst of countries considering the political and economic problems.

Argentina, the barn of the world, through breakdown and recovery

Argentina was at the turn of the 20th century one of the world's most prosperous nations. The country became known as "the barn of the world"[45] because of its agro-exports mainly of wheat and grains to the USA and to Europe, especially in the first half of the 20th century. Another popular description is to call Argentina "a generous country,"[46] which refers to its abundant natural resources and climate, hence optimal economic conditions for agricultural development. This latter saying stems from the times of massive immigration to Argentina in the late 19th and early 20th centuries, when immigrants arrived to cultivate the land from regions in the world where resources were scarce. This austral country is often considered to be one of the most developed and egalitarian countries in Latin America, illustrated by the existence of a large middle class, a social welfare system including for example compulsory and free education, and a strong civil society. In the 2010s, reforms of the Civil and Commercial Code in matters such as lesbian, gay, bisexual, and transgender rights, marriage and divorce (including the legalisation of same-sex marriage), reproductive rights, and indigenous property rights positioned Argentina as one of the most progressive countries in the region and even the world in many of these matters.[47] The notion of being a "civilised" society is part of Argentinian common sense. It can be traced to the state-led ideal from the times of modern formation in the late 19th century, of being a white, immigrant and cosmopolitan nation with few Indians and no

---

[44] The celebration of the bicentenary that was organised by the national government included a series of thematic forum called the Agenda Federal (Federal Agenda) arranged in a federal vein all over the country. The slogan of this campaign was "*La oportunidad de pensar la Argentina que viene*" (The opportunity to think [about] Argentina of the future) (Presidencia de la Nación Argentina 2010b). In the same vein, the Secretariat of Culture of the Presidency created the Casa Nacional del Bicentenario (National Home of the Bicentenary) (Secretaria de Cultura, Presidencia de la Nación 2010).
[45] In Spanish: *El granero del mundo*
[46] In Spanish: *Un país generoso*
[47] The legislative reform of the Argentinian Civil Code was intensively debated in 2012 and could be followed on line (Argentina.ar 2012).

Blacks (Briones and Guber 2008; Visacovsky and Garguin 2009). The Argentinian nation has been imagined by statesmen and intellectuals alike in terms of opposing factions such as civilisation-barbarism, centralism-federalism, authoritarianism-democracy, just to mention a few. Grimson has recently revived social theories reinforcing this imaginary (Briones and Guber ibid.) by describing an Argentinian national ethos, which is "myth maniac" in a bipolar fashion, always on the verge of either nationalist megalomania or absolute worthlessness (Grimson 2012). I prefer to understand this interplay between invocations of stereotypes, expressions of scepticism, the use of irony and humour as cultural critique as illustrative of what Herzfeld calls "cultural intimacy" (2004) referring to those discourses and performances that subvert official discourses while they at the same time reify them. By reproducing ideas of a grand past, a gloomy present and a potential future in and of Argentina, abstract categories of identity and belonging are transformed into intimate expressions of felt solidarities, sometimes within the national community and at other times within particular communities within the nation. Shared experiences of political and economic crises in the 20th century have contributed to such cultural intimacy (cf. DuBois 2008:8-9).

    The proud notions of being the "barn of the world" and a "generous country" in the first half of the 20th century, contrasts to the painful awareness of the economic decline in the second half of the century. It was the military mismanagement of the economy during the last dictatorship, which eventually led to increased indebtedness and ended in hyperinflation in 1989 that forced the sitting president Raúl Alfonsín to hand over government to the newly elected Carlos Menem before inauguration day. His government represented what at the time was internationally celebrated as a successful development, but what many Argentinians in hindsight would depict as the disaster leading to the disaster. Strictly following the recommendations of the IMF and other international financial institutions, the Menem government enacted "a neoliberal revolution" (Acuña 1994:31) in Argentina by devaluing the currency, suspending legal restrictions on foreign investment, dismantling union institutions, flexibilising the labour market, and privatising more than 90 percent of Argentina's state enterprises and public services (Shever 2012). The structural adjustments carried out in these years caused a sharp increase in the unemployment and underemployment rates, stagnant wage levels and increased levels of poverty (C. Acuña 1994). A new socio-economic category was produced during these years, the so-called "new poor" (Minujin and Kessler 1995; Powers 1995; DuBois 2008). In contrast to the "structural poor," a historical social category of Argentinian society (Powers 1995) of people who could not meet basic needs such as housing, food and education, the so-called new poor suffered declines in their relatively high-income levels which made previous levels of consumption impossible. The economic policies of the Menem government eventually led to the financial breakdown of the country. His successor, Fernando De la Rúa, was elected in 1999 but did not fulfil his mandate due the political turmoil and social upheaval generated by the continued economic problems. He literally fled from his post in the midst of violent street riots in December 2001.[48]

The structural adjustment programmes in the 1990s had produced increased structural poverty as well as new poverty, yet the economic breakdown of the years 2001-2002 was a real blow to almost all sectors of society. As a result of falling nominal incomes, low job creation and high levels of inequality preceding the breakdown, the incidence of poverty peaked in October 2002. More than half of the Argentinian population was then considered to live below the line of poverty in very vulnerable conditions (Novick, Lengyel, and Sarabia 2009:246). In contrast, post-crisis Argentina from 2002 and onwards has been characterised by an about-turn in economic strategy. This has coincided with a positive economic cycle experienced by Latin American economies in the 21st century (ibid.: 248). The governments of "the Kirchners,"[49] representing the largest Argentinian political party, namely the Peronist Party,[50] have pursued a macroeconomic regime which has focused on achieving a competitive exchange rate and on cleaning up the public accounts and reducing foreign debt, in combination with industrialisation efforts and redistributive measures. This economic model, based on the domestic market while simultaneously achieving a notable increase in exports, has produced a remarkable recovery from the past crises and a change in historical patterns (Frenkel and Rapetti 2008; Wylde 2011). The economic development in the 21st century certainly boosted the political support for the Kirchner presidential couple. Tens of thousands of people mourned at the lying in state of Néstor Kirchner, who died unexpectedly in November 2010. In October 2011, his then widow and sitting president, Cristina Fernández, won a landslide re-election as president with 54 percent of the votes, the widest margin of victory in a Argentinian presidential election since the return of democracy.[51]

---

[48] Demonstrations in Buenos Aires, Rosario and several other Argentinian cities in the end of 2001 culminated on the 20th and 21st of December, which led to violent confrontations with the police and ended with at least 30 dead protesters. Several of these victims were teenagers.

[49] Néstor Kirchner (2003-2007) was succeeded by his wife, the senator Cristina Fernández (2007-2011). She was re-elected in 2011 for a second term. In Argentina they are often referred to as a couple, as "the Kirchners." More contemptuously, political adversaries call them and their followers simply "the K" (*Los K*).

[50] The formal name of the Peronist Party is Partido Justicialista. It was founded by the late General Juan Domingo Perón in 1947. His importance and legacy quickly personalised the colloquial name of the party to Partido Peronista.

[51] President Fernández, or Cristina as she is colloquially called by supporters and adversaries alike, continues to rally support from large parts of the population, as manifested in April 2012 when her government expropriated the petrol company YPF from the Spanish company Repsol, claiming to recover a national resource. YPF, standing for Yacimientos Petrolíferos Fiscales (Treasury Petroleum Fields), is one of the oldest petrol companies in the world. It was the property of the Argentinian State until 1992 when the government of Menem had it privatised and sold to Repsol. Politically speaking, the Argentinian government under the Kirchner presidential couple has reinforced the country's relations with other Latin American countries and revived the notion of the *Patria Grande* (Great Fatherland), referring to the political idea of Latin American integration. This is manifested in numerous bilateral agreements, most notably with Brazil and Venezuela, but also in the multilateral Southern Common Market (Mercosur) and the newly formed Union of South American Nations (UNASUR).

The Argentinian political map of the 21st century

The political opposition to Peronism in Argentina has been weak and organisationally fragmented in later years. Opposition against government has rather been expressed in public opinion through street protests. Some of these protests have been organised by unions and NGOs, while other manifestations have been more spontaneous, largely motivated by a widespread political fatigue among Argentinians. This is not exclusively an Argentinian feature, as the anti-globalisation movement, the occupy movement and the *indignados* in Southern Europe have manifested in later years. In Argentina, a disappointment with and lack of trust in the political establishment grew especially strong during the 1990s. Fernando de la Rúa, representing the Radical Party, won the elections in 1999, allegedly because he promised to deal with political corruption. As he was driven off from his post in December 2001, the slogan of the people banging pots and pans in protest in the streets was "*¡Que se vayan todos!* All of them must go!" This statement referred not only to the sitting president and his government but to politicians in general. In spite of the crisis, not many of the politicians left; rather they just changed positions. This is the case in many societies, but it is indeed illustrative of how political life in Argentina is changeable and stable at the same time.

In the Argentinian society at large, Cristina Fernández and her government have enjoyed a strong support. Her re-election as president in 2011 certainly broke the historical record in number of votes. Yet at the same time there is an equally widespread fervent "anti-K"[52] sentiment among the other half of the population, which exacerbates public debate, political activism and social protest. Federalism is a central feature of the Argentinian political system that provides the country's provinces with a relatively large political power,[53] not least in fiscal terms (Tommasi 2006). Provinces are at the same time heavily dependent on central funding for their finances. This leads to a particular intertwining of national and regional politics and policies (ibid.). The federal governments led by the Kirchner presidential couple since 2003 have had political support in more than 50 percent of the provinces through governments that have been ruled by governors supporting their faction in the Peronist Party.[54] The Province of Santa Fe was ruled by Peronist governments since the return of democracy in 1983. At the time of *la Inundación* in Santa Fe City and other parts of

---

[52] While the Peronist Party has been fraught by internal divisions and alliances between wings and factions, there were political adversaries to the Peronist Party who supported the sitting government. In parties which were divided along Kirchnerist/Anti-Kirchnerist lines, the members of the Kirchnerist faction were often distinguished with the letter "K" (as in K-Peronists, K-Socialists, or K-Radicals), while the factions opposing Kirchnerism were similarly labelled with the expression "Anti-K."

[53] The Federal Republic of Argentina consists of 23 provinces and one autonomous city which is Buenos Aires. After emancipation from the Spanish Crown in 1816, the country was fraught with conflict between the provinces and the ruling power of Buenos Aires. Not until 1880 was Buenos Aires declared the city capital of the republic. The capital city and the provinces have their own constitutions within the federal system.

[54] The Frente para la Victoria (Front for Victory) was an electoral alliance and formally a faction of the Peronist Party, which was established by Néstor Kirchner for the presidential election in 2003.

the region, the governor at the time was Carlos Reutemann. He was succeeded by Jorge Obeid in the elections that same year. Not until 2007 did the political opposition manage to win the provincial elections. Since then, the Socialist Party has been in power in the provincial government of Santa Fe. As we shall see in forthcoming chapters, the particular political structure, partisan configurations and exacerbated relationship between the political establishment and the citizenry, have had implications for the case at hand. This particular dynamic has largely shaped how flood management has been handled and understood, but more importantly it has been significant for how the urban flood memoryscape in Santa Fe City has been formed. Before we delve into this process, I shall now describe more carefully the historical, economic and political context of Santa Fe City.

Santa Fe, generous province and the barn of Argentina

Santa Fe City, or Ciudad de Santa Fe in Spanish,[55] is located 476 km northwest of Buenos Aires. Santa Fe is the capital city of the homonymous Santa Fe Province, situated in the north-east of Argentina. The development of the agricultural economy in this province, the farming, dairy and livestock-rearing industries, was made possible largely because of its geographical conditions, epitomising the notion of Argentina as being the "generous country" and the "barn of the world." The agricultural economy of the region has also shaped urban life in this province. Santa Fe City was for example a port town from its very beginning, being declared *Puerto Preciso*[56] in colonial times, obliging all ships on the Paraná River to stop over here on their way to or from Asunción. Santa Fe is located on the eastern side of the province, in the Department La Capital. The province of Santa Fe is geographically differentiated into the southern and northern areas. The boundary between the two is considered to run north of Santa Fe City. The northern part of the province is classified as belonging to the semi-arid Chaqueño region[57] characterised by thorn brush jungle and whatever is

Figure 1 | Location of Santa Fe Province and Santa Fe City in Argentina (Map by Roberto Robuffo)

---

[55] The full name of the city is Santa Fe de la Vera Cruz. It is generally named ciudad de Santa Fe to differentiate it from the homonymous provincia de Santa Fe, of which it is the city capital. Throughout the study I use its English translation, Santa Fe City, or simply Santa Fe, if otherwise not stated.
[56] The *Puerto Preciso* was a Spanish Colonial institution consisting of the privilege given by the Spanish Crown to certain colonial port towns within the empire, to charge taxes on all passing ships.
[57] The Chaqueño region includes the region of Gran Chaco that stretches over eastern Bolivia, Paraguay, northern Argentina and part of Brazil.

left from forests of *quebracho* trees. The high quality of the *quebracho* timber gave rise to intensive forestry exploitation and exports in the 19th and 20th centuries. The timber was used for poles and railway sleepers, and the tannin was used to tan leather. By the mid-20th century, large forests in the province and in the North of Argentina had therefore virtually disappeared (cf. Gori 1965). The south of the province is ecologically classified as part of the humid plains, the so-called *pampa húmeda*; an exceptionally fertile area. The pastures found in this area are of high quality, making possible the production of the famous Argentinian beef. In provinces such as Santa Fe, Buenos Aires and Córdoba, the pampas grazing has also sustained a productive dairy industry. While cattle were the primary economic resource in the region during Spanish Colonial times,[58] agriculture was introduced at a large scale in the mid-19th century in the context of nation building.[59] Both agriculture and livestock still play significant roles in regional and national economy of the 21st century. This became clear in 2008, during the so-called farmers-government conflict between Cristina Fernández's government and the Argentinian farming sector. This political conflict over taxation escalated to strikes and violent street protests all over the country that engaged not only the farmers but virtually all of society, taking sides in the conflict (cf. Giarracca and Teubal 2010).

During the years of my fieldwork, when I travelled overland to Santa Fe by bus it did not matter whether I arrived in the city from the east, the south or the north. As far as my eye could see, surrounding the city were enormous fields everywhere, either filled with grazing cattle or cultivated with corn, wheat, sunflowers and soybean. My impression of this landscape was reinforced by reading the statistics. In 2005, agriculture provided 13% of Argentina's GDP (de Simone 2006:4). In the years 2005-2009, the province of Santa Fe was among the principal provinces contributing to the country's exports, being the one of the country's principal producers grains, beef, vegetable oils and dairy products ('Información Agropecuaria: Comercio Exterior 2005-2009' 2012) The output from agriculture in Santa Fe has been fairly stable throughout the years, except for the soybean production, which has been boosted not only in this province but in the entire country as well as in the region,[60] implying a major shift in Argentinian agriculture. The cultivation of this crop was doubled in the province of Santa Fe in the period 1993 2005. The province provided around 40% of the

---

[58] While the indigenous communities in the region at the time of the Spanish conquest lived from hunting, gathering, fishing and some agriculture, the Spaniards introduced livestock as the principal productive asset by bringing domestic cattle to the New World. The cattle population was introduced to what was later Argentina from Peru, Chile and Paraguay and proliferated both as livestock and as wild cattle. The cattle economy would be dominant in the region for centuries. It was sustained by the forced labour system of the *encomiendas* until the beginning of the 18th century (Nidia Areces and Tarragó 1999:65). Through the effects of this system even those indigenous communities who were still independent after the conquest were diminished, or perished in any of the diseases that was rife at the time (ibid.: 68).
[59] The process of "agriculturalisation" was part of the Argentinian territorial expansion into land yet not in control in the 19th and 20th centuries (cf. Martínez-Sarasola 1992; N. Areces 1999b; Barreira 2006).
[60] The 21st century soybean boom has also taken place in Bolivia, Brazil, Paraguay, and Uruguay, as well as in the USA (cf. Travasso et al. 2006; Grau and Aide 2008; Walker et al. 2009; Bartholdson et al. 2012).

Argentinian soybean production during these years (Instituto Nacional de Estadísticas y Censos 2005a). The increase is a response to a growing global demand as well as to the introduction of new technologies such as gene modified herbicide resistant seeds. Soybean cultivation has largely replaced the farming of other crops as well as livestock rearing. It has moved the historical agricultural frontier in Argentina into regions which were historically cattle producing, such as the North of the Province of Santa Fe among many other areas (Teubal and Palmisano 2010). It is well known that deforestation and the use of pesticides affect climate as well as soil and water qualities (Kupfer and Karimanzira 1990; Shukla, Nobre, and Sellers 1990; Magrin and Gay García 2007). It may also affect the absorption capacity of the soil. Instead of forests capturing rainfall, deforestation produces soil erosion and more direct runoff of water to the watercourses. This increases the risk for flooding (Teubal and Palmisano 2010:245).

Santa Fe City is situated on what can be described as a sort of peninsula in between two rivers: the Paraná River on the east and the Salado River on the west. Paraná is a Guaraní[61] word meaning approximately "like the sea," allegedly due to the size of this river, which is considered to be the second largest in South America after the Amazon River. It runs through Brazil, Paraguay and Argentina over a course of 2,500 kilometres, empties into the Río de la Plata and eventually flows into the Atlantic Ocean at the coast of Buenos Aires. The width of the primary river ranges between 300-600 metres but the entire flood plain of the Paraná River can reach 65 kilometres in width at its widest point. This is because the riverside on its western shores, which is where Santa Fe City is situated, consists of small and large islands separated by numerous creeks, streams, lagoons and channels making up a delta landscape. In times of flooding it becomes more of a wetland however. The watercourses closest to Santa Fe City are the Santa Fe Creek, the Setúbal Lagoon, and the Santa Fe River. In front of the harbour the watercourse is called the Bypass Channel[62] because it is dredged. So is the Access Channel running from Alto Verde to the mainstream of the Paraná River. On the western side of the city runs the Salado River. This river has its source in the Andes in the Northern Province of Salta and flows for more than 2000 km before it empties into the Paraná River. Despite its length it is a relatively small river and can hardly be compared to the Paraná. Both rivers have flooded regularly, albeit the Paraná River much more frequently than the Salado River.

Taken together, the vulnerability to climate induced disasters is prone to increase if this development continues. Santa Fe City, situated between two major rivers, is surrounded by extensive agricultural production and furthermore largely dependent on this regional agricultural economy, which promotes deforestation. Hence, the conditions of environmental vulnerability in the region of Santa Fe have been exacerbated in the last decades (Montenegro et al. 2005).

---

[61] Guaraní is a local indigenous language. It is one of the official languages of Paraguay and is also spoken in parts of southwestern Brazil, and in some northeastern Argentinian provinces, such as in that of Corrientes.
[62] The Canal de Derivación channel is divided in two. The North Channel is closest to the Suspension Bridge and the South Channel ends in the Santa Fe River and the outlet to the Salado River.

The Santafesinos and their city

Santa Fe City is at present the ninth largest city in Argentina. In the national census of 2010, 415.345 inhabitants were registered in Santa Fe City (Instituto Nacional de Estadísticas y Censos 2010a).[63] The population had increased approximately 12% since the previous census a decade earlier.[64] Historically, the rate of population growth since the time of the city's foundation in the 16th century had been rather stable.[65] An important peak in the population growth occurred at the turn of the 20th century however, due to the high influx of immigrants around that time.[66]

  A widespread notion I found talking to different people in Santa Fe was that, during the last decades, "things in this town have only become worse." People referred mostly to the economic and social development of the city after the return of democracy in 1983. The 2001 financial crisis in Argentina and the 2003 disastrous flood were part of their explanation as to why this was the case. These events epitomised the structural adjustments made to Argentinian economy in the 1990s, which largely affected the middle- and low-income sectors. This period was in Santa Fe characterised by low economic growth and increase in unemployment and poverty rates due to economic structural adjustments (Arrillaga, Grand, and Busso 2009). Many of the people I talked to were disappointed with what they saw as the decay of the city. Still, they also expressed a collective self-representation of a warm hearted community. I learned that the city had the nickname "The Cordial [City]"[67] because of the friendliness of its inhabitants. This remark was often made particularly by middle-class residents, who, more than others, wanted to show me their best qualities as Santafesinos. I later learned another slogan, usually used in governmental settings to highlight the political importance of the city and its residents, namely: "Santa Fe, Cradle of the Constitution"[68] (Mino 1998). This referred to the establishment of the first Constitution of the Argentinian Republic, which was adopted in Santa Fe City on May 1st 1853. The slogan also refers to some of the subsequent constitutional amendments adopted in conventions in Santa Fe, the last one in 1994. Another historical trait often referred to, when representing the idiosyncrasy of the Santafesinian community, was the so-called "Revolution of the Seven Chiefs"[69] This was the first insurrection against the Spanish rulers, carried out in Santa Fe

---

[63] 525,093 people were registered as inhabitants of the department La Capital to which the municipality of Santa Fe City and another 26 municipalities belong (Instituto Nacional de Estadísticas y Censos 2010b)

[64] In 2001, 369,589 inhabitants were registered in Santa Fe City (Instituto Nacional de Estadísticas y Censos 2001).

[65] By the time of the first local census in 1816, the same year as the La Plata provinces proclaimed independence from Spain, the town had approximately 6,000 inhabitants. When the first national census was carried out in 1869, this number had increased to 10,670 (Instituto Nacional de Estadísticas y Censos1869)

[66] The population of Santa Fe City almost trebled from approximately 60,000 inhabitants in 1914 to around 170,000 in 1947. In the National Census of 1970, 244,655 inhabitants were registered in the city (I am indebted to the local staff at the Provincial Statistical and Census Institute in Santa Fe City for providing me with historical census data).

[67] The nickname is *La Cordial* as in *La Ciudad Cordial*

[68] In Spanish: *Santa Fe, Cuna de la Constitución*

[69] In Spanish: *La Revolución de los Siete Jefes*

by native Creole soldiers in 1580. Among the signifiers for collective identification was also the depiction of a contrasting other. For the Santafesinos, the mirror of reference was the city of Rosario, located approximately 180 kilometres south of Santa Fe. While Santa Fe is the older town of the two and the administrative city capital of the province, Rosario is a much larger city with approximately one million inhabitants in the 21st century. The latter city has long enjoyed greater economic importance and is the third largest city in Argentina after Buenos Aires and Córdoba.

While many Santafesinos represented themselves as a community of friendly people with a fairly glorious past in the context of the Argentinian nation building, they also considered themselves to be living in a city which had suffered a generalised decay. The memories of *la Inundación* reinforced this collective self-identification of a cohesive community of sufferers by many of the city's dwellers. Yet, far from being characterised by social cohesion, the society of urban Santa Fe was characterised by large social inequalities. Since its foundation in colonial times, large differences in terms of social class have been a feature of Santa Fe City. The urban elite has consisted on the one hand of the local traditional Creole elites, who were many times large estate owners. On the other hand, there were families of European descent who had climbed the social ladder since their immigration at the turn of the 20th century to reach the top. The working class, which at the turn of the 21st century was rather a class of under- and unemployed, was largely constituted by less successful European immigrants and by internal immigrants from the Northern provinces in the mid-20th century.[70] The largest social category in numbers of people in Santa Fe City was that of the heterogeneous middle classes, something which can be said to be a reflection of Argentinian society in general (cf. Visacovsky and Garguin 2009).

As I walked the city extensively during my fieldwork, the urban landscape revealed to me how social class was spatialised in the community. The city is divided into eight districts called the Northside, the Northwest Side, the Northeast Side, the Westside, the Southwest Side, the Eastside, Downtown and the Coastside.[71]

---

[70] The indigenous peoples that lived here in pre-colonial times were killed, enslaved and marginalised. The communities living in and around Santa Fe City in the 21st century belong to the tobas, mocovíes and abipones ethnic groups, having arrived in this area from the northern Chaco region in different periods, beginning with the processes of industrialisation, urbanisation and internal migration from the 1940's onwards. Important waves of indigenous migration took place as a consecuence of the 1986 and 1987 floods (Garbulsky and Vicuña Martínez 2006:150-61). Despite certain improvements for these communities in the 20th and 21st centuries in terms of legal recognition and land restitution, they generally live in poverty and marginalisation as a result of having been subject to historical politics of invisibility (I owe this observation to my field assistant and colleague Eugenia Martínez Grieco who has carried out fieldwork for her doctoral thesis in the 2010s in the Mocoví community in the town of Recreo, north of Santa Fe City).

[71] This division corresponds to the municipal jurisdiction but also largely how people orient themselves. The exception to this colloquial use is that people generally say the Westside (*el Oeste*) when referring to all the districts on the western side. "The Westside" then generally refers to the low-income neighbourhoods in all the districts in this area. In this account I too use this notion unless otherwise specified.

Figure 2 | Santa Fe City[72] (Map by Roberto Robuffo)

---

[72] This map represents the city at large. The most recent work of the Westside ring road and flood embankment to Recreo is not marked here.

The Eastside, and in particular the Northeast Side, was predominantly a high-income area. In residential quarters, such as Guadalupe and Siete Jefes, people commonly lived in large or middle-sized villas with tiled roofs and well-maintained and fragrant gardens behind high fences. The streets were wide, clean and lined with huge Jacaranda trees. Along the western shores of the Setúbal Lagoon was the Costanera Oeste, an esplanade several kilometres long, which was also a flood embankment.

Figure 3 | Costanera Oeste in autumn (Photo by author 2005)

Across the waters, on the eastern side of the lagoon, was the Costanera Este. This was a recreational area with sand beaches where people sunbathed, and bars and restaurants. In the waters of the lagoon, not only small scale fishing was practiced, but all kinds of nautical sports such as windsurfing, water skiing, water scooter driving, kayaking and sailing.

Figure 4 | Costanera Este in summer (Photo by author 2005)

The middle-income districts were located in a strip from north to south in the middle of the city (Northside, part of the Westside and Downtown). At the northern end were *barrios* such as Guadalupe Oeste and Villa Maria Selva, and at the southern end were for example Candioti Norte and Candioti Sur, Adelanto Barranquitas, Mariano Comas, República del Oeste, Barrio Roma and Barrio Sur. The middle-income districts were characterised by one and two-storey brick houses, sometimes with a tiny garden in front of the house but more commonly with a small backyard. In some neighbourhoods, such as in Barrio Roma, most houses were built in the typically Argentinian *casa chorizo* style.[73] Some areas, such as the commercial areas Downtown and along the large avenues, were increasingly characterised by apartment buildings. These neighbourhoods thus ranged from being residential and quiet, to being full of commerce, traffic and noise.

Figure 5 | Municipal Female Traffic Brigade in Downtown (Photo by author 2005)

The Westside, referring to the districts on the western outskirts of the city, consisted predominantly of low-income districts, ranging from working-class quarters to shantytowns. Here, few streets were paved and in many neighbourhoods there was no sewage system. Houses were small and often precariously built in brick with no grout. The dwellings in the shantytowns were mostly shanties or *ranchos* as they are often called in Argentinian cities.[74] The deficit draining sys-

---

[73] The Argentinian *casa chorizo* type of house dates from the 19th century. It consists of a house built longwise on a long narrow plot. The rooms are built in line and are interconnected while facing a lateral yard. It is due to this arrangement that the building is likened to a *chorizo* sausage. Historically extended families lived several generations together in these dwellings or the owner family rented out one or a couple of rooms they did not use themselves to other families.
[74] To be more precise, the *rancho* refers to a humble dwelling both in rural and urban Argentina. Historically, the *rancho* was a rural dwelling built in thatch or reed and adobe which is still common for many poor families in rural Argentina. In this context, the word *rancho* is also used to denote a person's home. In the Littoral region, the rural *rancho* is traditionally built with poles, with the walls made

49

tem consisted of small ditches that ran along the dirt roads separating the lots from the street. More often than not, the ditches were filled with stagnant water and waste. A foul odour often filled the air, mixing with the smell of burning garbage from the many *cirujas* (scavengers) living and working on the Westside.

Figure 6 | *Ranchos* on the Westside (Photo by author 2005)

East of the city was the suburban Coastside. This was a lush and large district situated on the islands between the city and the mainstream of the Paraná River. Two bridges, the emblematic hanging bridge and a car bridge, crossed the Setúbal Lagoon to what used to be called the Tacurú Island where the *Costanera Este*, the campus of the National University of the Littoral and the housing estate El Pozo were located. This was where the National Routes 11 and 168 passed, the latter leading to the subfluvial tunnel that connects the Littoral region with that of the Mesopotamia. Most of the neighbourhoods in the Coastside were suburban and semirural at the same time, like that of Alto Verde, La Boca, and La Vuelta del Paraguayo, where many inhabitants commuted to work in the city while others were fishermen and cattlemen. Other *barrios*, such as Colastiné, were mainly residential areas that had been gentrified through the expansion of weekend cottages and summer houses, called *casas quintas*.[75] Some of the latter were in the process of becoming permanent residences during my fieldwork. The suburban

---

from clay mixed with water and straw, and the roof made of straw. As for the urban context, the *rancho* refers to the precarious dwellings in the shantytowns, which became increasingly common through the migration to the cities in the 20th century. The urban *rancho* is generally built in tin plates, wooden boards or other cheap materials.

[75] Literally translated to "garden house" in English, the Argentinian *casa quinta* is usually located outside a city. Such a property generally consists of a house with a large garden and often a swimming pool. It is mainly used for recreational purposes.

district of the Coastside therefore included low-, middle- and high-income neighbourhoods. Walking the city and talking to different interlocutors throughout my fieldwork I became aware of the social borders and material boundaries within the urban space that separated people and places from each other along lines of social class and place identity. The *barrio* was for many Santafesinos the basic unit of the urban life (cf. Gravano 2003).

A *barrio* in Santa Fe City

During my fieldwork in Santa Fe City in the year 2005, I rented a room at the home of a family in Barrio Roma. This was a lower-middle-class neighbourhood in the Westside district with approximately 3600 residents (Instituto Nacional de Estadísticas y Censos 2001). According to the statistics,[76] in 2001 a third of the residents were children under the age of 14. Close to half of the economically active population in the *barrio* had a job, while fifteen percent were unemployed and eleven percent were students. There were fourteen percent of pensioners in the neighbourhood. That year, the rate of social vulnerability in relation to occupation in Barrio Roma ranged from low to middle vulnerability (Arrillaga, Grand, and Busso 2009). Italian and Spanish descent predominated among the inhabitants, but there were also people with origins in the northern provinces of El Chaco and Formosa. Most residents were property owners and only a tenth were tenants. Approximately 75% of the households had private health insurance. Most houses were one storey buildings in grouted brick, many of which were in the *casa chorizo* style.

Figure 7 | Fish catch of the day on the shores of Alto Verde (Photo by author 2005)

The neighbourhood of Barrio Roma had been settled in the early 20th century. There had been a high demand for land and housing in Argentinian cities in those years, including Santa Fe City. Even the flood-prone lowlands on the Westside were increasingly occupied. This demand was largely due to demographic growth, mainly because the international immigration going on since the late 19th century. Before that, the population in Argentina had been relatively sparse.

---

[76] It is worth noting that these figures stem from the national census carried out on November 17th-18th 2001. This was before the financial crisis broke out which had serious effects on economic and social life. It is also noteworthy that the official statistics on employment on the scale of neighbourhood from 2003 onwards was not yet published or made available by the Provincial Institute of Statistics (IPEC).

Figure 8 | Sunday morning in Barrio Roma (Photo by author 2005)

Since independence from Spain in 1816, violent conflicts between different factions and regions had been dividing the new-born country, making it virtually impossible to govern. By the late 19th century, the Argentinian government implemented numerous strategies to gain control over the national territory and to defeat indigenous peoples who were still resisting conquest. One such strategy was to establish agricultural colonies in frontier areas, such as in the one in the province of Santa Fe. "To govern is to populate"[77] was the catch phrase of this policy. The ruling elite in Buenos Aires had little faith in the *criollos*,[78] the Creole inhabitants, or in the colonised indigenous communities to be capable of producing the social and economic development considered necessary. Settlers were thus recruited from Europe. The European recruits were promised plots of land in the frontier regions and technological and economic support in order to settle as colonising farmers, so-called *colonos*. This Argentinian immigrant policy attracted a large number of people from the then poverty stricken Europe and the Province of Santa Fe was one of the regions where the colonisers were settled. The *colono* was in general a property owner of his land who, in contrast to the large estate owner (*estanciero*), used to work the land himself side by side with his entire family and occasionally became a patron by employing farmhands (generally *criollos*) such as in times of harvest (see Archetti and Stølen 1974, 1976; Gallo 1976, 1984; Bartolomé 1990; Stølen 2004).

---

[77] "*Gobernar es poblar*" was allegedly the motto coined by the Argentinian politician and intellectual Juan Bautista Alberdi (1810-1884) who supported the idea to bring Europeans to America in order to civilise the new nation states.

[78] In colonial times, the category *criollo* referred to the people born in Spanish America by European parents. These were of lower rank than the *peninsulares*, the people born in the Spanish peninsula, in the social organisation of Colonial Spanish America. As the colonies emancipated in the 19th century, however, certain *criollo* families turned into social elite. The category *criollo* later came to include also the *mestizo*, that is, the child of a European born parent and an indigenous parent. While the latter category of *criollos* in general had a better position in the colonial countries, compared to the indigenous peoples that remained or to the African slaves and their descendants, the *mestizo criollo* was still at the lower end of the social hierarchy. This position was re-consolidated when European immigration took place in the 19th and 20th centuries.

While the bulk of the European immigrants ended up as agricultural settlers, many of them also settled in the thriving Argentinian cities. Immigrants arrived from all over the world to Santa Fe, although most of them came from Italy, Germany, Spain, France, England and Switzerland (Sonzogni 2006:20). A majority of these were Catholics, but there were also Protestants, Jews and Muslims. This contributed to an increased religious diversity in an urban community, which had been predominantly Catholic since the time of its foundation. During my fieldwork I found numerous churches represented in the city. Besides Catholics, Jews and Muslims I learned there were Evangelical Lutherans, Methodists, Mormons, Jehovah's Witnesses, Baptists, and members of the Universal Church of the Kingdom of God. The international immigration to Argentina and Santa Fe continued well into the 20th century as Europeans were pushed to emigrate from their home countries by war, poverty and political persecution. Immigration contributed heavily to the growth and expansion of Santa Fe City in this period.[79]

In 2005, I frequented the *vecinal* (neighbourhood association) in Barrio Roma hoping to make new acquaintances. I attended the aerobics classes once a week, where I got to know a group of women whom I interviewed. The aerobics class turned out to be basically the only activity going on in the *vecinal*. Other neighbours, who did not frequent the place at all, were annoyed by the fact that there were no activities of interest going on there, but more fundamentally, that the president of the association was "*haciendo política*" (making politics), through the association. By this was meant that he was using the association for political purposes. This was seen by many neighbours as morally despicable (cf. Frederic 2004). The neighbourhood associations in Santa Fe emerged as the city grew in the 20th century. Urbanisation required modern infrastructure such as potable water, electricity, sewage, the opening up of streets and pavement, and access to public transport. The neighbours were encouraged by the land owners and the real estate agencies to organise in neighbourhood commissions in order to collectively demand such infrastructure from the municipality (Gallasi 2006; Roldán 2006). The municipality, in turn, supported the establishment of such neighbourhood associations as a means of exerting governmental control of the new settlements located far away from the city centre and political power (Roldán ibid.). In Santa Fe City the *vecinales* were institutionalised in the 1970s by municipal bylaws that made them the formal representative entities for their respective neighbourhoods. The *vecinales* thus became the institutional intermediaries between the citizens in the *barrio* and the municipal government.

When I carried out fieldwork in the city, a common view in both middle- and low-income districts was that many (but not all) of the *vecinales* had become a venue for political brokerage, where favours were transacted for future votes, instead of being a meeting place for social intercourse and identity work. According to several of my interlocutors, what used to be a truly communal endeavour had been co-opted by the Peronist party affiliates during its years in gov-

---

[79] The population increased from 14,206 inhabitants in 1887 to 22,244 inhabitants in 1895 and to almost 60,000 in 1914 (Larrechea 2008).

ernment (1983-2007), who had used them as an extension of their clientistic political practice (cf. Auyero 2001, 2003; DuBois 2008; Quirós 2011).[80] This practice was questioned by many neighbours (although not necessarily by all of them) (cf. Frederic 2004), who therefore had chosen to distance themselves from the *vecinal* and its activities. Nevertheless, I could observe that these places were also venues for social interaction between neighbours celebrating feasts and organising different educational and social activities. The *vecinales* did provide a context for the construction of the *barrio* identity even if they no longer seemed to have the same power of community making as they used to have, from what I was told.

The women I met in the aerobics class in Barrio Roma certainly cultivated communality. They were between 30 and 50 years old. Many of them were born in the *barrio* and had kept residence there after being married and having children. They seemed to know each other well, when they chatted in class about themselves and their bodies, about family problems and issues with other neighbours who were not present. They talked about local events in the past, which confirmed that they had lived there for many years and about future projects, which indicated an intention to stay. Several families had left Barrio Roma after the 2003 flood. Diana, for instance, whom I met in the context of the *inundados* movement, had decided to leave the *barrio* after the disaster. She and her family thus rented an apartment on the Eastside for several years. When I spoke to her in 2005, she could not bear the thought of going back, because of the traumatic memories that her home evoked. In contrast, the women in the aerobics class explained to me that they could not afford to pay housing elsewhere even if they wanted to. They or their husbands had inherited their houses, and they did not have to pay mortgages on house loans, which gave them low housing costs. All the women expressed a strong identification with their *barrio* and claimed that this was another strong reason for them to stay put. Diana told me sadly that in spite of everything, she missed the quarters where she grew up and where she had raised her children. When I met her again in April 2009, she happily informed me that they had moved back to Barrio Roma.

Middle- and low-income economies in Santa Fe

According to my interlocutors in Barrio Roma, most of its inhabitants were either blue or white collar workers. Yet I observed that quite a few families kept family businesses in the front parts of their homes. There were bakeries, vegetable and fruit shops, kiosks, small warehouses, butcheries, or small hardware stores in

---

[80] It has been argued that the politicisation of the neighbourhood associations in Santa Fe is not a recent phenomenon however. Roldán (2006:81-89) describes how the *vecinalismo*, the creation of community associations which was initially an apolitical sociality, turned into a political movement in the city of Rosario in the 1930-40s. By changing their juridical figure from neighbourhood commissions to associations and candidate for office in municipal elections, the *vecinales* emerged as an alternative to the established political parties. The *vecinales*, on their part, now found themselves competing for votes, which was then countered by the political power at the time (the Radical Party) by inviting them to solve the problems of the neighbourhoods. Thus, the practice of political reciprocity, or clientelism, does not seem to be new or specific to any political party.

almost every block. I was told that many of these small shops were the result of the impoverishment of the *barrio* since the 1990s (cf. DuBois 2005:126-127). Families opened small shops to complement the regular income and were often attended by the woman in the household. In the past, the women in Barrio Roma had mostly been housewives. It seemed to me that this was still often the case, despite the number of female shop owners I observed and the women employees that I also befriended.

I was also told that many independent craftsmen lived in the *barrio*. Luis was one of them. He was a man in his fifties, living with his widow mother in a street next to mine. His deceased father had been of Sefardi Jewish origin, born in Santa Fe City in the beginning of the 20th century. The father had worked as an electrician of the Wholesale Market until he had retired in the late 1970s, just before the market was relocated from Barrio Roma to a place in the Northwest district. The Wholesale Market gathered all local producers of vegetables, meat and fish in the region. The market created a large economy around it of transport, restaurants, and service. Luis followed his father's footsteps by studying electrical engineering at the prestigious Industrial School and at the National University of the Littoral in the 1970s. Luis thought that he would most probably have inherited his father's office at the Market had it not by then decreased its volume of trade, hiring no new staff.

Santa Fe is the capital city of the province and consequently the bulk of governmental offices were located here. Thousands of Santafesinos were employed as white collar workers within the bureaucracy, the healthcare system and the educational system.[81] The municipality was a growing organisation with both white and blue collar employees. Public services, such as potable water provision, electricity and communications, had been privatised in Santa Fe like in the rest of the country in the 1990s. One of the effects of privatisation was that staff had been downsized in the public sector. The financial and institutional crisis of the country in 2001-2002 exacerbated this process, even if employment in the public sector increased slightly in the following years, according to some of the clerks that I interviewed.

The nearby city of Rosario has since long been the industrial city of the province of Santa Fe. Nevertheless, Santa Fe City has also had some important industries throughout history. Most of these have been small and medium enterprises, with up to 20 employees with a few exceptions. The municipal cold storage built in the late 19th century in the Northwest district employed hundreds of people until it closed down in the 1980s. The brewery Cervecería Santa Fe was founded in the beginning of the 20th century and was still operating, being the second largest brewery in the country at the time of my fieldwork. One of the largest factories in the city, employing some 5,000 operators at its peak, was owned by the Fiat Company. In the late 1960s, the car company established a tractor and truck plant in Sauce Viejo, a place southwest of the city. Germán, a neighbour of mine in Barrio Roma who was born in 1964, told me that when he

---

[81] 38,7% of the city's active population was employed in the public sector in 2006 (Instituto Provincial de Estadísticas y Censos 2006).

was a small boy he used to accompany his uncle to the Fiat factory. The uncle had moved to Santa Fe from the province of Entre Ríos and had set up a kiosk at the factory. As far as Germán could remember, the kiosk served the factory workers and was always full of customers in the breaks and in between shifts. He estimated that his uncle must have earned as much as a factory employee, if not more, because the uncle could afford a car and go for vacations in January when the factory workers had their holidays. Germán figured that several thousand of operators worked at the Fiat factory in the 1970s. Many of them had immigrated from other provinces to take up such jobs. According to Germán and other interlocutors, it was a real blow to the community when Fiat closed down the factory in 1981, leaving thousands of unemployed.

Intimately connected to the history of Santafesinian industries is that of the railways. The Argentinian railway system had developed in the late 19th century by the growing agricultural production nationwide and the incorporation of peripheral territories into the expanding Nation State. British and French capital was invested to build the railway network. Many foreign companies kept concessions to operate these lines for decades. The expansion of the railway system in the province of Santa Fe was directly related to the process of modernisation and agriculturalisation of Argentina. The first railway line to Santa Fe City was the so-called French Railway[82] constructed in the 1880s by the provincial government to connect the town with the agricultural colonies up north. Another two railways were later built to connect the people and the products of Santa Fe with the rest of the country. In 1948 the first Peronist government had nationalised virtually all railways (C. Lewis 1983; W. Smith 1991). These remained in state ownership until their privatisation in the 1990s during the presidency of Carlos Menem. In provinces where neither the provincial government nor any private investors were interested in taking over the services, they were simply cancelled. Such was the case of Santa Fe. When I did my fieldwork in the city in 2005, there was only one passenger train a week running between Santa Fe City and Buenos Aires. The freight traffic seemed to operate somewhat more frequently.[83] From where I lived in Barrio Roma during fieldwork, I could now and then hear the train whistle as it passed close to the neighbourhood. I visited the abandoned station houses several times as well as the Railway Museum in the city centre of Santa Fe. The museum guard was a man in his seventies, who had worked his entire life in the railways, starting off as a controller of train wagons and ending his career in the Telegraph Superintendence. He was one of the founders of the museum and the author of a book that he offered me to buy in support of the museum (Andreis 2003). He still had some hope for the reestablishment of the railways as he said to me:

> I had the fortune to retire from the railways before the privatisation, but hundreds of *compañeros* (workmates) lost their jobs here in San-

---

[82] The Ferrocarril Francés was the first railway company in town. After a couple of years it was franchised to the company Ferrocarriles Francesas de la Provincia de Santa Fe, by which it got this name. This name was later changed to Ferrocarriles Santa Fe (Santa Fe Railways).
[83] From what I heard, passenger traffic between Rosario and Santa Fe stopped again in 2006.

ta Fe in the 1990s. We need the railways! It is not only the best means of transport for our products, but it provides thousands of families in this city with food on the table.

During my field research in Santa Fe, I learned how the railway had in fact played a significant role in the flooding history of Santa Fe. The infrastructure had served to bar the floodwater, that is, the high embankments on top of which the railways were built, had served as flood embankments. They had even worked as a refuge for people escaping from the rising waters. The station houses and train wagons had been used throughout the 20th century as evacuation shelters, including in the 2003 flood. In 2005 the Mitre station had been partially transformed into a cultural centre, occasionally used by the Santafesinian civil society, including the flood victims of 2003 as we shall see in next chapter. In 2009, the rundown Belgrano train station on the Eastside was being completely restored by the municipality in order to become a public space for conventions and expositions.

Migration, industrialisation and urbanisation

The international immigration to Argentina in the 19th and 20th centuries gave rise to the saying allegedly coined by the Mexican writer Octavio Paz: "The Mexicans descend from the Aztecs, the Peruvians from the Incas and the Argentinians - from the ships." This phrase refers to the widespread idea that the country is above all an immigrant nation, constituted by descendants of Europeans. At the beginning of the 20th century, immigrants in Santa Fe City tended to live close to relatives or fellow countrymen, where they could get support and gain opportunities through reciprocal ethnic networks, as manifested, for example, by the social clubs and the mutual aid associations.[84] This seems to have been particularly so for the Italian and Spanish immigrants, the largest immigrant groups in Santa Fe. The case of the family of Julia is one case in point. I met her at the Barrio Roma Pensioners' Club in 2005. She was then in her eighties. Her parents had arrived in Argentina in the 1920s from Calabria in Southern Italy. They had travelled directly to Santa Fe City because they had fellow countrymen from their same village of origin there. Julia was born in 1928. Her father got a job as a driver of

---

[84] The *asociaciones de soccoro mutuo*, colloquially called *mutuales*, emerged all over Argentina with European immigration. Similar to the so-called fraternal societies in the USA (cf. Beito 2000) the *mutuales* were formal associations through which matters of health, education, work, and identity among those belonging to the ethnic diaspora were attended to in a cross class manner (S. Fernández 2006:21). Of importance in Santa Fe City were the Swiss Filantrópica Suiza de Santa Fe, the Spanish Asociación Española de Socorros Mutuos; the French Sociedad de Socorros Mutuos L'Union; the Italian Sociedad Italiana de Socorros Mutuos "Union y Benevolencia;" and the Jewish Hebrea y Sefaradía de Socorros Mutuos de Santa Fe. The aim of these associations was to institutionalise solidarity and mutuality between members of the diaspora on the basis of national identities, which in some cases were not even consolidated in their country of origin (such as in Italy, which did not become a republic until 1946). Similar to the mutual aid associations of the immigrants, the worker unions also established such *mutuales* for their members, constituting the embryo of 20th century syndicalism and workers movement (S. Fernández and Galassi 2006:63). Many of these *mutuales* continue to exist in Argentina.

the city's tramway and her mother was a housewife. They bought a plot of land in what was to become Barrio Roma because they had Italian friends who were also buying land there. Slowly they built their own house. Julia's mother later set up a small grocery shop in the front part of their house. Both her parents worked there until they retired. They never went back to Italy, not even to visit. "We were Italians but most of all we identified as Argentinians. This country gave us all we ever had," Julia explained. When she married in 1952, she and her husband went to live with her parents. Julia then inherited the house when her parents passed away. She had never left the *barrio* and hoped to end her days here.

The Argentinian population increased quickly at the turn of the 20th century,[85] as a consequence of immigration politics. Yet the idea referred to in the above cited expression also reveals an existing racial discourse in Argentina. In this discourse, which underpins the idea of a national identity, there is an emphasis of the White European descent of the population at the expense of the legacy from the indigenous peoples, the *criollos* and the immigrants from neighbouring countries.[86] In the initial conversations with my neighbours in Barrio Roma, many of them were keen on highlighting their identity as European descendants. This identity marker is rather typical for the Argentinian urban middle and upper classes. It is associated with historical representations of European immigrants and *criollos* mainly in racial and moral terms (cf. Visacovsky and Garguin 2009). The European immigrant was depicted as a hard worker and with a strong sense of innate responsibility, while the *criollo* was imagined as lazy, lacking initiative and responsibility. These racist notions have long roots in the history of Spanish conquest and colonisation of the indigenous peoples in the region, but have been discursively reproduced throughout Argentinian history. The governmental promotion of European immigration in the late 19th and early 20th centuries was one such point in time, even if this simultaneously prompted a nationalistic wave in Argentinian popular culture, romanticising the rural *criollo* embodied in the *gaucho*[87] (Civantos 2006:55; cf. Freidenberg 2009). Historical politics and discourses also shaped local relations such as those between immigrant *colono* farmers and rural *criollos* in the north of the Province of Santa Fe (Archetti 1988; Stølen 2004). These historical relations are spatialised in the notion of the *pampa gringa*,[88] referring precisely to the prairie region where the

---

[85] From 1,8 millions in 1869 to 4 millions in 1895 and 7,9 millions people in 1914 (Instituto Nacional de Estadísticas y Censos 2005b).

[86] Immigration from Bolivia, Chile, Paraguay, Uruguay and to a lesser extent from Brazil has been prominent in Argentina since the 1930s and in Santa Fe since the 1960's (cf. Giorgis 2004; Serafino 2010).

[87] The *gaucho* of Argentina, Uruguay, Paraguay and Brazil is a loose equivalent of the North American cowboy, the Chilean *huaso*, the Cuban *guajiro*, the Venezuelan or Colombian *llanero* or the Mexican *charro*. These Creole cattle workers and eminent horse riders, product of European colonisation of America, were discriminated as nomadic savages in the early 19th century. Later the *gaucho* as a figure became a strong nationalist symbol however, not least through the epic poem *Martín Fierro* written by the Argentinian writer José Hernández. The *gaucho* is a key social figure in Argentinian economic history, language and folklore. There are at present thousands of *gaucho* associations around the country aiming at preserving *gaucho* traditions.

[88] The *pampa gringa* refers to the European settlements in the region of the Argentinian plains, the *pampa*, in the late 19th and early 20th century. The word *gringo* means stranger in Spanish. In contrast to Central America, where the *gringo* is the North American, in Argentina the term has largely been

social process of agriculturalisation by European immigrants took place (Gallo 1984).

When industrialisation and urbanisation began in the 1930s and 1940s, these were processes that not only changed the Argentinian social structure but also the political landscape. This was when the social category of "*cabecitas negras*"[89] first appeared (Ratier 1971a; Guber 1999b). This category with racial connotations referred to the *criollo* urban migrants. Out of this social category emerged in the 1950s the notion of the "*villero*," referring to the inhabitant of the *villa miseria* (Ratier 1971b) as the Argentinian shantytown came to be called.[90] The *cabecitas negras* and the *villeros* became the work force in the industrialisation of the country. As such they also came to embody the social and political base for the growing Peronist party (Ratier 1971b:3), which since that time the largest political party in Argentina. The emergence of these new social categories threatened to transform the national self-image of the White European Immigrant Nation to a country of poor ignorant mestizos (Guber ibid.: 112) which is plausibly one reason as to why "*negro*," "*morocho*" and "*villero*" are categories still used today in contemptuous ways in Argentinian society.[91] Julia and many of her fellow pensioners at the Barrio Roma Pensioners' Club were proud of their European descent and keen on highlighting it, in order to differentiate themselves from their neighbours on the other side of the railways on the Westside.

Social stratification and urbanisation

International immigration and urban migration in the 20th century prompted the expansion of Santa Fe City. In all Argentinians cities, the shantytowns grew in number after the economic recession of 1955 (Guber 1999b:114). The entire Westside of Santa Fe City, on early official maps identified as municipal *bañados municipales* (marshlands), was in the 20th century gradually filled and drained, in order to gain land. This intensified the process of informal settlement by urban migrants, who most of the time had no other place of choice to dwell.

---

used to denote the immigrant who was European or of European descent. The category *gringo* is often put in dichotomy with the *criollo*

[89] *Cabecita negra* alludes to the often dark colour of the hair and of the skin of the *criollo*. In daily speech, the synonymous terms *negro* or *morocho* is used. It can be applied both contemptuously and respectfully, while the term *groncho* that is sometimes used, is only meant contemptuously. The British and Australian term "wog" seems like the most appropriate translation to English.

[90] The Argentinian writer and journalist Bernardo Verbitsky was allegedly the first to use the term in his novel *Villa Miseria también es América* (1957). In everyday speech the shantytowns are just called *villas*.

[91] This racial discourse of Argentina as a White European Creole society has only been challenged at the turn of the 21st century, producing a more diversified image of Argentinian identity. This change can be ascribed to several recent processes in Argentina. For example, indigenous politics of identity and redress are gaining momentum (cf. Briones 2005) and genetic studies have demonstrated that more than half of the Argentinian population have indigenous ancestry (Heguy 2005). Attention is increasingly paid to the history and current situation of African descendants in Argentina in both mass media (Downes 2005) and science (Colabella 2012). In the case of Santa Fe City, a recent study in the neighbourhood of Santa Rosa de Lima demonstrated that 2,2 % of the population had African descent (Pita 2006:8).

Some of these settlements have later been officially recognised by the municipality as urban neighbourhoods, which has entitled them to the provision of basic infrastructure such as electricity and potable water. This has also enabled some of the inhabitants in these districts to acquire title deeds for their properties. Still, into the 21st century, urban migrants in Argentina are pushed to settle in an unregulated way.[92] They generally have very little means to build a house; hence, in addition to their status as illegal settlers they have to dwell in poorly built *ranchos*. Local, regional and national authorities have throughout history applied different policies to deal with the problem of urban substandard housing, of which the campaigns to "eradicate the *rancho*"[93] have perhaps been the most common political strategy. In Santa Fe City, local NGOs such as the Movimiento Los Sin Techo,[94] founded by a Catholic priest in the mid-1980s, have been major stakeholders in advocating for and building housing for thousands of poor families living in such *ranchos* (Uno Santa Fe 2012a).

Much of my fieldwork took place in poverty stricken neighbourhoods on the Westside and the Coastside. One of my key interlocutors here was Pedro, a man in his early forties. He grew up in the neighbourhood of Yapeyú, on the Northwest Side, although he had lived in many other places as well during his lifetime. When I first met him in 2005, he had recently divorced and was renting a house in Barrio Roma. Pedro's mother was a native *santafesina*, while his father was from a small village in the neighbouring province of Entre Ríos. They had their firstborn child in Santa Fe after which they moved to Buenos Aires. There, Pedro's father was a factory worker and his mother worked as a house maid. Pedro himself was born in a shantytown in Avellaneda, a southern suburb of the city of Buenos Aires, in 1964. His strongest memory from Avellaneda was when their *rancho* caught fire and he saw his father and his grandfather (who lived with them) trying to put out the fire with buckets of water. They in fact rescued much of the humble dwelling. When Pedro was 11 years old, he moved back to Santa Fe with his mother and his siblings. They stayed with his grandmother, who lived in a *rancho* on the Salado riverbank together with her bachelor son, Pedro's uncle. She worked as a cook in the nearby Golf Club. She also held domestic animals such as laying hens. Pedro remembered having swum in the Salado River and also having self-evacuated when the river flooded her *rancho*. Pedro's father came back to Santa Fe a year or so later. The family went to live in a modest house on the Northwest side. Pedro himself said that his youth was tough but not bad. His mother joined the Jehovah's Witnesses at some point, while his father was more of a drinker. In Pedro's social life, alcohol and drugs were constantly present, but so was politics and music, in particular that of the carnival music *murga*.[95] Football was another passion. Pedro supported one of the

---

[92] This was tragically highlighted in December 2010 when Bolivian and Paraguayan immigrants occupied a square in a district in Buenos Aires as a protest and in order to call attention to their problem of housing. The protest ended in violent conflict between the occupants, the residents in the neighbourhood and the police forces (Jastreblansky 2010).
[93] In Spanish: *Campaña de erradicación del rancho*
[94] In English: The Movement of Those Without a Roof
[95] The *murga* is a typical musical rhythm in the Río de la Plata region normally played with percussive instruments. It stems from the musical theatre performed in Argentina and Uruguay during

city's two big football clubs, Colón,[96] and was a true *sabalero*. This was the name of the fans because the club had been founded in the urban outskirts, at the shores of the river where the *sábalo* fish was caught.[97] Pedro began working at the age of 16 in the nearby municipal cold storage. He engaged in the union which at the time was a thriving environment for young people with ideals of social change, like Pedro. This was during the military dictatorship however, and the workers movement in the entire country was systematically repressed (Yael Ríos 2006). In those years he was also engaged in the *vecinal* of the neighbourhood and was elected as the president of the association after a couple of years. He and other people in the *vecinal* promoted different infrastructure improvements and arranged cultural activities in the *barrio*.

Pedro became a father at 19 with a girl from the same district. They never shared roof but he described his relation with the girl and the child as good throughout the years. In the late 1980s, he got a job in the municipality as a traffic inspector. He became affiliated with one of the largest unions in the city, the ATE,[98] and engaged in syndicalism. He had also engaged in a street theatre group, with which he travelled all over Argentina and visited several other Latin American countries. Eventually, he married a *compañera*[99] girlfriend from this amateur theatre company, a girl from Barrio Roma. They had two sons and lived in the nearby town of Santo Tomé until they divorced in 2002. Pedro then moved back to Santa Fe.

Pedro can be said to embody social mobility in many senses; spatially from the shantytown to the middle-class district, economically from industrial work to white collar employment, and culturally from marginality and not having completed schooling to being a union worker and actor, involved in an intellectual and cosmopolitan network that stretches far beyond Santa Fe City. His life history can be seen an illustration of the late 20th century's possibilities of social mobility in the class divided society of Santa Fe City. Yet at the same time, Pedro seems to be more the exception than the rule. Most people in this city seem to have been far less mobile. When Pedro told me about his family and about his friends from youth, most of them turned out to still live in the poverty stricken Westside, struggling to make ends meet as blue collar workers or even unemployed.

---

the Carnival season. The Santafesinian *murga* is generally performed in the Uruguayan manner as a musical play consisting of a suite of songs, recitative speeches and percussion by a group of dress in colourful jester-like costumes.

[96] The formal name of the club is Club Atlético Colón. The other big football club is Club Atlético Unión, whose fans are called *tatengues*.

[97] Another myth of origin about the Club Colón was that in 1905, the year that the club had been founded, ocurred the so-called Great Flood in Santa Fe and the football ground was flooded, hence, full of *sábalo* fish.

[98] ATE stands for Asociación de Trabajadores del Estado (Union of State Workers).

[99] The use of the term *compañera* (female for comrade) and *compañero* (male for comrade) to denote one's sentimental partner (married or unmarried) is an identity marker of leftist ideology in Argentina. In many cases it signals identifying with Peronism.

Poverty and social assistance

According to official statistics, in 2005, the poverty rate in metropolitan Santa Fe[100] was 41% of the population with extreme poverty at 17.1%. In 2010, the poverty rates had decreased to 13,4% and 2,6% respectively (Instituto Provincial de Estadísticas y Censos 2012). These numbers had decreased significantly since the year 2003 when poverty rates hit the roof after the disastrous flood.

Historically, the *vecinales* and the *mutuales* were the social institutions through which local and personal problems were dealt with. In all of Argentina, structural poverty has historically also been remediated by means of social assistance. Such institutionalised practices are at least as old as the charity societies from the 19th century. Such an association was established in 1823 in Buenos Aires by the national government. In Santa Fe City, a charity society was created in 1860 to manage several public hospitals and the Girls' School. As such, it constituted the beginning of a new policy field in Argentina, namely that of social politics (Facciuto 2003). Such societies were from the very beginning charities run by the ladies of the local social elite (Facciuto 2003; S. Fernández and Galassi 2006:56-58). The institutions that advocated for private charity as a solution to social problems were not challenged until the first government of Juan Domingo Perón (1946-52). The First Lady at the time, Evita Perón, established a foundation to attend the needs of the poor. The Fundación Eva Perón was very effective in distributing material goods, as well as building schools, housing, hospitals, geriatric homes, among many other achievements. The government of Perón established several different institutions in matters of social security. In principle, they endure until this day at national, provincial and municipal levels, even if their names have changed over time (cf. Pantaleón 2004).

In the province of Santa Fe, the Ministry of Social Development is responsible for creating policies in this area. This ministry is furthermore responsible for running the School of Social Service located in the city, a tertiary level school in which social assistants are educated. In Santa Fe City it is the Department of Social Action of the municipality that is to implement national and provincial policies by way of social assistants visiting and organising different local institutions in the poor districts (cf. Faya 2004). In addition to these governmental institutions, I found a vast number of NGOs (both church organisations and secular ones) working with these matters in the city.[101] The actions of both governmental agencies and NGOs have been oriented towards alleviating poverty. Their strategies have ranged from providing clothes and meals, to managing projects of constructing one's own house, to supporting a local FM radio station, running day care centres or canteens for children to have their lunch and after-

---

[100] Metropolitan Santa Fe includes suburbs and nearby towns such as Santo Tomé, Recreo, Sauce Viejo, Villa Adelina, San José del Rincón, Rincón Norte and Arroyo Leyes.
[101] During my fieldwork there were several NGOs in Santa Fe City undertaking *acción social* (social work). Among the ones I interacted with during my fieldwork were the organisations Los Sin Techo and Caritas that were both associated to the Catholic church; Acción Educativa, a secular organisation inspired by the works of the Brazilian pedagogue and philosopher Paulo Freire; and CANOA, an interdisciplinary organisation that engaged in social and urban development in cooperation with the residents in the poor neighbourhoods.

noon snack (ibid.). I got to know people from some of these organisations while undertaking fieldwork in the Westside and the Coastside. I noted that the people of the NGOs were keen on separating themselves from the representatives of the governmental agencies. The latter were, by NGOs and Westside inhabitants alike, understood as politicised institutions. Similar to the *vecinales* in the neighbourhoods, many residents saw the social assistants as clientelist representatives of the Peronist Party (cf. Auyero 2001; Faya 2004:29; DuBois 2008:65-70; Quirós 2011). The aversion between the staff in non-governmental and governmental organisations in Santa Fe seemed to be a longstanding and mutual one (Faya ibid.: 40-41). As we shall see in Chapter Four, this relationship was manifested in the wake of *la Inundación*, when several of the city's NGOs sided with the *inundados/activists* in their claims on the government.

Among *changarines, cirujas* and *piqueteros*

Santa Fe was in 2008 the city with the highest unemployment rate in Argentina, with a rate of 12,6% (Instituto Nacional de Estadísticas y Censos 2012). Yet, the number had decreased since the Argentinian financial crisis of 2001/2002 when rates peaked.[102] The *changa*, referring to the occasional work of the day, was a common informal employment practice in both rural and urban Argentina before the advent of syndicalism at the beginning of the 20th century. The increasing flexibilisation of the labour market at the turn of the 21st century brought back the *changarines*, the informal day workers. In general they are males of all ages with little formal education. In Santa Fe many of the *changarines* lived in the low-income districts on the Westside of the city, as well as on the Coastside. These districts had the highest rates of unemployment and underemployment prior to and during my fieldwork. Several interlocutors in these neighbourhoods told me that the number of people working as *cirujas*[103] (scavengers) had increased in Santa Fe, especially since the crisis of 2001/2002. This trend corresponds with that observed in other Argentinian cities (cf. Schamber 2008).

The Northwest Side was one of the most socially vulnerable districts in the city (cf. Arrillaga, Grand, and Busso 2009; Viand 2009). Close to the neighbourhood where Pedro grew up, was now a new neighbourhood called La Nueva Tablada. It was built in the wake of the 2003 disaster, partly to offer families a place to live that had become homeless due to the flooding. It was a governmental relocation project especially for flooded families who had lived in La Tablada; a dispersed settlement of *ranchos* situated on the riverbanks of the Salado River, which had been virtually washed away in the 2003 flood. The housing project of La Nueva Tablada was co-financed by an Evangelical church and the municipal and provincial governments. It consisted of helping the relocated families build their new houses. The municipality and the provincial government would provide the infrastructure of drinking-water, sewage wells and electricity.

---

[102] The unemployment rate of the economically active population in Santa Fe City was 27,6% in 2001 (Giusti and Massé 2001).
[103] Another denomination of this occupation in Argentina is *cartonero,* which refers more specifically to the people collecting cardboard yet is sometimes used synonymously to *ciruja.*

I had met people in this district already on my first visit to Santa Fe in July 2004, when they still lived in Red Cross tents and shanties in the old Tablada. When I met them in 2005, they had moved to their new *barrio*, but were not particularly happy.

Lorena was 26 years old when I met her again in 2005. She was married to José, with whom she had four small children. Lorena took care of the children and was enrolled in a *plan*, meaning a social allowance programme.[104] José, who was a bricklayer, worked in the construction sector whenever there were any *changa* vacant. They tried to complement their unstable and low-income livelihoods by working as scavengers from time to time. They owned a horse cart and used it for *cirujeo*, that is, to recollect garbage in the city that they then sold to purchasers. They had rented a small house on the Westside when they had their first baby. When the second child arrived and with the scarcity of *changas* for José, they could not afford it any longer. That was when they decided to move to La Tablada, where they knew some people doing *cirujeo* and who lived on municipal land. Lorena and José then built a shanty there. When the 2003 flood ruined their house, they thought that things could not get worse. The relocation to the new district of La Nueva Tablada appeared promising as they would have a brick house of their own. Only later did they realise that even if they now had electricity and toilet in the new house, they also had to pay for these services. The new house in La Nueva Tablada had a small yard but not space enough for depositing and sorting the garbage they collected. There was a plot of public land just in front their house. José and Lorena however discarded the idea of using this plot of land for their business, because of the competition with neighbours who also carried out *cirujeo*. They gathered that their goods would most probably be stolen if they stored it there. The last time I met them in 2005, José had just found out that he had an illness that required treatment and would prevent him from working. He had applied for a job in a construction company and been required to undertake a medical examination. The results from this examination indicated a fatal disease. The fighting spirit of Lorena was understandably low, as she and her family made efforts to cope with yet another disaster in their lives.

In contrast to the case of Lorena was that of Marcelo. When I got to know him in 2005, he was in his late thirties and active within a local group of *piqueteros*. Picketing is a form of social protest or public manifestation. In Argentina, the *piqueteros* constitute a social movement since the late 1990s, characterised by the principal practice of protest, which is to block the roads. The *piqueteros* movement emerged throughout Argentina at the turn of the 21st century, having started with the protests against structural adjustment reforms in the southern town of Cutral-Co in 1996 (Auyero 2003). Increased unemployment rates in the wake of the privatisations and cutbacks of the 1990s were a reality also in Santa Fe City. Different picketer groups then organised road blocks and

---

[104] The many governmental social allowances programmes are generally all referred to as *planes* (plans) by their beneficiaries. The *plan* as a means of economic survival and daily practice of remembering is discussed in Chapter Seven.

street protests demanding jobs and rises in the social benefit allowances. I never observed or heard that any Santafesinian pickets took place during my fieldwork however. I nevertheless met people from one of these groups in the neighbourhood of Santa Rosa de Lima.

I was told that, in Santa Rosa de Lima, the protests had begun as a neighbourhood initiative in 1996, in reaction to the increasingly difficult economic situations due to unemployment and underemployment met by many families in their *barrio*. In 2001, this was still an important problem, indicated by the middle-high to high rates of social vulnerability at that time (Arrillaga, Grand, and Busso 2009; Viand 2009). The picketers decided to block the road as a way to bring public and political attention to this problem. Susana, a social worker, who was one of the founders and driving forces within the protest movement, told me that there used to be around 30-40 people in the movement. During the days that preceded the violent street protests in December of 2001, referred to as the *Argentinazo*,[105] the picketers in Santa Fe City protested in front of the municipality and in front of several supermarkets, demanding food (Viano and Armida 2006). When I attended a couple of their meetings in 2005 at the office of a local NGO in the *barrio*, the spirit of that protest seemed quite far away. I had been invited by one of my key interlocutors, Adriana, who was the spouse of Marcelo. The social worker Susana was always there as well as a dozen of other people, more men than women. People walked in and out. I could not really tell who was participating in their meeting and who was taking part of the activities next door. The meeting place was in the local radio station, which was also a community centre, where adult education, homework help, and community workshops took place. There were people who clearly belonged to the movement but who preferred to stay outside the meeting room, listening and making comments from there. After a while they left. The few people who remained in the meeting discussed the provincial government's threat to cut the number of existing *planes*, concluding that they needed to build strategies to defend these social allowances programmes. They realised they could not count on enough people to carry out a road block. Hence they decided instead to try to book a meeting with the Secretary of Work at the provincial government. Had they not heard anything from the Secretary by the following week, they would organise a picket. With this decision, the meeting ended. I never found out whether the activists managed to get an appointment with the Secretary or not, but to my knowledge, that picket never materialised.

The urban outskirts and notions of perilous places

The districts on the western side and some of the suburban neighbourhoods on the Coastside were not only the most socially vulnerable and exposed areas of the

---

[105] The *Argentinazo* refers to the street protests and riots that occurred in several Argentinian cities on the 19th and 20th of December 2001. In total there were more than 30 fatal victims after clashes with the police forces. The sitting president De la Rúa resigned and had to leave the governmental palace by helicopter due to the furious crowds in front of the building in the Plaza de Mayo square in Buenos Aires (cf. Viano and Armida 2006; Auyero 2007).

city, but also often imagined as lawless places. In particular, young people from these districts were depicted as drug addicts and criminals. When I told my middle-class interlocutors that I was doing fieldwork in these areas, they raised their eyebrows and asked me if I really went alone to these places. They suggested that I needed to be careful in how I dressed. I should not carry a camera or anything valuable. Such notions of risk were not only products of middle-class imaginaries, however. Many of my interlocutors living in these same districts pointed out to me that certain blocks in their *barrio* or other low-income districts in the city (other than their own) were godforsaken places where danger lingered, especially for a European woman like me. In 2008, I heard that several local taxi drivers and fast food delivery couriers defined many of these districts as dangerous zones where they refused to work. Police patrols in cars and pickups were ubiquitous all over the city. I observed them on several occasions in the high- and middle-income neighbourhoods Downtown and on the Eastside, driving slowly and carefully. When I saw patrols in the districts on the Westside and in the Coastside they would more often than not drive around excessively fast with armed police officers on the flatbed and with the blue lights on. The contrast between the different ways of patrolling was striking. The residents in the poor urban and suburban outskirts often talked about the police with fear and distrust. During my fieldwork in Santa Fe, several violent incidents, ranging from assaults to murder, including family and sexual violence occurred. Such events occurred in all kinds of social contexts, and all over the city. Yet the poverty stricken urban and suburban outskirts prevailed as the most dangerous places in the Santafesinian social imaginary; a notion which was reinforced by local mass media. It seems plausible that this placing of risk and danger is embedded in historical racial and social prejudices about the Westside *"negros"* the idea of Alto Verde as a kind of "Far West" of Santa Fe.

When I walked the sandy streets on the Coastside during my field research, I felt far from being at danger however. Along the main road of Alto Verde, one-storeyed houses stood one next to the other, with small gardens in between them bordered by small fences in front of the house. From the main street, named after a former president of the *vecinal*, narrow alleys reached out. There were plenty of trees and bushes on the island, offering pleasant shade during hot summer months. Small rowing boats sailed around or lay on the riverside. Alto Verde certainly lived up to its name of Green Hill. In La Vuelta del Paraguayo some of the buildings were rural dwellings, so-called *ranchos de paja*.[106] La Boca was like a village with its scattered small and humble wooden houses, fishing nets hanging at the back and the quiet pace of social life. The Coastside reminded me of rural Argentina, rather than of a suburban district.

---

[106] The *rancho de paja*, also called *rancho de adobe*, is the traditional rural dwelling that is generally made of reed and adobe in the Littoral region. For a more detailed description of the *rancho*, see footnote 74.

Figure 9 | *Rancho de paja* on the Coastside (Photo by author 2005)

The Coastside: The harbour and Alto Verde

The neighbourhood of Alto Verde was a product of the construction of the Santa Fe harbour at the turn of the 20th century. The year of the inauguration of the city harbour, 1910, is celebrated as the date of the foundation of the Alto Verde Island. The story goes as follows: At the end of the 19th century, large quantities of grains, timber and tannin, and, with the invention of the cold storage, meat, were shipped to Europe from the Santa Fe harbour, which was located in Colastiné at the time. These goods were largely transported by train to the harbour, crossing the waters of the Setúbal Lagoon on a large bridge. In times of flooding, the location of the harbour was inconvenient. The increase in production and exports at the turn of the 20th century required better facilities. A new modern harbour was built in the middle of the city and inaugurated in 1910. The sand, silt and mud that were dredged from the bottom of the brooks to build the harbour were deposited on a tiny island just in front of the area in construction. Slowly the island grew in length, breadth and height. Its leafy aspect motivated the name Alto Verde, meaning Green Hill. Numerous people who had worked and lived in the old port of Colastiné at the turn of the 20th century were employed in the construction of the city harbour and continued afterwards to work here as stevedores. Most of them settled in Alto Verde with their families. Most of my interlocutors in Alto Verde had relatives who had worked in the harbour, or they had worked there themselves. Large transatlantic ships brought European immigrants directly to Santa Fe and left with wheat and *quebracho colorado* timber. The building of the new harbour contributed to flood management Downtown and on the Southside, as the ground was elevated several metres above ground (and sea) level in order to build the quays. From the 1970s onwards, the port activities decreased as other harbours in the region expanded, most notably those of Rosario and San Martin. When I carried out fieldwork in 2005, the harbour was not operating. Upon my next visit, in 2008, part of the harbour facilities had been turned into a shopping mall. The harbour had been transformed into a commercial complex, consisting of a casino, a hotel and a shopping centre. I was told that this had been accomplished with the help of investments from the Santafesinian *sojeros*, as the soybean farmers were called. There were rumours that port activities would be promoted with the construction of a new harbour. In recent years the bidding for a public contract has in fact come closer (*El Litoral* 2012b).

Life on the islands

The western shores of the Paraná River are made up of a delta-like landscape with a myriad of islands, lagoons and creeks. The urban neighbourhoods of Alto Verde, La Boca, La Vuelta del Paraguayo, and others mentioned above are actually located on some of these islands. There are numerous other islands however. I was told that nobody lived permanently in them anymore. Only hunters and fishermen kept *ranchos* there to stay overnight.

Don Santiago, a resident of Alto Verde, was one of seven children, born on one of the islands south of Santa Fe City the in the early 1930s. His father worked as a *puestero*, a crofter who watched over the cattle belonging to a large estate in the province of Entre Ríos, grazing on the island. The humid environment of the islands provides abundant pastures for grazing and *engorde* fattening livestock before sale. In the Paraná River wetlands, island grazing is widely used by cattle breeders in the coastal provinces such as Santa Fe and Entre Ríos. They often hire the *isleros* or *isleños*, as the islanders are called,[107] to watch over the cattle (Rosato 1988; Boivin, Rosato, and Balbi 2012). In Argentinian farming, sharecropping[108] has since long been a common form of agreement between the large to medium estate property owners and the tenant farm worker. The latter are those who actually carry out the work of breeding and looking after the livestock, for which they are generally paid in-kind by the owner. They receive a share of the offspring and a possibility to live in a house on the estate. The subsistence economy of the *isleros* also included the rearing of horses, chicken, pigs and even goats in the islands. Fishing and hunting have been practiced along the Paraná and Salado river shores and wetlands since pre-colonial times, being important activities for the *isleros*, both for the purposes of subsistence and for sale (Rosato 1988). Among the hunting preferences were doves and ducks for meat, and capybaras,[109] caimans and otters for pelt. Otter hunting used to be particularly lucrative. In recent decades however, the otter is seasonally protected most of the year due to the risk of extinction (ibid.). Another lucrative activity that Don Santiago recalled from his childhood in the islands was the collection of mother of pearl plants,[110] which were sold for their nacre to a button factory in Entre Ríos. The mother of pearl is an aquatic plant carrying tiny shells. It was used in those years by the textile industry. Santiago emphasised that it was easy to collect these plants as they grew under water on the riverbank, and therefore was a task for children.

---

[107] Both terms mean islanders in Spanish. They were used interchangeably in Santa Fe.
[108] This is called *miedería* in Spanish.
[109] The capybara, or *carpincho* in Argentina, is a giant rodent animal found in most of South America. It can weigh up to 60 kg.
[110] The mother of pearl is referred to as the *cuchara del agua* (water spoon) or *conchilla del agua* (water shell).

Delia was in her early sixties when I met her in Alto Verde in 2005. She had also been born and raised in one of the islands of the Paraná River close to Santa Fe. She emphasised that there used to live plenty of people in the islands when she grew up in the 1950s. While Santiago and his siblings, who were born in the 1930s and 1940s, received a few years of primary education in a rural school on one of the islands, Delia had actually finished primary school. Santiago had left the school at the age of twelve to help his father with the cattle work and the fishing. With time, the rural schools had closed down which had forced many families to leave for the sake of their children's schooling. Without any kind of institutional life left on the islands, it became difficult to live there on a permanent basis. Many islanders moved to Santa Fe City, and particularly to the suburban island of Alto Verde. Delia recalled the flooding as stressful. They had to evacuate and ran the risk of losing everything. According to her, many *isleros* left the islands after the extraordinary floods in 1959 and 1961, and also after that of 1983. The scarcity of fish in the Paraná River at the turn of the 21st century, caused by overfishing and the building of dams upstream (Ortiz 2008), as well as general problems of contamination that affect the river ecosystem, make life in the islands even more difficult.

According to both Santiago and Delia, life on the islands had been quiet and plentiful, but also full of hardships. There was a lot of heavy work, mosquitoes, snakes, and other dangerous creatures. The dreams of a better life made Delia's parents leave for the city. Such visions were decisive also for Santiago when he left his family in search for a better life in Santa Fe. The city offered abundant job opportunities in the late 1950s. When I met him in 2005, he had since long retired from his work as a docker in the harbour. He was instead working as a *botero*, one of the rower men that transported people between the shores of Santa Fe across the Santa Fe Creek to Alto Verde. There was plenty of traffic with the rowboats as people commuted to school and work. Many inhabitants of Alto Verde worked or attended school in the city, just as the staff in schools and in the health centre in Alto Verde lived in the city. Most people took the rowboat because it was quick and arrived at a central location. The only local bus line was slow and expensive and offered a much longer ride. To cross the creek with the *boteros* took about ten to fifteen minutes, unless the weather was bad. Boats had been the only means of transport between Santa Fe and Alto Verde until the 1960s, which was when the first bridge, the *Puente Palito*,[111] was built between Alto Verde and El Pozo. Santiago remembered that the bridge represented important progress for the people in Alto Verde. They got a road to use in case of emergency, which meant less dependence on calm weather to go to the city. Another significant event in the improvement of the livelihood in the district and beyond was the building of the flood embankments in the 1990s around Alto Verde, El Pozo, La Guardia, Colastiné, Rincón, and Arroyo Leyes. Despite such

---

[111] The bridge that crosses from The Pozo Island to Alto Verde was built in concrete in the 1960s and replaced the old wooden bridge, the *Puente Palito*. Yet many people in Santa Fe still refer to this new bridge with the old name.

mitigative improvements in matters of flood protection, all neighbourhoods except for one on the Coastside scored middle-high to high rates of social vulnerability in 2001 (Arrillaga, Grand, and Busso 2009; Viand 2009).

Urban and suburban vulnerabilities in the past and in the present

In this chapter, I have outlined the historical and ethnographic context in which the Santafesinian flood memoryscape was configured. I can hardly pose any claims of being exhaustive in my description of the state of things in past and present Argentina, my review of the geography and economy of the region of Santa Fe, or my characterisation of social and economic life in Santa Fe City. I have instead focused on those key aspects of this historical and contemporary context that I argue have contributed both to the production of urban vulnerabilities and to the ways in which the flooding past of Santa Fe is remembered.

These aspects constitute what scholars have referred to as the "big picture" of disaster risk (Wisner, Gaillard, and Kelman 2011c). These are political, economic and social macro-issues that often go beyond national borders but that are always embedded in local contexts. In Argentina, social, political and economic processes driven by global forces in the past and the present have forged vulnerabilities in Santa Fe City. Agriculturalisation and industrialisation have affected the rural and urban environment as much as the economy. Colonisation, migration and urbanisation have put demographic pressure on urban land. People have settled legally and illegally in flood-prone lowland areas, despite the risks involved. Political and economic developments after the return to democracy in 1983, punctuated by several major crises, have also forged the conditions of vulnerability in Santa Fe. The downsizing of the harbour activities, the privatisation and partial closing down of the railways and the shutdown of local industries from the 1970s onward increased under- and employment in the city and exacerbated social vulnerability.

At the turn of the 21st century, Santa Fe City was a heterogeneous urban community and was known as one of the Argentinian cities with the largest social and economic inequalities. These divisions were, as we have seen in this chapter, ideational as much as spatial and material. The territorial organisation mirrored the social structure and cultural notions around this. The posh villas in the high-income neighbourhoods on the Eastside were secured by fences and sometimes by private guards, while the middle-income neighbourhoods on the Northside and Downtown were characterised by smaller houses or department buildings in less lush areas. The poor neighbourhoods on the entire Westside and the Coastside lacked much of basic infrastructure and the people with the most unfulfilled basic needs lived here. These poor districts in the periphery were also considered by most Santafesinos, including by the inhabitants themselves, to be perilous places. Such spatial notions were related to ideas about social and ethnic categories between European descendants and *criollos*. These racial notions can be traced back to the Spanish conquest and to the 19th century European immigration to Argentina in general and to Santa Fe in particular. These social categories were then reproduced, driven by the economic processes referred to above, as *criollo* migrant workers joined the industrial labour force, while many European descendants became professionals or entrepreneurs. Social and economic inequalities within the community were historically remediated through civil society organisations along these social and spatial lines. While civil society is still an important social actor in Santa Fe, such organisations have become increasingly intertwined with state institutions and political networks.

Such long existing cultural notions around and social relations between people, places and institutions in Santa Fe were, as we shall see in the forthcoming chapters, central to the configuration of the urban flood memoryscape. Yet it must be observed that the latter was forged in interaction with a larger national context, which had less to do with the particular problem of flooding but was more related to the current politics of regret taking place in Argentina.

As many scholars have observed, the causes of social vulnerability to disasters are both simple and complex (Bankoff and Hilhorst 2004; Oliver-Smith 2009; Wisner, Gaillard, and Kelman 2011d). It is the product of the past; it is dynamic and embedded in larger political and economic processes, as illustrated when discussing the 1970 earthquake in Peru as a "500-year earthquake" (Oliver-Smith 1994) or referring to the 1975 Guatemala City earthquake as a "classquake" (Susman, O'Keefe, and Wisner 1983). As this chapter has set out to describe, vulnerability was differentially distributed within the urban community of Santa Fe. Having sketched something of an objectivist view of risk in Santa Fe I now set out to explore the more subjectivist side of disaster. How do people make meaning of past disasters?

PART ONE

Chapter 3 | *La Inundación* and the making of an accidental community of memory

The post-disaster

During my fieldwork in Santa Fe City, *la Inundación* was constantly talked about and recalled in different ways. This occurred evocatively in daily life practices, in particular but not exclusively, in the neighbourhoods that had been affected by the disaster. The tragedy was also remembered in reminiscent and commemorative ways however. Later on in my fieldwork, in the years 2008-2011, the force and abundance of this memory-work abated somewhat, yet the many traces of *la Inundación* continued to be prominent in the Santafesinian flood memoryscape. In this chapter I will describe how this remembering took place through narration, place-making and the making of objects. Ethnographically, the focus is on the people who were directly affected by *la Inundación*. In this account I call them the *inundados/victims* to differentiate them analytically from other categories of *inundados* in Santa Fe. I shall argue that through their memory-work they constituted what Malkki (1997) calls an "accidental community of memory," that is, a community that is haphazardly and suddenly bound together by a "biographical, microhistorical, unevenly emerging sense of accidental sharings of memory and transitory experience" (ibid.: 91).

Even if disasters and crises can be analytically conceptualised as social processes, they are more often thought of by people experiencing them as temporally circumscribed events (Vigh 2008). As such they are constituted by a "before," a "during" and an "after." The "during" refers to the disruption of the emergency, a liminal experience or a transition in time.[112] Most of my interlocutors in Santa Fe who had been flooded in 2003 spoke about *la Inundación* in these terms, saying that the experience of the catastrophe meant a turning point in their lives. I arrived in Santa Fe for the first time one year after this event, in the time of the "after." In the field of disaster studies, this is generally called the "recovery phase" of the catastrophe (Rodriguez, Quarantelli, and Dynes 2007; B. Phillips 2009) or simply "the aftermath" (Keesing 1952; J. B. Miller 1974; Barsky, Trainor, and Torres 2006; Palser 2007). The term "post-disaster" is being increasingly used, sometimes in combination with any of the other terms (Oliver-Smith 1979a; Aldrich 2012; M. Clarke, Fanany, and Kenny 2012; G. Smith

---

[112] In disaster management, this temporality is often referred to as the "disaster cycle" consisting of the phases of mitigation, preparedness, response and recovery. Varying in time and context, these phases have been further divided in more categories: prevention, mitigation, preparedness, alert, response, rehabilitation and reconstruction (Coetzee 2009).

2012). I here use the latter term and conceptualise the post-disaster as something more than a temporal phase in such a process. In line with the notion of memoryscape as a configuration of memory-making, I see the 2003 post-disaster as a process of making meaning of a past critical event, a process which unfolded both in time and in space. In what follows, I shall describe some of the forms of remembering through which this was made.

Narrating *la Inundación*

Narratives are a central feature of socialisation; crucial in and for remembering (Fentress and Wickham 1992:49-51; Fabian 2007:84-85). Similarly, in the wake of disaster, narrativisation is crucial for people to reconstitute their disrupted life worlds (Camargo da Silva 2009). In Santa Fe, narrative practices such as informal conversation and telling stories were key in the making of an accidental community of memory *la Inundación*.

Withering weather

The weather in Santa Fe was a constant topic of conversation before and during my fieldwork. I was warned: "The weather in Santa Fe is terrible, you'll see!" In the course of fieldwork, I came to understand what they meant by "terrible." The heat and dampness in spring and summer almost knocked me out, and the mosquitoes that came with it drove me crazy! The climate in the entire La Plata basin, where Santa Fe City is located, is characterised by humidity and high temperatures. There are no clearly defined differences between the seasons, except for the summer season between the months of November and March when temperatures are constantly high (+30°C at an average). The average temperature for the rest of the year is around +20°C and the humidity is around 80% all year around. Normally there are a few days of low temperatures in winter. The climate in Santa Fe City is largely affected by its proximity to the rivers and is subject to the ENSO fluctuations over periods of time. The latter refers to the wet and dry climate cycles known as the El Niño and La Niña.[113] A tendency between the years 1961-2010 has been observed in the entire country but in particular in the Littoral region, in which the annual average rainfall level has increased in the summer, fall and spring, and decreased in winter (Servicio Meteorológico Nacional 2012). During my fieldwork most people agreed that they had observed recent signs of climate change. The variations of one warm week followed by a cold week that occurred in 2005 were commonly interpreted as exceptional. The walls and the floors in people's homes could on humid days be completely moist, which was not at all considered normal. The exceptionality and changes of the weather were preferred topics of conversation everywhere on drizzly days, when

---

[113] El Niño Southern Oscillation (ENSO) refers to a climate pattern that occurs across the tropical Pacific Ocean roughly every five years. The extremes of this climate pattern's oscillations, El Niño and La Niña, cause extreme weather (such as floods and droughts) in many regions of the world.

analogies to the days of the 2003 flood emerged in all kinds of conversations. "This was exactly how the weather was in those days, at the time of *la Inundación*," people in the city said. On such days, I was told, many people said they felt depressed and sad, sometimes even fearful, as *la Inundación* came to their minds. On such days, the 2003 disaster recurred as the main topic of conversations in all kinds of settings such as in the school, in the bakery and or at the bus stop. This was one of many examples of how memories of the disaster were evoked through the presence and absence of people, objects, smells, sounds and in other ways in the everyday lives of the *inundados/victims*, making them talk and share their memories from the event. I shall return to this everyday remembering but let us now take a closer look at the narratives that forged a particular story of the disaster.

The canonisation of *la Inundación*

In the introductory chapter, I mentioned Marta, a divorced mother in her fifties, who lived in the Barrio Roma neighbourhood. She and her family had been badly affected by the 2003 disaster. They were still recovering emotionally and economically when I got to know them in 2004. In the years that followed I shared many meals with them at their home, and they told me about their experiences from the disaster and after. During my fieldwork I was told numerous stories similar to theirs. The accounts were shaped by individual experiences and memories, yet the stories melted into one of collective and public narrative about this past event. This phenomenon is similar to other ethnographic contexts, such as the "consecrated narratives" told about the emblematic psychiatric hospital of Lanús in Buenos Aires (Visacovsky 2002) or the stories told about Nakba, the catastrophe that the Palestinians experienced in 1948 when they were expelled from their homeland as the Israeli State was created (Sa'Di and Abu-Lughod 2007; Gren 2009). Here, certain memories from this dramatic event have produced what Juliane Hammer has called a "canonisation" of particular stories and symbols (Hammer 2001). While Hammer by this concept refers to the making of collective memory through symbols and images in a more general sense (p.456), my take on canonised stories is more specific. I define it as the process of sanctioning a particular set of memories that are accepted as authentic and true within the group that reproduces them. Memories contesting these stories will find no place in this process (Sa'Di and Abu-Lughod 2007) and can thus be said to be forgotten. Canonisation also refers to the consecration of particular people and objects. This can be related to the process of sanctioning particular narratives which become more or less inviolable in a particular setting, which I found to be the case with *la Inundación* in Santa Fe.

In order to convey ethnographically the many specific stories, such as Marta's, that make out a collective narrative, Malkki suggests the making of "narrative panels" which standardise the many stories (1995:57-58). Yet, as she notes in a self-critical spirit, the analytical approach that tries to discern a social pattern amongst many individual stories tends to homogenise individual remembering and simplify singular memories, because it does not allow for neither variation of memories, nor contextualisation of them. I nevertheless consider that there is an analytical point in recalling the many stories through a collective narrative given that similar stories about *la Inundación* were told all the time and everywhere. It was the story I learned to recount myself, through the interaction with different interlocutors. It was the story largely mediated through radio recordings, newspaper accounts, videos, photographs and documents. In what follows, I have not used Malkki's elaborate strategy of narrative panels strictly, but rather been inspired by her thoughts on how to represent ethnographically the many stories about the 2003 disaster that I was told in Santa Fe in one single narrative as follows:

The disaster | When the Salado River flooded Santa Fe City on April 29th, 2003, Mayor Alvarez declared on the radio that while the city was in chaos and evacuation would be required in certain areas, mass evacuation would probably not be necessary, certainly not on the Westside and Southwest Side. Only a few hours later, both these districts were completely flooded. Many people had refrained from evacuating because of the mayor's declarations. As their homes were quickly flooded they had to escape in chaotic fashion. These were the districts that were the worst affected in the disaster, where 23 people drowned. On the Southwest Side, the water level reached several meters above ground, and up to seven meters in some areas. Despair increased as the day came to an end, and the waters continued to rise and the city was in darkness due to the power outage.

The municipality began to evacuate women and children in buses and lorries, taking them to different evacuation sites. Due to the scarcity of vehicles and rescue workers, many people were forced to self-evacuate. People took refuge at the homes of relatives or friends, in schools, factories and churches. Others sheltered at the premises of the neighbourhood associations or those of the municipal cemetery. Some people set up tents on bridges and roads. The Provincial Secretariat of Communitarian Promotion was in charge to care for both evacuees and self-evacuees. Food boxes, mattresses, blankets and clothes were distributed to the evacuation centres and to the self-evacuees at strategic points in the city. The response by public authorities to the disaster was chaotic, however. To secure governmental assistance was a virtual odyssey for flood victims. It was stressful having to register officially as an *inundado*, waiting in lines for hours, suffering the shortage of supplies in a context of generalised devastation. This stress contributed to people's anxiety. The military had been called upon by Governor Reutemann to carry out evacuations, to distribute food and to safeguard public order. The presence of the military on the ground, in the water and in the air nevertheless intensified the stress among the *inundados*, evoking the violent years of the Dirty War when cities were militarised.

Recovery and return | Public authorities wanted to ensure that the entire community of Santa Fe would go back to normal as soon as possible. Because many of the evacuation centres were located in public schools, school activities could not be resumed. This was considered a problem by those inhabitants who were not affected by the flooding and who were concerned because their children were losing school days. Hence, approximately one month after the flood, the authorities issued a campaign to make evacuees to return home. The *inundados* began to return to their destroyed homes. Many people, especially women and children, had not been back since the evacuation started. It was shocking for them to return. Many homes had been entirely destroyed by the water or were deformed, dirty and damp. Furniture, utensils, tools, toys, books, records, clothes and photographs had been submerged for a long time under the water. Many people had no choice but to throw everything away. The authorities recommended this measure for sanitary reasons. Dustcarts were required to clean the streets, once the *cirujas* (scavengers) had collected what could be used. Paradoxically, the extreme volumes of garbage in these months meant that the *cirujas* in the city had a hectic and productive time, trying to collect as much waste of any value as possible, and this helped them to rebuild their lives after the flooding. Many of the families that lived by *cirujeo* lived in shanties in the Westside outskirts. They literally lost their homes to the flooding when their shanties were washed away.

Reconstruction | The provincial government established a provisional agency to carry out the process of reconstruction. It was named the Executive Unit for the Repair from the Hydrological and Pluvial Emergency[114] but was colloquially called the Reconstruction Unit or simply the Unit.[115] This agency was responsible for implementing all policies aimed at recovery and reconstruction[116] and for administering all the reconstruction funds after the disaster, including the economic compensation to the *inundados*, issued by the provincial state.[117] This subsidy was officially called "benefit" and was allotted to people and companies that had been flooded, both in Santa Fe City and in other regions of the province. The flooded households were granted 4,000

---

[114] In Spanish: La Unidad Ejecutora de Reparación de la Emergencia Hídrica y Pluvial
[115] In Spanish: El Ente de la Reconstrucción or simply el Ente
[116] This agency was created to administer the process of reconstruction after the 2003 disaster.
[117] Two bills were passed in the provincial parliament that enacted the economic compensation to the flood victims (*Régimen de Reparación Excepcional Por El Desborde Del Río Salado* 2003; *Reparación Por Inundación - Modifica Ley 12.183* 2004).

Argentinian pesos.[118] The families of the 23 persons who perished during the flood received a compensation of 45,000 Argentinian pesos[119] per family. Later, another subsidy was granted the *inundados* to further compensate for their material losses.[120] In order to be granted the subsidy, the property owner or the tenant had to apply for it through a procedure at the offices of the Unit located in the city centre. For the victims the strenuous journeys to obtain attention at the Unit's offices started all over again, with reduced opening hours and less administrative personnel. A condition for receiving such help was to waive one's right to pursue legal claims against the State. The amount was calculated according to specific guidelines, namely the building's cadastral category, the height that the floodwater reached inside the house during the flooding, and the number of square meters affected. This estimate was made by the employees of the Unit. They visited the flooded neighbourhoods to verify the information provided by the *inundados* themselves. The information was then corroborated with the database of the Territorial Cadastral and Information Service of the provincial administration. Yet the *inundados* were far from satisfied with this calculation. Most people claimed that there had been more floodwater in their homes, and during a longer time, than the verifiers had assumed. Quite a few *inundados* were critical of the fact that some of them had received more money that others, given that they had "after all suffered the same flooding."

As can be appreciated, the narrative about *la Inundación* is not just a story about a traumatic natural disaster. It is a narrative about a moral order, namely one of understanding the public authorities as beliers, failing to protect and to take care of the flood victims, before, during and after the disaster. Such an "event history" (Comaroff 1985:17ff) articulates with a widespread negative notion that Argentinian citizens have of their State and its representatives, which reinforce the meaningfulness of the narratives about *la Inundación*. This narrative created a particular meaning about the disaster. As we have seen, the generalised point of view among the *inundados/victims* themselves and many other urban residents was far from an ecological understanding of the disaster. Instead, multiple stories creating this collective narrative framed the disaster as through a moral order. As we shall see in the next chapter, this order served as the ideological basis for the mobilisation in protest against the government that emerged. In the making of the accidental community of memory, this canonised narrative articulated with other practices of remembering the 2003 disaster. In what follows I will describe how memories were spatialised in particular places.

---

[118] This amounted to approximately 1,400 USD at the time.
[119] This was approximately 16,000 USD at the time.
[120] Until April of 2005, 17,594 payments had been issued to house owners and tenants, a total of approximately 74 million Argentinian pesos (Gobierno de la Provincia de Santa Fe 2005).

Placing memory

Scholars of memory, beginning with Halbwachs himself (1980), have long agreed on the spatial dimensions of and for memory. Memories are spatially embedded in landscapes that serve as evocative cues. Memories are also central in the social construction of places, as several ethnographies have shown (Bohlin 2001; L. Lewis 2001; Regis 2001; Orta 2002; Gordillo 2004; Paxson 2005; Riaño-Alcalá 2006; Weszkalnys 2010). Places were indeed central in the remembering of *la Inundación*.

A driveabout in the flood memoryscape

Juan was a young university teacher in Santa Fe and the friend of one of my first interlocutors in the city. In July 2004 he took me and my friend Maria for a drive around the city in his car, which was a driveabout of memory (cf. Riaño-Alcalá 2006) since the places we visited were key sites for remembering *la Inundación*. By visiting them, Juan, Maria and I engaged in making the urban flood memoryscape. Juan picked us up early on that winter morning. We grabbed our *mate* gourd[121] and a thermos with hot water and set out to see the traces of the disaster. Throughout our drive, Juan narrated the canonised story about *la Inundación*. His narrative also placed the memories of the disaster at the flood embankment, as he explained to us:

> Large parts of the Westside and the Southwest Side of the city were surrounded by flood embankments. At the northwestern end of this embankment, close to the Las Flores hippodrome and the Jockey Club golf course, the final piece of this embankment (which was supposed to reach as far as the village of Recreo 17 kilometres north of the city) had never been built. A fifteen metres wide gap thus yawned for years between the closed end of the embankment and the golf course. As a result of this, when the Salado River flooding reached Santa Fe City in April 2003, the waters gushed in through the gap. The flooding had really begun already two days earlier in the outskirts of the Northwest Side. This was the same day as provincial and municipal elections were being held. In spite of mass media reports from upriver towns, the municipal authorities in Santa Fe City at first only monitored the water levels. Not until the next day, on April 28th, did the municipality begin to fill the gap with stones and sand bags. This was a futile effort, however. Floodwater was already gushing into the city through the breach, making it even wider. Only then did the municipality begin to evacuate inhabitants on the affected Northwest Side. The very same embankments that were built to protect the city from flooding, instead worked

---

[121] The *mate* is a traditional South American infused drink, particularly in Argentina, Uruguay and Paraguay and in regions of Brazil, Chile and Bolivia. It is served in a gourd filled with dried leaves of *yerba mate* on which hot water is poured. *Mate* is typically drunk in particular social settings, such as family gatherings or with friends. The same gourd and straw are used by everyone drinking.

as a kind of a tub, containing the floodwater so it could not find its way back out into the river. The level of the floodwater was at one point of the disaster several metres higher in the city than in the flooding river. Only when the provincial government after a couple of days dynamited parts of the embankment at the southwestern end, did the waters begin to recede. By then, the worst flood ever in Santa Fe City had already occurred!

The first place where Juan took us was consequently the flood embankment on the Westside; more precisely the gap through which the river had flooded the city the year before. By the time of our visit, however, the gap had been filled and it was hard for us to imagine that there had been a hundreds of metres wide hole in this several-metres-high embankment. I visited the site of the gap several times during my fieldwork, accompanied by different interlocutors who wanted me to see the place in order to understand how the disaster happened. The breach in the embankment was not only a spatial cue that sparked memories of the disaster and governmental negligence, but the *inundados/victims* (and the *inundados/activists*, as we shall see in the next chapter) had turned this site from being merely one point of the Westside flood embankment into a memorial (Connerton 2009) of *la Inundación*.

City of comrades in the Cordial City

The car ride with Juan lasted the entire morning. It was quite cold on that day in July 2004. The sun did not warm much. We fetched some more hot water for our *mate* at a gas station and Juan assured that this weather was an exception to the otherwise warm weather of Santa Fe. As he drove southwards along the Planes y Lopez Avenue in the Westside, he spoke about those days of *la Inundación*. Juan lived with his family in the centre of town and had not been flooded himself. Since his wife worked as a teacher in the Cristo Obrero School in the neighbourhood of Villa del Parque, he had gone there as soon as he heard the news, in order to help people he knew. Juan emphasised another aspect of the 2003 disaster, namely the solidarity with the *inundados/victims* shown by those inhabitants who were not flooded:

> In *la Inundación*, it was the people who helped the people. The State was completely absent, instead it was the people [who collaborated]. . . Well, there's a reason behind the fact that this city is called *La Cordial*, you know!

Juan referred to the city slogan "Santa Fe, the Cordial [city]" half jokingly, but he nevertheless seemed to think that this solidarity was a product of a Santafesinian ethos, as in the slogan. While solidarity may have been widespread during the 2003 disaster, it can hardly be described as a particular Santafesinian trait. Social solidarity is observed in most disasters and has long been documented. This intense form of social cohesion has been called "city of comrades" (Prince 1920), "therapeutic community" (Fritz 1961), "altruistic community" (Allen 1969), "community of suffering" (Oliver-Smith 1986) and "brotherhood of pain" (Oliver-Smith 1999). These concepts aim at understanding the practices of collaboration and feelings of solidarity among the members of a community affected by a disaster, both among the victims themselves and by residents who have not been affected. This phenomenon, which tends to emerge despite differences of class, gender and ethnicity, is generally claimed to be produced during and right after the disaster (Quarantelli and Dynes 1985). Although such a claim has been challenged by other researchers on the point of universality (Button 1993), the Great East Japan Earthquake in 2011 illustrates that it is a phenomenon that keeps emerging (Okada 2012:59-61). The anthropological concept of *"communitas"* developed by Victor Turner (1969) also conveys this dynamic, as a property of a community in a liminal stage between one order of things and another. Beyond the fact that this seems to be a generalised phenomenon, what was relevant in Juan's comment was the articulation between the memories of how people acted during the disaster, the collective self-image as a heartfelt community and the notion of the deceitful State. This understanding of the actions of the inhabitants (and the authorities) in Santa Fe during *la Inundación* was widespread among my interlocutors and accounted for a particular social and moral order. Only a few people recalled that in those first weeks, certain shop owners, far from solidary, had taken advantage and overpriced certain goods to supply basic needs, such as bottled water, bread and candles. In addition, through official reports, photographs and interviews with public servants, I learned that there had in fact been a rescue operation organised by the Civil Defence in collaboration with municipal actors and the military, even if it had been inadequate, disorganised and completely overwhelmed. In the canonised narratives about *la Inundación*, these aspects were largely omitted.

Perilous people and places

Next stop on the ride with Juan was behind the stadium of the football club Unión and the Garay Park. Northwest of this huge and lush park with numerous lakes, the poor neighbourhood of Villa del Parque and the shantytown Villa Oculta were located. Here many people were scavengers. Because of this, there was garbage piled all around the area. Juan parked the car on the side of the railway embankment. From the street, only the roofs of the houses in Villa del Parque were visible. The embankment was several metres high and the ground level of the *barrio* was below that of the park. We got out of the car and followed Juan. He showed us a large hole in the embankment and explained that it had been made by the residents in Villa del Parque on the day of the disaster, in order to let the floodwater out to the other side of the embankment. As he was showing us this, he seemed a bit nervous and asked me to be careful with my camera, because the *inundados* did not like to be photographed, insinuating that people could be upset and angry. He was referring to the residents on the other side in Villa del Parque and Villa Oculta who had been flooded in 2003. He then suggested that we should continue, so we went back to the car.

At that moment I thought my new acquaintance was a bit paranoid. I only later realised that his comment resounded with local conceptions of the *inundados* as a social category and notions of risky places in Santa Fe City. It corresponded to a widespread image of those perilous others living on the dangerous other side of the railway, namely the poor people on the Westside. Such notions were also manifested by people who had been my first interlocutors in the city in 2004, a group of middle-class women living on the upper Eastside. Truly worried, they questioned my intentions and the methodological choice to seek residence for my fieldwork in a Westside neighbourhood that had been flooded in 2003, given the dangers they imagined I faced as a European woman. When I finally found a place to stay in the Barrio Roma neighbourhood, they reluctantly approved. Perhaps their acceptance was due to the fact that Barrio Roma was locally categorised as a lower-middle-class or working-class neighbourhood, or maybe it was because I found this residence thanks to the friend of a friend of one of these women. Even if Barrio Roma was located on the poorer Westside, from the point of view of these women, it was at least on the "right" side of the railways. Such cultural notions of spatial boundaries were largely shared by the inhabitants of Barrio Roma and in other working- and middle-class neighbourhoods in Santa Fe, as discussed in Chapter Two. In what follows is another ethnographic example of how memories from *la Inundación* interacted with already existing notions of people and places in Santa Fe.

Walking the embankment

Luis, whom I mentioned in the previous chapter, was a neighbour of mine in Barrio Roma. One day in 2005 he was waiting for me on the sidewalk outside my house. The day before we had agreed on walking to the flood embankments that were located west of Barrio Roma. We were both excited about the excursion. I was anxious to understand what these flood embankments were like and where they were actually located in relation to the neighbourhoods and to the river. Luis was eager to show me the authorities' abandonment of the embankments and floodwater pumps. He and his mother had been flooded in 2003, an experience which had affected Luis very badly. He often told me that it had turned his world upside down. He had a hard time forgetting and was committed to not forgive those he considered responsible for the disaster. That was why he had engaged in the *inundados/activist* movement, although with no particular group. This was also the reason why he so eagerly wanted me to meet as many people as possible to learn about the political fraud that led to the disaster. Luis and his mother had both urged me to dress down. They said that I should not wear brand new, nor too expensive, clothes. According to them, this was an absolutely necessary precaution when going into the Westside *barrios* due to the risk of robbery. I put on my usual outfit, moreover a very Argentinian urban one, consisting of a pair of jeans, a t-shirt and sneakers. As I dressed, I had to admit that the worries of Luis and his mother had made me a bit nervous. At that time, I had not yet visited Santa Rosa de Lima myself. Hence, I found myself wondering whether my jeans were worn-out enough and if my looks would let me pass unnoticed on the other side of the railways.

Luis and I set off for the embankment crossing the Lamadrid Street and climbing up on the embankment of the Mitre railway line. As I got up there, I looked out over the Santa Rosa de Lima neighbourhood. I recalled what Marta, another neighbour of mine in Barrio Roma, had replied to my question of whether she could recall other past floods:

> No, well, never in my *barrio* anyway, although as a girl I used to go with my friends to the railway embankment to watch when the Salado [River] used to flood [the close by neighbourhood of] Santa Rosa. I remember that sometimes only the roofs of the *rancho* dwellings closest to the river would emerge above the surface of the water.

As I stood there myself, I could definitely imagine that this was a good vantage point to make such observations. Several metres below us the Santa Rosa neighbourhood spread out. Only a steep earth slope led down there.

Figure 10 | View of Santa Rosa de Lima from the railway embankment (Photo by author 2005)

As we walked through the *barrio*, I was struck by the bad smell of stinking water. I then became acutely aware that the railways and the railway embankments made up a social boundary as much as a material border between two different life worlds. Surrounding the blocks and just in front of the brick houses were narrow ditches filled with stagnant water and rotten garbage. The smell got even worse as we approached the embankment of the abandoned Belgrano Railway, which marks the northern end of the neighbourhood. Here was a long ditch along the foot of the embankment, filled with dirty water and garbage of all kinds. The intense sunshine at the afternoon hour of the siesta seemed to intensify the stink. A feeling of disgust invaded me but did not seem to bother anybody else around me, not even Luis. Families were sitting in the shadow outside their houses, just in front of the ditch, chatting, smoking and sipping *mate*. Small children were playing in the dirt road in front of the houses, running up and down the slope of the embankment. Loud music of the popular *cumbia santafesina*[122] was heard from one of the houses. As we walked on the top of the railway embankment, we passed several houses and the people sitting there watched us. Luis grabbed his bag harder and kept walking decidedly. While the inhabitants of Santa Rosa quickly lost interest in us and turned back to their conversations, I realised that, to Luis and to Juan in the preceding example, these people embodied the urban imaginary of the dangerous Westside resident.

Place and inscription of disaster memories

On our way back, instead of walking through the *barrio*, we got up on the top of the railway embankment again. A couple of horses were grazing on the top. On the northern slope we found a small pig farm. It consisted of some ten pigsties made out of tin sheets which were, as far as I could see, all occupied by fat sows and their piglets. Next to it was a small *rancho*. I could see no people around, but it was clear that somebody lived there. Having passed the dwelling, we arrived at a small abandoned building on the top of the embankment, hidden in between trees. On the other side of the trees was what was left of a small tower. Luis told me that this had been a water tower for the trains passing on the Belgrano Railway. We looked into the half destroyed tower from below and saw many graffiti on the wall, as if the place was used by young people who wanted privacy. One of the biggest inscriptions in the abandoned water tower was a direct allusion to *la Inundación*.

Graffiti are basically scratchings on a wall, a practice probably as old as mankind (Höjer

Figure 11 | Graffiti in the abandoned water tower (Photo by author 2005)

2008). Yet, graffiti are particular inscriptions in the public space. As contemporary visual means of expression they challenge the order of this space by being writ-

---

[122] The Argentinian *cumbia* music and dance style is based on the Colombian *cumbia*, introduced in Argentina in the early 1960s. The *cumbia* became particularly popular in the Argentinian urban centres at the time. It has even become characteristic of Santafesinian popular music, referred to as *cumbia santafesina*.

ten on the premises of others. The phenomenon is thus often imbued with criminal and vandalistic notions (David and Wilson 2002:43). As a cultural phenomenon, folklorists have called this practice "folk epigraphy" (Read 1977) differentiating it from institutionalised decoration of the public space. Graffiti is an inscription of the self and a way of marking a place, a subjective as much as a territorial concern. Yet, more importantly in the context of *la Inundación*, their marking of presence and of self can be seen as a spatial inscription into the memoryscape, a memorial (Connerton 2009). As Sather-Wagstaff points out in her analysis of the memorials of the 9/11 in the USA, graffiti is an "active process of making… [a] site historically salient in individual and collective memories" (2011:120). She argues that this, however ephemeral, marking of place is a participatory process between the inscriber, the inscription and the reader which results in a collective reflection upon a past event, that which the inscription refers to (ibid.: 125).

The graffiti in the old water tower indicated that a number of people, most probably from the *barrio* Santa Rosa, evacuated on this site in the days of the 2003 disaster. The identification as "The Bosses" (*Los Capos*) suggested that it had been a group of young men, some of the ones who are identified by their last name (Monzón, Castro, Gonzales) and the rest by their first name (Mario, Ruben, Tucho). Tucho had apparently held the charcoal with which the graffiti was written, as it was signed by him. The neighbourhood Santa Rosa de Lima had in May 1st, 2003, been covered with one to two metres of dirty floodwater. I was told by numerous interlocutors that many people from this *barrio* had evacuated to the embankments on those first days of *la Inundación*.

Graffiti as a visual practice often provokes strong emotions over whether it embellishes or destroys the public space. As cultural artefact, a piece of graffiti can also produce strong emotions because of the memories it evokes (Sather-Wagstaff 2011:123-26). This was clear as Luis and I read the graffiti in the abandoned water tower. He was clearly upset and said to me with tears in his eyes: "[Do you] see what they did to us, these sons of bitches!?" referring to the political responsibility of *la Inundación*. He then turned his back on me and got out of the building as fast as he could without hurting his head at the low entrance. Luis had not been evacuated on the embankment during the 2003 disaster, but he told me that he had suffered being evacuated at his sister's comfortable place, knowing that his home and his *barrio* were destroyed and that he had never really recovered from this experience. The inscription evoked his own personal embodied memories from the event and enabled him to empathise with Tucho and all other *inundados*. The inscriber, the inscription and the reader thereby engaged visually in the mnemonic embodiment of *la Inundación*.

As we shall see in Chapter Four about the *inundados/activist* movement, the people who were active in the protest also used graffiti as a visual practice of protest in the urban landscape. Tucho's graffiti, located in a place where not many people would eventually read it, was of another kind however: it was a testimonial artefact (cf. Höjer 2008). The testimony is an important practice of remembering as it mediates individual experiences and collective events, personal remembering with social memories. In what follows, I shall discuss the theoretical concept of testimony in relation to another form of inscribed memory, namely written texts.

Writing and performing disaster memories: Testimonials

La Inundación was extensively written about in the years following the event. The disaster was for instance included in new editions of provincial school textbooks (Mérega 2008). During my fieldwork, several books about *la Inundación* were published in Santa Fe. I was recommended several of them by different interlocutors and I bought them in local book stores. Several of these books were publicly launched in venues such as the annual Book Fair of Santa Fe or in local theatres. Many of these books were journalistic accounts, written by local journalists. Several of these were critical to the government's role in the disaster. I shall return to the particular books in the next chapter when discussing the politisation of *la Inundación*. Other books were written in the manner of narrating first-hand experience of being flooded. This latter genre of literature is in literary and cultural studies called "testimonio." The Spanish word *testimonio* means to bear witness to something. As a narrative genre, it carries ethical and epistemological authority by claiming to have lived, directly or indirectly, the experiences that are narrated (Beverley 2004). The genre emerged in the wake of the Cuban Revolution as a medium for telling stories about the life and experiences of subaltern subjects (Allatson 2002:42) and has also been called "marginal literature," "resistance literature," "autobiographies," "life-history," and "memoirs," just to mention a few terms (Harlow 1987; Gugelberger 1996; Beverley 2004). The testimonio is typically told in first person by a narrator who is the protagonist of the story or a witness of the events that are being recounted in the text. One of the most well-known works in this genre, *I, Rigoberta Menchu: An Indian Woman in Guatemala* (Menchú and Burgos-Debray 1984) was widely debated in terms of truthfulness and representativity in the late 1990s (Carey-Webb and Benz 1996; Stoll 1999; Arias 2001; Grandin 2011). The events narrated in this genre are generally of a violent nature and the narrator has most often been subject to this violence him/herself. Hence, the testimonio attempts to put words to the traumatic effects of violence and is "oriented toward addressing wounds that have yet to heal because they have never fully been acknowledged" (Argenti 2007:25). In the context of memory studies, testimonio has been described as a category of oral history (Randall 1985; Carey-Webb and Benz 1996) and more recently as "historical narratives rooted in memory" (Roybal 2012). In this vein, I suggest that this kind of text can be seen as an inscribed form of narrative memory.

Telling *la Inundación*

On July 23rd 2012, the newly published book *Resiliencia - Vidas que Enseñan*[123] (Gorenstein 2012) was presented by its author at the well-known Ateneo

---

[123] In English: Resilience - Lives that Teach [us]

bookstore in the city centre of Buenos Aires. The book, written by a journalist from Buenos Aires, narrates the stories of 25 Argentinians who have faced different adversities in their lives and learned how to overcome such problems. One of these persons was Laura, one of my interlocutors in Santa Fe. She had been flooded in 2003 and had also been affected by the inundations due to the heavy rains in 2007. In the book, she tells her story of how she has overcome these disasters.

Laura's testimonio was the last in a row of published testimonies about *la Inundación* in Santa Fe City. In the years following this disaster, three books were published by the National University of the Littoral, perhaps because the authors were all faculty researchers in its humanities department. One of these books was *Raíces en el Agua*[124] (Vallejos 2004). It is a short reflection upon the trauma of being flooded, written by a female university professor who was flooded in 2003. Another one, *Contar la Inundación*[125] (Hechim and Falchini 2005), is a volume edited by two other female professors at the local university, of which one had her home in the neighbourhood Parque Juan de Garay flooded in 2003. This book is a compilation of the stories of 64 different *inundados* in that disaster. Some of them were interviewed by the research team, while others provided written testimonies. The stories are about the memories of these from the flood emergency. They describe the fear, the rotten smell, the sound of gun shots and helicopters of the emergency, and the experiences during evacuation, but also the feelings of returning home. This publication is actually linked to a third book, in which one of the above mentioned professors was involved. It is a photographical book called *Memorias y Olvidos de la Gente del Oeste*[126] (Claret et al. 2005). On April 27th, 2005, two days before the second anniversary of *la Inundación*, I attended the launch of this book.

Launching books, making memory

The old train station of the Mitre Railways, located in the Southwest Side, was built in the late 1880s in an English colonial style with tin roofs, wooden friezes and tall, slender iron posts, typical of the Argentinian railway architecture of the time. More than a decade had passed since the last train from Buenos Aires arrived here. In 2005 the railway station was used by a cultural and arts association, the Birri Foundation,[127] for various cultural events. The book *Memorias y Olvidos de la Gente del Oeste* was the true result of reminiscent memory-work. A group of local academics and journalists, several of whom had been flooded in 2003, had joined in a collaborative research project sponsored by the National University of the Littoral and the Ecumenical Movement for Human Rights[128] with the purpose of "fighting against the politics of oblivion" (p.5). In the book, twenty

---

[124] In English: Roots in the Water
[125] In English: Telling the Flood
[126] In English: Memories and Oblivions of the People on the Westside
[127] The foundation Fernando Birri de Artes Multimediales was created in Santa Fe in 1995 by one of Santa Fe's most prominent intellectuals, the filmmaker Fernando Birri (born in Santa Fe City in 1925). Birri is the director of the motion picture *Los Inundados* discussed in Chapter Six.
[128] In Spanish: Movimiento Ecuménico por los Derechos Humanos

people are portrayed in their homes by way of texts and photographs in black and white, having themselves chosen how to be depicted. The photographs are accompanied by each individual's reflections upon their experiences and losses in the disaster. A couple of pictures depict the streets full of trash taken when those of the *inundados/victims* who actually had a home to return to, were back and had to clean their homes:

> The rumour was that you had to take pictures of the state of the things that were left in the house [after the flooding]. And when I entered [the house], I began to take things out . . . and throw them away . . . and when I finished I realised that I had thrown away almost everything. Then I said to myself: [take] pictures inside the house? Of what? (p.23)

On the night of the presentation of the book, around 150 people were gathered in what used to be the waiting hall of the train station. I ran into several people that I had met in the Plaza de Mayo square during the *inundados/activists'* demonstrations, but also some neighbours from Barrio Roma. A couple of local journalists that I also recognised from the street demonstrations were there too. A table had been set up with microphones and spotlights in a corner, where a woman and a man were sitting. Soon after I arrived, they began to speak to the crowd. The woman, who was one of the editors of the book, made a short introduction of the book and its background. Then she introduced the middle-aged man next to her as one of the *inundados* depicted in the book. The man, who presented himself as an artist, talked for about fifteen minutes about his experiences and losses from *la Inundación*. He said that not only had he lost personal belongings such as family photographs, furniture inherited from his grandparents and his own artistic works, but also health and peace in life. His life had been destroyed, he said. As the man finished speaking, a middle-aged woman sitting in the audience, clearly moved by the man's talk, took the floor and introduced herself as a neighbour from the Santa Rosa neighbourhood. She said, "I will never again be the same [person] as before *la Inundación*" and added that she had lost herself through the loss of her belongings. She emphasised the importance of the book they were presenting, because it represented the experiences of all the *inundados/victims* in 2003. The couple at the table then nodded their heads in agreement. The woman at the table underscored that the book was "for memory, because we have to remember and fight against oblivion [of the disaster and the *inundados*]." Her remark received strong applauds and assent among the participants in the waiting hall.

After the oral presentations, a slide show based on the book was presented. It was screened on the wall in front of the audience. The slide show presented the portraits of the book, one after the other, accompanied by a recorded reading out of the texts in the book. Everybody in the audience remained in complete silence watching it. I observed the corporal and facial expressions of the people surrounding me, noticing that they looked moved. Others seemed tense and upset. A young woman on my right continuously shook her head as if she could not believe, nor accept, what had happened. A well-dressed middle-aged man next to her nodded in empathy when a man on the screen said how much he regretted the loss of his personal library. When the slide show ended, the audience burst out in standing ovations. I also joined in the applauding, which seemed to last forever.

Akin to literary readings that are carried out by writers in public places (Wulff 2008), the book launch at the Birri Foundation can be seen as a narrative performance (R. Bauman 1986) through which memories of *la Inundación* were reproduced and shared with the audience. The *inundados/victims* on stage performed their own memories as narrated in the book and shared them with the audience, turning the event into a performative moment of social remembering.

Writing and performing flood memories from Santa Rosa de Lima

In addition to the books and the book launch described above, other books of the kind were published and performed during my fieldwork. Two of them were written by people of Santa Rosa de Lima. The first, *Las Aguas Subían Turbias*[129] (Velásquez 2004), paraphrasing an old Argentinian movie,[130] includes poetries and short accounts about *la Inundación*, and testimonies from different people in this neighbourhood.[131] The other book titled *Entre Todos Escribimos, Dibujamos, Cantamos*[132] (Escuela nro 1298 Monseñor Vicente Zazpe 2006) is also a compilation but stems from the pedagogical work done with the pupils in one of the primary schools in the neighbourhood. I had been told that this particular school was historically a refuge to the residents in the *barrio* in times of flooding and so it was in 2003, until the school had to be evacuated as well. The book contains drawings, photographs and texts produced by the children and their teachers in the spirit of celebrating the capacity of the residents in the *barrio* to recover. It is explained in the book that the volume is really the result of a pedagogical project to deal with extensive learning and social problems carried out in this school in 2005. The teachers based their teaching on the pupils' everyday life in order to overcome the gap between the school and the home environments of these children, the latter strongly affected by the 2003 disaster. The book thus contains many a reference to *la Inundación*. One of the projects was a *murga* workshop, with the aim of having the children express their ideas and feelings through music.

The musical street theatre called *murga*, so typical in the Río de la Plata region, is generally performed in carnival season but is also considered something of an urban folklore expression in Santa Fe, and therefore performed on occasions the entire year. The pupils in the school in Santa Rosa worked with composing *murga* songs and costumes as part of the project (ibid.: 45-62). On

---

[129] In English: The Waters Rose Muddily
[130] The motion picture referenced is *Las Aguas Bajan Turbias* (1952). Abroad it was given the title *Rivers of Blood* although in the USA it was called *Dark River*.
[131] The book was edited by Angélica Velázquez, an elderly woman and resident in this neighbourhood, who was also the author of the poems in the book.
[132] In English: Together we Write, Paint, Sing

May 25th, 2005, I attended one the official commemorations of the May Revolution, organised by the Human Rights Secretariat of the Provincial Government, which was a *murga* festival held in the Parque de los Niños located next to the Costanera esplanade on the Eastside. Twelve children *murga* troupes, all dressed in colourful costumes and hats, and with their faces painted, marched a couple of blocks singing, dancing and playing their *redoblante* and *bombo de marcha* drums,[133] before arriving in the square which was really a small park.

Figure 12 | Children *murga* troupe on May 25th (Photo by author 2005)

A stage had been set up in the middle of the park equipped with a sound system. As hot chocolate and *churro* cakes were served in a typical way[134] to all children present, the *murga* troupes performed their songs on stage. One of these was the 6th graders of the school in Santa Rosa de Lima mentioned in the book. The name of their troupe was *El Poder de la Murga*[135] and they performed a song titled "Son Culpables"[136] that they wrote inspired by one of the songs by the Argentini-

---

[133] In *murga* performance, only percussive instruments are generally used, like the snare drum (*redoblante*) and the marching bass drum (*bombo de marcha*). Occasionally the guitar is used too.
[134] The *churro* is a fried pastry similar to the doughnut and is served with hot chocolate as breakfast or snack in Argentina and in other countries, in particular during cold winter months. In Argentina the *chocolate con churros* is also often served at the public celebrations of the National Holidays of May 25th, which commemorates the so-called May Revolution of 1810, and July 9th, which commemorates the declaration of independence in 1816.
[135] In English: The Power of Murga
[136] In English: They are Guilty

an pop singer Vicentico. The lyrics, which are also printed in the above mentioned book, recall *la Inundación* by accusing the mayor and the governor (whose nickname was Lole) of being responsible for the disaster as expressed in the refrain:

> Guilty,
> Mayor, you are guilty,
> I accuse you and I curse you
> You left me without my home, abandoned in a shed
> Guilty,
> You and Lole are guilty,
> I accuse you and I curse you
> From the bottom of my soul and of my heart

La Inundación was recalled by most *inundados/victims* as a political failure rather than a natural disaster. Remembering the disaster in this particular way was shared across generations, as this example makes clear. In contrast to the notions of "postmemory" (Hirsch 1997) and "intergenerational transmission of memory" (Argenti and Schramm 2012), which refer to the experience of one generation mediated through remembering to the next generation, in the case of the children in Santa Rosa de Lima in 2005, they were writing and performing their own disaster memories. Nevertheless, by sharing these with other children from other flooded and non-flooded districts of the city, the accidental community of memory around *la Inundación* was reinforced and enlarged.

The sounds of disaster

Music and musical performances were common means of remembering *la Inundación* in Santa Fe during my fieldwork. In addition to the example of the children *murga* discussed above, established local musicians wrote songs in memory of the tragedy. I heard Martin Sosa perform his song "Somos Todos Inundados"[137] on a couple of occasions. Then there was a song by the local *cumbia* orchestra Los Palmeras. This orchestra was famous in the entire country, having produced around forty records throughout the years, many of which had sold gold and platinum. The band was immensely popular in its hometown, to the extent that the city's Town Council declared the members of the orchestra Distinguished Citizens in 2002. In the wake of *la Inundación* they recorded the song "29/4/2003," which was the date of the disaster. I was told by my interlocutors in the Westside that Los Palmeras performed this song regularly in the dance halls, thereby reinforcing the memory community beyond the *inundados/victims*.

---

[137] In English: We are All Flooded

Charity concerts

In the context of disaster, music and musicians are in fact often used, either as means to raise funds or to highlight a situation. Fundraising shows are increasingly common worldwide in the wake of disasters aimed at producing solidarity with distant suffering of victims other than ourselves. The fundraising show format creates "a temporal space for participation and expressions of solidarity" (Olesen 2012:100) through moral and emotional engagement. Such ritual moments of engagement can also be thought of as moments of social remembering. In addition, musical artefacts such as records serve to evoke particular memories and the narrative of song lyrics can, as we have already seen, be commemorative.

In Santa Fe and Buenos Aires, several charity concerts were held in support of the *inundados/victims* of Santa Fe. Famous Argentinian pop singers like Fito Paez, Juan Carlos Baglietto and León Gieco, all three of them originally from the Province of Santa Fe, performed twice with their well-known songs in the Obras football stadium in Buenos Aires.[138] Only a couple of days later, one of them, León Gieco, visited Santa Fe City together with another popular singer, Victor Heredia, in an effort to express their solidarity and compassion for the people affected by the disaster. They gave several concerts in different evacuation centres around the city (*El Litoral* 2003). Both these pop and folk music singers/songwriters had been very popular in Argentina for many decades. They had throughout the years engaged actively in human rights issues and are considered to be politically committed artists. Before one of their concerts, Gieco and Heredia performed in the Cuban city capital Havana together with Silvio Rodriguez, the Cuban singer and principal figure in the Cuban Nueva Trova musical movement.[139] They decided to record the concert and produce a CD for the benefit of the flooded Children's Hospital (*Página/12* 2003). The CD, titled *Canciones con Santa Fe*[140] included songs recorded by many famous Argentinian and other Latin American artists.[141] The final track on the CD is a famous song called "Cita con Ángeles"[142] that Rodriguez composed after the terrorist attacks in the USA in 2001. The lyrics are a reflection on war, the abuse of power and the effects of such world relations, referring to people like Federico Garcia Lorca and Martin Luther King, and events like the Hiroshima bombings and the 1973 coup

---

[138] This double concert and a whip-round held on May 11th, 2003, was organised by an Argentinian NGO called Red Solidaria in order to collect money to buy milk for the child flood victims in Santa Fe City (Giubellino 2003).
[139] The *Nueva Trova* was a movement in Cuban music that emerged in the late sixties after the Cuban Revolution of 1959. By its lyrics it is very political, intimately connected to the revolution. In Argentina the *Nueva Trova* was linked to the development of the so-called *Nueva Canción* movement with the works such as that of Mercedes Sosa and León Gieco and many others. The *Nueva Trova* became very popular in Argentina as in the rest of Latin America. It was banned under the various dictatorships on the continent.
[140] In English: Songs with Santa Fe
[141] Performing on this CD are the Argentinians Fito Paez, Juan Carlos Baglietto, Lito Vitale, Liliana Herrero and Charly Garcia, as well as other Latin American artists like the Uruguayan Rubén Rada, the Chilean Isabel Parra, the Spaniard Ismael Serrano, the Peruvian Tania Libertad, the Puertoricans Danny Rivera and Roy Brown and the Cubans Carlos Varela and Santiago Feliú.
[142] In English: Date with Angels

d'état in Chile. In the concert recorded on the CD a new verse[143] was added to this song by the Argentinian Victor Heredia. The placing of *la Inundación* in the mnemonic context of these other major disasters and critical reflections upon the events as the product of skewed power relations contributed to framing the flood, not as a natural disaster, but as a political failure. The musical performances of Gieco and Heredia and other artists worked not just as practices of remembering *la Inundación*. Their respective former trajectories as singers committed to human rights and social injustices in Argentina gave a particular meaning to these commemorative fundraising actions. Their engagement for the situation of *la Inundación* of Santa Fe evokes memories of other sufferings and struggles in Argentina, including that of the violent political past, intensifying emotional and moral concerns for the wellbeing of the *inundados/victims*.

Voices from a tragedy

One audio media that was widely distributed in Santa Fe about *la Inundación* was different from the musical works. It was a CD recorded by the university radio station titled *la inundación | voces de una tragedia*[144] (LT10 Radio Universidad Nacional del Litoral 2003), which was a compilation from 200 hours of broadcasting from this radio between April 27th to May 4th, 2003. Dramatic pieces of music and sound effects frame the narrative sonically. A male broadcaster introduces and situates each and every statement and commentary during the hour-long CD compilation. The declarations of experts, politicians, public officials and desperate voices of ordinary people in those days make up a compelling oral narrative that shapes the imagination of how this disaster took place. Interviews with flood victims made by the radio journalists at the site of the flooding and phone calls made by radio listeners to the radio station in the height of the emergency constitute a story of despair and disinformation but also of solidarity and commitment.

This recorded story largely corresponds with the stories I was told by so many people during my fieldwork; that which I analyse in the beginning of this chapter as a canonised collective narrative that singles out *la Inundación* as a particular event in the urban flood memoryscape. The statements by government officials recorded on this CD also sustain the latter. Among the most emblematic story elements is that of the Mayor Marcelo Alvarez on April 29th. His public statement had disastrous effects because it made people refrain from evacuating. During my fieldwork, his declaration was frequently and mockingly referred to when recalling the poor governmental disaster management in 2003:

[It's] a totally atypical phenomenon . . . [yet] [the neighbourhood of] Villa del Parque…is still salvageable . . . [If there is a truck with sand this should] go to Villa del Parque because [this neighbour-

---

[143] The verse in English: "In Santa Fe the waters cover the dreams of sad children, flooding with uncontainable fury the pain of the evacuees. An angel falls in tears as he discovers the ravings of the dark wing of the Salado [River] that covers everything that is beloved."
[144] Lower case letters in original. In English: the flood | voices from a tragedy

hood] is still salvageable, especially because with water pump number 3 we can pump 10 million litres [of floodwater] per hour to the reservoir [which] is empty . . . we can save this sector. For those residents who call in [to the radio] from the Southside I can say that . . . we have no problem whatsoever with water pump 1, that is, all [neighbourhoods] of Barrio Centenario, Villa del Centenario, Barrio Chalet, Barrio San Lorenzo, Barrio El Arenal, all those will not have **any** problems, because [the floodwater] is extracted by the water pump 1 . . . the Southwest Side will have **no** problems . . . [The General Lopez Avenue and the embankment] is in good condition, there won't be **any** problem at all [in that area]. (Track 4. Emphasis added to denote the emphasis of the mayor).

Another statement recorded on the CD is that of the then Governor Carlos Reutemann on a press conference on May 3rd. His statement became emblematic of the lax disaster management of the municipal and provincial authorities.

Well, I have not received any of the information [about the studies and reports] you mention. Nobody, absolutely nobody has informed me [about this]. (Track 9).

As we shall see in next chapter, both these statements were used frequently by the *inundados* movement to highlight the governor's responsibility for the tragedy. They were also used and reiterated in other media about *la Inundación*, for example in the many documentaries produced.

Visualising *la Inundación*: The documentaries

Numerous documentary films were produced in the wake of *la Inundación*. I collected nine in the course of my fieldwork, but there were many more.[145] I have watched these documentaries several times during my fieldwork, both alone at home and some together with other people as they were publicly screened in Santa Fe. While the biographical ones are more emotionally framed than the analytical ones, it is equally moving to watch the images in all documentaries. As I walked the city and talked to people during fieldwork, I realised that the documentaries I had seen helped me to imagine and situate, hence remember, places and people of this event, though I had no personal experience with them myself. When I participated in public screening of these documentaries I could observe how people engaged emotionally with the images and sounds displayed by nodding their heads, crying, cursing or talking to each other. The documentaries

---

[145] In addition to the documentaries I collected, Acuña (2005) accounts for another ten documentaries about *la Inundación* that were produced in Santa Fe. In 2006 I was informed by an interlocutor that at a cultural symposium organised in the Cultural Centre Fundación Birri around the third anniversary of *la Inundación*, at least four new short documentaries were screened.

served as audiovisual testimonies of a past event, and as such they were cues for evoking these memories, both of individual experiences and of socially established narratives.

The documentaries about *la Inundación* that I have seen all included images from the city in emergency. Some of them contain images from the years of recovery that followed. Some of them, like *La Lección del Salado*[146] (Cable y Diario 2004) and *Agua de Nadie*[147] (Traffano and Pais 2005), mixed images from the emergency with interviews with the *inundados* on site, politicians, civil servants and technicians in the municipality and in the provincial government. Similar to the testimonial texts discussed above, the documentaries about *la Inundación* can be divided in two categories. One is journalistic, analytical and critical towards the government's role in the disaster. I shall return to these in the next chapter. The other category of documentaries is more personalised or biographical. Those are the films that we shall take a closer look at in what follows.

Inundaciones: Recording and recalling evacuation

One of the first documentaries produced and one of the most well known in Santa Fe was *Inundaciones*[148] (Santa Fe Documenta-Colectivo de Video 2003). This film conveys images and radio transmissions from the emergency on April 29th and onwards. The unfortunate statement of the mayor described above is reproduced. The film also includes interviews with evacuees in the evacuation centres, on the top of the roofs and back home cleaning their mud covered homes, who tell the camera about their experiences. This documentary was made by a group of young local filmmakers and journalists. My friend Maria and I originally met some of the members of this group during our first field trip in July 2004. They told us that they had gathered on those first days of *la Inundación* and had decided to document the events in order to contribute to the collective memory in Santa Fe. When they had finished the documentary, they first screened it publicly in September 2003 in the Plaza de Mayo square in Santa Fe City. As I shall write more about in the next chapter, the square was at this time being occupied by the flood victims protesting against the government's actions in relation to the disaster. According to the filmmakers, the emotional reaction among the demonstrators was impressive as the images and sounds from the emergency evoked traumatic memories and strong feelings in them.

Maria and I were invited to accompany the film crew as they were documenting the process of recovery of people in different parts of the city for a follow up video in collaboration with the Argentinian Workers' Central Union (CTA).[149] That afternoon we visited two neighbourhoods in the outskirts of the city, namely the Tablada in the Northwest district, on the banks of the Salado

---

[146] In English: The lesson from the Salado [River]
[147] In English: Nobody's Water
[148] In English: Flooding
[149] The acronym stands for Central de Trabajadores de la Argentina (Argentinian Workers' Central).

River, and Las Delicias in the North district. The first was a precarious settlement where the *ranchos* had been completely washed away on April 27th, two days before the rest of the city. The inhabitants had been evacuated to an evacuation centre and then re-evacuated to La Tablada neighbourhood. Many of them, like Lorena and José mentioned in Chapter Two, later moved to the new *barrio* of la Nueva Tablada, which was a one of the relocation projects that the municipality had established for flood victims from different neighbourhoods in the city. In the wake of *la Inundación*, the municipality, with the support of the Argentinian and the German Red Cross, the Humanitarian Aid Office of the European Union (ECHO) and different NGOs, created several "relocation neighbourhoods" in the Northside and Northwest Side districts. In addition to the above-mentioned, there was also the neighbourhood of Loyola Norte and 29 de Abril – the latter a place where *la Inundación* was ever-present in memory by the shere name of the *barrio*. In several of these neighbourhoods, families with many children were still living in Red Cross emergency shelters during my fieldwork. Several of my interlocutors referred ironically to each one of these neighbourhoods as *Barrio Plastiquito* because these shelters were made of plastic modules.

In our visit to La Tablada and Las Delicias in 2004, the inhabitants showed us around among their brittle evacuation sheds. The film crew asked them to stand in front the shelters for the camera interviews. The testimonies given by the residents were unanimously critical about the support provided by the provincial government and the municipality. They had been living in emergency shelters for more than a year by then, completely lacking infrastructure such as water, sewage and electricity. Their children had not yet returned to school. The schools were situated on the Southwest Side, approximately eight kilometres from where they lived now. These families could not afford to pay daily bus tickets for them and they had not yet been transferred to schools closer by. Similar problems persisted the year after, when I visited the *barrio* 29 de Abril together with Gabriel and others from the *inundados* movement and two young doctors from the Spanish NGO Médicos del Mundo.[150] Their grievances were not difficult to sympathise with.

The shootings that the film crew from the video collectivity took on that day in 2004 were edited to a short 11 minutes video called *Informe a 15 meses*[151] (Santa Fe Documenta-Colectivo de Video 2005). I was told it was screened in a cultural centre in Buenos Aires. I watched it upon my return to Santa Fe in 2005, together with another thousand people in the main square Plaza de Mayo, during the commemoration act of the second anniversary of *la Inundación* organised by the *inundados* movement, which will be addressed in Chapter Four. It was a rather impressive feeling for me to stand in such a large crowd in the dark night and observe how at first people watched the film in absolute silence. A couple of women next to me began crying after a while and were given comfort by people standing next to them. In one passage of the video, the

---

[150] This NGO is the Spanish branch of the international Doctors of the World.
[151] In English: Report after 15 months

public statement by the mayor mentioned above about not needing to evacuate on the Westside was reproduced. The voice of the Mayor Alvarez and his fateful words evoked memories of anxiety, fear and anger among the crowd, who suddenly burst out in a loud booing against the government which they held responsible for the tragedy. Their curse echoed in the urban night: "*¡Hijos de puta!* Sons of bitches!"

Inundados in an ethno-biographical gaze

In documentary film there is a genre among the more personalised approaches called "ethno-biography," a concept coined by the late Argentinian filmmaker Jorge Prelorán.[152] The ethno-biography is considered a sub-genre of ethnographic film in which individuals' personal stories are taken to represent a larger cultural context, similar to how life histories are used in ethnographic texts. The production of an ethno-biographic film is based on close collaborations between the filmmaker and the subjects of the film.

When I returned to Santa Fe in 2009, Mariana, one of the members of the video collectivity, had produced a new documentary as part of her thesis for a bachelor's degree in journalism. When we met in a café one day, she kindly gave me a copy of her film called *Vanesa* (Rabaini 2008). It is a compelling documentary about a young woman by that name, whose 12-day-old baby son Uriel was one of the 23 dead in *la Inundación*. Vanesa's little son drowned as she tried to escape the flood with all her three children. Only the two eldest survived. Mariana had met Vanesa in the first days of the disaster, when she worked as a TV-journalist and was covering the news. She told me that Vanesa's story had a strong impact on her. Mariana had wanted to make something more of it for the purposes of social memory, both of the fate of Vanesa and her family, and of the tragedy of *la Inundación*. She asked Vanesa if they could continue conversations in front of the camera and so they did. I did not attend any screenings of the documentary, but I was told that it had been presented several times in Santa Fe and in other Argentinian cities.

The year after, María Langhi, another young female filmmaker from the city of Rosario, made the documentary *Seguir Remando: La Tragedia Santafesina*[153] (2009). In this documentary there are three protagonists involved in the events of *la Inundación*. The principal character in this film is Lucia, a housemaid in her fifties from the neighbourhood San Lorenzo on the Southwest Side. The film follows her from the moment of *la Inundación* until 2009 back in her home in the *barrio*. It depicts her as she struggles to make ends meet in order to recover from the losses and the experiences from *la Inundación* and the minor

---

[152] Jorgé Prelorán (1933-2009) was a highly productive filmmaker who worked all over the world, but in particular in South and North America. Before he died he donated all his works to the Department of Anthropology at the Smithsonian Institute in the USA ('Jorge Prelorán Collection at Human Studies Film Archives' 2013). A recent documentary gives an account of Prelorán's own life in a similar way (Alvarez Rivera 2009).
[153] In English: *Keep On Rowing: The Tragedy of Santa Fe City*

flood of 2007 (which was due to heavy rain), in which she had to evacuate again. In addition there is Luciano, who is 20 years old and who engaged himself as a volunteer in one of the evacuation centres during the 2003 disaster. The final protagonist is six-year-old Sol, a charming little girl who was flooded with her grandmother and evacuated in the middle of the night by the gendarmerie.

Seguir remando was screened for the first time in the cinema América in Santa Fe the day before the seventh anniversary of the disaster, on April 28th, 2010. In a radio interview about her film, María referred to how the Santafesinian audience in particular had reacted to it:

> [The reception] was good, there was some audience there . . . like you say, this is where it [the disaster] occurred . . . [in the audience] was the people of the Assembly of the *inundados/activists*, [who] on that day were beginning their wake [for the anniversary commemoration on the following day] in the [Plaza de Mayo] square. When you screen a film [like this] in Santa Fe it is very powerful; people start crying, eh, you will hear from someone sitting behind you saying to somebody next [to him or her] "Do you remember [this], do you remember [that], uh, look what he said!" Yes, it's very powerful what is happening in Santa Fe (Radio Universidad - Universidad Nacional de Rosario 2010).

There are several interesting observations about all these personalised documentaries in the context of memory. One regards the images used, especially those from the very moment of the emergency. While some of the filmmakers shot the images themselves, many others have used the same images in the different documentaries. According to the latter, many images from the emergency were shot by the local cable television company, the Cable y Diario, which covered the disaster intensively and extensively in those days. Journalists from this company eventually edited the "documenting documentary" titled *La Lección del Salado* mentioned above and made available these and other images to different filmmakers. The video collectivity also filmed plenty during these first days. They used these images themselves in many different audiovisual productions. One example of this was a video that the famous Argentinian rock band Bersuit Vergarabat used in their show to perform a song called "Otra Sudestada."[154] While the song referred to different calamities such as storms and floods, it also referred to political corruption and violence and to how the Argentinians engaged in resistance to such things. This was represented in a video that was screened at the back of the stage, conveying different images such as from the social protests of the Argentinazo of 2001 and from la Inundación and the inundados movement

---

[154] In English: Another Sudestada [storm]. The *Sudestada* refers to the Southeast storm winds common during the winter in the Río de la Plata region. It consists of a sudden rotation of cold winds, which brings heavy rain, rough seas and, more often than not, flooding in urban areas.

in Santa Fe.155 Some of the filmmakers in the video collectivity provided for the images from la Inundación and participated in the making of this video, which was screened at hundreds of concerts by Bersuit Vergarabat in Argentina and abroad.

Secondly, several of the protagonists appear in different documentaries. Vanesa, for example, appeared already in the prior documentary *Inundaciones*. One of the interviewed women in *Inundaciones* was the grandmother of little Sol who was the protagonist of *Seguir Remando*. While this is probably simply the result of collaboration between the filmmakers, it is interesting to note how certain personal testimonies came to circulate in many different documentary productions. A third interesting observation is that several of these documentaries use images from other audiovisual works to make a narrative link to past floods in Santa Fe. The documentary *Inundaciones* for example, begins with fragment from the old Argentinian motion picture *Los Inundados* (Birri 1961).[156] This latter film depicts flooding precisely in Santa Fe and is central in the Santafesinian mythico-history of flooding, as we shall see in Chapter Six. In the documentary this piece is followed by a fragment of an interview with an old man now flooded, who recalls having acted as an extra in the old movie. The documentary *Seguir Remando* also starts with a fragment from this movie. In a similar vein, the documentary *Inundables* uses images from the Argentinian film *El Viaje*[157] (Solanas 1990) in which a city is completely flooded. While these images of a flooded city are not supposed to represent Santa Fe (but Buenos Aires) the film uses a surrealist language to evoke a critique against the Argentinian State, and the international economic and political system that produces asymmetrical relations of power and well-being. The argument conveyed in the fiction *El Viaje* supported the argument in the documentary *Seguir remando*.

Finally, the documentaries about *la Inundación* all have one thing in common, namely the goal of making memory. In one way or another allusions are made to this aim. Some of them, like *El Agua y la Sangre (Memorias de la Inundación)* (Alarcón et al. 2004), mention this ambition already in the title. Others do so in the forewords, credits or synopsis. In *La Lección del Salado* it is declared that "[t]his TV documentary intends to contribute to the necessary memory of what has occurred"; in *Inundaciones* the claim is to "call upon ourselves to maintain the collective and historical memory of our wet city." Finally in *Agua de Nadie* the purpose is to "exercise memory and open spaces for debate and reflection about the events, the documents and the testimonies from the worst tragedy that the Santafesinos have ever experienced." In a similar vein, Langhi in the radio interview about her film *Seguir Remando* said the following:

> It is a controversial film because, well, it addresses themes that are not closed, eh, it refers to people who are in the political limelight . . . it's good that this is made visible . . . that we talk about it . . . we

---

[155] The performance referred to is found on the DVD *Bersuit: La Argentinidad al palo* (2004) and is also available on line (*Bersuit - 'Otra Sudestada' - La Argentinidad Al Palo En Vivo (DVD)* 2010).
[156] This film was given the title *Flooded Out* in English speaking countries.
[157] In English: The Journey

might not have the same opinion [on why and how the disaster happened] but beyond this, the film is memory (Radio Universidad - Universidad Nacional de Rosario 2010).

The ethnobiography *Vanesa* ends with a section in which the director, Mariana, accompanying the images after the credits, speaks in a meta-communicative and reflexive manner about her role as a journalist and filmmaker in the engagement with Vanesa and the film:

> I don't know if I opted for her [Vanesa's] history or if the histories pick you. Maybe [it was] in order to not be abandoned in a journalistic moment in the midst of the abyss of chaos, cases and impacts and [instead] become part of another type of [media] communication. Five years after *la Inundación* of 2003, when the major claim is justice, as a communicator I find myself mediating between opinions, experiences, beliefs and imaginaries that give meaning to communities - and to the memory!

Returning to the relation of testimony and memory, there are multiple layers of testimonies in these documentary film productions. The protagonists in the biographical documentaries were eyewitnesses to the disaster and in most cases embodying these memories as *inundados/victims*. Being eyewitnesses, they were considered entitled to give their testimony in front of the camera. The filmmakers were in many cases, if not all, also eyewitnesses to the tragedy. Several of them were residents in the city and many worked as journalists in 2003 and later. The filmmakers were also witnesses to the testimonies of the protagonists, corroborating their narratives with their own experiences and memories of *la Inundación*. This is the case also with the audience of the different documentaries. Taken together, the witnessing of all these actors configure a process of sharing and reproducing memories in a memoryscape that branches out to other parts of Argentina.

La Inundación visualised: Photography in private and public

As we have seen above, visuality was involved in multiple ways in the memory-work of *la Inundación*. Several photography exhibitions were organised throughout the years. By the time of the 10th anniversary in 2013, a large exposition with the pictures of many a renown Santafesinian photographer was organised in Santa Fe called "Santa Fe *inundación*: A ten year gaze."[158]

Photographs played a role in remembering the disaster also in the private domain. As I have described, the return home had been a hardship to most *inundados/victims* in 2003. To actually see what had happened to their homes and belongings, most of them ruined, was an emotional blow and a sense of loss.

---

[158] In Spanish: *Santa Fe inundación: Mirada a 10 años*

The material losses mentioned by my interlocutors ranged from books, old letters, music records and school diplomas to grandmother's chest of drawers and "the house that my father built with his own hands." Ruined family photographs and family albums were mentioned almost on every occasion. Despite differences in how many albums or pictures had been lost, or what kind of pictures, people from the middle- and low-income neighbourhoods expressed the same grief over this loss. I was told by Carlos, a man in his forties from Barrio Centenario, that "those were the pictures of my dead parents, the only memory I had from them." Luisa, a woman in her sixties from Villa del Parque said almost crying: "I lost my wedding picture, you know." Nora, an architect in her fifties from the neighbourhood Parque Juan de Garay, said that she most lamented "the pictures of the kids throughout the years as they grew up, photos from our vacations in Córdoba and in Mar del Plata."

What does this say about family photography in contemporary Argentina? Family photography can be described as a primary means through which family identity and memory is perpetuated (Barthes 1982; Bourdieu 1996). Pictures visualise the past of a family and represent different belongings in social life. Family photographs deploy a "familial gaze" referring to "the conventions and ideologies of family through which they [the family members] see themselves" (Hirsch 1999:xi). This gaze is constituted through the social practices by which the pictures are produced and organised. The very act of taking the picture of family members and of particular familial situations is the first step in this. The images are then organised and displayed within family space, generally at home, either exposed on a chest of drawers or chronologically ordered in albums. Family photography conveys memories from our lives and reminds us about our own mortality. Photographs visualise how we understand ourselves and our past. Given this significance, which in the case of Santa Fe was common to people in different social contexts, it seems reasonable to say that memory and subjectivity are affected if family pictures are no longer there to remind us of who we were and who we are. Such absence can thus be said to refract the familial gaze by offering new conventions of who we are. For many of the Santafesinos, particularly from the middle classes, they suddenly belonged to the social category *inundados/victims,* an identity hitherto unknown to them. As Nora, the woman from Parque Juan de Garay, said: "I mean, our whole life was in those pictures and suddenly they were just gone!" Mirta, a woman in her fifties from Santa Rosa de Lima, expressed her grief in a similar way, saying:

> It was as if my whole life had vanished. The pictures were filled with clay and shit from the dirty floodwater. The thought of having to take them out of the house and just throw them away – there's no way I can explain the pain that I felt, a mix of pain, sadness, hate and anger.

In Santa Fe, this deflected understanding of life, family and self that came about unexpectedly did not stop with ruined portraits and the loss of family albums. In 2003, after having returned to their ruined homes and finding their belongings destroyed, people had to begin to clean up. Parallel to this arduous task, they had to carry out numerous bureaucratic tasks in order to get recognised as flood victims in order to be entitled for governmental support in the process of reconstruction. They had to register and to get an ID card that certified that they were indeed registered. Once entitled to support, they could acquire food and clothing, mattresses and bedclothes and health care for free. The provincial government later launched the process of economic compensation for material loss. To qualify for this, the people who had been flooded had to prove that their losses had been their property. For their properties, title deeds or rental contracts were required. For personal goods, authorities encouraged the *inundados/victims* to provide photographs of the objects; pictures both from before the disaster and after. Thus, the remnants of those ruined family albums, in which the car was depicted or in which the house and the garden were captured, came to play an important role for those affected, not that of representing home and years of effort, but as proof of those wasted efforts. Suddenly they came to convey loss, rather than life gains.

Thus, in 2003, people who still owned a camera that worked took pictures of the ruins. These pictures not only served the purpose of providing evidence of damages, but were from then on integrated into people's (new) family albums. A new familial gaze was in the making. The old photographs that were left after the 2003 disaster and the new ones taken in the aftermath, shaped new memories of the past and contributed to new self-understandings of many of the families who were flooded, not least of those in the middle-class districts. They had never before been flooded and for sure had never imagined that they could be. The material losses they suffered were not only a blow to their economy but also to their self-understanding and social identification within the Santafesinian society. Unexpectedly to many, they were *inundados/victims* of *la Inundación*. This category of identification articulated with another emerging social category, that of the *inundados/activists*, but also with the pre-existing social category of *inundados*, a category that I will address in Chapter Six.

For the *inundados/victims* the refraction of their familial gaze referred to the rupture of the social order and a new identification by accident; a different understanding of self, family and community. I suggest that the losses of personal belongings in general and of the family pictures in particular in this disaster contributed to this refracted gaze which enabled the constitution of an accidental community of memory. As we shall see in the forthcoming chapter, this refraction also allowed for people who had never before been politically active to imagine themselves as activists carrying out street protests and holding authorities accountable for their losses.

Materialising and placing disaster memories

Public monuments and memorials created in memory of major atrocities are found all over the world. Several of them have received scholarly attention, such as the Berlin Holocaust Memorial (Sion 2008), the Hiroshima Peace Memorial

Museum (Akiko 2002), the Memory Park and Monument to the Victims of State Terrorism in Buenos Aires (Huyssen 2003, Sion 2008), the memorial at the former site of the World Trade Center in New York, so-called Ground Zero (Sturken 1997; Sather-Wagstaff 2011), and the Lebanese war memorials (Volk 2010), just to mention a few. Several "natural" disasters have also prompted memorials around the world, such as the Tsunami Museum in Aceh, the Indian Ocean Tsunami Memorial in London, and the Tsunami Memorial Sculpture in Krabi, the Katrina memorials in New Orleans, and the Donghekou Earthquake Relics Park in Sichuan. Many memorials created in the aftermath of disasters do not receive global attention however, such as that in a small Tamil fishing village (F. Hastrup 2011). It is also increasingly common, in the wake of sudden loss, to find "spontaneous memorials" (Santino 2006), that is, places for commemoration that are created by ordinary people and not by any public institution. Sometimes such official and non-official spaces of memory coexist. After the tragic discotheque fire in Buenos Aires in 2004 a sanctuary consisting of all kinds of symbolic artefacts and pictures was created by survivors and relatives to the victims, while the local government created the Memory Square in remembrance of the victims next to this (Zenobi 2011:114).

Forgotten monuments?

In Santa Fe, several non-official monuments were created to commemorate *la Inundación*. As we shall see in the next chapter, some of these were used as venues in the politics of remembering. Other popular monuments were not politicised, or at least, were not intended to be, by the people creating them. Rather they were built to mourn the dead, to grieve the loss and to recall the disaster as a reminder to not repeat it. One of these memorials was placed in one of the few parks in the city, the Parque Garay.[159] This large leafy park, created in the early 20th century was located on the Westside between the homonymous upper-middle-class neighbourhood Parque Juan de Garay, the poor neighbourhood Villa del Parque and the working-middle-class Barrio Roma. In 2003 the entire area was completely flooded, including the park. To commemorate this, a monument was erected in the main entrance to the park. The monument to *la Inundación* consisted of a small bronze plaque sitting on a one-meter-high square pedestal. The inscription was dated with the first anniversary of the disaster on April 29th, 2004 saying:

> We recall the first anniversary of the day when the Salado River flooded our Roma neighbourhood. We pray to god that this will never occur again. In tribute to our victims. The neighbourhood associations of Parque Juan de Garay, Barrio Roma and República del Oeste.

The monument was placed in the centre of the avenue that leads into the park, not far from a statue of the Virgin of Guadalupe, the Patron Saint of Santa Fe City.

---

[159] The official name of the park is Parque Juan de Garay in memory of the founder of the city.

Right in front of the monument was of a bust of the city's founder, the Spanish Captain Juan de Garay, to whom the park owes its name, and a mural representing the Spanish colonisation of the region in the 16th century and the settlement of the town in 1573. This particular placement of the disaster monument in relation to some of the key symbols of Santafesinian upper and middle classes, Catholicism and its European descent, seemed to place *la Inundación* well in the hierarchy of social memories. On the occasions that I passed by the memorial, I never observed any movement around it, nor did I hear that any commemorative ceremony would have taken place there. It seemed like a rather forgotten place, in contrast to other memorials, especially the one in the square Plaza 29 de Abril.

The Flooded Mothers and the Plaza 29 de Abril square

In the corner of the highly trafficked Mosconi Avenue and Mendoza Street on the Southwest Side, just in front of the Children's Hospital, was a plot of land, approximately 50 metres wide and 100 metres long. I was told by the lady who owned the small grocery shop across the street that before 2003, neighbours used to walk their dogs here. In 2003, it was completely flooded, as were the hospital and the surrounding neighbourhoods. In 2004 it was turned into a square, the Plaza 29 de Abril, in memory of *la Inundación*. I visited the square several times during my fieldwork. At the back of the plot was a two metres high wall on which children had painted several colourful murals representing *la Inundación*. In one mural, children had painted houses with floodwater up to the roof, with people, adults and children standing on the roof with their hands lifted as if they were calling for help. On the roof were also TV sets, cupboards, cats and dogs. In the floodwater, several rowing boats with people rowing them were depicted. Helicopters were painted in the grey sky. One of the most compelling paintings was one depicting blue water and countless skin-coloured hands sticking out of the water as if they belonged to people who were drowning, calling them *desaparecidos*. By using this particular term to refer to the drowning people in the painting, an analogy was made between the victims of the Dirty War and those of *la Inundación*, making the latter resound in the memory of other past Argentinian horrors.

Figure 13 | Wall paintings at Plaza 29 de Abril (Photo by author 2005)

A couple of other paintings were more optimistic. One of these made a biblical analogy to *la Inundación* by depicting the Noah's Ark and the Great Flood. In the lower corner there was an inscription: "After the great flood, the new man is born."[160] Next to this mural was another inscription with an encouraging message in big capital letters: "Despite all odds, our losses our struggle continues! Santa Rosa de Lima on its feet."[161] All the murals were signed by the different public and private schools in the surrounding neighbourhood that had participated in the making of the paintings.

At the northern end of the wall, the name of the square was spelled out in big red capital letters commemorating the day of *la Inundación*: "Plaza 29 de Abril." Right under this inscription, the date of the paintings had been added, which had been the first anniversary of the 2003 disaster. Almost a year later, on April 20th, 2005, the commemorative character of the place was underlined by the inauguration of a monument in the middle of the square, the Monument to the Tribute of the Flooded People.[162] The Plaza 29 de Abril square was an open space only confined by the wall at the back. The front was circumscribed by the streets and by half metre high poles stuck into the ground every metre or so, indicating perhaps that a low fence had once been there (or would be set up). The only objects in the square were a couple of green wooden benches to sit on. The ground was a run-down lawn except for at the centre of the square where there was instead a yellow concrete pavement surrounded by a larger circle of red grit. It was in the centre of these circles that the monument had been placed. A two-meter-high white-painted pedestal carried a ceramic statue depicting a family standing on a square metre of tile roof, representing the *inundados/victims* in 2003 that had to take refuge on the roofs of their homes. The father was embracing his wife and their young son and a dog was lying at their

---

[160] In Spanish: *Después del diluvio nace el hombre nuevo*
[161] In Spanish: *A pesar de lo que hemos perdido ¡seguimos luchando! Santa Rosa de Lima está de pié*
[162] In Spanish: *Monumento Homenaje al Pueblo Inundado*

feet. I was told that the statue symbolised both the desolation that the flood victims felt through their grievances, but at the same time it represented the dignity and the nobleness of people who weathered the storm. This was expressed by the fact that the family was standing up (and not lying down, for example). Furthermore the family was standing close to each other, symbolising a united family which was central to successful recovery, according to my interlocutors. The family was in their mind the cornerstone of society and needed to stay united in times of despair. The monument had consequently been blessed by a Catholic priest on the day of its inauguration.

Figure 14 | *Monumento Homenaje al Pueblo Inundado* at Plaza 29 de Abril (Photo by author 2005)

The people behind the making of this square, who were also my interlocutors in this context, were a group of women, who called themselves the Movimiento de Madres Inundadas, that is, the Flooded Mothers Movement. At the end of June of 2005, I was invited to Mary's house in the Santa Rosa de Lima neighbourhood. She had promised me fifteen minutes to briefly explain to me what they, the Flooded Mothers, were doing and what motivated them. I ended up spending half a day at her home as she talked and finally invited me to join her family for lunch. She told me that this was a group of middle-aged women in the *barrio*, most of whom had known each other previously. Once they had returned home after weeks of evacuation in July 2003, they had begun to gather every week as a means to overcome the terrible memories from the disaster and to begin to look forward again despite the losses. Mary explained:

> On that April 29th, the future of our children was flooded and we felt the need to defend it. Therefore we decided to call ourselves "Mothers," in tribute to other Argentinian mothers who became symbols of heroic resistance and, above all, of peaceful struggle.

Mary emphasised that their struggle was nonviolent. They had decided to call themselves Flooded Mothers in allusion to the emblematic movement of human rights in Argentina, the Mothers of the Plaza de Mayo (cf. DuBois 2008:42).[163] Mary was careful to mention that on the day of the inauguration of the monument, a woman from the Santafesinian branch of this NGO had been present to represent that movement. As we shall see in the next chapter, in contrast to the groups that constitute the *inundados* movement, the Flooded Mothers did not want to associate with the political side of the Mothers of the Plaza de Mayo, but rather with their nonviolent way of demanding information about their disappeared children by walking around the square every week during the Dirty War. Mary told me that the making of the Plaza 29 de Abril square was an effort to make memory. Yet, instead of making it a monument over the past tragedy and the desolation, they wanted to commemorate the dignity of the people who had faced adversity. The Flooded Mothers aimed at recalling hope, endurance and the wish to rebuild. In some paradoxical way they commemorated the future. This was why several children and young people from the *barrio*, who in their consideration embodied the future, received diplomas during the inaugural ceremony of the square in 2005 for their outstanding efforts in sports despite the disaster.

I later learned that the wall paintings had been washed away. In 2006, a new mural had been painted by the same sculptor who had made the monument. The new mural was 16 metres long and depicted, among other things, skulls, garbage, cockroaches, prayer beads and flies. It alluded, not only to *la Inundación* but also to a new, albeit less severe, flood occurred on the Westside and Southwest Side in 2007. It bore an inscription, written in a spirit of criticism against the repeated governmental failure in flood management: "What about the water pumps? And the Contingency Plan? Another 29th and here we go again!" In May and June of 2007, during the political campaign for municipal and provincial elections to be held in September, the new mural was painted over with whitewash and painted with political slogans, a common Argentinian practice of political propaganda. The artist and residents of Santa Rosa de Lima accused the sitting Mayor Balbarrey, who was running for re-election, of having a hand in the destruction of the mural in a quest for oblivion of his municipal government's failures. Paradoxically the effect of the whitewashing was rather memory than oblivion, because the event gained a lot of attention in local mass media (*Página/12* 2007; *Notife* 2007; *El Litoral* 2007a). Mayor Balbarrey in the end lost the elections that year. By the time of the 8th anniversary of *la Inundación* in 2011, the artworks in the square were restored once again, by the sculptor himself and other artists, and with the assistance of students from the Art School, who also painted new murals on the wall. One of the women from the Flooded Mothers held a public speech at this occasion, and was quoted in a local newspaper:

---

[163] According to a recent study, groups of mothers of disappeared people have formed in more than a dozen countries other than Argentina since 1977. Many of these groups recognise the Mothers of the Plaza de Mayo as a key source of inspiration (Sikkink 2008:4).

> We want an emblematic place where to recall what happened ... in the neighbourhood Santa Rosa de Lima. Today [eight years after *la Inundación*] we have an encouraging spirit, in order to thrive (*Notife* 2011a).

Eventually, in 2012, the square was officially named Plaza de la Memoria 29 de Abril (Memory Square 29th of April) by a petition of the neighbours in Santa Rosa de Lima (Concejo Municipal de Santa Fe 2012a). This place had become a particular memorial of *la Inundación*. The Flooded Mothers aimed at recalling the experience as one of social resilience unfolding into the future, rather than one of vulnerability to the past.

The making of an accidental community of memory

In this chapter I have described the many ways in which *la Inundación* was remembered in Santa Fe by the *inundados/victims* in the years following this disaster. *La Inundación* was extensively remembered through the interaction of evocative, reminiscent and commemorative ways. This intense memory-work shaped an "accidental community of memory" (Malkki 1997). It should be made clear that by the term "accidental" in this concept is not meant the event in itself, but the constitution of the community by accident. In the words of Malkki: "There is indeterminacy here not because these or other historical occurrences are haphazard, but because they bring together people who might not otherwise, or in the ordinary course of their lives, have met." (ibid.: 92). This was the case with the *inundados/victims* in Santa Fe who were brought together in the process of remembering their experiences of *la Inundación*. Malkki holds that the importance of these communities lays not only in the psychological and emotional scars, but also the afterlives the communities shape. The shared memory has the power to shape identities, ideas, desires and beliefs, "all powerfully formed and transformed in transitory circumstances shared by persons who might be strangers." (ibid.: 92). In Santa Fe, for most people in the middle classes, this was the first time ever they had been flooded. In contrast, for the people in the poor neighbourhoods on the Westside, this was far from the first flood they had coped with. The memory-work that these *inundados/victims* engaged in brought people together who had previously not shared life experiences because they lived in different social and physical worlds separated by relations of class and spatial boundaries. As illustrated ethnographically throughout this chapter, this community of *inundados/victims* was created through a "modality of sociation" (Amit 2002, 2012). That is, the memories that bound together the community were made through imagination by way of memorials, books and documentaries, but also construed in daily life practices and conversations in face to face relations. *La Inundación* was an event that changed the lives of 130,000 people in multiple ways. Next, I will look into how *la Inundación* became a politicised disaster and how memory played a critical role in this process.

Chapter 4 | Post-disaster protests and the making of a polity of remembering

Disaster politics and politics of memory

The previous chapter discussed how *la Inundación* was remembered at large in Santa Fe by people who were affected by the disaster, those which I call the *inundados/victims*. I shall now turn to a social protest that was undertaken by people whom I call the *inundados/activists*. Many groups in the protest movement was formally part of what was called the Asamblea Permanente de Afectados por la Inundación (Permanent Assembly of People Affected by the Flood). In this account I call them the *inundados* protest movement. It consisted of a heterogeneous cluster of different people and NGOs. The number of activists varied between groups and over time, and according to what type of protest was undertaken. Some protests gathered a handful of people while other manifestations, such as the anniversary actions on every April 29th, gathered thousands of demonstrators. Most of the *inundados/activists* were indeed *inundados/victims* themselves. Others had not been directly affected by the disaster. Most activists had scarce or no experience at all with street protests or political activism prior to *la Inundación*, although those who participated as representatives of NGOs often had such knowledge. This chapter analyses how this protest movement formed in the post-disaster and how commemorative practices were particularly used as a means of protest. I argue that this created a "polity of remembering" in Santa Fe.

Narrating inundation and indignation

In 2013, ten years had passed since *la Inundación*. In the months preceding the 10th anniversary on April 29th, the *inundados/activists* organised meetings and were active on Facebook posting comments and photos about this event. They also underscored that, from their point of view of claiming justice and compensation for the losses in the disaster, not much had happened in a decade. For them, "*la lucha continuaba*," that is, the struggle continued. In order to grasp this struggle we need to return to the beginning and to the constitution of the *inundados* protest movement.

When my interlocutors among the *inundados/activists* told me about how their claims came about, they all first narrated their experience of *la Inundación*. Not all activists had been flooded themselves but most of them had been in the city during the disaster and vividly recalled those days. An overwhelming majority of these stories were of the kind of canonised narrative about *la Inundación* that I analysed in the previous chapter. They then proceeded to tell me about their acts of protest and how they had encountered community and understanding with equally traumatised, frustrated and angered people at the evacuation centres and in the lines waiting for assistance. Silvia, one of the activists, was from the *barrio* Alfonso, one of the affected middle-income neighbourhoods. When I asked her, she recalled that in that moment "everybody felt the need to do something. If we didn't act, nobody was going to worry about us, least of all the government!" At the meetings and in the street protests, they had been able to voice their indignation. Similar to the previous chapter's canonised narrative by the *inundados/victims*, the following is the collective narrative about how the *inundados* protest movement was formed. This is based on narratives from my interlocutors among the *inundados/activists*, on their written documents and on my own observations from participating in the making of this polity of remembering.

Grievances | During the evacuation, irritation began to grow among evacuees. In certain evacuation centres, the evacuees and the volunteer help workers began to feel frustrated with the problems of distributing aid. An assembly was organised by the evacuees in the Simon de Iriondo School where problems were discussed. Simultaneously, some self-evacuated neighbours in the Barrio Roma neighbourhood took the initiative to call for a meeting at the centre of the *vecinal*. The call was spread by word of mouth between neighbours as they were cleaning their flooded houses with bleach or queuing for the government's food boxes. People also heard about the meeting when they ran into neighbours at the grocery or other shops that either had been spared by the flooding or had managed to reopen and take up their activities again, in an attempt to overcome the situation. There was a shared feeling of disorder, ineffectiveness and negligence on the part of the State against the *inundados* in the disaster and afterwards. The discussions at the meeting served to offer relief and catharsis for the participants. Yet the meeting was also a forum for reflections on how to demand better assistance from the authorities during the process of reconstruction.

Meanwhile, the authorities continued to deny responsibility for what had happened. Mayor Alvarez and Governor Reutemann insisted publicly that this had been an absolutely unpredictable disaster brought on by the uncontrollable forces of nature, specifically, excessive rainfall. Several inquiries and reports nevertheless suggested the contrary, namely that both the provincial and the municipal authorities had failed in accomplishing their responsibility in prevention and mitigation. In light of this, the public declarations about the unpredictability of nature were interpreted as blatant efforts to justify negligence in order to escape responsibility. The surmounting evidence, contrary to the governmental claims of an unexpected disaster, raised claims of political accountability. Although none of the politicians or involved decision makers resigned from their posts, their public declarations ceased. In December 2003, eight months after the disaster, they were both succeeded. Mayor Alvarez then left politics while Governor Reutemann was elected to represent the Province of Santa Fe in the National Senate. Neither in the provincial legislative body, nor in the Municipal Council, was there any quorum to set up an inquiry commission to investigate the accusations of mismanagement and corruption surrounding the disaster. The governor had, before he left his post, promoted a project of economic support for the victims of the disaster. One condition for victims to be entitled to this support was that the beneficiary had to waive any legal claims against the State. In the public eye, these direct and indirect messages from the authorities was changing the framing of the 2003 flood from one being an unforeseeable tragedy caused by the whims of nature to one of a fully predictable, maybe even preventable, disaster caused by political and administrative incompetence and negligence.

Indignation, interaction and a tent | The indignation over the governmental negligence and mismanagement thus grew among the *inundados/victims* and other Santafesinos. New assemblies were organised in other neighbourhoods and the numbers of activists increased. At some point an inter-neighbourhood meeting was arranged. At one of the meetings, the idea of staging a protest emerged. It was organised through motions, discussions and votes. There were proposals of carrying out road pickets and street protests against local politicians. Other proposals suggested making peaceful road blocks and banging pots. Some activists wanted to form work commissions, while others suggested that one ought to present lists of demands to the governor. Some of the *inundados/activists* suggested that everybody should refuse to receive the government's economic aid.

A Neighbourhood Coordination Committee was established and the idea of setting up a tent in protest was born. Three months after the disaster, on July 29th, 2003, the *Carpa Negra de la Memoria y la Dignidad* (Black Tent of Memory and Dignity) was set up on the city's principal square, the Plaza de Mayo. They had chosen the black colour for the tent to represent the mourning and the grievances. The black tent was inaugurated with the following words:

"April 29th transformed our lives in every sense. One's life was lost, [our] everyday life, [our] life that, now when we can't enjoy it anymore, we have discovered that it is this [the everyday life] that gives us meaning, that which everyone of us gradually puts together, in our homes, in our neighbourhood, with our plants, with our animals, with our corners, with our backyards, with the sidewalk, with the neighbours. Everyday life became something strange. We realised that, from now on, to live would be a difficult task. In this way, we met in the [street] corners, we improvised meetings, we talked all together because everything was mixed up: the necessity, the pain, the anger, the powerlessness. We felt that the floodwater only had been the beginning of the flooding. We brutally understood that we were alone . . . The census, the queues [to search for food, clothes, cleaning utensils], the share-outs . . . Everything turned to torture. The cries were many but few were listening. Every 29th, a street meeting took place. We were more and more worried and rebelled in view of the certainty that we were sinking into oblivion . . . So it was with the support of the people in the square, the tent of the *inundados* was set up. Without water, without mud, but with the same grief and helplessness: for dignity, for justice, for recovery, for our sick and dead people. No to impunity! The tent of pain, but also of dignity! We do not want to be *inundados* the whole life . . . Here we are, learning to fight for us and for all. This is not about another box [of food aid]. This is about our catastrophe, as a way of manifesting that we live in an unsafe city, with rulers who do not show consideration for a large part of the population, and with citizens that claim to be treated as such." The group Carpa Negra (Black Tent) was formed in this setting.

The Memory Museum | At the same time as the black tent was set up, an exhibition called the *Museo de la Memoria* (memory museum) was inaugurated in the same square. The *inundados* brought their destroyed belongings from their flooded homes to exhibit at this museum. These were things that were unusable after they had lain in the dirty water and had been dumped on the street, such as coffee machines, books, dolls, microwaves, [music] discs, chairs, pictures, typewriters and other objects. It was all muddy, wrecked and damaged. The things were placed on the ground and along the paths of the square, like an exhibition and a message to the provincial government, located in the same square: "Look what you've done to us!" In the months to come, the *inundados/activists* took turns guarding the tent and the memory museum. At first there were not even enough available shifts for so many volunteers. Mirta, Silvia and all the other activists hurried to and fro between the square, their homes and their jobs, keeping guard day and night. The anger and the determination to make the city remember the disaster and its victims had kept them going. Nevertheless, the number of activists decreased rapidly. The remaining activists kept up the tent for almost six months despite several inconveniences. They had been threatened with an eviction order and with the arrest of their members for energy fraud, since the light bulb hanging at the tent's entrance was fed by the power of the square's streetlamps. With increasing fatigue, caused by internal discussions as well as bad weather, the will to fight slowly faded away. There were many internal differences and tensions between the activists regarding which strategies to follow, some of which turned into open conflicts.

The Torches' March | The conflicts contributed to the formation of different groups. One was the Black Tent. Another was the Marcha de las Antorchas (Torches' March), often colloquially called the Marcha (March). While taking guards at the tent and the memory museum during those cold winter days, some of the activists got the idea of walking around the square with burning torches. They decided to hold marches every Tuesday because Tuesday had been the day of the week on which the Salado River flooded the city. In the first months, they walked around the square, chanting and demanding justice at the stairs of the Provincial Court Hall and in front of the House of Government. With time, other elements were added to the place and to the ritual. The March activists set up small wooden crosses on the lawn next the obelisk, one cross for every casualty in the disaster. They made banners and posters to deploy as they walked around the square and stopped in different places. They read out loud the names of the casualties according to a list. When rounding the square, the participants sang the well-known protest song "No nos moverán."[164] In front of the Court Hall and the House of Government, the members of the March would raise their Argentinian flags and sing the national anthem. Sometimes they turned their backs to the buildings, symbolically questioning the legitimacy of these institutions of power.

The Asamblea | The Asamblea Permanente de Afectados por la Inundación, colloquially called the *Asamblea*, was constituted in 2004 to organise the activities of claim and protest. The Asamblea gathered the NGOs, groups and networks[165] that made up the core of the *inundados* protest movement. Over time, the number of *inundados/activists* participating in public protests and activities varied from a dozen key individuals to a thousand or more people on some occasions, depending on the kind of activity undertaken. Over the years, several *inundados/activists* stopped participating. Many of the remaining activists saw this as a betrayal and accused them of having received governmental subsidies and social welfare benefits. To the activists this was a mayor offense, given that the State had been identified as their adversary in the struggle for

---

[164] This song, in English known as "We Shall Not Be Moved" is an old protest tune sung during the Spanish Civil War and during the widespread social and political conflicts in Latin America in the 1960s and 1970s. It was made famous outside the Spanish speaking world in the 1980s by the North American protest singer Joan Baez.

[165] The Asamblea gathered many of the organisations and groups that had participated in a Solidarity Committee formed in the acute phase of the 2003 disaster. Among the organisations that made up the Assembly in 2005 were: Carpa Negra de la Memoria y la Dignidad, Marcha de las Antorchas, Empresas Afectadas, Movimiento de Madres Inundadas, Inundados Autoconvocados, Casa de los Derechos Humanos, Familiares de Víctimas de la Inundación, Asociación 29 de Abril Barrio Roma, Madres de Plaza de Mayo, Acción Educativa, CANOA, Comité de Movilización del Foro Social Mundial en Santa Fe, Primera Escuela de Psicología Social Dr. Pichón Riviere and INuMás.

recognition and compensation from the disaster. Despite of splits and divisions, the *inundados* movement lived on with the Black Tent, the March, and the House of Human Rights of Santa Fe[166] being among its principal actors.

Victims as activists

The *inundados* protest movement emerged from the accidental community of memory and transformed partly into what I have termed a "polity of remembering." By "polity" I refer here to a specific form of association in which its members pursue a goal through collective organised action. How this transformation took place can be analysed from various angles. On the one hand, it can be interpreted from a national perspective seeing it as part of a genealogy of social protests in Argentina at the turn of the 21st century. This was a period of generalised annoyance and distrust towards the rulers and politicians in this country (cf. Frederic 2005:315-341). For many Santafesinos, the governmental mismanagement of the flooding in 2003 was the last straw. On the other hand, the formation of this protest movement can be regarded as part of a global trend towards demand for accountability in general terms (Boström and Garsten 2008) and in particular after disasters and political crises (Boin et al. 2005; Boin, McConnell, and Hart 2008).[167] This may be connected to the phenomenon of victimisation in post conflict and post-disaster contexts. In many cases the only way for affected people to secure societal support and repair is to appeal for moral, social and political recognition as a social category of sufferers (cf. Kleinman, Das, and Lock 1997; Das 2001; Fortun 2001; Petryna 2002; Chatterjee 2006:57; Dahl 2009; Camargo da Silva 2009; Zenobi 2011).

The *inundados* protest movement in the national context

Argentina of the last decades offers countless examples of social protests expressed through street demonstrations. The protest marches of the Mothers of the Plaza de Mayo in Buenos Aires in the 1970s and 1980s are the most emblematic and well-known demonstrations worldwide. As described in Chapter Two, after the return of democracy in 1983, there have also been the pickets of the *piqueteros* (Auyero 2003; Catela da Silva 2004; Quirós 2011); the pickets and street protests in the conflict between the farmers and the government in 2008 (Giarracca and Teubal 2010) and during the crisis of 2001-2002 there were riots, loot-

---

[166] The Casa de Derechos Humanos de Santa Fe consisted of several humans rights organisations namely the Madres de Plaza de Mayo de Santa Fe, Familiares de Desaparecidos y Detenidos Por Razones Políticas and the Movimiento Ecuménico por los Derechos Humanos.
[167] For example, the Popular Party's defeat in the Spanish elections of 2004 reflected dissatisfaction with the government's actions during the terrorist attacks in Madrid on March 11th, 2004. The removal from office by impeachment of the Head of the Government of Buenos Aires, Anibal Ibarra, can be interpreted as a consequence of the allegations against him due to the Cromañón disaster in 2004 (cf. Zenobi 2011).

ing and pot-banging protests (cf. Auyero 2003). The pot-banging protests were repeated again in different parts of the country and abroad in 2012, targeted at the government of Cristina Fernández. There have regularly been demonstrations by the teachers' union for a rise in salary and by the veterans of the Falklands War for recognition and economic support. Numerous cases of insecurity, that is, extortive kidnappings and murders, have throughout the years also caused massive street protests and even violent assaults on police stations.[168] There have also been post-disaster claims for accountability, similar to that of Santa Fe City. Examples of such protests are those in the wake of the bombings of the Jewish *mutual* AMIA in 1994; during the Buenos Aires blackout in the summer of 1999; after the Buenos Aires discotheque fire in 2004 and after the Buenos Aires rail disaster in 2012. The human rights organisation H.I.J.O.S was the first to carry out so-called *escraches* as a form of protest (Kaiser 2002). This type of protest refers to a public demonstration that a group of activists carry out through sit-down protests, songs or graffiti, usually in front of the home or work place of somebody held accountable. The purpose is to unveil the accused and make public his/her alleged wrongdoings. From the 1980s onwards, the human rights movement has been active in occupying certain areas of the urban space, including in Santa Fe City, in order to make their demands public (Alonso, Boumerá, and Citroni 2007). It has been argued that the emergence of massive social protest stand for a new style of political protest (Catela da Silva 2004). Yet, numerous historical examples indicate that this is not an entirely new phenomenon in Argentina.[169] In the words of Robben (2007): "[P]olitical rallies, street demonstrations, and protest marches [are] so typical of Argentine political culture, and so mesmerizing to the Argentine people and their leaders" (p.xi).

From disaster solidarity to accountability

In the sociology and anthropology of disaster, the concept of "emergent citizen groups" has been used to describe how people organise in order to help disaster victims (Quarantelli and Dynes 1977; Neal 1984; Stallings and Quarantelli 1985; Button 1993). The concept is defined as the congregation of citizens who are formally or informally organised and work together locally to achieve objectives related to disaster management (Neal ibid.: 252). These groups often emerge early in the disaster's response phase, immediately following the disaster, but can also be formed in the early post-disaster phase of recovery. Only in rare cases do they continue from the acute phase of rescue to the post-disaster recovery and

---

[168] Certain cases of extortive kidnappings, increasingly common in the 2000s, ended in murder, such as that of the engineering student Axel Blumberg, who was kidnapped and killed in March 2004. This case caused massive demonstrations, protesting against impunity and supporting Axel's father, Juan Carlos Blumberg, in his search for justice.
[169] Among the historical examples are the riots during the so-called the Tragic Week in 1919; the massive popular support in Buenos Aires in 1945 to liberate the then jailed Juan Domingo Perón who was at that moment the Secretary of Work in the sitting government; the *Rosariazo* and the *Cordobazo* in 1969, which were civil uprisings to the military dictatorship; and the massive support to receive General Perón from his exile in Spain, which ended in the so-called Ezeiza Massacre in 1973.

reconstruction phase (Stallings and Quarantelli ibid.: 95). As described in the previous chapter, the canonised narratives about *la Inundación* included such notions about an altruistic community in which the people helped the people.

For analysing the case of the *inundados/activists*, the concept of emergent citizen groups only helps us part of the way. While the notion of "emergent" is significant to describe how people organised in new groups in response to the disastrous flood, it does not capture the diversity and dynamic of the *inundados* protest movement over time. During my fieldwork in Santa Fe, the protest movement included *inundados/victims* that had helped other *inundados/victims* out during the emergency and then engaged in the protest movement. Then there were people who had **not** been flooded, but who had been active in the emergency and who were now in the protest movement. Finally were there many *inundados/victims* that neither helped others, nor took to the streets protesting.

In the disaster sociology literature, emergent citizen groups have been analysed as extraordinary expressions of social cohesion because of the emergent and non-institutional nature of this phenomenon (Stallings and Quarantelli ibid.: 94-97). What it rarely addresses is the political aspects of the recovery and reconstruction processes, in which emergent groups often constitute stakeholders. Political science and public administration studying crises and disasters address this as processes of accountability. Here, particular attention has been paid to the phenomenon of "scapegoating" or "blame games" (Brändström and Kuipers 2003; Boin et al. 2005; Boin, McConnell, and Hart 2008). The opportunity to investigate and assign responsibility to political representatives and public employees is a feature of democracy as well as a social process that allows certain facts to acquire specific meanings. This process of meaning-making[170] takes place in different spheres of the affected society, from the heart of people's homes and familial places in the neighbourhood such as the bakery or the grocery shop, to more public venues such as intermediate organisations, the media, bureaucratic agencies, political realms and inquiry commissions. Increasingly, processes of accountability involve multiple social actors, ranging from the state to the private sector and civil society (Boström and Garsten 2008). Today such processes tend to go beyond national borders, turning the issues to transnational disputes (Fortun 2001; Ullberg 2001, 2005; Boström and Garsten 2008) or "framing contests" (Boin, McConnell, and Hart 2008). The latter concept refers to the processes of intense meaning-making in crisis situations (Oliver-Smith 1986; Button 2010; Revet 2013). In terms of collective action and social mobilisation, the role of citizens for post-disaster processes such as those in Santa Fe has been observed in many different contexts (see for example Button 1993; Fortun 2001; Petryna 2002; Kofman Bos, Ullberg, and 't Hart 2005; Zenobi 2011), displaying

---

[170] In the crisis literature this phenomenon has been differentiated between "sense making" when it is about cognitive or ontological dimensions and "meaning-making" when the focus is on the [political] communication process (Boin et al. 2005:69-90). Others use the concept of "sensemaking" to refer to both the cognitive and the communicative dimensions of this phenomena (Kendra and Wachtendorf 2003:324-325), which comes closer to an anthropological conception of culture as meaning-making (cf. Hannerz 1992). In this study I use "meaning-making" in this latter sense.

characteristics of contemporary social movements (cf. Tilly and Wood 2013). In Santa Fe, the *inundados/activists* came from different social and economic backgrounds, identified with different ideologies and rejected any attempt from the established political parties to represent them. They rallied around a couple of claims, namely that political responsibility for the flooding should be tried in court and that the disaster victims should get full compensation for their losses. Yet there were many different and contradictory interests, ideologies and opinions about how the protests should be carried out within the *inundados* protest movement. Kim Fortun (2001) has used the concept "enunciatory community" to describe the protest movement in Bhopal, India, after the 1984 industrial disaster in this city. By this concept she refers to a "collectivity [that] is not a matter of shared values, interests, or even culture, but a response to a temporally specific paradox" (p.11). This concept seems to capture the heterogeneous and contradictory nature of many post-disaster movements that try to make sense out of the causes as much as of the responsibilities of the calamity. Yet it does not sufficiently grasp the temporality of the dynamics of collective action. While the *inundados* protest movement indeed mobilised to achieve future goals, such as getting decision makers to trial and to get economic compensation, more important for the movement's cohesion and endurance was a common past. This consists of the experiences of the 2003 disaster and the indignation growing out of this memory, that is, of their belonging to the accidental community of memory analysed in Chapter Three. It was the memories that the activists shared of the disaster, which constituted their principal tools of protest, and which were enacted in anniversaries, monuments and rituals. This shared past was a driving force of protest. Resorting to victimisation, as the *inundados* movement did, was used to question the moral authority of the State (Gilligan 2003). This brings us to take a closer look at the connection between politics and morality.

Morality, memory and mobilisation

According to Olick, the forces shaping post conflict demands can be understood as the outcome of relations of power, trauma and "*ressentiment*"[171] (2007). The memory of the past wrong is what keeps up indignation over the injustice. Memory becomes the tool for claiming future justice in collective action. Just as the phenomenon of social remembering enables us to remember things we have not experienced, one can be morally indignant and make claims on behalf of others without actually having suffered the particular trauma or injustice oneself. As a morality, *ressentiment* is produced and shared through the articulation of emotion, identity and memory. It is in particular the emotional component of *ressentiment* that provides it with a political potential that can forge collective action.

---

[171] The term is translated to resentment in English but is normally used in French. Originally the concept referred to the particular morality of revenge that produced from the frustrated experience of an injustice. It has been critically dealt with by scholars like Kierkegaard, Nietzsche, Weber and Ranulf just to mention a few. For a detailed overview, see Olick (2007).

In the context of memory, which concerns us here, processes of post-disaster protests are of particular interest, given that demands for redress and justice increasingly draw on what Olick calls "mnemonic resistance," referring to the on-going struggles of claim and counterclaim, memory and counter memory (ibid.:139). Central to the notion of *ressentiment* is that such emotions and moralities are produced in particular configurations of time. Along a temporal axis, guilt is placed in the past whilst the distribution of responsibility is future oriented. This conceptual framework can help us understand why the activists in the *inundados* movement mobilised in protest of the governmental mismanagement of *la Inundación* and how their polity of remembering was formed. For many of the *inundados/victims* in 2003, being flooded was a cause of moral indignation. This was particularly the case for those Santafesinos who had never been affected by flooding before, most notably people from the urban working and middle classes. In effect, they were among the most active in the movement. Memory was crucial in and for their mobilisation. On the one hand, the shared memories of a traumatic experience and *ressentiment* were the emotional force of the polity. On the other hand, they were forced to remind society about their positions as victims in order to achieve moral recognition and thereby political legitimacy by the larger urban community. In what follows I shall give account of some of the ways through which the polity of remembering have formed.

Work of memory, work of protest

During my fieldwork, especially in the years 2004-2006, the *inundados/activists* were very active in their protests. Many of the practices and symbols of protest used had links to pre-existing Argentinian cultural and political repertoires of symbols and images. For example, the tent has been a recurrent symbol in Argentinian political life at least since the 1990s,[172] representing both a peaceful demonstration and a protest that may well endure. And of course, more pragmatically, such tents also serve as lodging when protests are staged outdoors. By mobilising the tent symbol in Santa Fe, the *inundados/activists* situated their claims in a political context, which went beyond the process of mourning. In what follows, I will describe in further ethnographic detail how the memory-work of the *inundados/activists* drew upon genealogies of protest while also developing their own.

---

[172] The tent has long been used as a central symbol in social protest. In 1968 the so-called Resurrection City saw hundreds of tents set up by anti-poverty campaigners in Washington D.C. as a reaction to the murder of Martin Luther King. Anti-nuclear peace camps were set up across Europe and North America in the 1970s and 1980s. Among the protests in Argentina on which the tent has been a key symbol are those of the Teachers' Union with their White Tent and the Malvinas War Veterans with their Green tent.

Anniversaries: The 29th

Almost nine years after *la Inundación*, on April 24th, 2012, an interview with Laura, one of the members in the group the Black Tent, was broadcast in a morning news show called *Santa Fe Directo* on the local TV-station Canal 13. She was asked to tell about the petition that her own organisation and a number of others in the *inundados* movement had submitted to the sitting Governor Bonfatti, namely a proposal to incorporate April 29th among the commemorative days of the provincial official calendar. The title of the interview was "For the memory."[173] Laura was interviewed in front of a house, possibly her own. The camera at first zoomed in on the roof of the house. A line had been painted on the water tank as a watermark. Under this was written with big letters: "[The water reached up] to here. April 29th 2003. Lole did it."[174] The inscription referred to the fact that the house had been completely flooded by the time the floodwater had reached its height. It also referred to the claim of the *inundados/victims* that former Governor "Lole" Reutemann was responsible for the poor public preparedness and management in relation to the catastrophe. Laura told the reporter that she and other activists considered that this day ought to be formally declared a commemorative date, as part of the struggle against the city's forgetfulness about *la Inundación*. The purpose would be to enact an official memory-work around this past event, especially in the schools. She said:

> Nine years has passed since *la Inundación*. The small children have only been told about [the disaster that they did not experience themselves]. We want them to hear the story and we consider the school to be the best place for this. The same way that March 24th was made the Memory Day [of the Dirty War] we think that April 29th can be the Day of Solidarity - a day to understand what really happened to us on that day in 2003.

The proposal by Laura and her fellow activists is illustrative of how central the date was to the polity of remembering. Commemorative dates are temporal markers of and for memory. In Argentina, the calendar structuring the idea of the Nation includes key dates such as May 25th, symbolising resurrection against the colonial power of Spain and July 9th, representing independence. Current national holidays include also more recent political events such as March 24th, in commemoration of the coup d'état in 1976 and the Dirty War. Commemorative dates created the temporal regularity required for remembering and for reproducing the claims of the *inundados/activists*. As we shall see next, space was equally important to place them on the local political agenda.

---

[173] In Spanish: *Por la memoria*
[174] In Spanish: *Hasta acá. 29 de Abril 2003. Lole lo hizo*

Making memorable places

The afternoon sun was still high on that autumn afternoon on April 29th, 2005, when a group of people gathered on the Westside, on Gorostiaga Street next to the hippodrome, the golf course and the poverty-stricken *barrio* San Pantaleón. This was where the Westside ring road ended. This was close to the site on the flood embankment where Juan had taken me and Maria the year before to see the place where the Salado River had entered the city. Among the 40-something people were a handful of journalists and I. The other participants were *inundados/activists*. Women and men, young and old, had arrived by car, local bus transport and even by a hired bus. One family with four small children had arrived in their horse cart that they normally used for *cirujeo* scavenging. Everybody who arrived was handed a placard by the activists of the March, which was the group that had organised the ceremony. I was offered a placard in black and white that said: "Reutemann, Chabán, Cromañón, Flooding. One single explanation. Murderous irresponsibility."[175] These words associated *la Inundación* and the issue of political responsibility with those of the discotheque fire disaster in Buenos Aires in 2004.[176] As the participants slowly walked up on the top of the embankment, Silvia and another woman from the March stopped and gave a short speech through a loudspeaker tied to the roof of one of the cars. They explained why they had chosen to carry out their commemoration of the second anniversary in this place:

> This embankment was never built. Yet it was inaugurated by Governor Reutemann in 1992. Nine years later we were flooded. [He said] nobody had informed him! That's why we call him a liar, a perverse and guilty! They [the provincial government] knew that if the defence was not finished, this is where the Salado River would enter [the city]. And so it was, because the embankment was transformed into a retaining trap and turned the town into a washbowl.

A row of placards had been placed along the path leading up to the top of the embankment. Each of them stated the year, the content of and the politician responsible for a political decision in regard to flood management policies in Santa Fe. Together they constituted a walk in the memoryscape of political omissions that eventually led to the 2003 flooding.[177] The walk was reminiscent of the Sta-

---

[175] In Spanish: *Reutemann, Chabán, Cromañón, Inundación. Una sóla explicación. Irresponsabilidad asesina*

[176] This disaster occurred in the discotheque Cromañón in Buenos Aires on December 30th, 2004, when a fire broke out during a concert with the Argentinian rock band Los Callejeros. The blaze started when a pyrotechnic flare was set off and ignited foam in the ceiling, killing 194 young people and injuring hundreds more. Among the people charged and later judged for the responsibility of the disaster was the owner of the night club, Omar Chabán. For an anthropological analysis of this case and the politics around the post-disaster, see Zenobi (2011).

[177] The first placard stated, for example, that Governor Reutemann back in 1992 had in fact taken part of a study that foresaw the geographical impact of a flood of the magnitude of that of 2003. At the bottom end it said "Didn't he know [this]?" referring ironically to the public statement by Reutemann in a press conference during *la Inundación,* when he claimed he had not been informed abouth the risk for flooding.The study referred to was made by the National Water Institute in 1992, in which vulnera-

tions of the Cross processions[178] that are commonly found in numerous towns and villages all over Argentina, made by the Catholic Church and its congregations. On that embankment on the Westside district of Santa Fe, there were seven stations and the procession of the March did not stop at each station on its way up to the top of it. The arrangement nevertheless reminded me of this religious practice, as each placard, placed in a row with some 5-10 metres in between and along that path, recalled key moments in the political construction of flood vulnerability. Indeed, they seemed like a hyperbole aimed at stressing the injustice of this disaster, the culpability of the State and the suffering of its victims. On the top of the embankment, instead of ending the row of stations with a cross, a stick with a torch had been stuck into the ground and lit. The torches, giving name to the group, were the key element of the March's ritual devices, symbolically illuminating their claim for "Justice, in all and for all!"[179] (cf. Guala 2005:147). On the top of the embankment, the activists of the March read out loud the more than 100 names of the fatal victims of the 2003 disaster, to which the crowd responded "¡Presente!" (Present!). This was a ritual that they repeated on all their demonstrations. For this particular occasion, they had also made small floating devices decorated with flowers. Some of the participants had candles in transparent plastic boats. As the names were read out loud, they went down to the river to put these light boats and throw flowers into the Salado River, recalling how the river had taken the lives of those being named. When the commemorative ceremony on the top of the embankment was finished, we all walked back down to the street. The entire ritual with the placards, the speeches and the recalling of the dead, had turned this place of the flood embankment into a memorial of *la Inundación*.

The efforts to locate disaster memory in this particular place continued throughout the years. Seven years later, a message was posted on the Facebook site of one of the members of the March to commemorate the nine years and five months that had passed since *la Inundación*. It was a post in reference to a recent proposal by the legislators in the Municipality of Santa Fe City and the Provincial Parliament to name the Westside ring road after the late former president of Argentina, Raúl Alfonsín. The ring road had been repaired after the 2003 disaster. A 14 kilometres long extension of the road, connecting it with Provincial Route 70 north of the city, was inaugurated in May 2012. The legislators considered that the ring road at that point deserved a memorable name. So did the people in the March. To them, the repaired flood embankment that surrounded the ring road on its Westside was a place of their memory of *la Inundación*. Hence, the post on Facebook said:

---

ble areas of the town to floods of different magnitude and probability from both the Paraná and the Salado Rivers were identified.

[178] The *Via Crucis* generally consists of a walk or a path in a natural landscape (in the mountain or in the forest for example) along 14 stations that represent the final hours of Jesus Christ, for the purpose of allowing the visitor to make a spiritual pilgrimage by remembering the Savior's sufferings and death.

[179] In Spanish: *Justicia en todo y para todos*

THE WESTSIDE RING ROAD: "April 29th"
[In view of] the [recent] decisions by the City Council of the Santa Fe City and the Senate of the Province . . . in relation to the proposed name of the Westside ring road . . . we want to bring our proposal to the legislative fore, convinced that there is no need to elaborate on arguments . . . the only name that fits this work is "April 29th." We all know this.

The day after this post, on September 29th, 2012, the March carried out its habitual manifestation as on every 29th on the Plaza de Mayo square. Here, they again voiced the claim of the place name of the ring road. A local newspaper cited a participant in the street manifestation in reference to the importance of the memory of *la Inundación*:

If public spaces harbour the noisy passing of everyday life, if the ring roads and transit systems are part of that space and contribute to the identity and character of the city, then such spaces should also preserve the memory of its inhabitants (Phillippis de 2012).

Making memory in memorable places

On April 29th, 2005, after the ceremony on the top of the embankment, the activists in the March headed towards the Plaza de Mayo square. Here the large anniversary act, organised by the Asamblea, was held that evening. It was about six o'clock when we drove in caravan towards the city centre. The sun was setting but it was still hot in the city, especially in the centre with its multi-storey buildings. It was Friday, normally the day when the pedestrian San Martín Street and other streets in the commercial Downtown were crowded. Teenagers hung around after school. Men and women toasted the weekend drinking a *liso* beer. Families walked about, shopping in the many stores. On this particular day, this light-hearted middle-class landscape was slightly changed through the presence of more unusual passers-by. Activists from different popular organisations[180] as well as from other less identifiable groups were walking down the street. Families with children, young couples and elderly people headed towards the square. From several blocks away, it was possible to hear the gathering crowd: the car

---

[180] Among the organisations represented that night was Los Sin Techo, a NGO that was active in Santa Fe City since 1985 dealing with problems such as housing, household drinking-water supply, urban development, vocational training, child and mother health, community development, care for children with nutritional and educational deficiencies and family violence. From 2000 onwards, it established maternal and child health centres, kindergartens and provided community centres with computers and wireless internet in the neighbourhoods where the organisation was active. Another organisation present that night in the square was the Corriente Clasista y Combativa, an Argentinian labour and political grouping led by the Revolutionary Communist Party, officially formed in 1994 in opposition to the government of Carlos Menem. Since 1996, it became a means for organising unemployed workers, turning into one of the most important groups of the *piquetero* movement. Finally, the Federación Tierra, Vivienda y Habitat was also there, a national NGO established in 1997 as a result of the demands and needs of the people in the poor neighbourhoods and settlements in the larger Argentinian cities, as well as in rural communities and villages, especially regarding matters of housing and habitat, subsistence and employment programmes.

horns, the murmur, the megaphone roars and the drums beating the typical *murga* beat. The square and the buildings around it were surrounded by the provincial riot police that evening. A metal fence stood out, separating the square from the government building. Nearly two years earlier, members of the March had placed numerous wooden crosses in the square to remember those who perished during the flooding of 2003.

Figure 15 | Wooden crosses in Plaza de Mayo (Photo by author 2005)

The night before that second anniversary in 2005, the members of the Black Tent had set up their black tent and other protesters had hung banners between trees and street lanterns next to the flat white memory stone erected the year before, in commemoration of the first anniversary of the Black Tent. The stone was reminiscent of a gravestone, yet its inscription with black paint was the commemoration of life and presence of the *inundados/activists*, saying: "29-07-03 Neither oblivion, nor pardon. Our faith and our struggle shall never be flooded. The Black Tent M[emory] and D[ignity] 29-07-04."

As dusk fell, thousands of people gathered in front of the governmental building, the Grey House, to commemorate the second anniversary of the 2003

Figure 16 | *Inundados/activists*' memory stone in Plaza de Mayo (Photo by author 2005)

flood and to shout their claims in protest of the flaws of the provincial government in this disaster: "Full compensation for all the victims! Trial and jail for the responsible people! Confiscation of all their goods! Justice for our dead!"

Figure 17 | Commemorating *la Inundación* in Plaza de Mayo on April 29th (Photo by author 2005)

As described in the canonised narrative in the beginning of the chapter, the Plaza de Mayo square had been central in the protests of the *inundados/activists* from the very beginning. Most commemorative actions organised by any group or all of them were carried out here, such as the anniversaries organised by the Permanent Assembly every year on April 29th or the demonstrations of the March. This particular square was already a key symbolic place in Santafesinian social and political life, as well as in other cities where there is a square with this name. The one of Buenos Aires is the most well known, but there is a Plaza de Mayo square in several other Argentinian cities. They are emblematic in many ways. They were the first squares in the colonial towns of the Viceroyalty of the Río de la Plata. In Santa Fe, the square had several names before it was named Plaza de Mayo in commemoration of the May Revolution and national independence.[181] Hence the square is a central place in the context of Argentinian nation-building not only by its name, but also because here is where political power is spatialised and materialised. Key institutional buildings are located around this square in all

---

[181] The square dates from the time of foundation of the town of Santa Fe. In 1887 it was named Plaza de Mayo, or more correctly, Plaza 25 de Mayo because it was on May 25th, 1810 when the Primera Junta, the first local government, of what had up until then been the Viceroyalty of Río de la Plata was established in Buenos Aires. For a historical overview of the Plaza de Mayo in Santa Fe see Mino (1998) and Calvo (2006).

the cities. In Santa Fe City, enclosing that Plaza de Mayo square is the so-called Grey House which is the government's building, the Supreme Court, the private School of the Immaculate Conception, the Metropolitan Cathedral and the Church of the Miracles.

As I have already mentioned, many of the historical social protests in Argentina, key presidential speeches and public manifestations of political support have taken place in the Plaza de Mayo of Buenos Aires. In Santa Fe City, the Plaza de Mayo square has also been the provincial stage of political performance. The local human rights movement, which emerged publicly in the latter days of the last dictatorship, carried out several manifestations there claiming for the end of the military regime, even if another square, the Plaza del Soldado, for particular reasons came to be the spatial centre of this movement in the city (Alonso, Boumerá, and Citroni 2007). Both these squares were confined to the urban space of the Santafesinian middle classes, namely the centre and the Southside. Such was also the case of the *inundados/activists'* appropriation of the urban space. While to the latter, the Plaza the Mayo was the hub and the principle place for meetings and protests, they also carried out marches and *escraches* in other places.[182] Similar to the Santafesinian human rights movement, to which some of the groups in the *inundados* protest movement in fact belonged, these *inundados/activists* spatialised memories of *la Inundación* throughout particular areas of Santa Fe City. These were mainly the middle-income districts, and where institutional power was located. The people and places flooded in 2003 were located on the impoverished Westside and to some extent in the southern outskirts of the city. By occupying the urban space that had not been affected, but where power was located, the *inundados/activists* aimed at bringing the past to the present also to these areas, where no traces from the disaster had been left.

Inscriptions of blame: Four examples

This spatialisation of memory was, as we have seen above, carried out by the *inundados/activists* by appropriating, occupying and circulating through particular places. Another way of recalling the issue of responsibilities, as we shall see next, was through inscriptions both in space, via the artefacts on which they appeared and by way of the social practice of making and presenting texts.

1· *Escraches* and street graffiti

During my fieldwork I attended a couple of *escrache* protests. One, carried out by the March in 2005, was outside the office of the governmental so-called Reconstruction Unit. This office was established sometime around the end of 2003 to attend to the claims of losses due to the disaster. From here, the staff at the

---

[182] During my fieldwork I participated in protests staged in front of different institutional buildings such as the Municipality in Salta Street, the Provincial Chamber of Deputies and the Chamber of Senators in General López Street, the Ministry of Water and Public Services in the Almirante Brown Avenue and the offices of the so-called Unit. I was told that protests had also been undertaken in other cities such as in Buenos Aires and in Rosario. In February 2009 a demonstration was held in front of the health clinic in the city of Rosario where the former governor Reutemann was hospitalised.

Unit also administered the programme of recovery, ranging from psychological attention to victims to art and swim classes for children in affected areas of the city (Perez, Lastra, and Forconi 2005). The Unit dealt with claims from all the departments in the province, which had been affected by the 2003 flood, though I was told that the bulk of what the staff called "beneficiaries" came from the city. The office was located on the Freyre Avenue in the Southwest Side. This avenue constituted the border between the impoverished Westside and the middle-income Downtown. During *la Inundación* the avenue had been the border between water and land, as the flood had reached only to this point. Numerous interlocutors told me that on those days of the disaster, the Freyre Avenue had been like the riverside. People were evacuated from their flooded homes to this point and from there taken elsewhere. Many people wandered along the avenue aimlessly waiting for kin to be evacuated or searching for their missing ones. Many people were said to have stood there just watching the flood, as if they could not believe what was happening. Thus, the Unit office's location on this street also had a symbolical meaning, situated as it was on the border between disaster and safety, between the traumatic and the ordinary.

On that afternoon when the March carried out their *escrache* in front of the office, memories from the days of *la Inundación* lingered among the participants. When I arrived, the group had gathered on the promenade in the centre of the avenue in front of the office. They held up banners and placards, of which one stated their slogan "Justice in all and for all!" The purpose of the entire *escrache* was to demonstrate what the activists considered to be blameworthy in this context, namely the business around and the corruption involved in the public management of *la Inundación*. The activists in the March saw the Unit as just a spectacle to legitimise the corrupt government and the salaries of the civil servants working there, wasting the funds that really belonged to the *inundados/victims*. They wanted to voice that their claim for accountability could not be bought with money, by which they meant the subsidies granted by the Unit to disaster victims.

The avenue was heavily trafficked as always around that hour. After a while, the activists crossed the street from the promenade to the sidewalk, where the Unit's office was located. Seven policemen were on guard to protect it from any disturbances. They stood in their dark blue uniforms in a row along the fenced windows of the office facing the street. During the entire *escrache*, I did not see them move a finger nor change their facial expression. The *inundados/activists*, facing the policemen and the office, displayed their banner and started shouting:

> We want justice and compensation! The Unit is a corrupt and sick body! Get rid of it! Forconi [the president of the Unit], get out of there!

It was rather difficult to hear the shouting, because of the heavy traffic. After a while the protesting crowd turned silent. They walked closer to the street with their signboards and started clapping their hands. One of the participants, Pablo, stepped out in the street and while the cars tooted as they tried to pass him, he started to spray graffiti on the street with white spray paint. The graffiti consisted of an economic calculation estimating the costs of setting up and administering the Unit. This money, the *inundados/activists* claimed, could be better used by the disaster victims. As Pablo finished his street graffiti and returned to the crowd, a journalist and a cameraman crossed the street. I do not know if they had just arrived in the scene or if they had been there observing and most probably recording the *escrache*. They wanted to interview members of the *inundados/activists*. The crowd crossed the street again to the promenade in the centre of the avenue where a local TV-team had arrived. As some of the activists were interviewed, others laughed and talked, preparing themselves to leave. They agreed that it had been a successful *escrache* given the attention they had received after all. The traffic continued and the cars ran over the street graffiti. When I passed by the site a couple of days later, only scattered white lines were left of the painting.

Inscriptions like the above were commonly used in Santa Fe as a means of recalling the conflict. Painting and writing on the walls with spray paint is, as we saw in the previous chapter, a common political practice in Argentina in times of elections. Apart from the official posters with the pictures and the names of the candidates that are set up on house walls, graffiti-like spraying in all colours is also a common form of propaganda made by campaign workers for the political parties. In 2005, the different visual messages were juxtaposed. I found several propaganda posters from the campaign for the elections to the Chamber of Deputies that same year, overwritten with white paint. This was especially the case with the posters on which the former Governor Reutemann was depicted. Reutemann was a National Senator in 2005. Even if he was not a candidate himself on this occasion, he appeared on posters in support of the candidates of his faction.[183] On these posters, found all over town, the faces were overwritten with big uppercase letters calling Reutemann *inundador* (flood maker) and *asesino* (murderer) (see Figure 18).

Earlier that year, in the autumn of 2005, I found one particular slogan painted on many different streets with big red and black letters, and signed by the regional student federation, the Federación Universitaria del Litoral:

> NO TO THE IMPUNITY OF THE FLOOD MAKERS! 29TH OF APRIL 18HS PLAZA DE MAYO SQUARE: MEETING FOR JUSTICE. THE STUDENTS DO NOT FORGET! (Upper case letters in original).

---

[183] In 2005, Senator Reutemann supported the sitting national government of President Kirchner and the Frente para la Victoria (Front for Victory) faction. But Senator Reutemann and several of his senator colleagues in the national parliament withdrew their support to this parliamentary bloc in 2009 due to the farmer-government conflict (see Chapter Two). Reutemann since then ran his own bloc called Santa Fe Federal (Federal Santa Fe).

Figure 18 | Street propaganda in the 2005 political campaign overwritten (Photo by author 2005)

Another student organisation, the Franja Morada,[184] similarly recalled *la Inundación* in the university campus:

> APRIL 29th . . . 2 YEARS FROM THE WATER CATASTROPHE: No to the IMPUNITY of the FLOOD MAKERS! (Upper and lower case letters in original).

Another type of graffiti was also widely seen on street walls in 2005. Its aesthetics was more like art than the partisan calligraphy I was used to seeing. The language of protest and critique was also more subtle and ironic, bearing some similarity to the *pixação* graffiti in the city of São Paulo through which the young male *pixadores* express their anarchic ideological stance in regard to Brazilian social and political processes (Caldeira 2012), or to the self-claimed "non-political" works among Tehrani graffiti artists of the post-revolutionary "Third Generation" in Iran (Khosravi 2013). Even aesthetically speaking, there were similarities between the graffiti made by the *inundados/activists* and that made by the artists in the cited examples. Using the technique of cutting a template and then spraying through this on the wall, the Santafesinian graffiti seemed like a very quick and efficient way of covering large areas of the urban space with a message. I observed many different graffiti of this kind in different parts of the city, mainly Downtown (see Figure 19).

---

[184] The Franja Morada (Murray Fringe) is one of the strongest university student unions in Argentina. It was founded in the 1960s and is associated with the political party Unión Cívica Radical (Radical Civic Union), which has been the main opponent to the Peronist Party in the 20th century.

Figure 19 | Making memory through street graffiti (Photos by author 2005)

The graffiti drew on different metaphors and metonyms to convey the message. The diving helmet and the inscription "Danger: Flood-prone city" referred to the risk of being flooded in Santa Fe City, to the point of having to need a diving suit. The inscription "Black Tent" referred both to the group Carpa Negra in the *inundados* movement and the black tent as a key symbol of protest. The inscription "Where does the Unit go when it Rains" alluded to the well-known Argentinian pop ballade "Where do the people go when it rains?" This song is about the unequal possibilities people in society have to cope when facing ordinary crises such as a downpour. It was written and recorded in the 1970s by the Argentinian duo Pedro y Pablo, associated with the country's musical protest movement against the military dictatorship. They were also the authors of the well-known song "Marcha de la Bronca"[185] from the 1970s, which was also performed in the protests of the *inundados/activists*.

In contrast to the graffiti painted on the walls of the abandoned water tower on the old railway embankment and the children's murals in the Plaza 29 de Abril square (see Chapter Three), the graffiti made by the *inundados/activists* was a particular imprint on the public space aimed at calling the attention to *la Inundación*. While using aesthetics and idioms similar to that of the Brazilian *pixadores*, the graffiti made the by Santafesinian *inundados/activists*, unlike the latter, had a political meaning. The transgressive character of the graffiti in itself, and the messages conveyed, played directly into the politics of memory in which the *inundados* movement was engaged.

II: Juxtaposed artefacts of memory

In Chapter Three I described the memorial created by the group the Flooded Mothers in the Plaza 29 de Abril square. In an e-mail exchange in 2012 with one of my interlocutors in the *inundados* movement, I learned that a new plaque had been added to the monument in tribute to the *inundados/victims*. A small red-

---

[185] In English: March of the Fury

brown tile had been placed below the existing plaques, stating: "Flooded in 2003 and it was not the fault of the Salado [River]," and it was signed by the March activists. I was a bit surprised to find out that the two groups suddenly shared this symbolic space of remembering, because of the ideological differences between the apolitical Flooded Mothers and politicised March activists. I mailed one of my interlocutors and received the following explanation:

From: Marta
To: Susann Ullberg
Date: 21 June 2012
I can tell you about the tile [on the monument] in the Plaza 29 de Abril [square], next to the Children's Hospital, that [we in] the Torches March stuck up several such messages in different places that were flooded [in 2003], another was [on the monument in] the Juan de Garay Park. [We did this] around the time of the 7th anniversary of April 29th in 2010, and we did it to keep making memory. Unfortunately, of all places, the only one left is the monument of the Plaza [29 de Abril], because the tiles we put up in the Park, on the walls of the [Children's] Hospital and on street walls in other neighbourhoods, were withdrawn. It seems that the monument has a special value for most [people] which is why I think they left it there. The struggle continues. Some [of the *inundados/activists*] have died and others are sick. We are becoming fewer and fewer. In the commemoration of April 29th [in 2012] very few neighbours (who are the most important [people] in this claim) gathered [in the Plaza de Mayo square]. Yet we are still resisting!" (E-mail communication, June 21st, 2012).

Even if the Flooded Mothers had been involved in the legal demand for economic compensation,[186] and actually formed part of the Permanent Assembly of Flood Victims, they had never voiced any critique publicly against the government or participated in the street protests. They were consequently not really considered part of the protest movement, neither by themselves, nor by the *inundados/activists*. In contrast, the activists all clearly situated themselves on the scale of resistance and critique against the government. The Flooded Mothers actually associated with the municipality to achieve their goals. Their commemorative actions were, in contrast to those of the *inundados/activists*, more of a ritual way of making meaning of the disaster. Yet, they left the tile that had been placed by the March on "their" monument. Hence, the different positions of one group and another, between one stance and another, between the community and the polity of remembering, were juxtaposed and negotiated over time.

---

[186] The Flooded Mothers had been instrumental in helping flood victims like themselves to get involved in the class action lawsuit against the Government of the Province of Santa Fe in demand for economic compensation for the damages. The lawsuits are discussed below and in Chapter Five.

III: Pamphlets and books

Written texts were central to the struggle of the *inundados/activists*, both as artefacts of memory and documents of claim. Many texts were printed and handed out as leaflets during the street protests. Examples of this were the satire bulletin called *El Inundador*[187] and the satire *Manual del Buen Inundador: El Pequeño Inundador Ilustrado*.[188] The latter alluded to the old and well-known encyclopaedia *Petit Larousse*,[189] and listed instructions of "the best and most efficient ways to flood Santa Fe City."

In Chapter Three, I described some of the many books about *la Inundación* published during my fieldwork. There were several books published in a more documentary or journalistic vein. The authors discussed did not write from the position of being victims themselves, but rather as eye witnesses, citizens and journalists. Some of these authors were *inundados/activists* while others did not participate actively in the protests. The activists often referred to their books as the "truth written."

Among these was the book *Agua de Nadie: La Historia de Cómo el Salado Inundó Santa Fe*[190] (Pais 2008), based on the above-mentioned documentary film with the same name (Traffano and Pais 2005). Pais was local journalist who had not been flooded himself in 2003. Instead he became an eyewitness to the disaster as he was in the street in those days, covering the events for the local radio station of the university, the LT10. The spirit of his book can be summarised in its final sentence which is: "Memory and Justice" (ibid.: 233). Another book in this vein was *La Tragedia Santafesina*[191] (Oberlin 2005) in which the author formulates a political and ideological analysis of the disaster, similar to a third book called *29-A: 29 de Abril de 2003 / Inundación en Santa Fe*[192] (Moro, Benito, and Moreno 2005). The latter was written by three young local journalists who argued that the 2003 disaster had been far from a natural disaster. Instead, they claimed that it had been a "water crime" or a terrorist attack, enacted by corrupt politicians protected by impunity. To make their argument they used the symbolic numeronym "29-A," standing for April 29th, in analogy with those used when talking about the terrorist attacks of 11-S[193] and the 11-M.[194] The last book in the vein of public accusation was published in 2011. One of the *inundados/activists* wrote the book *Verdades Locas Contra Impunes Mentiras: Fábula Política Inundada Bajo "El Reino de los Fangos." Inundaciones 2003-2007*[195] (Castro 2011). The book, with a foreword written by

---

[187] In English: The Flood Maker
[188] In English: The Manual of the Efficient Flood Maker: The Little Flood Maker Illustrated
[189] The first Spanish edition of the encyclopaedia *Pequeño Larousse Ilustrado* was published in 1912. The dictionary was a bestseller in Argentina, widely used in homes and schools.
[190] In English: Nobody's Water: The History of How the Salado [River] Flooded Santa Fe
[191] In English: The Santafesinian Tragedy
[192] In English: 29-A: April 29th 2003 / [The] Flood in Santa Fe
[193] "11-S" is the Spanish equivalent of the numeronym "9/11" to denote the terrorist attacks in the USA in 2001.
[194] "11-M" refers to March 11th, which was the day in 2004 in which the Madrid train bombings occurred.
[195] In English: Crazy Truths Against Unpunished Lies: A Political Fable Flooded in the "Kingdom of Mire." Floods 2003-2007

one of the Santafesinian *Madres* in the Mothers of the Plaza de Mayo, received a lot of attention in local mass media and the author presented it several times at press conferences in Rosario, Santo Tomé and in Santa Fe City. The 10th anniversary of *la Inundación* was commemorated with yet another book to be published, *Lo que el Salado Sigue Gritando: Diez Años Después* (Frade del, Haidar, and Cello forthcoming), written by two Santafesinian journalists and a political scientist. It was presented in public on the Plaza de Mayo square on April 27th, 2013, within the programme of activities arranged by the Asamblea. The title of the book certainly seemed appropriate in this context: *What the Salado River Continues to Cry: Ten years After.*

IV: *Documentos* and reports

The *inundados/activists* produced numerous texts or short reports issued as *documentos*. Representatives of some or all of the organisations, which formed part of the Permanent Assembly, and individuals who represented only themselves, participated in the elaboration of these documents. This was done among a group of organisations, but also in open meetings, *asambleas*, where the content and order of the texts were discussed by all present. The *documentos* were presented at press conferences or read out loud during the demonstrations, most notably the anniversary commemorations in the Plaza de Mayo square. The *documentos* were then kept as written declarations, artefacts of memory of the protest movement. I do not have a complete register of all these documents but a list of fourteen documents that I collected during my fieldwork in 2004 and 2005. The first one is dated six months after *la Inundación* and the last one 27 months after the disaster. I have been told by interlocutors in the movement that the same practice has continued, at least for the anniversary demonstrations organised every year. The *documentos* I have read and heard read out loud in the square are of different length, ranging from one or two pages to seven or eight pages long. The statements differ from document to document, depending on the point in time that they were written. The claims of justice are the same through them all, but the details reflect and denounce recent decisions (or non-decisions) by the provincial and municipal governments or the judicial system regarding the situation of the *inundados/victims*. In what follows we shall see how some of these texts were produced and presented.

Assembling *documentos*

The creation of the *documentos* was a collective endeavour that mostly took place in *asambleas*. These were meetings that anybody in the movement could participate in, regardless of whether they were representing an organisation or themselves. The assembly as a form of political action and memory-work is a particular trait of social movements. While assemblies are in essence a meeting form carried out in all kinds of formal and informal organisations, the *asamblea* referred to in this context refers to a democratic principle of "all inclusiveness." In Argentina, the emergence of the *asamblea* as a form of political action is associated with the widespread dissatisfaction with how representative democracy has been carried out since its return in 1983. The social protests in the country in 2001-2002 gave rise to numerous initiatives of participative democracy such as *asambleas barriales* (neighbourhood assemblies), which aimed to transform the many street protests into political proposals (A. M. Fernández 2008; Helmus 2009). Among the *inundados/activists*, the *asamblea* was the arena in which the different tactics of protest of the different groups and individuals were turned into careful considerations of what was to be declared publicly. The constitution of and participation in these assemblies was, like the movement itself, dynamic and changing, even if there was a formal frame for it, which was the Permanent Assembly, colloquially called the Assembly. Some groups such as the March, the Black Tent and the House were almost always represented in the *asambleas*. Others showed up only occasionally. In principle, I was told, every group and activist in the movement was welcome to participate, in spite of differences and conflicts within the movement. Everybody who had something to say, individuals and groups alike, was considered. Single specific phrases suggested by one group or participant were discussed in the *asamblea*, sometimes ardently. The documents, just as the commemorative acts on the anniversaries, had to be made despite internal divisions and conflicts. This was why it was so important to be inclusive, but also to scrutinise what was done and said publicly. I attended one such meeting prior to the second anniversary, when the content and the formulation of the document to be read out loud were discussed.

It was late in the evening on April 28th, 2005, when I arrived in the Plaza de Mayo square, where representatives from the Assembly were planning the commemorative act to take place the next day. I had spent the afternoon in Recreo, a small town north of Santa Fe City, to attend another related meeting. That town had also been severely flooded in 2003. According to my interlocutors among the *inundados/activists*, in contrast to Santa Fe City, it was not until 2005 that some of the *inundados* in Recreo had begun to make claims concerning public disaster management during the 2003 disastrous flood. The commemoration there on that day[196] was the first of its kind. Several *inundados/activists* from Santa Fe City had been invited to speak, so as to inspire protest in this town. When we returned to Santa Fe that night, and arrived in the square, the *asamblea* was already engaged in the planning. Laura and Lucia from the Black Tent had already set up the tent. This year it was a small igloo camping tent in a military green colour. In order to turn it into the Black Tent, they had hung a black tarpaulin on the top of it. The white stone with the inscription, made the year before, had been placed next to the tent, which was facing the House of Government. Between the trees in the square hung the large white banner, by now greyish and ragged, from the first year of protest, saying Black Tent of [the] Memory and [the] Dignity.

---

[196] The town of Recreo, just north of Santa Fe City, had been flooded on April 28th, 2003.

Figure 20 | *Asamblea* of the *inundados/activists* in the Plaza de Mayo (Photo by author 2005)

Laura and Lucia, activists in the Black Tent, were planning to stand vigil in the tent overnight and start early in the morning with the broadcasting from a *radio abierta*, a kind of street radio broadcasting directly from the square. The radio was to be working there during the entire day of commemoration. Anybody participating in the activities in the square, or just passing by, could sit down and speak from their heart. The speech would be broadcast through a local FM channel. In the meeting, representatives from the March and from the House were present, as well as people from a couple of NGOs who were active in the movement. Several other activists, who were not members of any particular organisation, participated in the meeting. When I asked, they said they were simply there because they were *inundados/activists*.

A draft of the *documento* to be read the day after was the key topic of discussion in the *asamblea*. Many different authors had written different pieces of text that now had to be put together into one single text. Emilio, one of the independent *inundados/activists*, read the draft out loud. I recognised a passage from a report issued by the House and presented at the press conference that same morning. One phrase came to be heavily discussed in the *asamblea*. It was a rhetorical question of whether to continue voting for the same politicians in charge before and during *la Inundación*. Luis, who was the author of the phrase, argued that it was imperative to remind the people of Santa Fe that power holders blamed for the disaster, were still occupying posts in the government or the public administration. He wanted to remind people to think about whom they voted for in the elections. Those who opposed this phrase argued that it focused exclusively on the act of voting, as if this was the only means of achieving justice: there were other means to change things in the city, such as their own demonstrations. Hence, to them the phrase presented a too-narrow conception of how to contest power. After some arguing, voting took place. It was decided not to include the particular phrase in the document. Luis grabbed his bag and left the square, upset with having his phrase removed, even if other parts of his authorship remained in the *documento*. The meeting continued and was concluded with a final draft, to be read out loud the next day. In what follows is an extract of this five-page long *documento*:

> TWO YEARS SINCE APRIL 29TH
> Yet another April 29th. Yet another date that we can't nor want to forget, we can't because the pain and the anger come together like blood in an open wound, we won't because to forget would be to deny or ignore what hurts or kills.
>
> They stole the life projects of us 130,000 Santafesinos, part of our history. The remains of those stories were degraded and discarded like old rags. What else can be said about us? For two years we have been informing and denouncing, from the [Black] Tent, the March, the demonstrations [carried out] on every 29th, the reports about the consequences and the dead, what happened and what continues to happen.
>
> [Yet] we remain [in the] same [situation]: No one knew, no one answered. Nobody knows, nobody answers. What else can be said about *los inundados*? We: those of us who are here, those who are not because they can't be here and those of us who will never [again] be with us. We are the *inundados* of Santa Fe . . .
>
> We will continue the struggle of holding the truth and demanding justice on top of the ruins of our lost stuff, our photos, our homes ruined, our sick [and] unemployed neighbours, and those who are gone. We will not leave the flood makers in peace, wherever they go we will search for them. And we will continue to demand compensation for all the people affected, compensation that recognises the material, physical [and] psychological damage, and [that] recognises the magnitude of the disaster. We will continue to set up tents, marches, demonstrations, reports, books, videos, reports, documenting the neglect, injustice and pain.
>
> We can't, nor want to forget. Justice for our dead and sick! Trial and punishment to the flood maker! Confiscation of their property! Disqualification from holding public office! Total compensation for those affected!

In the manifestation on the next day, the evening of April 29th, the *inundados/activists* read the *documento* out loud through the loudspeakers from a stage set up next to the House of Government. Thousands of people in the Plaza de Mayo square listened in silence to the statements, which brought *la Inundación* back to the present in their minds and bodies. As the final words resounded in the warm and crowded night, the people present in the square joined in the cries for justice.

Presenting results

Some of the groups in the *inundados* movement carried out or hired inquiries regarding some issue at stake, which were presented in *documentos* or other reports. These presentations were crucial in the struggle, not only of allocating responsibility, but to establish the political and legal responsibilities as well. Several of these reports were provided as evidence by the activists for the judicial and the political hearings. The public knowledge about the reports was also seen as important by the activists. They tried to get as much public attention as possible, generally by presenting the reports in press conferences. During my fieldwork in 2005 I attended two such press conferences.

One of them was arranged on a sunny spring morning in October by the human rights organisations that were members of the House of Human Rights of Santa Fe, referred to colloquially by the activists as simply the House. The conference was held in the Methodist Church in the centre of the city. One of the organisations in the House was an ecumenical organisation,[197] which had its headquarters in this church. Approximately fifteen people were sitting in the church when I arrived, of which a few seemed to be journalists. I recognised other people from the street protests. The press conference was organised to present an independent technical inquiry into the causes of *la Inundación*, commissioned by the plaintiffs in the so-called *Causa Inundación*, the flood lawsuit.[198] Two of these plaintiffs,[199] Diana and Guillermo, were members of the ecumenical organisation. The press conference was introduced by Diana. She sat at a table covered with a white cloth set up close to the altar and in front of a large map of the city. On her left sat one of the *Madres* from the Mothers of the Plaza de Mayo dressed in her white head scarf and on her right sat two young women, who were the two lawyers representing the plaintiffs. Next to them was an older man who was the technical expert they had commissioned. He was a professor in water engineering from the city's university and himself an *inundado/victim*. Before presenting his inquiry, Diana read out loud a declaration on behalf of all the human rights organisations involved. Her words, of which the following is an excerpt, echoed in the church hall:

> We [the organisations of human rights in Santa Fe] believe with deep conviction that politics is primarily an act of service, for the most humble, for the most needed, for the entire people, for progress, for the equality of opportunities and, in essence, for a much more just present and future. When politics becomes a contest of

---

[197] Movimiento Ecuménico por los Derechos Humanos (Ecumenical Movement for Humans Rights)

[198] The so-called Flood Lawsuit actually referred to two different legal processes. One was pursued according to the Criminal Law to establish responsibility of public officials before, during and after the 2003 disaster. This was the one in which the *inundados/activists*' plaintiffs claimed that former Governor Reutemann should also be interrogated. The other was pursued according to the Civil Code by around 6,000 *inundados* plaintiffs who demanded economic compensation. The provincial state prosecutors answered to the demand in 2009, denying any responsibility and alleging that the "criminal case" should be solved first before settling the "civil case." The Supreme Court of the Province of Santa Fe revoked this claim in 2011 however and the lawsuit was instructed to proceed (*Notife* 2011b).

[199] In the legal process pursued according to Criminal Law, they were not really plaintiffs in the juridical sense. In contrast to National Criminal Law in Argentina, the legislation of the Province of Santa Fe does not allow an individual citizen to constitute him/herself as a *querellante* and bring legal action to the accused. This is only the faculty of the prosecutor. The individual citizen can only constitute him/herself as a so-called civil actor and appeal to the prosecutor to proceed with a lawsuit. This was why these inquiries were so important to the *inundados/activists* in their quest for accountability.

loyalties on the backs of the people, [then] truth [and] reality is the first victim.

The sad reality of April 29th, 2003, with its voices silenced, with its cries submerged, with its groans for help, [the voices and cries] rises today before this concert of cover-ups, of what we call the lies of the true story.

We ask [you] for a moment to think about the place that this citizen, this unique human being, identifiable by her way of living, her job, her affections, by life itself, what she must have felt in the last moment before drowning, [a fate] not chosen, not expected, not deserved. Think for a moment [about] the real possibility of that human being, how she could be with [us] today and her affections, her work and her life.

From there [the vantage point of the victim], only from there, can we identify with the truth. That's why we say that anyone who does not start this story from that point, who doesn't ask himself why she died, he will begin to walk the path of covering up of political, corrupt and mafia-like loyalties; ultimately the path of true lies.

Because, truly, you have to lie well in order to justify this story.

. . .

A [commemorative] stone ought to be placed, as in the Antique, in Gorostiaga Street where the [flood] water entered [the city] and [it should] say:

This is where the Salado River happily entered [the city], the capital of water engineers, and flooded mostly poor people, over a hundred people died according to the numbers of a [bunch of] lunatics, as the governor Obeid remarked. They [the dead victims] did not know, no one warned them that they lived in flood-prone lowlands and that they forgot to sign [a statement] to the province that they would not accuse [the government] of their death. Only the horses at the [nearby] racecourse realised [the danger of the flood] and left. The judicial system has not yet processed [those responsible]

After Diana's introductory speech, the technical expert presented his report, which was actually an evaluation of another expert inquiry of the events of *la Inundación* (Bacchiega, Bertoni, and Maza 2005a). The latter had been commissioned by the provincial state prosecutor who would use the conclusions to establish whether any politician or public official, who had been in charge at the time of the disaster, would actually be prosecuted. This expert inquiry pointed to the many flaws in the governmental flood preparedness such as not having finished the flood embankment, not having kept up an existing early warning system, and the lack of a contingency plan. Hence, the separate inquiry, presented in the press conference in the church, was commissioned by the plaintiffs of the *inundados/activists* to have their own expert's view on the experts' analysis. The professor's study confirmed and even sharpened the conclusions of the other expert inquiry. Both reports contributed to the legal argument of the plaintiffs and to the moral argument of the *inundados/activists*. This was the reason it was publicly presented at a press conference: to reach as wide an audience as possible and to gain legitimacy and support for the legal claims.

        Earlier that year, another press conference had been held by the activists in the House to present a *documento* referring to the victims of the disaster. This press conference was held Downtown at the headquarters of the House, on the day before the second anniversary in 2005. The date had been carefully chosen to maximise symbolic impact. Local mass media had been invited to attend the press conference. I arrived just before ten o'clock. The small office at the ground floor of an ordinary two storey house was already full of people; members in the organisations, journalists and cameramen. I offered to help in the preparations and was asked to organise and to staple the printed copies of the *documento* so that the people attending the press conference could have one. This *documento* was a six-page update on previous *documentos* about the state of victims of the 2003 disaster. It was written by some of the NGOs which formed part of the *inundados* protest movement. The report added new names to the list of fatal victims, claiming a total of 115 dead persons. It was argued that there were an overwhelming number of *inundados/victims* who had suffered from depression which in combination with prior health problems had led to death. More than sixty cases of persons suffering other physical or psychological consequences had also been registered. The *documento* ended by way of five conclusions:

> [The Government] ought to consider that those affected by the avoidable disastrous flooding suffer from five damages:
> a. The damage of having been flooded, experienced at the time of flooding.
> b. The damage that occurs when one knows that [the disaster] should not have occurred and that nothing was done to avoid it.
> c. The damage that impunity leads to, knowing that those responsible have not only escaped punishment but [that they] have been recycled in positions with immunity.
> d. The damage of knowing that one is vulnerable, that again other terrible things can happen [to you].
> e. The damage produced due to the permanent manipulation of the pressing needs of victims. Expectations are generated regarding payments or refunds that never materialise or [that] are just charities."

After the organisers had presented the statistics and read out loud the denunciation of the lack of disaster policies, the short press conference was over. Several activists were interviewed by the journalists present, interviews that were broadcast to all Santafesinos in the local news that same evening.

Voicing blame

Along with memorials, *escraches*, graffiti and texts, the *inundados/activists* also used music to convey their message. In larger street manifestations, such as in the anniversary commemorations every April 29th, the *bombo de marcha* and *redoblante* drums were often carried and played, not least when political and syndicalist organisations, which also used drums in their manifestations, participated in the protests. The members in the March always sang certain songs of protest during their Tuesday ritual in the Plaza de Mayo. Sometimes, recorded music was also played. In 2005, I received a CD with different recorded songs of protest. The CD included seventeen tracks of protest songs typically associated to social protest in Argentina, and in particular those performed during the Dirty War years. One was the song "El Pueblo Unido Jamás Será Vencido"[200] one of the most internationally renowned songs of protest written by the Chilean folk music group Quilapayún in 1973 in support of the government of Salvador Allende. Among the Argentinian songs included on the CD were the well-known songs from the years of the Dirty War, "Sólo le Pido a Dios"[201] and "Todavía Cantamos,"[202] written and performed by the protest singers León Gieco and Victor Heredia, mentioned in Chapter Three. Another song associated with the history of violence and struggle for democracy in Argentina was that written by the immensely popular Argentinian singer-songwriter, Maria Elena Walsh, in 1972, namely "Como la Cigarra."[203] In addition to these well-known and symbolically significant songs, there was another song included on the CD which was repeated three times. It had been recorded by the *inundados/activists* themselves, performing under the name of Los Piragüeros del Salado,[204] ironically referring to the fact that many people had been rescued in canoes during the 2003 flood. The song is a cover of the song "Matador"[205] from the 1990s by the popular Argentinian rock band Los Fabulosos Cadillacs, but with new lyrics and renamed "Inundador" (Flood maker). An extract of the song:

> They call me the *inundador* and I'm a bastard
> If we talk about flooding, my [building] works kill you
> We inaugurated the [flood] embankment a long time ago
> Without finishing it, I don't care – they'll be flooded!
> *Inundador, inundador*
> Where are you, trickster?
> Governor, *inundador*
>
> REFRAIN
> *Matador, inundador*, nobody fucked you up better [than I did]

---

[200] Known in English as "The People United Will Never Be Defeated!"
[201] In English: I Only Pray to God
[202] In English: We are Still Singing
[203] In English: Like the Cicada
[204] In English: The Canoeists of the Salado [River]
[205] In English: Killer

Matador, inundador, where are you going, killer?
Bookmaker and traitor...Look bastard, how you flooded me!

CHORUS
Reutemann, present! Look, bastard, how you flooded me!
Mercier, present! Look, bastard, how you flooded me!
Obeid, present! Look, bastard, how you flooded me!

Drawing on this song about a killer, "Inundador" blames the provincial political decision makers for intentionally having flooded the people of Santa Fe. Three politicians are named at the end of the song: Carlos Reutemann, Jorge Obeid and Juan Carlos Mercier. At the time of *la Inundación*, Reutemann was the governor and Mercier was the minister of finance. Obeid was a National Deputy at that time but preceded and succeeded Reutemann as governor. As Reutemann's successor, Obeid managed much of the disaster reconstruction policies. All of them have represented the Peronist Party (and different factions within this party) at different stages in their political careers. Their faces, and the faces of other accused politicians, were continuously made visible during my fieldwork by ways of images and sounds. In several street demonstrations held by the *inundados/activists*, I heard these songs being played in loudspeakers. They worked as a soundtrack of memory in the making of the polity of remembering.

Visualising blame

The *inundados/activists* used different means to visualise their claims. Among the many documentaries produced about *la Inundación*, there were a few that addressed responsibilities in a more accusing way. The film *Agua de Nadie: La Historia de Cómo el Salado Inundó Santa Fe* mentioned earlier claimed that *la Inundación* was foreseeable and thus preventable. This argument was also made in the already mentioned documentary *El Agua y la Sangre (Memorias de la Inundación)* produced and publicly screened several times during my fieldwork by a group of students in media and communication from the National University of Entre Ríos in the neighbouring city of Paraná. These filmmakers argued that this disaster was, like previous floods, a matter of business for the economic and political establishment. Both documentaries were screened a number of times during my fieldwork in the context of an activity of the *inundados/activists*.

Another means of visualisation was to plaster the whole city with posters depicting the *inundadores*. One of the activists owned a printing press so the printing was for free. Different images were used, such as pictures from political events and digitally manipulated images from Argentinian popular culture. One of the most widespread posters was created for the demonstrations of the second anniversary of *la Inundación* in 2005. This poster was a digital makeover of the cover of a CD of the popular contemporary Argentinian rock band Bersuit

Vergarabat. Their CD (2004) was called *La Argentinidad al Palo*[206] and the leading track had the same name. The song deals with the historical and cultural particularities of the Argentinian identity, such as strong nationalism and patriotism parallel to the occurrence of numerous violent crises and corruption throughout history. The phrase and the song is an example of that cultural intimacy (Herzfeld 2004) that the Argentinians often engage with, as discussed in Chapter Two. The *inundados/activists* drew on the work of Bersuit Vergarabat and the notion of unlimitedness by writing "Impunity Flat Out" on the poster. This referred to the fact that none of the decision makers depicted in the poster had yet been tried for their eventual responsibility in the disaster. The *inundados/activists* argued that this was yet another expression of absolute political impunity, so typical of Santa Fe and Argentina.

Figure 21 | "Impunity flat out" (Photo by author 2005)

For the parliamentary elections in 2005, several different pamphlets typical of election campaigns were designed. In these, official pictures of Reutemann and some of his allies were reproduced. The statements were phrased in a language of political satire, with the following as an example: "In order to keep up impunity in Santa Fe: [Vote for] Reutemann [and] Rossi [of the] Flood Maker Front." This pamphlet referred to the fact that Reutemann had been in charge of the disaster management but not held accountable for his responsibility. Agustin Rossi really had nothing to do with *la Inundación* or even the provincial government at that point in time, as he had been a member of the town council of the city of Rosario. Yet, in 2005 he was running for office as a national senator for the Province of Santa Fe representing the Peronist faction that Reutemann was associated with. This was enough to accuse Rossi too of being a flood maker. Another pamphlet stated: "The Water and Fire Party. Vote for Reutemann [and] Chabán, a killing formula" This statement made an analogy between *la Inundación* and the disco-

---

[206] To "*estar al palo*" literally means "to be to the stick" and refers to having an erection. This is illustrated in the cover of Bersuit Vergarabat's CD and in the activists' poster. *Al palo* also refers to an idea of full force to the point of being beyond limit. This is the second sense of the title of the CD. Drawing on the latter sense of the word, the translation to English could then be "The Argentineness Flat Out."

theque fire disaster in Buenos Aires in 2004. Chabán was a businessman and the owner of the discotheque that caught fire and killed hundreds of young people. To the *inundados/activists*, Reutemann as a politician at the time of *la Inundación* was equally responsible as Chabán for the calamities he had been involved in.

Another poster also drew on the image of the flood makers (see Figure 22). It depicted the official inauguration of the Westside flood embankment in 1997. This inauguration proved to be something of an anticipated celebration, given that the final section of the embankment was never built, which made possible the 2003 disaster. By naming the different decision makers involved in this public work, the *inundados/activists* held them accountable for *la Inundación*:

> THE FLOOD MAKERS. Inauguration of the Westside flood embankments – August 1997. Jorge Obeid, Carlos Reutemann, Gualtieri, Rosatti, Pennisi and Lamberto uncovered the memorial plaque during the inauguration, alongside Gutiérrez, Mercier and Morín. SO THAT THEY WON'T CONTINUE TO LAUGH AT US. JUSTICE AND PUNISHMENT.

Figure 22 | "The Flood Makers" (Photo by author 2005)

In 2013, around the 10th anniversary of *la Inundación*, the same poster was recycled and published on the internet. Over the image it had been added with big letters: "2003-2013 – The lost decade – Impunity flat out," making reference to the lawsuits and to the fact that in ten years, nothing had really happened in the trial of the political decision makers

On the making of a polity of remembering

This chapter has analysed the emergence and action of the *inundados* movement in the wake of *la Inundación*. By describing some of the ways protests were undertaken by the *inundados/activists* against the municipal and provincial governments, I have argued that they formed a particular polity of remembering in Santa Fe. I agree with Button (1993:54) that if post-disaster protest movements like that of the *inundados* emerge in the first place, it is due to a claim regarding the flaws of the formal institutions set to see to such societal needs. This is why I use the concept of "polity" to describe this expression of collective action. The people involved in these movements have demands, and are therefore by definition pursuing political goals, even if they do this by way of tactics and not necessarily even define themselves as political subjects. This is particularly true in the Argentinian context where *haciendo política*, that is, making politics, has come to signify something of an invective to many people, in view of widespread corruption and clientelism in political life. In fact, and as we shall see, the protest movement became fragmented with time, precisely because of schisms regarding how to organise the struggle and with whom to collaborate. Some people within the movement opted for cooperating with the municipality or the provincial government, seeing such interaction as an opportunity, while other *inundados/activists* interpreted this as *haciendo política* which to them was an act of betrayal and moral corruption (cf. Guala 2005).

Approaching social protest from this angle, we have seen how memory played a vital role in processes of post-disaster mobilisation. On the one hand, by remembering past experiences and grievances evocatively, reminiscently and commemoratively, anger and indignation over the lack of preparedness could be reproduced. This *ressentiment* formed the moral and emotional basis for the *inundados/activists*' engagement in social protest. Activism was not only driven by the need to recover material assets, but by the necessity of recover dignity as citizens (cf. Auyero 2003). On the other hand, memory was used as a mobilising resource by the activists. As we have seen, victimisation shaped the tactics of mobilisation of the *inundados* movement, both in court and in street protests. Hence, in order to uphold the status as victims of political negligence, *la Inundación* had to be maintained in public memory. The memory-work undertaken by the *inundados/activists* drew on two symbolically relevant repertoires of action, which contributed to the public memory of *la Inundación* as much as to the political legitimacy of the *inundados* movement. One was to use moments, names and places that were temporally and spatially reminiscent and commemorative of *la Inundación*. The other was to use symbols, practices and idioms of grief and claim, which were well established in the Argentinian social and political life. This gave the claim of the *inundados/activists* a temporal and spatial resonance with other prior social protests, most notably that of the human rights movement, both in Santa Fe and in other parts of the country (cf. Alonso, Boumerá, and Citroni 2007). The presence of the Mothers of the Plaza de Mayo in the manifestations of the *inundados/activists* in Santa Fe mobilised a symbolic power of social protest in Argentina that was "supported by the acknowledgement of a genealogy of struggles" (Catela da Silva 2004:141). The *inundados* protest movement emerged and endured through active memory-work, and because the institutions of power largely ignored their claims. The effect of this was that *la Inundación* became a highly politicised event at both local and provincial levels,[207] which also contributed to the predominance of this particular disaster in the Santafesinian flood memoryscape. We shall next take a look at how political actors responded to the politicisation of *la Inundación* and how flooding in general was remembered within the realm of bureaucracy.

---

[207] The politicisation of *la Inundación* did transcend regional boundaries on a few occasions, for example when activists in the Black Tent demonstrated in Rosario and Buenos Aires and when the case was discussed on a couple of national TV broadcast shows in the first years following the disaster. In April 2013, heavy rains caused severe flooding in several Argentinian cities, Santa Fe City, Buenos Aires and La Plata City. These events were discussed intensively in national media in analogy to the 2003 disaster in Santa Fe. Given that these disasters occurred just before the 10th anniversary of *la Inundación,* this prompted much memory-work about this particular event.

Chapter 5 | Flood management and the logic of omission

Politics of memory / oblivion in politics

Upon my return to Santa Fe in 2008, Gabriel, a key interlocutor of mine in the *inundados* movement told me in passing about the monument to the *inundados* that had been built by the government. In his opinion it was ironic, but not quite laughable, that the government, which had never acknowledged any responsibility of the disaster, should build a memorial at all. Another aspect that bothered him and other people in the movement was the choice of location of the monument. It was placed on a traffic island in the midst of the Eastside ring road, a highly trafficked road and thus not a contemplative place for such a memorial at all. Finally, the aesthetics of the monument was considered by them to be a *mamaracho*, a daub, which was absolutely tasteless. Gabriel was upset when he spoke to me:

> How can it occur to them to use water for aesthetic purposes when it was the water that flooded us!? And representing the dead people with cubes in concrete?! This monument is like laughing in our faces!

This chapter addresses how the remembering and forgetting of past flooding took place in the political and bureaucratic realms of Santa Fe. I begin this chapter by describing an instance of interaction between the municipal government and groups of *inundados/victims* and *inundados/activists* in terms of commemorative politics of *la Inundación*. After this I shall delve more into the bureaucratic context and illustrate ethnographically how the making of official memory and oblivion follow a particular pattern of selective remembering and forgetting, which I call the "logic of omission."

The official memorial of *la Inundación*?

Monuments are materialised commemoration and both literally and conceptually a memorial (Connerton 2009). As objects of memory they make us recall our knowledge of a particular event or person of the past, but it also instils in us memories of somebody we did not know or of events we did not experience ourselves. The social meaning of places is constituted through remembering. Memory in turn is shaped by places. Lucia Volk, in her analysis of the politics of memory surrounding Lebanese public memorials, argues that memorials simultaneously constitute "rhetorical spaces," "real physical places" and "ritual spaces" (2010) that shape particular understandings of the past through narratives, symbolic artefacts and embodied ceremonies. Such places and practices of remembering are central to any making of community and identity, which can be seen not least in efforts of nation-building (B. Anderson 1991; Guber 1999a; Volk ibid.).

One day in 2008, I went to see the alleged official monument of *la Inundación* myself. As I approached the intersection of the 27 de Febrero Street and the Alem Avenue, next to the Plaza de las Palomas square, I noticed the many cars and heavy trucks that passed in high speed. I certainly agreed with Gabriel that this was really an awkward place for a memorial of a tragedy, both due to the noise but also considering the symbolic dimension of the choice of site, given that the 2003 flood struck the Westside and not the Eastside. It would have made more sense to place it on the Westside where the "non-official" monuments were located (see Chapter Three). The memorial consisted of a kind of small dam built in concrete with geometrical forms:

Figure 23 | Monument at the Alem Avenue (Photo by author 2008)

The memorial was quite a big construction, approximately twenty metres long and ten metres wide, occupying a large portion of the grass-covered traffic island. One end of the construction was a concrete floor sloping down towards the lawn and to the dam. On this floor some fifteen cubes in concrete had been placed in an asymmetrical way, as if they were boulders thrown out on that slope. Another three cubes had been placed in the dam as if they had fallen into the water. A long conductor was built above the dam, presumably to catch rain water and to make it fall into the dam like a cascade. When I visited the place no water was falling from there, but then it had not rained for several days. Instead the dam was filled with stagnant water and furthermore with trash, whereas the surrounding lawn and trees seemed to be attended to. The memorial itself and its deafening location gave me the impression not of remembrance, but rather of oblivion, in the sense of abandonment. I walked on top on the memorial and approached the marble plaque placed at eye level on the rainwater conductor. It had a bronze shield with the coat of arms of the Municipality of Santa Fe on the top. Below this it was written with capital letters:

THE MUNICIPALITY OF THE CITY OF SANTA FE DE LA VERA
CRUZ AND THE SANTA FE BREWERY WORKING FOR
THE PROGRESS OF OUR CITY
ENGINEER EZEQUIEL MARTÍN BALBARREY, MAYOR
22 SEPTEMBER 2006

Only then did I realise that this monument had nothing to do with *la Inundación*! When I searched for information about it in the archives of the local newspapers, I found an article that reported that it was the winning proposal in an urban design contest arranged by the municipality and the Association of Architects of Santa Fe, and financed by the city's oldest brewery, the Cervecería Santa Fe. This factory was in fact located only a few blocks from the monument which made the site suddenly seem very appropriate. According to the newspaper, the brewery had received a plot of municipal land next to the factory in exchange for the sponsorship (*El Litoral* 2006b). I later found out that the brewery had recently accomplished a big restoration of the factory and that the company had also opened a museum the same year as the inauguration of the monument. Given the company's importance in the local economy, such an exchange between the public and the private sectors seemed to make sense. I now became curious to know how the widespread idea had come about that this was an official monument of *la Inundación*. Gabriel told me that he had heard this from another activist in the movement. When I asked other interlocutors among the *inundados/activists* they told me the same story as Gabriel had and that they had heard it from someone else. Other people I asked, not involved in the *inundados* movement, hardly knew about the existence of the public work, however. Thus, while it was still unclear to me how the rumour had begun, it was interesting to note that it was interpreted as such within the protest movement. The will to recall among these activists seemed to have disposed them to interpret this public work in terms of the antagonistic relationship with the local government. As I read more about the contest, another newspaper article, I began to grasp their particular interpretation and, hence their indignation. The explanation of the symbolism of the public work was published in the widely read local newspaper *El Litoral*:

> [T]he presence of water will be made visible [in the artwork]. Marking an optimistic view about the dialectical relationship that exists in our city with it [the water], the proposed design is intended to sym-

bolise this co-existence. This is why the perforated beam that runs throughout it . . . symbolises the control . . . that mankind has over such an essential natural resource. The shape and volume of great magnitude and materiality captures this meaning; represented in this case as the act of control and domination. Also, within this set, cubes in concrete are emerging with the purpose of identifying the different actors or actions taken by man in nature. Therefore, as artefacts . . . some [of these] icons operate within and others outside the [water] with the idea of reflecting the different relationships that every [culture] has [with nature]. At night these cubes are illuminated by submersible lights as a metaphor that reinforces the character of the limitations of urban life but, at the same time, it serves to connect the idea of the canal as a permanent renewal, which apart from collecting water in the bottom for recycling, establishes the meaning of the life cycle as an effective way to make sense of the eternal return, or start and end without interruption (*El Litoral* 2006a).

Reading these explanations of the symbolism of the work, it became clear to me how the *inundados* could interpret this as offensive. Far from having been able to "control" or "dominate" the waters of the Salado River in 2003, their view of this "dialectic relationship" was not at all "optimistic." Representing "actors" and "actions" in nature as cubes falling down a slope into the water with some cubes submerged, was interpreted by them as depicting people drowning. Thus, the public work that was not built as a monument at all, turned into a memorial for the *inundados* to whom it represented a painful reminder of the disaster.

But what about the intentions of this work? Neither the municipality nor the provincial government had until that moment built any monuments to commemorate the disaster, even though there had been a couple of political initiatives to do so.[208] As we have seen in the preceding chapters, the *inundados/victims* had built several non-official memorials on the Westside and the *inundados/activists* had placed numerous artefacts and images of memory throughout the city. At first, the governmental non-action toward commemorating *la Inundación* seemed to me as an institutional will to promote forgetting about it. Yet as I continued to find information about the "non-monument" at the Alem Avenue, I came to change my frame of interpretation. While the 2003 flood, or any other flood, was never referred to in the urban design contest, there was an explicit intention to reframe how the city's relationship with the surrounding rivers should be remembered, as stated in the rules of the contest:

[T]he project should seek to enhance the quality of the place, including the treatment of green areas and the incorporation of sculptural

---

[208] One parliamentary member of the Province of Santa Fe actually presented several bills in the years 2006-2008, addressing the need to build an official memorial to the victims of the 2003 disaster ('Hugo Marcucci - Senador Del Departamento La Capital / Santa Fe' 2012).

> and/or architectural elements generally known as "urban landmarks." Among these alternatives, the municipality considers important the inclusion of water and all references to its decisive role in a sustainable environment, as a theme…of great currency and symbolic value, capable of representing the positive relationships that intertwine humans and nature (Municipalidad de la Ciudad de Santa Fe de la Vera Cruz et al. 2005:2).

Considering the timing of organisation of this contest, in late 2005, when the claims for accountability by the *inundados* movement were resounding in the entire city of Santa Fe and the rivers were being recalled as places of risk and danger, it is feasible to think that the municipality would support any idea that countered this representation. If so, even if it was a rather concealed counter memory to that of the *inundados/activists*, the municipality was in fact contesting the commemorative imagery brought by the flood victims. In fact, oblivion about the disastrous *la Inundación*, and all issues around accountability, could be achieved by creating other memories about the river. Here, Scott's concept of "hidden transcripts" can help us to grasp how this relates to the notion of logic of omission. Scott (1992) analyses how power relations, and resistance to them, takes place through what he calls "public and hidden transcripts." The first refers to the open performance of power and a deliberate display of its signs, and the second to the exercise of power (and resistance) in disguise, that is, those discourses and actions that are not directly displayed in public, but which largely forge the relations between those exercising dominance and those being dominated. As Carol Greenhouse has observed, "the metaphor of the 'transcript' implies that the action has already taken place elsewhere. In this sense, the hidden transcript is not speech as such . . . but, rather, a shorthand term for the interpretive doubts – second thoughts – about what has just been said" (2005:357). Connecting these ideas to my study and the logic of omission constituting the Santafesinian flood memoryscape, the transcript can thus be seen as memory, and the monument to the progress of the city and to its relation with the river; as materialising public and hidden transcripts.

Unveiling hidden transcripts

Eventually, six years and two mayors later, things seemed to have changed slightly regarding the governmental stance of not commemorating *la Inundación*. By the time of the 8th anniversary of the disaster in 2011, the municipality had supported economically the restoration of the memorial created by the Flooded Mothers. In the inauguration of the restored murals and monument, the municipal representative and soon to be mayor, José Corral, gave a speech in which he took the path of the politics of regret:

> [H]onestly, I think what the government should have done then, is to have recognised the reality and ask for forgiveness, regardless of the economic possibilities of repair, because people have a right to the

truth. And the truth tells us that there were two problems . . . The first was that the third section of the embankment was not finished. The report by Deputy Marcucci clearly shows that shows that if this had been completed it would never have been surpassed and no water had entered the city. But the other thing that happened is that once the contingency was produced, we were not prepared to deal with it, and that's the responsibility of government . . . Therefore . . . is [this] an act of memory that serves to put things as they should have been. And the government, instead of appealing to lawyers and legal strategies seeking an excuse or an argument, should have told the truth, and recognise that what happened was because we had not done what we should have (*Notife*, 2011).

The city council participated again in the 9th anniversary commemorations organised by the Flooded Mothers. On this occasion, representatives from this organisation handed over a petition to the public officials signed by hundreds of residents in the Santa Rosa de Lima neighbourhood to officially name the square the Plaza de la Memoria 29 de Abril. In August that same year, the town council passed a bill to make this the official name of the square (Concejo Municipal de Santa Fe 2012b). In addition to this initiative, in October 2012, the municipal council approved a bill on the creation of the *Circuíto Urbano 29 de Abril*. The idea of the Urban Circuit April 29th was to place memory of *la Inundación* through particular landmarks indicating which places the floodwater had reached and through marking the height reached by the 2003 floodwater on emblematic buildings and private homes. The councilwoman who proposed the bill was cited in a local newspaper explaining that the project aimed at keeping alive the memory about the solidarity and the mutual aid that had framed the 2003 disaster (Uno Santa Fe 2012b).

A decade after *la Inundación,* therefore, a gradual shift in the official stance had occurred, from one of no commemoration and "hidden transcripts," to that of participating in the non-official commemorations of the Flooded Mothers, and creating official memorials and spaces of remembering in order to never forget. While the discourses of the municipal representatives were framed in a reconciliatory way, the regret was not expressed by the accused "flood makers" themselves, but by their successors who represented the political opposition. The politics of regret is enabled by the logic of omission, which is always selective in what is remembered and what is forgotten. With time, the urban space in Santa Fe had come to lodge juxtaposed memories about *la Inundación*, some struggling to recall a disastrous past, others making memory for what they imagined as a resilient future.

In 2013, the stance of the municipal and the provincial governments completed its shift. At the end of February that year, the then mayor, José Corral, and the vice governor, Jorge Henn, in company with a number of public officials and legislators, declared in a public act that a vast programme of commemoration would be organised for the 10th anniversary of the tragedy. The official commemoration involved numerous activities in order to "keep memory alive" and to "encourage the reflection and awareness [among citizens] about the relation between the city and the river, risk management and culture of prevention" (*Notife* 2013). These activities ranged from building an official memorial, the *Memorial de la Inundación*, arranging exhibitions in city museums and presenting cultural activities, to reinforcing citizen campaigns about the risk for flooding in schools and neighbourhoods. The mayor declared that this ambitious programme was due to the international award that the city had won in 2011 as a resilient city[209] and to the fact that "the city itself has to rebuild its own memory, and above all rely on that experience [of *la Inundación*] and the solidarity that emerged, so that from here on, every time we face such challenges from nature, we will be better prepared" (*Notife* 2013). To this official statement and the whole commemorative endeavour, my interlocutor Laura posted an angered comment on Facebook that same day:

> Years of struggle in the Plaza de Mayo square in Santa Fe in order to unmask the kings of impunity, "the *Inundadores*." [We] are now close to reaching 10 years of marches, acts, claims, demanding justice. You don't steal a struggle [like that], you respect it!

Laura was referring to the fact that the *inundados/activists* had undertaken the memory-work of *la Inundación* for such a long time and for the sake of seeking justice. Now she felt that the municipality suddenly was co-opting this work in order to transform the ways in which the disaster was remembered. In the following months, the *inundados/activists* mobilised by way of *asambleas*, street manifestations, *documentos* and social media to protect their entitlement to make memory of *la Inundación*. In the month of March, a photo album called *Así Construímos la Memoria [de la Inundación]* (This is How we Constructed the Memory [of *la Inundación*]) were posted on the Facebook site of the Torches' March, accompanied by captions that not only described the different photos, but also made statements about the struggle of the March. The caption of one of the pictures was particularly telling about the stance of the *inundados/activists* towards the recent official initiative of commemorating *la Inundación*:

> [We] the *inundados* of the Torches' March already went to the hole where the [flood] water entered [the city]. [It] was in 2005, we were there, explaining how the water had entered the city. There in Gorostiaga [Street], where we also paid tribute to those killed by the flood by throwing flowers into the river. And that [act] wasn't part of any political campaign, such as the one they are doing, [Mayor] Corral, [Vice Governor] Henn and company. That was how we built memory, from below, and with the conviction that so many deaths could have been avoided.

---

[209] In 2011, Santa Fe City was awarded the prestigious Sasakawa Award and appointed a Role Model City in the UN campaign "Making Cities Resilient: My City is Getting Ready" (United Nations International Strategy for Disaster Risk Reduction 2011a).

Figure 24 | Torches' March's post on Facebook (Screenshot by author 2013)

The picture posted on Facebook was taken on the flood embankment on April 29th, 2005. It took me a few seconds to realise that I had taken that photo and several others in the album. I recalled that after completing the first period of fieldwork in late 2005, I had indeed left with these interlocutors, in the spirit of maintaining fieldwork rapport, a CD-ROM with all my pictures from the activities of the *inundados* movement. These pictures, depicting the memory-work by the *inundados/activists* were initially taken for my own memory as field notes. The images were now used by the activists to remind others about their effort to remember. This way they could make the claim of having been the first and only to have undertaken this important task. My ethnography had turned into artefacts of remembrance, or devices of testimony, and was forming part of the Santafesinian flood memoryscape.

Bureaucratic practices and cycles of exclusion

Getting inside the Santafesinian bureaucracy was both easier and harder than I had imagined. On my first field trip to Santa Fe in July 2004, I had identified a list of people in the municipal and provincial government, who were responsible for disaster management in general and flood management in particular in Santa Fe City, whom I would like to interview upon my return to the city the following year. In March 2005 I began this endeavour. With the help of Germán, one of my key interlocutors, I was able to get in contact with one person I had previously identified, specifically in the area of the 2003 post-disaster public administration. One of the directors of the Unit had been a friend of Germán's since the 1970s. They had worked together as young militants for the Peronist Party. While Germán had long since left partisan politics, this *compañera* of his had advanced from partisan social work at grassroots' level to work as a civil servant in provincial government, more specifically in the Secretariat for Community Promotion, which was in charge of social development. Thus, after the 2003 flood she was appointed to manage the private compensation process that this provisional agency was partly designed for. Nevertheless, she had not forgotten about her old *compañeros* from the years of activism. Therefore, I presume, she accepted to meet with me that same week. By then I was encouraged and predicted that I would be able to make many interviews fairly soon. Yet I was proved wrong.

As I began to contact the other people on my list, I was asked by their secretaries to call back again and again, or to submit a formal letter of request. It took me several weeks to get many of the appointments. When I finally managed to get the interviews, I found that many of the interviewees were reluctant to talk about anything before their time in office. All the people I interviewed in 2005, except for three, had been appointed when the new government assumed office in December 2003. This meant that I was not able to ask them anything about the 2003 disaster or about any prior flood. When I asked the interviewee if he or she could give me the names and current positions of their predecessors, I was told that they had no idea what had become of them. A couple of interlocutors suggested, off the record, that giving me their names would be futile, because these people would probably not be willing to talk to me anyway given the deplorable disaster management the municipal and provincial governments had provided during *la Inundación*. In fact, when I tried to locate some of the officials whose names I could retrieve from the newspapers of the time of the 2003 disaster, I failed in all cases except one.

What I felt at the time was a methodological problem points to an interesting phenomenon, which seems to be of relevance to this analysis of remembering and forgetting in bureaucratic organisations. In Argentina, as in other countries (cf. Lundgren 2000), there is an established political practice that when a newly elected government assumes power, there is a considerable turnover of staff at all levels (municipal, provincial or national). People in politically appointed positions are exchanged as well as civil servants, because they too are identified with the former political leader, party or policy (cf. Frederic 2004). There is of course a natural staff turnover in every organisation everywhere, but the turnover in the public administration of Argentina represents a larger movement than can be accounted for by individual careers and pension retirements. New and fresh, or old but recycled, employees loyal to the new government are taken in as the new government assumes power. The discarded staff are simply removed or transferred to other less important positions within the administration. This practice is based on an asymmetrical yet reciprocal relationship and can be seen as part of a larger political phenomenon generally labelled "clientelism." Political clientelism in Latin America and in Argentina in particular, is a phenomenon so vastly studied in the social sciences that it has become something of a regional characteristic, close to a "gatekeeping concept" (Appadurai 1986). The analytical point of departure of political clientelism is more often than not a normative stance, that is, clientelism is inherently bad. Those political systems of which clientelism is part are often seen as morally inferior, not least from the perspective of societies where clientelism is less practiced. Such judgements indicate the intrinsic and deep relation between morality and politics (cf. Frederic

2004, 2005; Balbi 2007). As a pattern of relations between politicians and the citizens, clientelism is generally classified as populism. When it takes place within public administration it is often labelled corruption and nepotism, far from a normative Weberian ideal type of bureaucracy. An anthropological take on this however leaves the normative judgment aside in order to examine the meanings and effects of clientelism. The cyclical turnover of staff in Argentinian public administration raises interesting questions about political change, continuity, accountability and how this is related to memory and oblivion within organisations and in the public realm.

Guber (1999a) has suggested that the Argentinian past is of particular importance in the political struggle to define what the Argentinian Nation is, could have been and should be, as illustrated in the commemoration of the bicentenary in 2010 described in Chapter Two. This, argues Guber, locate processes of social remembering and forgetting at the centre of politics and the creation of the Nation State. She likens this struggle with a geological cataclysm (ibid.: 66), in which political periods are abruptly marked by forced exclusion of people and memories. This takes place not only at a discursive level but also within the State in the public administration. The former outgoing administration is regarded as a political enemy by the new administration, and this idea justifies the purge of staff, policies and symbols that can serve as reminders of the former. The new administration picks up and revitalises symbols and narratives from its own political legacies and predecessors, which have been buried in layers of the past, while forgetting, and making forget, those of the immediately preceding administration by in effect erasing both people and policies. The entering of a new administration and the beginning of a new political cycle is represented as a rupture with the former administration, which is why the boundaries to this must be clear (ibid.: 66-67). A pertinent historical example of this logic of omission was the pressure that the government exerted on all state employees (already employed or wanting to become one) to enrol in the Peronist Party, if they wanted to keep their jobs or get one (Balbi 2007). After Perón had been overthrown in 1955 by a military uprising, the so-called *Revolución Libertadora* (Liberating Revolution), the Peronist Party suffered proscription. Perón himself was forced to leave the country in exile and all Peronist symbols were prohibited by the new government, imposing societal and bureaucratic oblivion about that recent regime (Guber ibid.: 69-70). In order to establish a new administration and enable a fresh start, selected portions of the past needed to be purged, or in other words, omitted from memory.

Archives and the materialisation of selective remembering

In 2006, Jorge Obeid, the then sitting governor of the province of Santa Fe, issued a decree by which the Provincial Archive of Memory was created within the realm of the Secretariat of Human Rights (Gobierno de la Provincia de Santa Fe 2006b). Shortly thereafter I met with Fernando, one of my interlocutors who worked at the Secretariat. He had been a political prisoner during the dictatorship and, after his release, had been devoted to the cause of human rights in Santa Fe.

As we have seen in Chapter Two, the issue of human rights has been highly ranked on the national political agenda in the 21st century, but also in the provincial realm. In the Province of Santa Fe, the Secretariat of Human Rights was created in 2003. Among the many activities carried out at this secretariat, the most important was perhaps the promotion of trials of local military leaders for human rights violations during the dictatorship. Fernando was deeply involved in preparing for these trials as part of his tasks at work, but he also testified in some of them, having been a political prisoner himself.

When I met with him in 2008, he told me about the Memory Archive that had been established at the Secretariat. While he considered it important to reproduce the social memory about the Dirty War atrocities in Santa Fe, he was less enthusiastic about including other issues. He told me, quite annoyed on that occasion, that the *inundados* were to share the place of memory with the Dirty War *desaparecidos* in this public archive. The Memory Archive was to include not only documents from and about the Dirty War, but also material about *la Inundación* compiled by a specific committee. He clearly thought the two were not comparable in terms of violations of human rights and lamented that he was forced to let office space to staff that would collect material about the natural disaster instead of working on the memory of the Dirty War. Despite being a political activist in the Peronist Party which had "social justice" as its motto,[210] Fernando had little sympathy for the *inundados* movement and its claims. Maybe this was because he was actually working in the government, which was the target of the *inundados/activists*. He never told me what the reasons were. Ultimately, neither the *inundados* committee, nor the documentation about *la Inundación* was included in the Memory Archive. When I asked Fernando why this never materialised, he just replied that he didn't know, nor did he care.

Santafesinian archives

The archive is perhaps the most emblematic technology both of memory and for accountability. In fact, the archive is often used as a trope when conceptualising memory. The archive is where governance becomes the past objectified, as it is filed and classified. Archives are often associated with modern bureaucracy, just like the practice of filing and keeping documents (Dery 1998). Yet the practice of governing through documenting the past has a longer history. Ketelaar (2007) has suggested that there is no [political] power without archives. The modern aspect of the archive as an institution is its public character. Historians date the birth of the modern archive to July 25th, 1794, when the French National Archives were opened up and made public (Osborne 1999). The role of this institution in the making of the values of the French Republic, and its role for social memory, has been addressed by historians (Pomian 2010).

My own understanding of the archive in the bureaucracy as a public site of memory was put on trial during my fieldwork in Santa Fe as I pursued

---

[210] This is even included in its official name, which is the Justicialist Party (Partido Justicialista) appealing to the notion of social justice.

answers to my questions about disaster preparedness within the local public administration. More often than not, the civil servants that I interviewed replied that they had no knowledge about this or that issue because it concerned a period prior to their employment within the administration. I figured that if I could only access the municipal archive, I could find out about past policies and regulations myself. Yet nobody was willing to help me gain access to the archive. It only later became clear to me that there was no neat archive for me to visit. Presumably there had once been a municipal archive, but in 2005, documents and files were stored in boxes and drawers here and there in the different departments of the municipality. I was told that they had been ruined by damp while standing in the basement of the municipal building. In combination with oblivious civil servants, the municipal past seemed to have passed into the terrain of forgetting. This situation changed however when Mario Barletta assumed power as the new Mayor of the Municipality of Santa Fe in December of 2007.

Barletta had been the head of the National University of the Littoral in 2003. When he was elected mayor, he set out to modernise the municipal administration in a more transparent vein. One way of doing this was to establish an archive, a Centre for Documentation (Gobierno de la Ciudad de Santa Fe 2008b). This included the digitalisation of documents and to provide open access to all documents from 2003 and onwards from the municipality's web site (Gobierno de la Ciudad de Santa Fe 2008a). This electronic service was operating fairly well in 2012, especially in terms of accessing municipal legislation. Yet all that seems transparent is not necessarily so. To access documents regarding particular proceedings, the applicant had to download a form, fill it in and submit it personally at the registrar's office. Even if the municipal archive was set up to enhance democratisation and public administration (in contrast to the Memory Archive of the Provincial Government discussed above, which was created akin to a museum), the archive was far from being accessible to everybody. Furthermore, it was not evident which documents had been cleared for open access, and which had not. This illustrates that as much as there is no political power without a public archive, there is no public archive without politics (Osborne 1999). Even if an archive is public (as opposed to private), it is not necessarily accessible to the public. In this sense, the archive can be thought of as materialising the logic of omission because it is a selection of what is to be saved, hence remembered, and what can be discarded and thereby forgotten. Another aspect of the virtual archive, in which documents are digitalised, is that it implies a certain degree of technological vulnerability. A computer virus, a software bug or a power outage poses the risk of passing memory into oblivion in a twinkle. There will be further discussion about electronic documents, technology and memory later in this chapter.

The Memory Archive was equally subject to the logic of omission. In 2012, I found that numerous legal documents involved in the so-called *Causa Inundación*, the lawsuits against the public administration regarding the 2003 disaster, had been published in a digital archive on the website of the Provincial Government of Santa Fe, more specifically on the site of the State Attorney. The reason for this was explained as follows:

In relation to Decree 0692/2009 (regulating the mechanisms of Access to Public Information), the State Attorney of the Province of Santa Fe decided to make available to the public, permanently and in digital format, all relevant and available documentation in regard to the lawsuits of the 2003 flooding. This measure is a response to the claim of a number of citizens affected by the water catastrophe to the State Prosecutor and [which] was advised [to follow] by Dictum 0076:2011, implemented by Resolution 26-11, and ratified by Governmental Decree 2812/2011 (Gobierno de la Provincia de Santa Fe 2011).

Having followed the case and knowing about the problems of the plaintiffs among *the inundados/activists* in gaining access to the files of the investigation, this decision seemed like a mayor achievement for them. I became curious to know who these "number of citizens" behind the claim had been. Gabriel, one of my key informants among the activists, confirmed to me in a long e-mail what I had imagined, namely that it had been the activists in the *inundados* protest movement who had presented this claim:

From: Gabriel
To: Susann Ullberg
Tuesday, 12 June 2012, 1:22
Where do I start? . . . When [Governor to be] Binner was campaigning [in 2007], he met with [us] the *inundados/activists* and promised that he would cooperate with the plaintiffs [in the civil case], providing us with the documentation which had not yet been made public . . . Obviously, this collaboration was in exchange for our support for his candidacy (at least vote for him). When Binner assumed office [in December 2007], "*le pasamos la factura,*"[211] that is, we asked him to open the archives of the provincial government for us to search for any information relevant to the legal process. That's when the troubles began. Our interlocutor was the state attorney. Basically what he said was that he by no means could provide us with information that later would become evidence against the province, because for him to do this would be a case of misconduct as a public servant. We [the *inundados/activists*] argued that this information was public [and that they would have to publish it] The thing is that we never agreed and in the meantime we found out, by [Governor] Binner himself, that at the same time as he was negotiating with us and promising us support in the court case, he was negotiating the appointment of ministers in his cabinet with [former Governor and at this time Senator] Reutemann. You can imagine our insults [against Binner] when we found out about this! Amid all this, the [activists of] the March began to demand that the state attorney publish the docu-

---

[211] The literal translation to English is "We passed him the bill," meaning that it was payback time for the governor.

mentation related to the lawsuits on the [attorney's] website. That's what you found posted. I had already provided you with many of these documents or they are posted on the website of the House [of Human Rights]. Other, from what I saw today when I checked, are not really relevant. And of course, the really important documents, which caused the conflict with the state attorney, are not there.

What Gabriel was unaware of (and what Fernando was ignorant of too, or was just unwilling to tell me) was that this selection of documents, related to the lawsuits had in fact been incorporated to the Memory Archive, as publicly stated on the government's website. According to Gabriel, this documentation was nevertheless incomplete, missing important information and hence constituting a skewed institutional memory or a memory that would benefit the government in future hindsight. Here we have an illustration of how the logic of omission governs the politics of the archive. An exacerbated historical analogy of this phenomenon in the Argentinian context was one of the last laws issued by the military regime, the so-called Pacification Law (*Ley de Pacificación Nacional* 1983). This act pursued amnesty for the militaries involved in any action of fight against political subversion in 1976-83. In support of this law, a presidential decree determined that all documents relevant to the regime's detention of people carried out in the framework of the Process of National Reorganisation and under the §23 of the National Constitution, which regulates the possibility of declaring state of siege, should be declared missing from the archives or destroyed (Torres Molina 2008). The detainees referred to had by then already been murdered by the regime in most cases. In view of a forthcoming democratisation, the military regime considered that they could never be held accountable for this crime if the documentary traces of these actions and the people involved disappeared. By discarding all documents, amnesia and thereby amnesty would be achieved. What is gathered, filed, authorised, certified, classified and made public (or not), and hence remembered or forgotten, is always a matter of evaluation, negotiation and decision (Lynch 1999).

Public infrastructure of memory and oblivion

Numerous public works and physical facilities in Santa Fe City and its surroundings are related to the historical relationship between the fluvial environment and the urban community. Some of them, the works of development, have created vulnerability to flooding while others, the works of defence, have in principle served to mitigate such risks. The exception to the latter was the 2003 disaster. As I have explained, on this occasion the Westside flood embankments worked as walls containing the waters that flooded the city. From the perspective of the logic of omission, one can see these works of infrastructure as artefacts that make both memory and oblivion. On the one hand, they operate as cues for remembering past disasters. Particular places and artefacts constitute material historical traces of such past events at the same time as they operate evocatively to remind us of these events. On the other hand, some of these works of infrastructure are techniques to control hazardous forces, and are sometimes described as creating false security. In this context it is possible to say that they promote the oblivion of risk.

Works of development, works of risk

The city's economic and demographic growth in the late 19th century and early 20th century accelerated the process of urbanisation and occupation of the flood-plain, both within the city limits and in its surroundings. In 1886 the first railroad line from Santa Fe to the harbour in Colastiné on the shores of the Paraná River was built (Paoli and Schreider 2000). A new overseas harbour was later built in the city centre and was inaugurated in 1910. The dredging of the Santa Fe Creek due to this major public works project left a large embankment right in front of the harbour where the suburb of Alto Verde would develop. In the first decades of the 20th century, the suspension bridge at the outlet of the Setúbal Lagoon was built as a viaduct to bring potable water from Colastiné to Santa Fe (Mino 1998:397). The viaduct suspension bridge was inaugurated in 1928. In those years, close to where this bridge was being built, the first example of a public park took shape in Santa Fe. This was the small park Parque Oroño, which was situated on elevated ground on the shores of the channel leading to the harbour. From the park an avenue and an esplanade were built, both of which were extended northwards in the late 20th century. Both the park and the esplanade served aesthetical and recreational purposes, at least for the wealthy families in the city (Collado 2007). They also served the purpose of flood prevention, having refilled land, elevated ground and reinforced walls and embankments.

Figure 25 | Fountain in Parque Oroño with the *Puente Colgante* bridge ca. 1960 (Photo courtesy Archivo General de la Provincia de Santa Fe-Hemeroteca-Fototeca)

Outside the city, the National Route 168, which runs between Santa Fe City and the entrance to the subfluvial tunnel leading to the city of Paraná, was built in 1936. A couple of years later, the so-called *Camino de la Costa* (Coastside Road), which was later named Provincial Route Nr. 1, was built partly on the embankments from the small town of La Guardia, east of Santa Fe City. Later this road was extended to the city of Reconquista in the neighbouring province of el Chaco.

The floodplain on the Westside was also increasingly urbanised, although not in recreational terms as on the Eastside. Several bridges were built to connect Santa Fe City southwards, crossing the Salado River. The first of them were the three bridges built in the 19th century for the railways leading to Buenos Aires. On the side of Santa Fe City, railways were built on the top of embankments running parallel to the river. These embankments enclosed flood-prone lowland that was partially refilled, which made it attractive to real estate speculation and increased the number of so-called spontaneous settlements in the form of shantytowns. Bridges in wood or iron crossed the Salado River between Santa Fe City and the town of Santo Tomé as can be observed in photographs from the early 20th century. These bridges were later replaced by others built in reinforced concrete. The first was the *Puente Carretero* between the town of Santo Tomé and Santa Fe, which was inaugurated in 1939. The bridge to the provincial highway AP01 running between Santa Fe City and the city of Rosario was inaugurated in 1972 (Mino 1998:576).

The public works built in the floodplain shaped the urban landscape of Santa Fe City and its surroundings. While some of them protected areas from being flooded as land was refilled and ground elevated, the occupation of the floodplain simultaneously constituted an obstacle to the flow of the rivers. This has throughout the 20th century generated repeated destruction of infrastructure. Old pictures show how the railway bridge crossing the Setúbal Lagoon was seriously damaged by enormous chunks of water plants, sticks and reeds in the 1926 flood. This bridge was later abandoned and left to collapse. The very construction of the suspension bridge, the esplanade and the Parque Oroño was delayed because of the 1905 flood, which actually destroyed much of the works in progress, which then had to be rebuilt (Mino 1998; Collado 2007). The Paraná River floods of 1959, 1961, 1966 and 1977 caused serious damage to the highways northeast of the city (Paoli and Schreider 2000). That of 1966 destroyed the Parque Oroño and provoked severe erosion in several parts of both of the highways involved and threatened to destroy further infrastructure in Santa Fe City. Hence, in order to release pressure on the suspension bridge, the provincial government, with the support of the national government, decided to open up sections of the National Route 168 by blasting it.

The suspension bridge finally collapsed in the flood of 1982/83. While the Parque Oroño was some years later built over with a road junction and was only remembered as a park by the older of my interlocutors, the suspension bridge was rebuilt, although not until 2001. The 1982-83 flood also caused the destruction of several bridges over National Route 168. This destruction affected the entire drinking water and sewage systems of Santa Fe City as pipes and bridges carrying the pipes were destroyed (Paoli and Schreider 2000). The impact of the Paraná River floods in 1992 and 1998 was less on infrastructure while coastal communities were harshly affected (ibid.). On the Westside, the railway bridges were repeatedly subject to damage in times of flooding, both of the Salado River and of the Paraná River. The bridge of the highway that was inaugurated in 1972 was destroyed only one year later, in the Salado River flood in June 1973. This bridge was rebuilt in the years following. Unfortunately, its design was not reconsidered and it was rebuilt with the exact same dimensions. This proved to be a fatal mistake. Again in 2003, the bridge obstructed the flow of the flooding river which forced the water in to the city instead. This significantly contributed to the impact of the 2003 disaster (Bacchiega, Bertoni, and Maza 2005b:11).

Works of defence

Among the public works in the flood plain are the ones specifically created for the purpose of flood control and mitigation. One increasingly common mitigative strategy is the implementation of warning systems. The River Plate basin, of which the Paraná River is part, has been monitored through hydrometric and sensor technology since the mid-1980s. According to staff at the National Water Institute this was established following the severe floods of the Paraná River in 1982/1983. A Hydrological Warning Operative Centre was set up and the operation was entrusted to what was then called the National Institute of Hydrological Science and Technology (today the National Water Institute). Since its establishment, the River Plate basin warning system[212] improved its methods and forecasts, enhancing the response to different floods in the basin and also to ebb. The latter was of particular interest to the port activities in relation to river navigation. For this reason, the system also included forecasts of drought.

The Salado River Basin had also been monitored. In the context of the research carried out on the ecosystems of the Paraná and the Salado Rivers, the National Limnological Institute located in Santa Fe, had several sites of study. One of these was located at the outlet of the Salado River in between Santa Fe City and the town of Santo Tomé. Here, the current water level of the river was also registered. In 1978, during the military regime, the National Water Institute set up several hydrometric stations in different places along the river to measure water levels. These stations replaced the ones which since 1928 had been operated by another national agency, namely the National Directorate of Port Constructions and Navegable Routes, but which had ceased to operate in the 1970s (Paoli and Goniadzki 2003:15). Due to financial constraints in the context of the Argentinian hyperinflation in the late 1980s, only one of the five hydro-

---

[212] The Systems of Hydrological Information and Warning is managed by the National Water Institute. Its main objective is to develop and operate the hydrological forecasting and warning service for the River Plate Basin and to coordinate information and documentation around these water resources (Instituto Nacional del Agua 2012).

metric stations of the National Water Institute was left in 1988. This was located in the town of Esperanza upstream 30 kilometres north of Santa Fe City. In comparison then, the Paraná River has throughout the last decades received constant institutional attention while the Salado River was largely left unattended since the late 1980s. In 2003, the only device left to forecast the disaster was insufficient. Hence, any warning system created to remind the governmental institutions about the risk for flooding from this river had been omitted.

In addition to warning systems as a means of protection, there are works of what Birkland calls "project mitigation" (2010:109). These refer to any physical construction or material gadgets to reduce or avoid possible impacts of hazards, which include engineering measures and construction of hazard-resistant and protective structures and infrastructure. In Santa Fe there were channels, embankments, reservoirs and water pump stations, constituting a system of defence against fluvial and pluvial flooding. The actual flood mitigation system of Santa Fe City began to be built in the 1930s, beginning with the so-called Irigoyen Embankment.[213] According to some of my interlocutors, the purpose of this public work was not to protect dwellers in this area from being flooded, but rather to gain land in the context of increased urbanisation and the real estate market's demand for land. By building the embankment, the lowland could be filled out and built on. Nevertheless this embankment served as a flood mitigation device. The embankment joined the road that lead to the bridge crossing the river to Santo Tomé, and reached northwards from the place called Cuatro Bocas on the Southwest Side. It ended in a juncture with the railway embankment of the Belgrano Railway, close to the neighbourhood of Villa del Parque and the Parque Garay park. While the embankment protected this district from flooding, paradoxically it also constituted an obstruction for the rain water to drain back to the river. Hence, drainage channels and water reservoirs were built to solve this problem.

Later, in the 1970s, pumping stations were built to pump out excessive water back to the river. Three pumps were established along the Irigoyen Embankment and one north of the levee. In the wake of the severe 1991-92 floods, the World Bank financed a large flood protection project.[214] The project was ambitions and consisted of the rehabilitation of damaged infrastructure and housing, but was also focused on the future by providing technical assistance to strengthen and improve the capacity of institutions responsible for project implementation, flood forecasting and increasing flood control works in the affected provinces. The Provincial Government of Santa Fe at the time decided to invest most of the money in infrastructure, that is, project mitigation. In Santa Fe, another six pump stations were built around the city. On the Coastside and on the city's eastern side, existing embankments were reinforced by concrete blocks and geo-textiles to withstand erosion. New embankments were also built with these

---

[213] The *Terraplén Irigoyen*.
[214] The World Bank's five-year project "Flood Rehabilitation Project (Loan 3521-AR)" involved a loan of USD170.0 million to mitigate the damages from the floods in 1991-92 which created USD905 million in economic losses in the seven littoral provinces of Argentina, namely Buenos Aires, el Chaco, Corrientes, Entre Rios, Formosa, Misiones and Santa Fe (World Bank 1999).

materials. On the western side, the flood defence works were combined with a road work with additional funding.[215] The Irigoyen Embankment was reinforced and extended, both in height and in length, even if only built with stones and compacted soil. Drainage channels and reservoirs were built along the new embankment. The new section of the embankment spanned from where the Irigoyen Embankment ended (between the neighbourhoods of Santa Rosa de Lima and Villa del Parque) to the slip road of the Santa Fe-Rosario highway and further up north, almost reaching the hippodrome and the golf course.

Figure 26 | Westside flood embankment, the Salado River and the ring road (Photo by author 2005)

In the embankment building project, it was planned that from the hippodrome it would be extended all the way to the town of Recreo, 17 kilometres north of Santa Fe City. This part was to be built in a third and final phase of the construction process; however, it was never carried out. While the embankment was inaugurated officially in 1997, as mentioned in Chapter Four, this equally vital part of the flood protection works was never even budgeted for in the following years. Other pressing issues were on the political agenda and the third section forgotten. Meanwhile, the second section of the embankment ended abruptly, leaving a breach of fifteen metres between the end of it and higher ground. In the case of flooding, a provisional closure had to be provided for, until the building of the third section. When the Paraná River flooded in 1998, the outlet of the Salado River also flooded and the entire Westside was at risk. The municipality then carried out a provisional closure by placing stones and sandbags in the breach (Marcucci 2004:25).

       This was not the case in April 2003 however. While it had been evident to technicians, decision makers and inhabitants, months and weeks prior

---

[215] The ring road was built with a credit issued by the Government of Kuwait to the Provincial Government (Marcucci 2004:23).

to the disaster that this could cause a major flood, neither provincial nor municipal authorities decided to carry out this closure until it was too late. Not until April 28th, when the water was already flowing into the city through this gap, did the municipality send excavators to tap it. This was a futile effort however. As floodwater gushed into the city, the embankment eroded quickly. The speed of destruction of the embankment had to do with the fact that on the western side of the city the embankment consisted of compacted soil and not concrete as on the eastern side. The breach in the embankment, originally fifteen metres wide, was soon a hundred meter wide. The water pumps were sized to extract water due to excessive rain but hardly the amounts of a flooding river. Furthermore, the pumps were badly maintained and hence malfunctioning, and they quickly overheated and stopped working. The embankments contained the water akin to a city wall. Some lowland places on the Westside were covered with five to seven meters of water. In the wake of the 2003 disaster, the fact that the Westside embankment had been incomplete was on everybody's lips.

As described in preceding chapters, this caused major indignation among the city's inhabitants, not least those directly affected. Several independent inquiries concluded that had the embankments been properly built, the disaster would not have occurred at all, or at least, it would have been of less magnitude (Bronstein et al. 2003:163) or delayed (Bacchiega, Bertoni and Maza 2005c:17). By the time of my fieldwork, the embankment gap had been closed. As I visited the place, it was difficult for me to imagine such a gap. Had it not been for the photographs and the videos from the 2003 disaster that I watched, and for the memory-work carried out there by *inundados/victims* and *inundados/activists*, it would have been even more difficult for me to imagine *la Inundación*, given that the physical marks of the gap were no longer there.

In the years that followed, this was how things remained, until 2008 when there was a change in government. When I returned to Santa Fe that year, the works with the so-called third section of flood embankments on the Westside and Northwest Side were intensively underway. The new provincial government, under the power of Hermes Binner from the Socialist Party, undertook the building of the so-called third section of the Westside embankment from the hippodrome all the way to the town of Recreo, including the continuation of the ring road,[216] and additional flood defence works such as channels, flood gates and reservoirs. The existing embankments on the Westside and on the Eastside, as well as the Coastside, which had been dimensioned for a 100-year flood were now reinforced and made higher to withstand a 1,000-year flood.[217] For the Westside embankments, this reinforcement implied the application of the same techniques that had been used on the Eastside and the Coastside, that is, geotextile blankets and concrete blocks that better resist erosion.

---

[216] The *Circunvalación Oeste* (Westside ring road) nowadays runs between the National Route 11 and the Provincial Route 70. The latter begins in the town of Recreo and ends in the town of Coronel Fraga.
[217] A 100-year flood is calculated to be the level of flood water expected to be equalled or exceeded every 100 years on average. Similarly, a flood level expected to be equalled or exceeded every 10 years on average is known as a 10-year flood and one every 1,000 years is called a 1,000-year flood.

By 2012 Santa Fe City was becoming an almost completely enclosed urban space through the flood embankments. These and other works of defence against flooding constitute material aspects of the local flood memoryscape in several ways. Connerton's (2009) argument that modern technology promotes forgetting about natural phenomena such as the river and the risk for flooding seems to be only partially true. The public works of defence carried out in the 1990s and in the 2000s aimed at controlling the effects of hazardous forces. This policy promoted the oblivion of risk, most notably epitomised on April 29th, 2003, when the provisory or neglected piece of embankment brutally reminded the people of Santa Fe that the risk remained. Yet, the landscape of defence was simultaneously a reminder to urban residents about past disasters as much as future risks. People had thought they were safe. It was therefore an unpleasant surprise to the urban citizens to learn that provincial and municipal institutions had not acted properly in line with legislation and electoral promises to safeguard them.

Flood control technologies can be seen as inherent to the "risk society" (Beck 1992), that is, as means of taming a hazardous and threatening nature. It can also be regarded as an index of changing modes of governance, which aim at regulating the public space (Harvey 2010). The quality of a government is judged by way of its achievements. Among the most tangible outputs to the eyes of the citizenry are infrastructures such as roads, dams and bridges, for which concrete is the preferred material in modern states because it is cheap and malleable, and above all enduring (ibid.). In a post-disaster context such as that of Santa Fe City, the investment in infrastructural development was politically significant. Urban residents (and voters) had such expectations, even if such expectations were also imbued with distrust. On the Facebook page about the 10th anniversary of *la Inundación* described earlier, a thread of conversation started in support of Laura's statement against the governmental intentions to commemorate the disaster. One of these posts said:

> Keep the memory alive [ha!] . . . [T]hey [the municipal and provincial governments] haven't even finished the infrastructure we need in order to be protected from floods!

This comment illustrates the prevailing lack of trust among the *inundados/activists* in particular, and among Santafesinos or even Argentinians in general, in the capacities of public officials to achieve safety and in governmental willingness to invest in this area, even in hindsight of the effects of *la Inundación*. Yet, similar to the faith put in the use of concrete in works of development (because they lodge promises of progress, strength and stability), flood control technologies have "an enduring appeal" (Harvey 2010:37).

In the context of memory, the endurance of modern infrastructure is a key feature. This enables them to be seen as monuments of governance, and of particular government officials. Infrastructural works stand for state power and useful spending of public money. In addition, particular works of infrastructure correspond to particular governments. Thus, ceremonial inaugurations are undertaken and plaques, stating the name of the governor or mayor and the date of inauguration, are normally placed somewhere on the work, in order to recall over time which particular government was the author of it.

In the case of Santafesinian flood control, the then Governor Jorge Obeid and his predecessor (and successor), Carlos Reutemann, and a number of other public officials were present when the unfinished Westside embankment was officially inaugurated by cutting the ribbon in 1997. The image from this ceremony was the one used in the poster referred to in Chapter Four, which was made by the *inundados/activists* to point to the boldness of the decision makers of celebrating an unfinished work that had become a trap to the people flooded in 2003. Fifteen years later, in 2012, the Governor Antonio Bonfatti and his staff of the Socialist Party, and representatives of the municipal government, inaugurated the finally finished third section of the embankment and the ring road cutting the light blue and white strap (*El Litoral* 2012a). In this setting, municipal and provincial legislators proposed that the ring road deserved a new and a more distinguished name. Their proposal was to name it after the former president Raúl Alfonsín, who came to symbolise democracy in Argentina when in 1983 he became the first elected president following the last military dictatorship. Alfonsín had passed away in 2009. The 30th anniversary of democracy celebrated this year was an opportunity to render both Alfonsín and democracy a place in the Santafesinian memory. As described in Chapter Four, the *inundados/activists* objected to this proposal, arguing that the ring road could not be named anything else but "April 29th," thereby contesting the official logic of omission. The choice of the politicians nevertheless illustrates the resonance of local memory-making within the larger context of politics of regret in Argentina, in which the memory of the Dirty War and the advent of democracy was dominant. It also echoes the Santafesinian governmental amnesia regarding the ambiguous commemoration of *la Inundación*, as accounted for above. The logic of omission in the Santafesinian bureaucracy seemed to be operating rather in favour of other past events that had less at stake in the local context and in the present.

Law and memory

There were a number of federal and provincial laws and decrees, as well as municipal regulations, which ruled how disasters in general and flooding in particular, were to be managed by the government in Santa Fe. Law as a form of social ordering or enforceable norms, has long been an object of anthropological study,[218] yet it remains a rather marginal field within the larger anthropological enterprise (Riles 2006; Moore 2007). Durkheim, from a sociological vantage point and in his concern with social solidarity, connected law to [collective] memory (1984). On the one hand he saw modern law like "traditional custom," as the past codified and a historical product. On the other hand he saw the instrumentality of law to [collective] memory, which in turn was instrumental in the creation of social cohesion. This view of law and memory as reciprocal has been developed

---

[218] For an overview of law as an anthropological object of study, see Moore (2007).

by later sociologists, for example by seeing judicial procedures such as trials, not only to be historical products but, in a more presentist vein, as theatres of history writing. The various truth and reconciliation commissions that have been established in several countries in the wake of authoritarian and violent regimes, such as in Argentina (see Chapter Two), are telling of this way of forging social remembering about a violent past (cf. Wilson 2001; Shaw 2007). In the same way, key legal documents such as national constitutions are at the core of the foundational myths of many nation states, as Misztal points out (2003:132). Yet, I see legislation as more than just constituting collective memory, as Durkheim would have it, but rather as the outcome of a situated political process and thus as containing both institutional memory and oblivion. In the legislative process, certain ideas and opinions are excluded and not visible in the final bill. They thus risk being forgotten. Furthermore legislation can and often does change over time. Even national constitutions are amended every now and then.

In Argentina in particular, a more complex view of law as a dialectical struggle of memory and oblivion becomes even more relevant in line with the reasoning of Guber (1999a). She speaks of a turbulent continuous process of turnovers in the public sector of Argentina. Like in other presidential regimes the rule by decree, more than by parliamentary legislative practices, is a legitimate governance practice in this country. In addition, since the inception of the Argentinian State in the early 19th century, the country has lived through several long periods of non-democratic government, when authoritarian rule by decree has been applied. Rule by decree allows the ruler to arbitrarily create law, without approval by a legislative assembly. As Agamben (2005) has pointed out, the state of exception is a rule by decree through which governments legitimise their own noncompliance with or suspension of existing laws. This can be seen as an institutionalised form of oblivion in line with the logic of omission.[219] In the case of Santa Fe, two things are noteworthy regarding legislation. One is that the current national and provincial legislation that regulates the public administrative roles and responsibilities of disaster management in Santa Fe follows a military legacy in the form of a hierarchical "command and control" structure.[220] The other is the constitutional possibility (in federal and provincial constitutions alike) of declaring a state of emergency. I will now describe in more details this legal space of memory and oblivion.

Risk reduction and regulation in Argentina

Article 2339 of the Argentinian Civil Code from 1871 establishes that public goods are the property of the Federal State or of the particular Provincial States

---

[219] This can be connected to the ideas of Hobbes who held that amnesia is a cornerstone of the social contract between citizens and government (Lowenthal 2001) and of Benjamin who claimed that states of emergency were the rule, not the exception (Fassin och Pandolfi 2010:22).

[220] "Command and control" refers in a military organisation to the exercise of authority by a commanding officer over assigned forces of soldiers to accomplish a mission. In organisational management, the concept refers more generally to the maintenance of authority with somewhat more distributed decision making. In the world of disasters, a so-called Incident Command System (ICS) consists of a standard management hierarchy and procedures for managing temporary incident(s) of any size. The latter is a worldwide institutional practice with origins in the USA of the 1970s.

of which this is composed, according to the distribution of powers established in the Argentinian Constitution. Article 2340 states that among such public goods are the rivers, streams, and waters. Hence, in the Federal State of Argentina the rivers are the responsibility of the provincial domain at all times, flooding or not.

As in many countries around the world, disaster management in terms of civil protection in Argentina was early on the responsibility of the military.[221] In 1968 this responsibility was passed from the Armed Forces to the Ministry of Defence and the Directorate of Civil Defence was created. The severe earthquake in the town of Caucete in the northeast of Argentina in 1977 for the first time seriously put this organisation to work. The return of democracy in 1983 implied the beginning of a process of demilitarisation of Argentinian civil defence (ibid.: 4). This was symbolically expressed by changing its focus from "defence" to "protection." In 1996, during the second public administration reform in Argentina, the civil defence organisation was reorganised as the National Directorate for Planning and Civil Protection and fell under the Ministry of Interior. After the disastrous flooding of the Paraná River in 1998, which affected most northeastern provinces, including Santa Fe, the Federal Emergency System (SIFEM) was created. The purpose was to coordinate planning and administration of federal, provincial and local mitigation resources (Zagalsky 2004; Celis et al. 2009). This initiative was due to the pressure from the Inter-American Development Bank in exchange for a USD 300 million loan to support reconstruction of public transportation, housing and infrastructure in six affected provinces (Inter-American Development Bank 1998:12). Yet, the SIFEM has never been operative in any of the disasters that have occurred since the time of its inception (Román 2013). Since 2007 both SIFEM and the National Directorate for Civil Protection has been the responsibility of the Secretariat of Provinces within the Ministry of Interior (Celis et al. 2009:13). None of these agencies were in effect involved in the disaster management of the 2003 flood of the Salado River. It has been claimed that had SIFEM been developed as planned, the 2003 disaster would have been of much lesser impact in Santa Fe City (Zagalsky 2004). The only federal support to the affected areas consisted basically in the then sitting president, Eduardo Duhalde's declaration of a State of Emergency in the affected provinces. The latter made possible the allocation of funds for attending to disaster victims and reconstruction of the affected provinces of Santa Fe and Entre Rios.

Legislation regarding flood management in Santa Fe

In the wake of *la Inundación*, an amendment was made of the provincial Ministries' Act (*Ley Orgánica de Ministerios* 2003). This bill created the Ministry of

---

[221] This dates back to the 1940s with the creation of the Air Defence Command and the Passive Defence Division and the establishment of general measures designed to limit risk and reduce the effects of any enemy attack against people, property, wealth and sources of production within the country (Barrenechea and Natenzon 1997). In this context, military authorities should attend the effects of natural disasters with the same systems and procedures that had been created to reduce the possible effects of enemy bombings on the country.

Water Affairs[222] and stated that this ministry was responsible for assisting the provincial government formulating water policies within the provincial jurisdiction (§2.4) and for implementing measures for flood prevention, coastal defence and control, and regulating all activities that may take place in flood-prone areas that correspond to the territory of the province (§2.6). This was not only the responsibility of the provincial government however. The responsibilities of the local municipalities are regulated in the provincial Organic Law of Municipalities (*Ley Orgánica de Las Municipalidades* 1939), which establishes that the Town Council is responsible for preventing flooding, fires and collapses (§39.33), while the mayor is responsible for taking all necessary measures to prevent disasters in order to protect and maintain the health and the well-being of the population (§41.24).

Another law that specifically regulates disaster management in the province of Santa Fe is the Civil Defence Act (*Ley de Defensa Civil* 1977). This Act establishes the responsibilities of the provincial and of the municipal governments as well as those of all NGOs, private companies and citizens, in case of emergency. Key in this bill was the creation of a provincial Civil Defence Board that shall assess regional and local decision makers and a Directorate of Civil Defence to work out the policies for disaster management. The provincial Civil Defence Act states clearly that the governor has the responsibility to see that civil defence policies are developed in connection with national policies. This includes emergency planning and the establishment of early warning systems. It also includes the ability to declare a state of emergency in parts or the totality of the territory.

The mayor has the same authority and obligations when it comes to the municipal jurisdiction, including the establishment of a Municipal Civil Defence Board. In Santa Fe City, this had been established in a municipal regulation (*Ordenanza Municipal Sobre Defensa Civil* 1976).[223] For the organisation of disaster management in Argentina, the principle of proximity is here legally established, meaning that a disaster should be managed as close to the affected citizens as possible. This implies that within the hierarchy of responsibilities, the mayor is first in charge when a disaster occurs. In case the event surpasses the capacity of the municipality, the provincial government is obliged to assist. In the last instance the national government has to provide assistance.

Governmental amnesia and judicial amnesty during *la Inundación*

Having described the institutional and legal structures that frame disaster management responsibilities in Santa Fe, let us now take a look at the ways in which these materialised in the 2003 disaster, or more specifically, how the processes of meaning-making around these issues took place in the public arena. This will

---

[222] A new amendment of this act changed this ministry for the Ministry of Waters, Public Services and Environment (*Ley de Ministerios* 2007).
[223] This regulation was later amanded by the town council as part of the development of a new disaster preparedness policy in the municipality (*Ordenanza Municipal: Creación de La Junta Municipal de Defensa Civil* 2000; *Ordenanza Municipal: Creación Del Sistema de Defensa Civil* 2005).

show how governmental amnesia was contested yet simultaneously reinforced by a selective distribution of amnesty to responsible individuals.

The municipal and provincial governments in Santa Fe argued from day one that the 2003 flood had been a natural disaster, with an emphasis on natural. The rains had been extraordinary that month and were suggested to be connected to global climate change without specifying how exactly this affected local weather. Therefore, the governor and the mayor argued, nobody could have foreseen a disaster of this magnitude. As the river was flooding the city, the mayor in a radio broadcast asked for calm and solidarity. He underscored that this was a completely atypical event, unexpected and unimaginable to everybody, and added: "Long timers tell me that this has not occurred in the Salado River for some fifty, sixty or seventy years."

Political leaders and officials in Santa Fe thus placed responsibility for the disaster on "nature's unpredictability." Furthermore, by the authorities' habit of systematically naming the disaster an *emergencia hídrica* (water emergency) or *fenómeno hídrico* (water phenomenon) in official speeches as well as in legislation and policy documents, *la Inundación* was framed in a discourse that naturalised flooding by focusing on the natural hazard. In a number of press conferences during the acute phase, the governor repeatedly sidestepped pressing questions from local reporters who wondered how disaster preparedness could have been so poor. Reutemann denied any knowledge about the risks. He insisted that "nobody had informed him," a statement that became infamous through the memory-work of the *inundados/victims* and *inundados/activists* (see Chapter Four). In one press conference he replied in a clearly annoyed fashion to the question of a journalist about past projects to regulate the Salado River:

> There is no project [to regulate] the Salado River! Bring it and show me such a project if you can find one! The only thing we know in this town about flooding comes from someone sticking down a peg in the ground saying "The water reached up to here [last time the city was flooded]!"

By appealing to the "naturalness" and "unpredictability" of the hazard, the political decision makers evaded the legal, political and moral responsibility for the flaws of their own performance prior to, during and after the disaster. Yet in the weeks, months and years following the disaster, information about the deficiencies in preparedness successively became public knowledge. Serious omissions made by municipal and provincial authorities, such as not building the third and final section of the Westside flood embankments, in combination with a number of other administrative flaws such as the lack of monitoring of the Salado River and the lack of a municipal contingency plan revealed that existing civil defence legislation in Argentina and in the Province of Santa Fe had not been followed. No actions had been taken to prevent or mitigate disasters of this kind in spite of being a historical problem. Despite extraordinary rains and reported high river levels upstream in those days of April 2003, politicians and public officials seemed to have been more preoccupied with the political campaign and the presidential elections on Sunday, April 27th.

Yet the official stance of denying any knowledge of the risk for flooding did not stand unchallenged for long. The statements of the governor and other official declarations made the entire staff at the Hydrological Faculty at the National University of the Littoral go through the roof. Barletta, who was later elected as mayor, was at the time the vice-chancellor of the university and a professor at the mentioned faculty. He called for a press conference in which he gave an account of all the studies on the risk of flooding in the city that had been carried out by this university and others since the 1990s. Many of these studies had in fact been commissioned by the provincial government.

Another crucial evaluation, contesting the governmental standpoint of the unpredictability of the flooding, was the independent technical inquiry commissioned by the Provincial Court prosecutor in the lawsuit referred to as *Causa Inundación*. As described in Chapter Four, this involved a couple of *inundados/activists*. What had started out as a number of legal denunciations shortly after the 2003 disaster, turned into a year-long judicial process. Twelve civil servants from the municipal and the provincial public administration were eventually called to hearings in the provincial court in 2005 by the appointed judge. He finally reached the conclusion that only three of these[224] were imputable for "culpable havoc,"[225] which is the judicial term for causing a catastrophe due to negligence. In this case it was aggravated by the death of 23 people. The judge dismissed virtually all the evidence presented by the plaintiffs, on the basis of his own inquiry and established that only these three public officials could be subject to lawsuit.

Some of the *inundados/activists* had as plaintiffs demanded that more politicians should also be tried and called to testify in court. The principal politicians they had in mind were the former governors Reutemann and Obeid. This claim was refused both in the Provincial Supreme Court (Corte Suprema de la Provincia de Santa Fe and Corte Suprema de la Nación de la República Argentina 2007; *Página/12* 2008) and in the National Supreme Court (Corte Suprema de la Provincia de Santa Fe and Corte Suprema de la Nación de la República Argentina 2007; Maggi 2008). The judicial process was protracted by continuous substitutions of the presiding judges and due to different manoeuvres by the defendants' lawyers, but also by the above mentioned appeals in higher instances made by the *inundados/activists* plaintiffs to charge Reutemann. Hence, from the resolution of April 2006 in which three public officials were determined as defendants, it took another six years for the Provincial Court to consider the charges. In May 2012, a new judge finally closed the investigation in order to declare the final sentences (*Página/12* 2012). Almost a year later, in the days before the 10th anniversary of *la Inundación*, the state attorney appointed two prosecutors to pursue the case, hoping to close it before the end of that year (Tizziani 2013).

---

[224] The three imputed persons were the then minister of Public Works, Edgardo Berli, the then director of Hydraulics, Ricardo Fratti, and the then mayor of Santa Fe, Marcelo Alvarez.
[225] The legal term for this type of crime is *estrago culposo* in the Argentinian Criminal Code.

This judicial process, including the denunciations, the investigations, the lawsuit, the sentences and the omissions, can be understood from the perspective of memory and oblivion. The inquiries brought to the fore this state of institutional oblivion; this neglect and indifference in regard to risk management within the Santafesinian bureaucracy. Given that the existing laws were not complied with by the institutions, this case proves that laws and their uses are far from the mere materialisation of collective memory, as Durkheim would have it. Instead law constitutes situated social processes of interpretation and negotiation. The legal process can also be seen as the making of memory; as theatres of history writing. In Santa Fe, the legal conflict was not only a matter of accountability but a battle about whether this disastrous flood should be remembered as a natural misfortune or as an instance of politically produced havoc. This struggle of meaning is crucial to the legal outcome. Despite abundant evidence of the municipal and provincial governments' noncompliance with established federal and provincial legislation in this case, the courts decided to try the burden of responsibility only on middle-range public servants.

Forgiving and forgetting go hand in hand as indicated in the words "amnesty" and "amnesia." The official amnesty granted by the judges to the remaining nine public officials investigated and the informal amnesty granted to former Governor Reutemann since he was not even called to testify, can be seen as forging amnesia about their role and responsibility for the events in the Santafesinian flood memoryscape. This highlights the connection between accountability, memory and oblivion, as observed in relation to the politics of regret (cf. Olick 2007). Yet, things can change in this regard. What seems forgotten (and forgiven), can be subject to reconsideration. The former dictators in Argentina are well aware of this as they are finally being tried in court after amnesty laws were revoked (see Chapter Two). In Santa Fe, the inundados/activists hope that the new appointed judge will call both former governors (Reutemann and Obeid), as well as members of their cabinets, to testify. It is difficult to establish the causality between this new decision and the memory-work enacted by the plaintiffs and the *inundados* protest movement at large. It is nevertheless reasonable to expect that this polity of remembering has had some effect on Santafesinian politics in this sense.

The Contingency Plan: Launching a new disaster management policy

During my fieldwork in Santa Fe, a new municipal contingency plan, the *Plan de Contingencia de la Ciudad de Santa Fe*, was launched in public at a press conference in the municipality in July 2005. The then mayor of the city, Martín Balbarrey, who was himself a hydrological engineer, explained that such a plan was "imperative, because even if Santa Fe is protected by surrounding levees, the city is [also] surrounded by rivers." At the podium the mayor was accompanied by representatives from both the municipal and provincial administrations. Next to the mayor sat a consultant who was the mastermind of the new contingency plan.

The consultant was a native Venezuelan who had arrived in Santa Fe in 2005 after working for the German Red Cross. He had been hired to design and implement a new system of disaster management in the city. Among my interlocutors in Santa Fe, he was simply referred to as *el Venezolano* (the Venezuelan). When I met him at his office a couple of weeks after the launching of the plan, he told me that it entailed a completely new approach to the problem of flooding in Santa Fe City. He had recently been appointed as the director of the new municipal Office of Risk Management, created in 2005 by a town council regulation which was part of the development of a municipal policy for civil defence.[226] The office responded directly to the mayor's office and was to collaborate closely with the municipal Department of Water Affairs. While the Office for Risk Management had an "all hazard approach"[227] and was not preparing only for flooding, the close articulation with the Department of Water Affairs was a result of how flood risk was prioritised in this setting.

Plans as social artefacts

From an anthropological perspective, plans are documents and can be seen as "artefacts of modern knowledge" (Riles 2006), referring to the materialisation of knowledge and information that pervade modern life. Others have defined the practice of documenting as technologies of government (Scott 1999; Nyqvist 2008) and "intersections of exchanges and meetings of different [discursive] domains" (Weszkalnys 2010). A contingency plan can be said to materialise such modern knowledge as it communicates notions of risk and how to deal with it. It has been suggested that contingency plans, in particular, are symbolic "fantasy documents" (L. B. Clarke 1999). They represent an organisational rationality that is in control over processes that it can never completely be in control of, simply because risk is such a complex phenomenon and uncertainty and unpredictability are at its core. Recognising the relative instrumentality or efficiency of plans, in order to understand them as cultural artefacts we need to look into the process of their production, that is, the planning process. Planning takes place within the bureaucracies of national states as well as in supranational organisations (cf. Ferguson and Gupta 2002; Thedvall 2006; Nyqvist 2008).

      Disaster management planning in particular has certain similarities with spatial planning,[228] at least when it comes to the management of so-called natural disasters which are always geographically situated. Spatial planning would seem to be a more stable and less uncertain practice compared to the planning of emergency management, but it has been argued that, for example, urban planning is in fact a rather messy world in which "visions and plans never straightforwardly translate into built realities" (Weszkalnys 2010). In a similar vein disaster management planning is a social and political process that connects

---

[226] See footnote 223.
[227] The "all hazard approach" refers to a policy in the field of disaster and emergency management, in which organisations are prepared in the same way for all kinds of emergencies, as opposed to organising differently for different kinds of hazards.
[228] Among the professional disciplines that involve spatial planning can be mentioned land use planning, urban planning, regional planning, transport planning and environmental planning.

various discourses, practices and subject positions from which risk can be configured in multiple ways in a society. Yet plans are not only representations of ideas or processual outcomes. As objects they shape thinking and acting (Nyqvist 2008). Their very purpose is to coordinate action and intervention. Plans can thus also be seen as artefacts that gain meaning through context, as objects with social lives (Appadurai 1988; D. Miller 2009). Emergency plans are in this vein part of the technology of contemporary risk society in which risk is thought of as something to be governed (Beck 1992). Contingency plans structure the organisation of disaster management even if the decisions made and action taken do not always work out as planned. The fact that a plan and a policy exist at all, is generally seen as a reassuring action of safety; a badge of rationality (L. B. Clarke 1999).

In the 2003 post-disaster context of Santa Fe City, the issue of safety, or rather lack of safety, had been no minor issue. Besides the flaws of appropriate flood protection infrastructure in 2003, an important part of the explanation as to why the governmental response in the 2003 disaster was such a failure in the first place was the lack of a contingency plan. I was told by several interlocutors that there had been no contingency plan in place at all before 2003. This was also addressed in the inquiry, referred to in Chapter Four, which was commissioned by the judge in the lawsuit of the *Causa Inundación*. The experts in the inquiry reached the following conclusion:

> [I]t was found that [in the 2003 flood] there was no appropriate plan in place [that would have specified] the assignment of specific roles, the definition of actions [to be taken] at certain levels of warning, the allocation of technical and human resources, training, capacity building and updating of staff and procedures, information and advice to the population, among other aspects (Bacchiega, Bertoni, and Maza 2005c:8).

The 2005 contingency plan for Santa Fe: Remembering risk

While plans are future oriented as they anticipate risk and action, they are simultaneously historical objects in the sense that an existing plan materialises the outcome of a past process of negotiating ideas and interests. In this sense, plans can be seen as time objectified. They collapse the past, the present and the future into one single time. The contingency plan captures ideas about what is ordinary and extraordinary in life, identifying certain past events as exceptional and unlikely to recur and others as repetitive and constant risks. The 2005 contingency plan for Santa Fe tells us something of how risk as a past experience and a future threat was defined, circumscribed and imagined in a particular moment of time. Approaching a plan as a historical object created in a particular time and place will not only evoke memories but will also imply scrutinising the particular interpretations of the past that it represents. This past includes the identification of places and practices considered as risky. Remembering risk therefore also entails the reifying of social categories. The making of risky subjects in the contingency plan articulates with particular social categories pre-existing in the urban imaginary, as we shall see in Chapter Six.

A plan, form or content?

I got hold of a copy of the 2005 contingency plan in digital format. In fact, during my fieldwork I never saw the actual plan published or in any way printed until I printed a copy myself. The CD-ROM I received was an ordinary disc on which it was handwritten "Contingency Plan" with a red marker pen. The CD-ROM contained eight folders with 36 documents in total, in several formats: Word, Power Point, Adobe Acrobat as well as one dwg-file.[229] My consternation over the electronic version of the contingency plan was both similar to and different from the surprise that Weszkalnys experienced when she discovered that the urban development plan she was studying was a visual drawing instead of a text (Weszkalnys 2010). In part this sensation had to do with my preconceived idea of what "a plan" should look like. This is because there is a certain aesthetic to the design of a bureaucratic document, both in terms of form and of order (Riles 2006). The fact that there was no particular order outlined for the files I received, made it seem to have something disordered and unfinished about it. It appeared more like what we like to think of as a "work in progress." Such a dynamic view of a plan made further sense when the Venezuelan consultant at the press conference in 2005 underscored that the plan was not the final product of anything, but rather the materialisation of a continuous process, adding that: "these papers now need to be given life – they certainly won't help [us when the disaster strikes] by simply existing."

While seeing the plan as a process places this artefact in a constant present, the electronic nature of such an artefact seems to carry specific temporal aspects. The electronic document as opposed to the paper copy appears less stable, given its immateriality. A fire or a flood can destroy an archive, but a virus in an IT-system can make data disappear from a hard disk or a server in just a moment. Even intentionally, an electronic document is easily hidden, if not erased completely.[230] The lack of backup can in any case have irremediable consequences. The speed of technological development can also put valuable information at risk, as new technologies are introduced and old ones discarded. For example, operative systems and software are updated and documents in old versions run the risk of not being accessible. Another example relates to storage of information and the archive discussed above. The floppy disk that was used as a ubiquitous form of data storage in the first decades of the personal computer has in the 21st century been largely superseded by storage methods such as computer networks, USB flash drives, portable external hard disk drives and memory cards. The floppy drive support is hardly manufactured anymore, making the retrieval of such data difficult for the ordinary user. The flux and volatility of

---

[229] DWG (drawing) is a file format used for storing two and three dimensional design data used in Computer-Aided Design (CAD) software used in spatial planning, architecture and engineering.
[230] Whether data can be erased completely or always leave a physical trace seems to be a disputed matter in the world of computers however (C. Harris 2013).

data documented electronically thus seems to open up for the possibility for forgetting in terms of virtual or visual absence. Another aspect of electronic documentation is legality, that is, whether or not digital documents are to be considered "akin to" paper documents in terms of legal validity (Riles ibid.:6). The volatility of the electronic document hence seems to pose legal challenges in terms of validity. The 2005 contingency plan under consideration is a case in point. A few years later, it was replaced by a new plan, which contained no major changes (Gobierno de la Ciudad de Santa Fe 2009).

The folder that contained the files that constituted the actual contingency plan had been simply and uninformatively named "Documents." Far from the *documentos* produced by the *inundados/activists* in the *asamblea,* these documents were the result of a top-down policy process. The folder contained several key international policy documents of reference for the policy world of disaster risk reduction (e.g. "Conference Statement from the Second International Conference Early Warning II, 16-18 October 2003" 2003; "The Manizales Declaration" 2004; United Nations International Strategy for Disaster Reduction 2005). Other documents therein covered different aspects of the contingency plan such as the legal framework, the warning system, evacuation procedures, communication strategies and community education, many of which were written in line with the international policies in the abovementioned documents. There was also the Power Point presentation that was used at the press conference when the plan was publicly launched. The plan, as I received it, consisted of both process and product. The documents constituted both form and content of the plan. Contrary to what is often expected when we speak about plans as products, it seems that rather than being fixed objects, plans are dynamic and never complete (Weszkalnys ibid.: 99).

Planning for disaster risk reduction

Among all the files in the Documents folder, one file seemed to be a key document. The 52-page document was called "Conceptual framework" and summarised all aspects included in the contingency plan. The framework included a risk and vulnerability analysis of Santa Fe City and its surroundings. Flooding from the Paraná River and the Salado River was defined as the principal risk scenario for the city, although heavy rainfall, mist, tornadoes and toxic transports were also identified as significant risks to the community. Similar to the expert inquiry involved in the 2003 disaster lawsuit mentioned above, the principal risk factor identified in this analysis was "human intervention in nature." This referred to inhabiting and building infrastructure in the flood plain, which was seen as modifying and obstructing natural processes such as the flow of rivers:

> Regarding the "culture" of occupying territory, it must be admitted that [the people of] Santa Fe City and its surroundings have not been able to accept that [its] urban development has taken place in a very fragile medium as . . . is . . . the flood plain.

The risk for flooding was described as a historically natural given, due to the city's geographical location. Causality was also being attributed to natural and societal transformations on a global level, yet without going into any particular local or regional conditions:

> It is becoming more common to read news about the effects on the population of different emergencies and disasters in the world. Indiscriminate growth of population, environmental damage, pollution, climate change, poverty and marginalisation, make each event that takes place in populated areas more and more impressive, with collateral damage to social, economic and political of cities, regions or countries concerned.

Social vulnerability at the local level was also framed as constituting risk:

> Santa Fe City has not escaped social deterioration as a result of the economic crisis that hit the country and the structural changes in the economy during the late 1990s. The urban agglomeration of Santa Fe has about 60% of its population under the poverty line and a high rate of unemployment. The pyramid of the population that live in risk areas of the city corresponds to a young age profile: 46% of the population are under 18 years, 48% of the population are between 18 and 64, and 6% of the population are over 65 years. The average size of households is between 3 and 4 persons. Approximately half of the surveyed households are constituted by nuclear families yet approximately 1 in 4 is a single parent family. 41% of these households are female headed. The employment status of this population shows strong instability, lack of jobs. The State is the largest employer due to low [industrial] production and commerce [in these urban and suburban areas]. While the province of Santa Fe is one of the most important production centres of the nation, it is also true that poverty affects a large percentage of people in the capital, where there are large pockets [of poverty] in the urban periphery and on disused public land. About 40% of the population live in slum areas and much of this population establish their livelihoods through social welfare programmes.

It was emphasised that risk management and disaster prevention was a political priority that required the appropriate use of early warning technologies as much as of crisis communication, but more importantly, it was a matter of joining all forces and sectors in society in order to "instil a 'culture of prevention,' to train [people and organisations] and . . . in the medium- and long-term, achieve self-management and self-protection." Hence, it was considered necessary to standardise the practices of citizens and institutions in order to create the self-managing and self-protective subject of risk management. Notions of governmentality ring familiar here (Burchell, Gordon, and Miller 1991) and echoes of contemporary global policies for disaster risk reduction in which "prevention culture" and "community resilience" are concepts marking the way forward to manage disaster risk (Manyena 2006:434; Revet 2013). Risk reduction in this vein is largely framed as a matter of public information and citizenly motivation (United Nations International Strategy for Disaster Reduction 2005), making "community participation" a central component. This was expressed in the Santafesinian contingency plan. What exactly this participation consisted of and how it was to be achieved was not described in the plan, except for stating that there was a need of a common frame of knowledge. Thus, a dictionary was presented at the beginning of the document. Every key term that constituted the disaster management discourse (or "language of prevention" to paraphrase the above concept) such as "risk assessment," "preparedness," "resilience," "vulnerability" and another 35 key concepts were defined in this dictionary.

When it came to the implementation of this part of the plan, this proved to be easier said than done. What has been called "process mitigation" (Birkland 2010:109), referring to getting people engaged in the development of their own resilience to disasters, was not easily achieved. In 2005 and 2006, the municipality in Santa Fe City organised workshops in the different districts in collaboration with the *vecinales* and various NGOs working in the different neighbourhoods. My interlocutors in the *inundados* movement dismissed such collaboration with the municipal government however, considering it to be like a kind of betrayal to engage with the State that had deceived them. Many neighbourhood associations in the city were equally dismissed by many residents as corrupt and politicised. Hence, very few people turned up on these workshops. The aim of making the community participate, as stated in the Santa Fe contingency plan and in international policies, seemed more like wishful thinking in the wake of *la Inundación*.

The 2005 contingency plan of Santa Fe City forecasted risky places, people and practices by remembering the past and the present in particular ways. By describing selected aspects of the past and the present of social life and flood management in Santa Fe, other aspects were omitted. Nothing was mentioned about those economic and political processes that put people and places at risk by forcing them to live in risky places. Nor were the significant human effects on natural processes, such as deforestation, agricultural technologies or regulation of rivers for energy production, considered in this analysis. This is perhaps not surprising if we consider a plan to be part of the disaster risk reduction "anti-politics machine" (Ferguson 1990). The logic of omission can in this vein be seen as constitutive of this apparatus. The plan can be read as a historical artefact in itself: a post-disaster product that was considered absolutely necessary from a local and regional political perspective. The incoming mayor of Santa Fe could rather easily earn credits for setting it in motion.

Flood management and shelved plans
What actually existed before the 2005 contingency plan was difficult for me to discern during my fieldwork. As I have described, archives were not accessible

and my interlocutors within the public administration were reluctant to speak about the past. Yet, when I least expected it, traces from the past emerged in the Santafesinian flood memoryscape. In April 2005, the director of the municipal Department of Pumping Stations had a bit reluctantly agreed to meet with me. Rolando Perez was an acquaintance of my friend Pablo, one of the activists in the *inundados* protest movement. Pablo had provided me with the contact, in spite of them not being on very good terms at that time. This was because Pablo considered that Rolando was among those responsible for the mismanagement of the events leading to the 2003 disaster and had told him so. Because I referred to Pablo when I contacted Rolando to ask for an interview, the latter possibly assumed that I was also in the *inundados* movement and thus prone to criticise him. Finally I managed to convince him that I was an impartial scholar, genuinely interested in understanding the point of view of municipal employees regarding the problem of flooding in the city.

We met at Rolando's office located in a store building, presumably an old train shed, on the Eastside, only a few blocks from the Costanera esplanade. A large yard surrounded the building. Several trucks were parked there and large pieces of machines were leaned against the walls. Rolando's office was dark and gloomy, perhaps due to the bookshelves in oak wood and the large desk. Rolando himself was sitting behind the desk but stood up as I entered the office. He politely invited me to sit on the wooden chair in front of the desk. As I began asking him questions about the technologies of flood prevention in the city, he seemed to relax and told me about this system. By the end of my interview with him I was invited to accompany him and his employees to join their inspection of the state of the embankments and the pump station devices. This excursion came about a couple of months later in June 2005, when I joined them in their van to the Coastside.

Figure 27 | Checking the state of flooding preparedness on the Coastside (Photo by author 2005)

We drove slowly on the crest of the embankments which were several meters wide. Occasionally, we stopped when we reached a pumping station or any of the drainage ditches that ran parallel to the embankments. As we drove and stopped, Rolando and his assistant checked the installations. More frequently than not they expressed irritation over finding cables missing, broken floodgates, garbage filling the drainage ditches and the embankments eroded by grazing cattle and horses or used as roads by motor vehicles. There were even a couple of large holes in the embankments as if someone had removed sand with a shovel. On our way back to the city, Rolando commented on his view of this sabotage:

> These people [who live in the suburban islands] know perfectly well how to deal with the flooding. They can predict the magnitude of the flood by looking at what height the river snail laid its eggs on the reed. They are used to flooding. Yet nowadays, they want to be protected [by the municipality] against the floods so we do [protect them], but then what is a mystery to me is that they continue to settle outside the protecting embankments and furthermore that they actually destroy the very same defences that are for their protection. This destruction occurs on the Westside too . . . Why should we [the municipality] then bother, if they [the inhabitants] don't care?

Rolando's view resonated with contemporary ideas in the context of infrastructure investments in the developing world, in which townspeople are seen as savages because they use public works in ways other than intended by the engineers, which cause damage to the work (cf. Harvey 2010:35-36). His comment also echoed the views of those in the world of disaster management in which disaster victims are seen as passive and not taking responsibility for their own mitigation (cf. Revet 2013).

Rolando shrugged his shoulders. He looked angered and resigned at the same time. This was the same face he had put up at the end of my interview in April 2005. We were talking about the state of disaster preparedness within the municipality. I asked him about the flood contingency plan, stating that I had been told by many Santafesinos that before 2003 there had been none. Without saying a word he first looked at me and then opened a drawer in his desk. In silence he threw a tiny green booklet and a thin spiral bound folder with a transparent cover on the desk in front of me. I read the title on the first page of the booklet: *C.I.M.A Flooding and Environmental Control*.[231] It had been published by the Secretariat of Water Affairs of the municipality of Santa Fe and was a summary of the purposes of this programme, which was to control, maintain and operate the flood defence system.

As I picked up the spiral bound folder and it struck me that it looked like – a plan! It consisted of nine pages, in which the CIMA programme for the management of the flood defence infrastructure was outlined. This pro-

---

[231] The acronym C.I.M.A. stood for *Control de Inundaciones y Medio Ambiente*.

gramme described in terms of equipment, personnel and time needed to operate and maintain the embankments, the canals, the reservoirs, the floodgates and the pump stations in order to mitigate future floods. It also considered an early warning system. This flood management plan was not dated, so I asked Rolando when it was from. He laconically replied that he and his colleagues had formulated it after the 1992 floods, but that it was closed down in 1996. He continued:

> ¡Fue cajoneado! Our plan was shelved and forgotten. Then, the 2003 flood occurred and here we are. Now they are trying to invent the wheel again.

Indeed, for Rolando to keep a copy of this plan in the drawer of his desk, in the *cajón*, struck me as symbolic to what he just told me. *Cajón* means box or drawer in Spanish and the verb *cajonear* is used in Argentina to denote a hindrance, delay or holding back of a question or a procedure within a public organisation. In this respect, Rolando keeping his own copy of the plan in the drawer seemed symbolical, not to say ironic, of a process of institutional oblivion. To what extent Rolando himself was contributing to this process of forgetting is difficult to say. Two years later, in July 2007, I read in a local newspaper that he had been reported for omissions as a public official, theft of public property, cover-up and menace to a subordinate (*El Litoral* 2007b).

On the political and bureaucratic logic of omission

This chapter has discussed how the historical problem of flooding in Santa Fe was addressed within the political realm of the city. I have argued that different political and bureaucratic practices follow and reproduce a logic of omission regarding flooding. As has been illustrated ethnographically throughout this chapter, this logic refers to a pattern of selective remembering and forgetting that enabled new governments and decision makers to cyclically start over. As other scholars have observed (Guber 1999a), this logic can be said to characterise political life in Argentina in general. I have shown in this chapter that the logic features in the Santafesinian political world as well. It shaped how the flooding past of Santa Fe was handled within the municipal and provincial spheres of action, which in turn forged flood management policies (or the absence of them). The logic of omission also enabled the noncompliance of laws and policies. Numerous official efforts of forgetting *la Inundación* were set in motion which helped highly ranked officials to escape political and juridical accountability.

As we have seen, memory within the public administration was shaped by practice of exchanging administrative staff within the public agencies following the electoral time cycle, not because individual experiences are forgotten when people are exchanged, but because there are incentives to not remember past decisions and arguments. This pattern of forced exclusion also involved materialised memory of the bureaucracy, that is, documents such as plans and maps in public archives, in processes of selective remembering and forgetting.

Public works of infrastructure also operated according to this logic, constituting the material traces of past disastrous events at the same time as they evoked such events. In addition, works of infrastructure are techniques to control hazardous forces such as flooding and forged the memory of past floods as well as oblivion of future risks. Technocratic narratives and calculations of risk framed how the flooding past was addressed. Future oriented contingency plans omitted addressing root causes of social vulnerability to flooding and instead framed the problem as one of human obstruction to the course of nature. The responsibility for this infliction on the environment was placed with particular people, practices and places, most notably at the urban outskirts. As we shall see in the next chapter, this stigmatisation articulated with myths and stories in making the urban flood memoryscape.

PART TWO

Chapter 6 | Urban flooding as mythico-history

Floods in the past

Flooding is a historical problem of Santa Fe City dating back to the days of its foundation by Spanish conquerors. *La Inundación* was only the last in a row of floods to strike the city even if it was one of the worst disasters in terms of the number of victims and material losses. In this chapter I change focus from the memory-work around *la Inundación* to take a closer look on how other past floods and the flooding past were remembered in different forms ranging from myths to memorials. I will argue that this remembering constitute what Malkki (1995) calls a "mythico-history" around flooding in Santa Fe. She defines this as "a set of moral and cosmological ordering stories: stories which classify the world according to certain principles, thereby simultaneously creating it" (ibid.: 54). Such stories are meaningful collective narratives that are situated betwixt and between history and myth. "Narratives" are in the concept's most basic sense stories that are framed and expressed in a particular order, which makes meaning out of a particular situation. Narratives can be expressed through language, images, music and performances, yet in the context of memory, the discursive dimension is particularly salient, given that language is a key feature of socialisation in general and consequently of remembering.

Malkki underscores that the use of the mythico-history concept is not to establish whether these narratives are true or false (ibid.: 54). I agree that in order to grasp how people make meaning of the past, there is no point in using the dichotomy of veracity as an analytical tool because of its normativeness. What are identified as "false" statements will be disqualified as bad, in favour of the good, "true" ones. Yet I think that aiming at understanding how memory and oblivion operate in tandem, it is significant to establish what existed and what did not (cf. Fentress and Wickham 1992:xi). Historicity becomes important, not as a normative judgement of good and bad versions of the past, but to see what is included or excluded in selective remembering. Notwithstanding, historicity is not what is in focus when applying the concept of mythico-history, but rather the aspects that make narratives about particular past circumstances so compelling. This is because such narrative are "concerned with *order* in a fundamental, cosmological sense" (Malkki ibid.: 55. Italics in original.), which "seized historical events, processes and relationships, and reinterpreted them within a deeply moral scheme of good and evil" (ibid.: 56). What makes the mythico-history powerful is both the repetitiveness and the thematic unity of narratives creating a sense of a collective voice. I argue that the mythico-history around past flooding in Santa

Fe, constructed through myths, legends, literature, film and popular music, has forged a particular cultural order in which the social category of the *inundado* was created and reproduced over time; a social category central to the flood memoryscape.

Commemorating origins

The well-known Argentinian saying "a Peronist day"[232] would have been a suitable way to describe that early spring morning of November 15th, 2005, in Santa Fe City. The sun was already high. There was not one single cloud in the sky. A warm breeze embraced us in the square Plaza de las Dos Culturas. A perfect day for celebrating the anniversary of the foundation of the city! The Santa Fe Police Band played the Aurora Hymn and the National Anthem, as both the provincial and national flags were raised under the eye of the statue of the town's founder himself, the Spanish Captain Juan de Garay, and the city's patron saint, the Virgin of Guadalupe. Mayor Balbarrey spoke before the crowd, followed by a monk from the nearby Franciscan monastery. There were around fifty people gathered, among which were political representatives and civil servants; representatives from the armed forces, the police and the Catholic Church; a couple of journalists; and me. Later in the evening, the celebrations continued with more speeches, musical presentations and regional food nearby the village of Cayastá, north of Santa Fe de la Vera Cruz, where the town of Santa Fe had been founded 432 years earlier.

Figure 28 | 432nd anniversary of the foundation of Santa Fe City (Photo by author 2005)

---

[232] The expression *"un día Peronista"* was allegedly coined by an Argentinian motor sports journalist, who was very close to the Peronist movement at the time of the first government of Perón (1946-51). The image of a beautiful day is often taken to represent October 17th, 1945, which was a sunny and warm spring day in Buenos Aires, and the day on which thousands of Argentinian workers invaded the city capital to protest the arrest of Perón. It has later come to stand as a metaphor for the Peronist movement itself.

In 1573, Juan de Garay set out by ship with his expedition consisting of Spaniards and *mancebos*[233] from the town of Asunción, city capital of the then Governorate of Paraguay-Río de la Plata within the Viceroyalty of Peru. The purpose was to explore new sites along the shores of the Paraná River, to determine where to settle a new town and from where to "open up doors to the land"[234] (Areces 1999:23; Barreira 2006:41-50). The aboriginal peoples living in this region at the time gave de Garay and his men a hard time, but the conquerors finally managed to establish on the western banks of the river. The town of Santa Fe was eventually founded at the outlet of the Paraná tributary known as the Quiloazas River on November 15th, 1573, with the following words:

> I, Juan de Garay, captain and Supreme justice in this conquest and population of the Río Paraná and the Río de la Plata, I say in the name of the Holy Trinity and of the Mary Saint and of the university of all Saints and in the name of the Royal Majesty hereby found and name this town of Santa Fe, in this province of Calchines and Mocoretáes, because it seems to me that here are the necessary parts and things for it to perpetuate as a town in terms of water and firewood and pastures, fishing and houses and land and farms for the neighbours and the dwellers of it, and I divide among them, as His Majesty has ordered, and I settle it and inhabit it with the addition that every time another place is found that appears to be more convenient and beneficial for the perpetuation, I can do this [again] in accordance with the Council and Justice that will exist in this town, in order to serve the benefit of God and of His Majesty; and because His Majesty commands the Governors and the Captains to settle new villages and towns, he gives them the power and the commission to do this in his royal name.[235]

De Garay planned the new town according to the then popular colonial checkerboard grid design.[236] He distributed land for dwelling and agriculture to his fellow conquerors. The new settlers would not have an easy time in the site they chose however. Numerous problems posed serious challenges to the continuity of the new town, such as insect plagues, drought and colonial politics (Barreira 2006:171-98). The indigenous people in the area, who still resisted the Spanish

---

[233] *Mancebo de la tierra* is literally translated to "slave of the land" in ancient Spanish. This was the name of the social category *mestizo*, that is, the children of a Spanish father and an indigenous mother, in the colonial Río de la Plata region. This term was later abandoned for the term *criollo*, which at present refers to the descendants of this category.
[234] The expression *abrir caminos a la tierra* was used at the time of colonisation to denote the intention to expand territory and to find a shorter way between Spain and the colonies in Spanish America.
[235] The complete foundational speech in Spanish can be found on line ("Acta de Fundación de Santa Fe" 2013).
[236] The so-called checkerboard design is called *trazado en damero* in Spanish. It refers to the Spanish colonial urban planning model as a grid of streets with the square as its centre stamped on rectangularity upon any terrain.

conquest, also constituted a constant threat to the inhabitants of Santa Fe. Recurrent flooding eroded the banks where the town was situated and threatened its physical existence (ibid.: 184). Furthermore, the flooding seriously complicated everyday life and commerce in the small colony. When the Paraná River flooded, the town became completely isolated for long periods. The difficulties that the inhabitants in Santa Fe were constantly facing prompted a rather radical idea,[237] namely to move the entire settlement to a safer place. Such an action needed the approval of the Spanish Crown. After several years of desperate insistence by correspondence, the Crown finally agreed. A new site, suitable for resettlement, was identified 80 kilometres south of the existing town. In 1660 the new town was finally settled. To differentiate it from the original settlement, the new town was named Santa Fe de la Vera Cruz (ibid.: 193-97).

Despite the existence of historical documents, the first foundation of Santa Fe City was for centuries akin to a myth rather than a historical fact. There were no vestiges of the Old Town. Nobody could identify where the first town had been located, making it a matter of serious discussion among local historians for decades (Aldao 1999:4). The ruins were not found until the mid-20th century when a local historian, Agustín Zapata Gollán, carried out excavations close to the village of Cayastá. The discovery of the ruins then turned the myth of the Old Town into history. In 1957, the site was declared a National Historical Monument. With time, an archaeological park and a large museum was built on the site.

The 432nd anniversary celebration that I attended in 2005 was a special celebration. The provincial authorities had for years pursued the idea that the ruins of the Old Town Santa Fe should be declared a World Heritage by UNESCO. In 2005, the proposal had reached the stage of a first nomination. This was highlighted in the anniversary celebrations by the presence of a Spanish historian who had been invited especially for the occasion. All speakers during the celebrations emphasised the importance of commemorating the foundation of Santa Fe City and of supporting the World Heritage project, not only because of the general historical significance, but also because of the value that the Santafesinian society represented throughout history: the power to resist the and capacity to cope with adversity. The foundation is commemorated every anniversary. The story about the settlement is recounted in academic historiography (Cervera 1979; Zapata Gollán 1990; Calvo 1992; Areces 1999; Barreira 2006), in popular history books (Mino 1998) and in school books (Mérega 2008; Gonzalez 2008).

Myths and legends

Foundational and settler myths and myths of origin have long been well documented and analysed in anthropology (e.g. Boas and Tate 1916; Malinowski 1926; Lévi-Strauss 1955). Myths have conventionally been taken to represent a

---

[237] Barreira reminds us that moving settlements was nevertheless a common practice in Colonial times, both by the Spanish and the Portuguese Crowns (2006:194).

timeless memory in opposition to chronological historiography. I have pointed out in the introductory chapter that the dichotomy of memory-history can better be understood as representing different ways of remembering on a continuum, and as ideal types that serve analytical purposes (Cole 2001).

The legend of the angry Paraná River

During one of my short field trips to Santa Fe in 2009, I asked the young school teacher Ana, one of my interlocutors in the Centenario neighbourhood, about how she approached the issue of urban flooding in her teaching. She recommended that I take a look at a new schoolbook in which *la Inundación* was a topic. It was a social sciences textbook for students in the 4th grade, focusing on the geography, history and society of the Province of Santa Fe (Mérega 2008). The 2003 disaster was indeed discussed as an extraordinary event in the history of the city (pp.32-33). Nowhere else in the book was the issue of flooding discussed, except for a story at the end of the book in a section called "Let's read a story from our province." The story was an indigenous Toba legend about the anger of the Paraná [River], as follows:

> Thousands of years ago, when the Toba nation was strong and powerful, the Tupá God had provided the Toba people with good hunting and fishing. The Toba territory became larger and larger, as they had increased it by scaring their neighbours. Tupá not only provided the Toba people with food security, but he also provided them with laws that they had to comply with. The laws included rights and obligations. Tupá had told them that they had the right to hunt and fish when they wanted for the purpose of food, but not just for fun, given that they had to care for what nature provided them with. He [Tupá] furthermore prohibited them from touching *Pirayú* (which is the Guaraní name for the Golden Dorado fish), the father of the Paraná [River], when he retired to rest in the shadows of the *Palo Borracho* tree. One day the Toba chief returned with his men from the river. They had been away to fight another tribe. The [Toba] had managed to take their [enemies'] land by which they expanded the [Toba] territory. They [the chief and his men] arrived in an arrogant mood, feeling invincible and as masters of the world. Suddenly they saw a golden brightness in the water [of the river]. *Pirayú* was there. They prepared their spears to hunt him, but *Pirayú* was much faster and he escaped. The chief, who wanted to have some fun and to show [the other men] that he was not only the best warrior but also the best fisherman, forgot the recommendation of Tupá as he started to chase the fish. The fish reached a huge *Palo Borracho* tree and thought he was safe as he plunged in under the trunk. But the chief, blind by his own pride, lifted his arm and drove his spear violently. In that moment, the sky got dark, the river opened its brown mouth and from the waters emerged a deafening groan. The waters rose and rose. The riverbed was flooded and washed down everything. Tupá was punishing [the Toba] for their disobedience. The flood

lasted for several months. When the waters lowered, not much was left from the Toba power. Many centuries have passed since then, but when the *Palo Borracho* tree is flowering, the neighbours of the Paraná [River] know that the time is coming when the waters get angry, to recall Tupá's punishment (p.102).

Several interesting observations can be made regarding this legend. The first concerns the possible sources of the legend. The Toba people in Argentina actually refer to themselves as such but also use the self-designation Qom, which means "people" in their native language (Gordillo 2004). Had a representative from any Toba/Qom community been involved in contributing to the textbook, it is reasonable to think that this would have been stated, given the contemporary redress of indigenous communities in Argentina (cf. Briones 2005). The second observation concerns the historicity of the legend. In order to corroborate it, I checked several sources, including interlocutors in Santa Fe[238] and existing studies (Métraux 1946; Colombres 2001; Gordillo 2005). None of these mentioned or corroborated this particular myth. Instead I discovered that, according to these sources, the characters mentioned in the Toba legend (the Tupá God and the *Pirayú*) belong to the Mbyá-Guaraní mythology, distinguishing the latter from the Toba/Qom mythology. The reference to a supreme god furthermore seems to be a Christian element, far from original Toba/Qom cosmology.[239] In the textbook, however, no references were made to the source of the legend. This, of course, is the general rule when it comes to the myth as a genre of narratives. Such stories cannot be placed or dated, nor ascribed to any particular author. Yet it seemed unlikely that the authors of the textbook themselves would have recorded this legend, thus they must have used some source for it. This is left unknown however. On the other hand, the textbook cites no sources at all for the rest of the content either, which can be said to be typical of schoolbook texts. A third aspect concerns the context of the publication of the legend. The publisher of the textbook was Ediciones Santillana Argentina, which is one of the biggest textbook publishers in the country. Their textbooks have long been widely used in both public and private Argentinian schools. This particular book, especially designed to suit the syllabus of the primary school in the Province of Santa Fe, was published in 2008, in the post-disaster context. The 2003 disaster is described on two entire pages, while the Toba legend is placed at the end of it, in the activity pages. At the foot of the page where the legend is written, there is an assignment for the students, namely to reflect and discuss what kind of phenomenon the legend is about and how this is explained. Even if I did not get the chance to discuss this with Ana or any other Santafesinian school teacher, it seems reasonable to think that this assignment opened up the topic of flooding for classroom discussions.

---

[238] I also tried to establish how widespread the local awareness about it was, both among the Toba/Qom themselves and in the City of Santa Fe at large. During my fieldwork, I never heard of this legend from any of my interlocutors, but then, none of them were of Toba origin. My later inquiries through my research assistant who carried out fieldwork in the Toba community in Recreo, unfortunately led nowhere in determining whether this legend actually existed in this form.

[239] Thanks to Gastón Gordillo for pointing this out to me (e-mail communication, 2012-07-19).

The moral of the Toba legend is that if people did not respect nature (or God), it strikes back violently. In the context of post-disaster Santa Fe, the analogy to the 2003 disaster but also to other past floods is at hand. From the perspective of memory, by using the genre of an aboriginal legend, the phenomenon of flooding was here recounted as a timeless and depoliticised yet everlasting problem in the region.

The Catholic and the Atlantis

In the end of May, 1914, Santa Fe was hit by a severe flood. This time it was the Salado River that flooded after days of heavy rainfall in the province and in other parts of the country. According to local newspaper reports in those days, hundreds of families were evacuated in train wagons and in warehouses during the weeks that the flood lasted. Various bridges and buildings were razed, and the ripe wheat fields just waiting to be reaped and shipped to the USA and Europe, were destroyed. In one of the local newspapers, letters to the editor were published. One day, there was a column in one of the city newspapers urging city residents to apologise, and it was signed *Un Católico* (A Catholic) (*Nueva Época* 1914). The writer claimed that through various immoral acts, not least a declining religiosity in the city, Santa Fe had insulted God. The rains and the flooding were the punishment. To illustrate the argument, the city's inhabitants were given a short version of the story in the Genesis about the destruction of the sinful city of Sodom. The writer then argued that divine justice had been carried out, and which could only be repaid by praying to the Lord. The writer urged: "Let us make a novena so solemn and so full of confidence that something like it will never have been seen before in Santa Fe."

    A day or two later, this same writer, in another column, warned that the flood was the fulfilment of the commonly known prophecy by the patron saint San Francisco Solano. This prophecy predicted that the Salado River and the Paraná River would flood at the same time and completely submerge Santa Fe City, because of its location between the two rivers. However, this prophecy was refuted a few days later in the same newspaper, when another, less superstitious, reader called on the newspaper's editorial staff to issue a correction. This reader questioned whether the prophecy referred to could possibly have anything to do with the saint in question. San Francisco Solano died in Lima (Peru) in 1610, while Santa Fe City was founded on its present site between the two rivers in 1651. Thus, the critical reader argued, it stood to reason that St. Solano could not have pronounced this prophecy, because the city did not even exist in its current location.

    During my fieldwork, a couple of interlocutors told me that the 2003 flood was actually the fulfilment of an apocalyptic prophecy which predicted that, of the three cities in the world that have the name Santa Fe,[240] one was

---

[240] Apart from Santa Fe de la Vera Cruz (founded 1573), there is Santa Fe, capital city of the state of New Mexico in the USA (founded 1609) and the town of Santa Fe in the province of Granada in Spain (founded 1491). They were all founded within the period of the Catholic Monarchs and their heirs, and the Spanish colonisation of the Americas.

doomed to disappear, like the Atlantis island. One woman assured me that it was the medieval prophet Nostradamus who had made this prophecy. By connecting the Atlantis island, which sank after having angered the gods, and Nostradamus, whose prophecies of doom were based on the idea of moral decay according to astronomical calculations, this contemporary myth of Santa Fe recovered the idea that "A Catholic" had argued for a century earlier, namely that the inhabitants of Santa Fe were punished for their pride and arrogance. The pride and ungodly behaviour of the Santafesinos, and a widespread notion of a city since long in decay, was embedded in this particular meaning-making of the 2003 disaster.

Flooding and myth

Taken together, these myths, legends and prophecies circulating in different media and at different points in time were parts of the Santafesinian flood memoryscape. Different aboriginal, Greek and Christian myths, sometimes a mix of them, recounted flooding as an everlasting risk in Santa Fe City. Their circulation and reproduction were contingent on class, gender and age in the heterogeneous urban setting, yet such narratives of memory were important in the formation of cultural identity (cf. Assmann 2011a) and the configuration of place.

The notion of time is particularly salient in the case of the prophecies. Interestingly, in both cases (1914 and 2005) these prophecies were retold in post-disaster contexts, as if they constituted fulfilled past and future risk at the same time. That is, the prophecies had been fulfilled, yet even worse disasters were foreseen: the final flood and destruction. Eschatological reasoning about the disastrous flooding of Santa Fe City thus seemed to be reproduced over time. The mythical prophecies articulated with the foundational myth of Santa Fe. The Old Town Santa Fe fitted well in the analogy to the Atlantis, disappeared as the city was for centuries. Yet my interlocutors, who told me about this prophecy, rather associated it to the 2003 flood in Santa Fe de la Vera Cruz, by saying that this disaster was more of a warning of future scenarios.

While myths are often thought of as timeless narratives, it is important to note that they are nevertheless also historical narratives, that is, they are created and circulated in a particular time and place. This does not mean that past myths belong entirely to "another country" (cf. Ingold et al. 1996). Rather it points to the fact that different memories and practices of remembering are temporally and spatially situated. Even if mythical narratives display a certain degree of continuity over time, it is true that they also contain the possibility of change over time (Gow 2001; Canessa 2008).

The Great Flood

"So, you're doing research on *la Inundación*?" Vera asked me when we first met in 2004. When I explained to her that I was exploring the memory of all past floods in the city, she was at first surprised but almost immediately she said: "Oh, I guess you mean the 1905 flood then?!" Most of my interlocutors referred to this particular disaster when I made clear that I was interested not only in *la In-*

undación as an object of inquiry. It seemed that the Great Flood, as it had been called, was a disaster fairly well remembered. Vera was a woman in her fifties. She was a lawyer at that moment working in one of the NGOs of the *inundados* protest movement. One afternoon in late April 2005 she received me in her home (and the headquarters of the NGO) situated on the well-off Eastside. We talked about my research project. She was very enthusiastic and encouraging. She was the one who first mentioned the monument of the 1905 flood to me, saying: "You know, there is a plate in town that commemorates the 1905 flood. It's placed in the Plaza España square. You should definitely go and see it!" So I did.

The quest for artefacts of disaster memory

According to the city map, the Plaza España square was not very far from Vera's house on the Eastside. When I arrived, it seemed to me like a rather abandoned square with few flower beds and scarce illumination. I learnt later that this particular square was built at the time of the Santafesinian *belle époque* at the turn of the 20th century, constituting the hub within a lively commercial area in connection to the nearby French Railway Station as well as to the harbour. A semicircular stage had been built in the middle of the square, presumably to stage musical bands. Park benches were distributed along the red gravelled paths of the square. While the traffic was quite hectic around the plaza at that evening hour, with cars and buses passing and stopping, only a few people were in the square at that moment. I began to look for the commemorative plate Vera had told me about, but found nothing of the kind. As I walked around the square, I ran into the municipal road sweeper. He looked surprised when I asked if he knew where the 1905 flood plate could be located. To my satisfaction he promised to show me where it was. I followed him as we stepped out on the withered lawn and arrived at a flat squared stone on the ground that I had not noticed as I walked around. The road sweeper seemed as happy as I felt to find the flood memorial. The excitement did not last for long however. When I looked closer at the large two-square-metre stone, I realised that it was a military signpost that indicated the altitude above sea level.

I was both embarrassed and disappointed but could not let go of the thought of finding the 1905 flood monument. I asked virtually everybody I ran into, if they knew anything about it or where it was located. While many people knew about the 1905 flood, they had never heard of any monument. A couple of interlocutors said that they had heard about a memorial but had no idea where to find it. After a few days I went back to Plaza España and began asking people haphazardly. One man indicated that he had indeed seen a plate many years ago up the street, sitting on the wall, as a watermark indicating the level of the floodwater. However, he could not recall exactly where he had seen it, but thought it could be on Rivadavia Street. As I walked up this street and passed the two storey buildings, I screened the walls for a plate, but with no luck. Disappointed and tired, I finally stepped rather willy-nilly into one of the shops along the street. A young man behind the desk was taking an order to repair a washing machine by a customer. I waited for my turn and then asked if he might know anything about a flood commemorative plate. He smiled and asked me to wait a second for him to fetch his father at the back of the shop. A few minutes later, he returned with a man in his fifties who greeted me by saying "So, you're looking for the tile from the flood? Follow me!" As I tried to explain my inquiry briefly, he walked out to the sidewalk and began staring at the pavement tiles while mumbling "Let's see, was it this one, or this?" He finally decided. "This is the tile," he said pointing to one of the tiles on his part of the sidewalk. I looked down at it. It was an ordinary grey ceramic tile, 25 centimetres times 25 centimetres with one corner broken. It had no inscriptions or anything that would make it a monument in my view. I looked up at him and asked him to explain. He said:

> Well, there used to be another tile here, one that had an inscription that the water [of the 1905 flood] had reached this point. I remember having stepped on it a million times as I was a kid, growing up in the *barrio*. The former shopkeeper replaced the pavement of the sidewalk at some point, although I can't remember when this was. I guess he must have discarded the tile along with the others. But it used to sit right here, that much I can remember!

Forty and Küchler (2001) have questioned the Aristotelian assumption that destroyed or disappeared memorials necessarily imply forgetting (pp.4-7). So-called "ephemeral monuments," that is, memorials which are built to decay, and the phenomenon of iconoclasm, have been suggested to make memory through their absence (Forty and Küchler, ibid.: 10-11; Argenti 2001; Küchler 2001). This is because the artefact's inherent capacity to make a place of memory in a space that it has previously occupied. Thus, even if the artefact of memory in itself is gone and disappeared, the place where it was serves to evoke memories. In the case of the memorial tile of the Great Flood of 1905, it had been placed to serve as a watermark and hence it was a commemorative artefact. Its removal and absence did not stop it from being remembered however, both as the artefact and the meaning it carried, that is, memorialising this particular disaster. While its exact location was unclear, it was nevertheless striking that numerous people remembered having seen it. This was made possible through the articulation of this particular place of absence with other memories of the Great Flood.

Disaster on display

In 2005, the centenary of the Great Flood occurred. I read in the local newspaper that an exhibition was going to be held in the Municipal Cultural Centre to commemorate the centenary. Exhibitions in museums and fairs not only represent the world through the display of particular objects, but also "recreate their object of attention in a perfect and desirable form" (Harvey 1995:89). Hence, there are ideological and aesthetic dimensions of exhibitions that cannot be ignored (Vergo 1989:2). In the context of memory, exhibitions about the past can be seen as ordering it in both temporal and spatial terms through the way certain past epochs or events are put on display. In Santa Fe City, the Great Flood was, as I have underscored, such a particular event. Its place of importance in the Santafesinian flood memoryscape was enhanced through the centenary exhibition in 2005. In July that year, I stopped by the Centre to see the exhibition titled *[The] Flood of 1905. Reality and Fantasy*[241] organised by the Historical Archive of the Province of Santa Fe in collaboration with a local artist.

I stepped into a large hall furnished with old wooden cabinets and desks. Some copies of newspaper articles from 1905 had been posted on panels standing in the middle of the hall. Along the walls there were some glass cabinets with old photographs. Photographs also posted on the wall depicted different places in Santa Fe City which were being severely flooded at that point in time in 1905. At the turn of the 20th century, large districts on the Eastside, Downtown, Southeast Side and Westside were flooded. The photographs from 1905 depicted only the Eastside and Downtown however. Places like the French Railroad Station, the new harbour that was being built and fashionable buildings in the city centre were depicted, as were men in rowboats and horse carriages, and women washing clothes from the sidewalk. Only one photograph depicted a few more modest dwellings even if they were not really visible in the picture, because they were covered with floodwater up to the roof. Instead there were several pictures of flooded upper-class families. One depicted a family of well-dressed adults and at least six children standing at the entrance of their big elegant home, watching people passing in rowboats on the street. Another sequence of photographs depicted a well-dressed lady and her two children dressed in white, who were being evacuated by a driver in a black horse-drawn carriage in the flooded street with water almost up to the floor of the carriage. One of the photographs depicted a family standing in a rowboat in their own courtyard, with the water hyacinths surrounding them, as if they were about to make an pleasant excursion.

Figure 29 | Family portrait on display in the Great Flood century exhibition (Photo by author 2005)

---

[241] In Spanish: *Inundación de 1905. Realidad y Fantasía*

In spite of it being a major flood with severe consequences, recalled as the Great Flood, it is striking that the photographs express neither distress nor fear. The upper-class families, on the contrary, seemed surprised to the point of amusement of the extraordinary event. Far from depicting a disaster, the photographer was representing a city in the making of modernity, finally rising from the burden of colonial vulnerability. The photographer, Augusto Lutsch, was an Austrian immigrant who had in 1905 become something of an official photographer of the municipal and provincial governments of Santa Fe. He had registered the most important public works in the city at that time, such as those related to the railway lines, the harbour and the modern urban developments. In the words of Collado (2007):

> "[His] urban images always portrayed the most prestigious locations [of Santa Fe City], the most fashionable images of urban life (parks and promenades, the shopping street, the area of the Plaza de Mayo square) or places that testify to the change [of the urban image], trying to exalt the monumental scale of new buildings and significant urban areas from the same frame of the image, in line with the laudatory descriptions of some travellers and commemorative albums. When the Mayor Irigoyen sends him to document the Great Flood of 1905, Lutsch removes the urban drama from all his portraits and [instead] a bucolic scene appears, akin to a South American Venice, with the [flooded] Santafesinos smartly dressed and riding in canoes or carriages in flooded streets" (p.299).

The visual documentation of the 1905 flood was of a different character from that of *la Inundación* in 2003, as I describe in previous chapters. To begin with, the task of documenting the first was entrusted by the municipal government, while the latter was hardly officially documented at all.[242] Secondly, while the images that were taken in 2003 depicted loss and despair of the people flooded, the pictures taken in 1905 only show the least vulnerable people. Lutsch documented fashionable people and flooded places (such as the Plaza España square where a resident later placed the commemorative tile), but he did not depict any of the many distressful situations described in the newspaper articles posted in the exhibition, which conveyed a tragedy. Several people had drowned; several hundreds of families from lowland neighbourhoods and surrounding villages had been evacuated to train wagons, warehouses and tents; houses had collapsed and hospitals were completely flooded; the train and telegraph services were interrupted; and a lot of livestock had been lost (Union Provincial 1905). Lutsch's photographs were widely reproduced in different local mass media and in popu-

---

[242] While the visual documentation of *la Inundación* was overwhelming, this task was undertaken by mass media and independent journalists, by NGOs, and by individual citizens. In my fieldwork research I came across one exception to the lack of official documentation, which were the photographs taken by the Argentinian Naval Prefecture.

lar history books (Mino 1998) when referring to flooding in Santa Fe City. No other historical flood in Santa Fe seems to have been as well documented until the advent of amateur and family photography, but more importantly, the digital camera. This was striking in the case of la Inundación in 2003 when thousands of professional and amateur photographs were taken of the disaster, of which many were published in local mass media and in social media, as well as put on display in several exhibitions (see Chapter Three). Lutsch's photographs were also public property. While the negatives were kept by the Provincial General Archive, many other museums, such as the Provincial Historical Museum of Santa Fe and the Regional Railway Museum of Santa Fe, guarded or exhibited copies of these pictures. Lutsch's images have contributed in placing the Great Flood in the Santafesinian flood memoryscape, and also to a particular image of flooding in the past, as an extraordinary yet fairly harmless disaster. There was also an art display in one corner of the exhibition in the Cultural Centre. Twelve of Lutsch's pictures in black and white had been re-elaborated digitally to colour by local artist Zulma Molaro, making the photographs appear psychedelic or dreamlike. The juxtaposition of Molaro's art works and the original photos were the reason to the title of the exhibition, Reality and Fantasy. A text written by the artist was posted next to her pictures:

> [T]he exhibited [art] works serve to situate us in a time in which Santafesinos experienced as much distress as the one not long ago [in 2003]. While the forms [the original images] are real, the colours and textures [of my pictures] are non-real; I imagined them as a phantasmagorical figure entering the city.

In Molaro's pictures, she superimposed the traumatic memories from the more recent 2003 disaster onto memories of the Great Flood. The result was a collapse of time between two extraordinary events, bringing the past to the present and vice versa. In contrast to Lutsch's pictures, triggering images of a South American Venice, Molaro's pictures evoked the distress of the 2003 disaster. Yet the dreamlike aesthetics made the real seem fantasy. In this visual representation and in the context of the exhibition, the boundary between myth and history was blurred.

Los inundados in Santafesinian literature and art

Art as a cultural form not only reflects society but also engages in commenting on social reality and in negotiating meanings around it. Literature, dance, theatre, and visual arts are shaped by their social, cultural, political and economic contexts and in turn shape the ways we understand these conditions. In discussing literature as such a particular cultural form, Archetti says, "[A] literary product is not only a substantive part of the real world but also a key element in the configuration of the world itself" (Archetti 1994:13). We have already seen in previous chapters how books and films were prominent in the memory-making around *la Inundación*. In what follows I will describe how flooding has been conveyed and dealt with in other previous Santafesinian works of art, more specifically novels, motion pictures and music.

On my first field trip to Santa Fe in July 2004, I visited my good friends and anthropologists Germán and Laura on my way. During conversations in their home in La Plata City, we talked about ethnography, about their experiences from fieldwork and about my forthcoming study in Santa Fe. They had searched in their home library for books about Santa Fe to help me get started in the field. They both urged me to read the books by the Santafesinian writer Juan José Saer because of what they described as his almost ethnographic descriptions of Santa Fe. One year later, during my fieldwork in Santa Fe City, Saer died at the age of 67 in Paris where he had lived since the late 1960s, working as a writer and a professor of literature. Born in the small village of Seradino, Saer grew up in Santa Fe City. He lived there and worked as a teacher at the National University of the Littoral until he left for France in the wake of the so-called Night of the Long Batons in 1966.[243] Saer's vast literary production consists of a dozen novels and a hundred published short stories and essays, yet he was not acknowledged as a prominent writer until the 1980s. He has of late been lauded as one of the best Argentinian writers, second to the most famous worldwide, Jorge Luis Borges (Libertella 2010; Cleary 2012).

Saer's fiction takes place almost exclusively in Santa Fe City and the surrounding littoral landscape of the Paraná River. He evokes places and characters in extreme detail in his often rather dreamlike stories. The stories are all located in a well delimited literary universe that Saer refers to as the "zone," consisting of Downtown Santa Fe and some of the coast areas such as Colastiné, Rincón and the Paraná River islands, either in present-day forms or in incarnations dating as far back as the 16th century (Riera 2006:28). The "zone" seems to be a space of eternal return for Saer, who provides a steady cast of characters whose lives can be traced from one work to the next. Yet he makes clear in a self-reflexive manner, that the use of such a space is really only a literary device "where narration can encounter the real and approach universal themes" (ibid.: 29).

Wulff (2009), contributing to the growing field of literary anthropology, makes the case for the genre of "ethnografiction." She defines this as a literary work of fiction based on research, even on ethnographic methods (pp.245-46). I argue that Saer's works can be placed in this genre. Despite the claimed universality of his works, the detailed descriptions of people, practices

---

[243] Since the university reform of 1918, Argentinian universityes were autonomous and run in a tripartite government of students, professors and graduates. After the coup d'etat in 1966, the military government carried out interventions against the universities and revoked this reform. In protest, several faculty buildings at the University of Buenos Aires were occupied by the students and professors, but were violent dislodged of by the police the night of July 29th that year. The name given to the event, the *Noche de los Bastones Largos,* refers to the long batons used by the police to hit the occupants in the dislodgement. Laboratories and libraries were completely destroyed, and hundreds of protesters were arrested. In the following months and years, hundreds of professors were fired or they resigned from their positions, Many, like Saer, exiled abroad.

and places make them at the same time very site-specific and ethnographic. As I read some of them during and after my fieldwork, it was easy to imagine and remember the city with all its colours, smells and sounds. Venturing another anthropological analogy it could perhaps be argued that since Saer was a native of Santa Fe yet an exile for many years, his gaze was that of an "ex-native" (Wulff 1998), an insider and an outsider at the same time or shifting in between the two categories (Narayan 1993; Björklund-Larsen 2010:53-54).

In Santa Fe, several of my interlocutors in the middle classes also recommended that I read Saer's work, not only because of his literary qualities (which some of them considered deserved the Nobel Prize), but in particular because of the references he makes to flooding in his stories. Floods are not so much the subject matter of any of his texts, but often mentioned in passing, as a background to the plot, as for example in his novels *El Entenado* (1983) and *Las Nubes* (1997), as well as in the novellas *Cosas Soñadas* (2000) and *A Medio Borrar* (1976). Alejandra, an architect working at the university, told me that she could remember, "just as in Saer's story" having visited the harbour together with her father during the Paraná River flood of 1966. She had heard the explosions when the National Route 168 was blasted to mitigate the pressure of the floodwater on the city centre (see Chapter Five). In the moment when she mentioned this to me, she could not recall exactly in which of Saer's stories these events were told. She knew that her husband had the story in his collection of Saer's works. After a few days she mailed me and said that I would find it in the novella *A Medio Borrar* (1976). It is ethnographically interesting in terms of remembering that nowhere in this particular story does Saer state that he is actually describing the 1966 flood, even if it is easy to imagine this, given the details of the story and the time of its writing, around the time of this particular flood.[244] Nevertheless, Alejandra associated Saer's story with her own personal memories, illustrating how such narratives serve his Santafesinian readers as mnemonic cues, almost as if they were historiography.

The social category of *inundados*

If *la Inundación* was dominant in the urban flood memoryscape during my fieldwork, so was the social category of "*inundados.*" In Chapter Three and Four I have described how this category operated in the creation of an accidental community of memory and a polity of remembering respectively. While the municipal and provincial authorities preferred the denomination "Affected by the Water Emergency"[245] when they referred officially to the 2003 flood victims, the most used term to talk about them, in public and in private, was simply "those who were flooded." The activists in the protest movement purposely identified themselves as such, turning the label into a political identity. Yet, as my fieldwork elapsed, I became aware that the term *inundados* was not a particularity of *la*

---

[244] According to Litvan (2012) the draft and first version of this novella was written in the years 1964-67.
[245] *Afectados por la Emergencia Hídrica* in Spanish.

Inundacíon, but a long-standing social category in the city. Through interviews and conversations with different interlocutors, and through the archives, I learned that in Santa Fe, *los inundados* also referred to those people who were "always flooded." This referred to the poor inhabitants who lived in the urban outskirts on the Westside, the suburban Coastside and the islands. The use of the category *inundados* emerged every time there was a new flood in the city, yet I found that this term resounded widely with certain narratives in popular culture. In Santa Fe, stories about *los inundados* were widespread, reproducing the mythico-history of urban flooding. As we shall see next, these stories, created by artists belonging to the local intellectual elite in different historical periods, reinforced middle- and upper-class understandings of the people living in the poor flood-prone outskirts as morally inferior.

Los Inundados – the novella

Mateo Booz[246] was a local writer and journalist born in the city of Rosario in 1881. As a young man he moved to Santa Fe City where he lived until his death in 1943. He wrote in all genres but it was for his novellas that he was known to the public at large (Booz 1999:513). These were published in the major Argentinian newspapers and journals of the time, such as *Caras y Caretas* and *La Nación*, as well as in the local newspaper *El Litoral* (ibid.). The works of Mateo Booz were thus widely known in Argentina in the first half of the 20th century. He has been acknowledged as among the most important writers of the province of Santa Fe. One of his best known novellas is called *Los Inundados* (Booz 1999b) a satire about the whereabouts of a poor family in the outskirts of Santa Fe when they are flooded. It tells the story about Dolores Gaitán, commonly called Don Dolorcito, and his wife, Doña Óptima, who lived with their four children in a *rancho* in a neighbourhood called Boca del Tigre. This place actually existed and was located at the banks of where the Salado River meets the Santa Fe Creek on the Southwest Side, approximately where the *barrio* Chalet is located nowadays. When Booz wrote this novella, Boca del Tigre was very much in the outskirts of the city and almost of a rural character.

In the novella, Don Dolorcito is depicted as a man in poverty but who takes these precarious material conditions rather light-heartedly. He worked only from time to time as a day-worker, a *changarín*. Occasionally he fished in the Salado River. His preferred job, however, was to engage in political campaigns. He would offer his services to any political party that could meet his interests, disregarding ideology, although he preferred the party in power because "in this [party], the resources would be abundant and the chances of receiving the emoluments on time were better" (ibid.:20). Don Dolorcito can be said to embody what in Argentina and in other Latin American countries is generally referred to as the *viveza criolla* (Creole mischief). This concept refers to a moral property of craftiness or smartness practiced by an individual to attain his or her ends, especially in an asymmetrical relationship of power, as to the State or to a

---

[246] This was his pseudonym. His real name was Miguel Ángel Correa.

patron. This property can either be a virtue or a vice, depending on the context and the eyes of the beholder. While this category of morality can be traced to the Spanish literary picaresque tradition of the 16th century (Alabarces 2006:78), the use of the adjective "Creole" situates the notion in the Latin American context. It indicates the asymmetric interethnic relations between the *mestizo* Creoles and the Spanish ruling elite, as well as the relations between the Creoles and the European immigrants of the 19th and 20th centuries. In Argentina, the concept is often used as a cliché in order to explain different social phenomena such as corruption, the style of Argentinian football (Archetti 1999) and even the Argentinian ethos or at least that of the Porteño, that is, the Buenos Aires inhabitant (Alabarces ibid.:ff12). In the novella *Los Inundados*, Mateo Booz drew heavily on this stereotype to portray Don Dolorcito and his entire family when depicting their ways of coping with poverty. Doña Óptima worked only occasionally as a maid and a cook in the well-off families Downtown or on the Eastside. Their offspring contributed to the household economy by crossing the bridge over the Salado River to the town of Santo Tomé to catch *chingolo* birds with wired traps. Their father then dyed them yellow and sold them as canaries at a high price to the visiting foreign sailors in the harbour. Booz underscored that the family worked only if absolutely necessary. Otherwise Don Dolorcito dedicated himself to his favourite activity, to observe the clouds from the vantage point of his *catre* folding bed, while Doña Óptima patiently cared for the delousing of her children. Booz portrayed the Gaitáns as a very poor but fairly happy family in their humble *rancho* home on the shores of the Salado River. This changed, however, on the day the river flooded.

One morning the Gaitán family woke up in the *rancho* with water to their ankles. Don Dolorcito took off for the city centre to see if he could find a place where to evacuate the family. Doña Óptima urged him to find them a safe lair, "the closer to [the convent of] San Fransisco the better, because there not even the Great Flood reached" (Booz 1999b:22) referring to the flood of 1905.[247] The Convent of San Fransisco is located in the Downtown neighbourhood of Barrio Sur, which is where the colonial city was resettled in the 1660s and one of the most highly elevated places of the urban terrain. In the novel, Don Dolorcito parried the worries of Doña Óptima by reassuring her that he had learned from the flood of 1905 that the best strategy in these cases was to keep still. So, while the neighbours packed their belongings and evacuated by horse wagon or canoe, the Gaitáns calmly stayed in their *rancho* with the floodwaters rising. By the time the firemen arrived in their canoes, the floodwater reached their knees. Don Dolorcito was nevertheless pleased to see that he had been right, saying: "Didn't I say so? One shouldn't be foolish, nor rush . . . Others shall see to it that we get out of this hardship" (ibid.:23). The firemen rescued the Gaitán family and their belongings. They evacuated the family in a truck to the place where the other inhabitants of Boca del Tigre had been evacuated, namely a row of train wagons at a dead-end track next to the Central North Railway station.

---

[247] This disaster occurred some 15-25 years before Booz must have written the novel, so it is possible that Booz actually experienced it himself, given that he by then lived in Santa Fe City.

Once installed in one of the wagons with some of their furniture, the Gaitán family declared that they were more comfortable there than they had ever been in their *rancho*. They even made nice new friends with other evacuees in the wagons next door. When Doña Óptima reminded her husband that he needed to find a *change* job to get something on the table, he replied cockily, as an excuse to refrain from carrying out such a task: "We are *inundados*!" Doña Óptima realised what he meant, when a couple of men from the Popular Commission for the Flood Victims arrived in the railway station with vans filled with food and clothing. In the novel, this was the beginning of the best days ever of the Gaitán family's life:

> No supplies or goods would lack in the train wagon in order to assure the well-being of the dwellers. The public powers and the local trade, sensible to such disgrace, tried to display generosity towards the poor flood victims. The journalists cooperated to generate this generalised spirit, lecturing about the damages of the calamity and about the proper obligations of human solidarity. Don Dolorcito, in circle with his neighbours, drinking mate and biting crackers, read this lucubration, which to all of them – reader and listeners alike – was both moving and convincing regarding their disgrace and their need to be well stocked. But what interested these troubled people most of all was the news and prognostics regarding the flood. It was not difficult to find an air of annoyance in these get-togethers if it was announced that the water level in the upstream Paraná [River] was descending (ibid.: 24-25).

When a group of foremen from the harbour came to recruit dock workers and another group of men came searching for agricultural workers, Don Dolorcito insisted conceitedly that he was not planning to work. "I'm an *inundado*!" he said, as did all his fellow *inundados*. Doña Óptima also put forward the hardship of the evacuation when the upper-class ladies came and requested her services. The flood had provoked a deep crisis in the supply of housemaids in town. When the evacuees were notified that they had to fetch their food portions themselves at the residence of the president of the Popular Commission, Don Dolorcito reacted with offence. When instructed to leave the train wagons, which were needed to transport the harvest from the hinterland to the harbour and obliged to move to another accommodation provided by the Popular Commission, the Gaitáns resisted. While all the other evacuees moved to other places such as the police station, Don Dolorcito and his family stayed put in what they now considered to be their train wagon. Following the advice of Procurator Canudas, they claimed their legal rights to be protected as flood victims.

One morning Don Dolorcito woke up noticing that the wagon was shaking strangely. Looking out through the half-open sliding door he saw the flat landscape of the *pampa* grass fields pass by quickly. He realised that their wagon had been connected to a train set and that they had left Santa Fe far behind. While this was a completely unexpected worry to Don Dolorcito and Doña Óptima, their children were delighted with the caravan. The train travelled day and night and the flat landscape changed to a mountainous view with rocky ground and shallow rivers. Don Dolorcito began to enjoy the ride, just like his children. Finally the train stopped in the small town of Cosquín, in the neighbouring province of Córdoba. The director of the railway station was surprised to find a family in one of the train wagons and inquired into their origin. Don Dolorcito informed him authoritatively that they were *inundados* from Santa Fe. The director informed the railway superintendence about the out-of-the-way wagon, but not until after eight days did he get a reply. But the answer was clear. He was ordered to connect the wagon onto the next train. One day as Don Dolorcito was strolling around the area, he realised that the wagon was moving again. He had to run after the train and managed to hop on with the help of his wife and children. The train did not return to Santa Fe however. Instead, it went westwards to the town of Cruz del Eje, where another train took them to the city of San Juan on the border to Chile and from there northwards close to Bolivia. Not until then was their wagon connected to a train that headed back to Santa Fe. After two months "on the road" the Gaitáns finally arrived in their hometown. In the meantime, the flood had passed and in Boca del Tigre things were back to normal. With the help of the Procurator, the Gaitán family was compensated by the Railway Company for the incident and returned home to ordinary life in the *rancho*, yearning for those fantastic days and hopefully considering the possibilities of a new flood.

Booz's work can be seen as yet another Santafesinian example of the genre of ethnografiction. Booz made a living as a journalist and was trained in searching for information. He became famous throughout the country for his published stories that depicted in ethnographic detail the life of the people in Santa Fe, most notably in the volume *Santa Fe, Mi País*[248] (Booz 1944). *Los Inundados* depicted Santafesinian society of the time from his own vantage point as part of the local intellectual elite. His representation of the urban under-class as mischievous and taking advantage of the solidarity of the people in the middle- and upper-classes, has to be interpreted from this angle. This view resounds with historical moral notions around social class in Argentina in general and in Santa Fe in particular, where the *negros del Oeste* (Westside "wogs") were the people "always flooded" and *los inundados*.

Los Inundados – the movie

The novella was a literary success at the time of its publication in the 1930s. It was made even more famous years later through the feature film made by the Santafesinian filmmaker Fernando Birri. The movie *Los Inundados*[249] was shot in Santa Fe City between December 1960 and March 1961. In fact, the Westside outskirts where the film was to be shot were flooded in those months (Birri 2008:165). *Los Inundados* had its première in Santa Fe on November 30th, 1961, and the opening night was a true popular celebration. A distinguished delegation of film critics and intellectuals from Buenos Aires were present on that night, but above all the locals were there to see a movie from their city. The number of

---

[248] In English: Santa Fe, My Country
[249] The film was titled *Flooded out* in English.

people by far overwhelmed the facilities of the cinema Cine de Mayo and many could not even get in to see the film. As a measure of its success, it can be said that the audience and the income of the first week of running *Los Inundados* surpassed by far those of the Oscar-awarded movie *The Ten Commandments*, which was also running in Santa Fe in those days (ibid.: 165-66).

The movie *Los Inundados* was the first feature film directed by Birri, who was known as a documentary filmmaker. The idea had occurred to him during his years in the early 1950s as a cinema student at the Centro Sperimentale di Cinematografía in Rome, Italy. In his own words, being a visitor in this country, the nostalgia for his homeland was sometimes pressing and he would take comfort in Argentinian literature. Among the books he read and re-read was Mateo Booz's complete works. *Los Inundados* by Booz was one of Birri's favourite novels and he thought that this ought to be his first film when he got back to Argentina (Birri ibid.: 162). So it was. Before this occurred, however, Birri devoted a couple of years to building up an institutional platform for his ideas and projects. Upon his return home to Santa Fe, he founded, together with a group of friends and colleagues, the Cinematographic Institute at the National University of the Littoral in 1956. This was timely in a context of reinforcing national cinema. In 1957 the bill to create the National Cinematographic Institute was passed, aiming at recovering the Argentinian cinema industry (Bravi 2010). These events constituted the beginning of what is known as the "New Argentinian Cinema" in the history of Argentinian film and the so-called Third Cinema produced in and by third world countries (Bravi ibid.; Berger and Wisner 2011:128).

Figure 30 | Film poster of *Los Inundados* advertising its première in 1961 (From Birri 2008: 123)

The Santafesinian institute was based on the model of the Italian film school, where Birri and others had studied. This school applied a neorealist aesthetics and pedagogy to the production and teachings of cinema. This would become a hallmark of the film production of the Santafesinian institute, as well as of the future works of Birri. The overall aim of the Cinematographic Institute was to put cinema at the service of social, political and economic change by documenting the underdevelopment in the country (Neil and Peralta 2007:20; Birri ibid.: 27-30). Such images and topics were unknown in Argentinian cinema until then, making this institute a national reference as "the documentary school of the Littoral" (Birri ibid.: 26). With time, however, this hallmark would tarnish the image of the institute, branding it as subversive. It was associated with the political activism and militancy of Argentina in the 1960s and 1970s, so when the military regime seized power in 1976 the institute was closed down and most of its archives were destroyed (Priamo 2007:83).

The film *Los Inundados* was based on the narrative of Booz's novella but built the argument and the script on the lives of "real people" who lived on the Santafesinian Westside, all of whom had participated in the documentary film *Tire Dié* (Birri 1987:61). The latter was a documentary film made at the Cinematographic Institute in the late 1950s. It depicted the poor people living in the shantytowns on the flood-prone banks of the Salado River on the Westside, in what would later become the neighbourhood of Santa Rosa de Lima. The film conveyed the poverty of this city and the children who lived in the Westside neighbourhoods were the protagonists. The expression *Tire dié* referred to the calls that these begging children, *mangueritos*, used to shout to the train passengers arriving in Santa Fe City. *Tire dié* is colloquial for *Tire diez [centavos]* which literally means "Toss [me] ten [cents]" but can be translated as "Toss me a dime." The children used to climb up to the bridge that crossed the Salado River as the train approached the city. Then they ran beside it along the railway tracks or they jumped up onto the steps of the slowly moving train. Other children followed the train running on the beach under the bridge when it was low tide in the river. As they were running and shouting "*¡Tire dié, tire dié!*" the passengers curiously stuck their heads out through the train windows and tossed coins to the children. This particular practice was so common in Santa Fe in the mid-20th century that the neighbourhood where the begging children lived, was at that time even called Barrio Tire Dié. I was told that this practice was abandoned even before the trains stopped reaching Santa Fe in the 1990s. Even if I, during my fieldwork, did see many children begging in particular at crossroads or in the commercial areas of Santa Fe, I never heard this expression on those occasions.

Tire Dié was a documentary film and *Los Inundados* a feature film, yet the bulk of the actors in the latter were amateurs casted locally in the outskirts of Santa Fe through the *vecinales* and social clubs (ibid.). I was told by my interlocutors living in the *barrio* Centenario that several of the amateurs had been from this neighbourhood, which was located close to Boca del Tigre described in Booz's novel. The leading role as Dolorcito Gaitán was played by Pirucho Gómez, a guitar player, *payador*,[250] folk dancer and singer who himself lived in a *rancho* in Boca del Tigre. The oldest daughter in the Gaitán family,

---

[250] The *payada* is part of the folklore on the Southern Cone (Argentina, Uruguay, Southern Brazil and Chile). The *payador*, traditionally a man, recites a rhyme by improvisation to the strum of a guitar. When the *payada* is performed by two people it is called *contrapunto* and is enacted like a sung duel in which the *payadores* are required to "reply to" the *payada* of the other. A duel can continue for hours and days until one of the *payadores* "loses" if he has not "replied" quickly enough.

Pilar,[251] was played by a fifteen-year-old girl from Santa Rosa de Lima who used to act in her father's amateur theatre group. Her boyfriend Raúl was played by Roberto Pérez, a young member of the *murga* troupe of Alto Verde on the Coastside. Only the role as Doña Óptima was performed by a professional actress. Lola Palombo had worked since a young girl in the Creole circus[252] and later in musical companies performing comedies and *sainetes*[253] (Birri 2008:164).

The film by Birri can be interpreted from several angles. The fiction conveys in a documentary mode the social and material relations that constitute social vulnerability in the city and the use of the disaster, by the local political establishment as much as by the *inundados* themselves. In contrast to Booz's novel, the attitude of the politicians and the charity ladies is depicted in the film as cynical, while the *inundados* (and in particular Dolorcito Gaitán himself) are depicted as conserving the idiosyncratic *viveza criolla* character. The movie aims at constituting a social critique (Berger and Wisner 2011:128) by using a realist language, local amateur actors and a visual aesthetics that comes close to the documentary, yet Bravi (2010) has argued that the film remains a fictional representation that reflects the gaze of Birri, himself a descendant of European immigrants. I agree with this argument, adding that it is precisely the documentary aesthetics and the heavy drawing on stereotypes that reinforce the cultural imaginary and these social categories, not least that of the *inundado*. It is nevertheless true that by making a satirical fiction and drawing on the picaresque tradition in Argentinian popular culture, the social critique reached a larger audience than what a documentary would have (ibid.).

Los Inundados was an important film and is today considered among the Argentinian film classics. It has even been claimed that it was this film that actually sparked the movement of the Third Cinema, referring to a form of filmmaking that combined fiction and documentary, professional and amateur actors and, most importantly, that saw film as a tool for social change (Bravi 2010; Berger and Wisner ibid). As for the local impact, I found during my fieldwork that the film was widely known in Santa Fe City, 45 years after its première. It had been screened in the cinema as well as broadcast on local television many times throughout the years. It was for example screened and debated during a photography workshop arranged in an art gallery in Santa Fe on May 10th as part of the commemorative activities around the 10th anniversary of *la Inundación* in 2013. On the book launch I attended in April 2005 (see Chapter Three), the movie was screened again after the presentation of the book. Of the people attending the event in the former train station waiting hall, many left the place after the presentation, while others, like me, stayed. I bought a *liso* beer in the bar and approached a group of people with whom I had already become acquainted, to ask about their impression of the event. After some small talk they

---

[251] This character does not exist in the short story by Mateo Booz, but in Birri's film this adolescent daughter gets involved in a love story in the evacuation site.
[252] The *circo criollo* was a type of circus show, developed and performed in Argentina in the 19th and 20th centuries, which also included a theatre play.
[253] A *sainete* was a popular comic opera piece, a one-act dramatic vignette, with music, popular in Spain and Spanish America between the 18th-20th centuries.

decided to leave. I asked if they were not staying to see the movie, but the unanimous answer was: "Oh no, that old movie – we have seen it a thousand times already!"

Los Inundados – the song

The soundtrack of Birri's film was a folk music tune composed for the film by another native Santafesino, Ariel Ramírez. He was born in the city in 1921 and became one of Argentina's most prestigious composers and musicians. He studied the piano at the conservatories in Buenos Aires, Madrid, Rome and Vienna, and early in his career became devoted to South American folk music which he made famous worldwide.[254] In 1960, Ramírez composed the song "*Los Inundados*," a song is in the folk music genre of Littoral Songs.[255] It was originally called "Boca del Tigre" (Birri 2008:162), making reference to the place where *los inundados* lived. For the film the accordion was played by a young folk musician, Raúl Barbosa, who later became a successful accordionist abroad and made the Littoral music known outside Argentina. Ramírez collaborated with another fellow Santafesino, Isaac Aizemberg, who wrote the lyrics:

> Roaring comes the water of the Paraná [River],
> flooding steadily day and night
> Homestead, gully, trunk it will take,
> with wind and heavy rain, the Paraná
> My *rancho* to the roof is already flooded,
> both the *ceibo* [tree] and the *aromo* [tree] lost their flowers
> I was sad that afternoon when I left,
> the *yerutí* [bird] singing its sweet lament
>
> Chorus:
> Navigating on the river, the rowboat is packed,
> I saved [fishing] nets, sticks, rigs from my home
> By the river I'll be back to Santa Fe
>
> The water of the Paraná [river] came roaring and left me poor,
> no *rancho* or shelter is probably left
> They won't get me out of this place where I was born,
> struggling with the streams I will live
> The sky is clearing [and] the *chajá* [bird] is flying
> [the] *calandria* [birds] and *crestudo* [birds] are already singing

---

[254] The most famous work by Ariel Ramírez is probably the *Misa Criolla*, a catholic mass set to music with rhythms from South American folklore that he composed in the 1960s, performed by numerous Argentinian and international artists throughout the years. Apart from this, Ariel Ramírez composed numerous songs that are very popular all over Argentina.

[255] The music from the Littoral region of Argentina can be defined as a blend of many historical influences, from the aborigines, the Spanish colonisers, the African slaves, and immigrants from all over Europe. While the *chamamé*, sprung from the central European polka, is perhaps the most emblematic music of the region, there are others. The subgenre *canción litoraleña* is characterised by its melancholic tune and by the lyrics which speak of the natural landscape of the region.

> So the day will come when I'll return
> to build my *rancho* again in Santa Fe

The song has been interpreted in numerous performances and recordings by many Argentinian artists throughout the years,[256] except for Ariel Ramírez himself, to the extent of being included in lists of traditional or most popular songs in the country (cf. *Cancionero Popular Argentino* 2000:216). Many Argentinians are not aware that the song is actually the soundtrack of the movie, which both have contributed to the making of the Santafesinian mythico-history of flooding.

Narrating *los inundados* in images, texts and songs

These three *Los Inundados* works – novella, film and song – had long been widely known in Santa Fe and in the rest of the country. The novella was read in literature classes in school; the song was performed by numerous Argentinian folk music artists; and the film was periodically broadcast on local TV, and screened on particular occasions. During my fieldwork, several interlocutors in the middle classes suggested that I should read the novella and watch the movie to understand how the people who were "always flooded" faced flooding. I found myself in a similar situation to that of Rivkin-Fish when her middle-class Russian interlocutors referred to an old well-known Russian novel to explain class relations in Soviet and contemporary Russia to her (Rivkin-Fish 2009:84). This novel depicted Soviet working-class people and Communist leaders contemptuously and so did her middle-class interlocutors.

When I had read Booz's novel and seen Birri's film, I raised the narrative as a topic of discussion with some of my interlocutors. Similar to Rivkin-Fish's reaction to her interlocutors' interpretation (ibid.: 84), my response to how Santafesinos interpreted *Los Inundados* was also consternation. Most of them, including government officials, agreed that both the novella and the film truthfully represented how those Santafesinos who lived in the flood-prone outskirts of the city coped with flooding, that was, taking advantage of the extraordinary to improve their ordinary poverty-stricken livelihood. In general, they saw this category of people, *los inundados*, as mischievous scroungers, rather than vulnerable to disasters. The director of the Unit whom I interviewed in 2005 (see Chapter Five), for example, explained to me that the reason that there were so many people making claims for compensation after the 2003 disaster was that poverty was such a big general problem in Santa Fe. The flood victims, she claimed, were actually taking advantage of the possibility offered by the government, just like the theme in the story of *Los Inundados*. Another illustration of this articulation was the existence of certain place names. The precarious jetty for taking the rowboats going between Santa Fe and Alto Verde was located Down-

---

[256] Among the artists making the song *Los Inundados* widely known and popular was one of the most popular and famous Argentinian folk singers, Mercedes Sosa, who recorded the song several times. Other well-known and popular artists who have recorded the song by Ramirez and Guizenberg are Los Fronterizos, Antonio Tarragó Ros, Las Voces Blancas, Los Cantores de Quilla Huasi, Liliana Herrero, and more recently Los Carabajal with Chango Spasiuk. Among the regionally known folk music singers are the Hermanos Cuestas and Maria Ofelia.

town, next to the Eastside ring road, the *Circunvalación Este*. The place was called Puerto Piojo, meaning Louse Harbour. According to some of my interlocutors, the name was due to the use of this area as a jetty of the poor (hence lousy) people living in Alto Verde. Interestingly enough, in the film *Los Inundados*, the evacuation camp where Don Dolorcito and his family and all the other *inundados* are evacuated is called Villa Piojo (Birri 2008:164), making the connection between the misery in an evacuation camp and the *villa miseria*. To the Santafesinos, the place that connected the city with Alto Verde was clearly imagined also through the film. A final example was the woman in her fifties and her husband who I met in an *asado*, a typical Argentinian barbecue, in their summer residence in Colastiné. They emphasised that Booz's novel was to the point because "everybody knew that they [the *inundados*] were just waiting for the next flood to come so that they could provide themselves with new tin roof plates, mattresses and stuff."

The narrative created by Booz and Birri had broad resonance among urban middle- and working-class Santafesinos and had forged their ways of remembering past flooding in the city. Their interpretations of the story reveal that it fixed the imagined social category of *los inundados* within a local moral economy of class. This category emerged in public discourse every time there was a disastrous flood and linked metonymically to other entwined urban categories in the socially stratified Santa Fe, such as *negros*, *morochos* and sometimes even *sabaleros*. People seen to belong to these categories were not only understood as poor, but as a morally inferior underclass, which was taken to be most clearly manifested through their mischievous *viveza criolla* in times of adversity. In contrast, my interlocutors in the middle and working classes considered themselves as morally superior, showing solidarity with flood victims and identifying with the notion of belonging to a generous community epitomised in the slogan "Santa Fe, the Cordial [City]." Hence, the moral economy of class was expressed and reified through the narrative of *Los Inundados*, contributing to the reproduction of the mythico-history. Similar processes of social categorisation connected to ethnicity and morality in the context of disaster was observed also in the Peruvian town of Yungay in the wake of the 1970 earthquake. Here the *sobrevivientes* (survivors) from the avalanche and the *damnificados* (victims) from the earthquake were identified within pre-existing relations of rural-urban and Indian-nonIndian categories (Oliver-Smith 1986:136-37). In Santa Fe, reading, watching, listening to and then discussing *Los Inundados* was evocative of the city's flooding past. It manifested how the mythico-history of urban flooding was largely forged through historical relations of class. While the resonance of this narrative was wide among urban residents, it did not create any accidental community of memory, as the narratives around *la Inundación* had done. Rather, the story of *Los Inundados* reified past and present relations of class, imbuing the urban flood memoryscape with moral connotations.

On the mythico-history of flooding in Santa Fe

This chapter has analysed how the Santafesinian flooding past, including other floods than *la Inundación,* was remembered in the city in different forms ranging from myths, novels and motion pictures to absent memorials and museum exhibitions. I have suggested that we can understand this remembering as mythico-history because, similar to other ethnographic cases (Malkki 1995; Cole 2001; Basu 2007), it was produced by historiography as much as memory. This confirms the notion that the dichotomy of memory and history is an intertwined process of different ways of remembering. The Santafesinos clearly drew on both these ideal type sources when they recalled the past by citing books, referring to movies or retelling myths. Some narratives, such as the story about *Los Inundados*, addressed flooding directly. Others, such as that about the city's foundation and replacement, dealt with flooding in an indirect manner, yet it was recalled as a central problem to the urban community from the very beginning. The mythico-history of flooding, I argue, gave account of a particular understanding of the urban community's relation to the rivers, one that from the beginning was signed by vulnerability and resilience to flooding.

In the mythico-history, most past floods were not recalled as singular events, with a few exceptions. The 1905 Great Flood was recalled through reminiscence and commemoration. In contrast, most other past disastrous floods seemed to rest in some kind of forgetful remembering (Fabian 2003), that is, a known yet not acknowledged problem of risk for the low-income sectors of the urban community. Upon my asking, most people, young and old, had notions about flooding as being a longstanding problem of the city. In these conversations I was often retold the foundational history of Santa Fe, and on some occasions, the mythical prophecies of future calamities, as a proof of this. Yet, most past floods were not remembered as singular disasters at all, that is, they were not chronologically situated events but were rather narratively placed in a timeless flooding past.

The mythico-history produced a central social category in the context of the flood memoryscape, that of the *inundados*. It was common knowledge among my interlocutors in the middle and working classes that it was that the poor inhabitants living on the Westside and the Coastside, who embodied this category. Yet the *inundados* were rarely considered as vulnerable subjects who were constantly exposed to risk by living in conditions of poverty in flood-prone places, but rather they were blamed for using flooding as a means of living by claiming disaster aid. Such actions were instead largely framed as a form of negative agency, which morally disqualified them as innocent objects of aid (Oliver-Smith 1986; Midré 1990; Dahl 2001). In the next chapter I shall turn to how the people who embody this category of *inundados* themselves remember the many floods they have coped with throughout history.

Chapter 7 | Flooding and embedded remembrance in the urban outskirts

Remembering recurrent flooding

On April 29th, 2005, after the commemorative act carried out by the March activists at the top of the embankment, I received a text message on my cell phone. It was from Germán, one of my interlocutors, saying that he would soon arrive to take me on his motorbike to the Plaza de Mayo square where the big anniversary manifestation was held. The women of the March invited us to keep the banners we had been given when we walked up to the embankment and to take them with us to the square. I got up on Germán's bike, trying to hold my banner and his as well, while he started the engine. I grabbed onto him as we set off for the city centre. Driving southwards along Blas Parera Avenue and turning on to Presidente Perón Avenue, we passed many of the low-income neighbourhoods of the Westside: San Pantaleón, Barranquitas and Villa del Parque. A lot of people were standing or sitting on chairs outside their homes and children were playing in the streets. They watched us as we drove by. Maybe the banners I held in my hand caught their attention. More likely it was the fact that Germán repeatedly shouted "*¡Justicia por los inundados!*" as we drove by. Nobody cheered us as we were advocating for their rights. They just watched us and talked to each other. I suddenly felt embarrassed to be carrying those banners and claiming for justice. Even if I could easily identify with the frustration and anger of the *inundados/activists*, I had to admit that I participated in their activities more for the sake of ethnography. After all, I had not been flooded while they had. I would later that evening find that many of the Westside residents were in the Plaza de Mayo square to participate in the second anniversary commemoration of *la Inundación*. Yet many more of them were **not** out in the streets protesting on that day. Driving through the Westside and watching the people as we went by them, I was utterly puzzled by their absence in the polity of remembering of which I was myself taking part.

This chapter takes a closer look at how past flooding is remembered in the flood-prone urban outskirts of Santa Fe. When the 2003 disaster occurred, it was not the first time that the people living in the poor *barrios* on the Westside had to cope with flooding. In contrast to the *inundados/victims* and the *inundados/activists*, the people who live in the low-income neighbourhoods of La Tablada, Barranquitas Oeste, Villa del Parque, Santa Rosa de Lima, Chalet or Centenario on the Westside and La Boca, Alto Verde, La Vuelta del Paraguayo or Colastiné on the Coastside, have been recurrently flooded throughout history.

In this account I call them the *flood-prone/inundados*. This chapter discusses how they remember past flooding in ways that I will describe as "embedded remembrance" because memories were eminently part of daily practices, places and other past events.

Historicising floods through media reports

Many floods have affected the districts on the Westside and the Coastside since the new settlement of Santa Fe City. Pistone gives an historical account of 19 extraordinary floods occurring between 1658 and 1878 (1989:73-75). In historical archives, I found photographs as early as from the 1878 flood. In the local newspapers, I retrieved accounts about the many floods that occurred only in the 20th century. The newspapers describe fluvial flooding as historical and recurrent disasters in these areas of the city.[257] As I read these accounts in the local historical archives, it struck me that the descriptions of the disasters did not vary much over time, although some of the floods had particular traits.[258]

The newspaper reports followed a narrative pattern – in effect reflecting that the history repeated itself. The reporting usually started with news from flooded towns up the Paraná or the Salado Rivers and observations on the rising level in the rivers, followed by reports on the families evacuating to higher spots nearby or being evacuated by the authorities to train wagons and warehouses located in the harbour, the premises of the Rural Society and the railroad yard. Reports from later dates (from the 1940s and onwards) often included dramatic accounts of how the embankments were reinforced by placing sand bags on top of them or with excavators shovelling sand and gravel on them. Many reports recounted how inhabitants were hoping to escape evacuation. Daily reports about how many centimetres the water level had risen or fallen, references to past records and prognostics about when the flood would peak were also part of the accounts. The neighbourhoods affected were pretty much the same in every account: San José de Rincón, Colastiné, La Guardia, Farrell, El Pozo, La Vuelta del Paraguayo, Alto Verde and La Boca on the suburban Coastside. On the Westside, the neighbourhoods Centenario, Santa Rosa de Lima, El Triángulo, Villa del Parque, Barranquitas and Villa Yapeyú were the most frequently mentioned. Which districts were affected depended to a certain degree on which one of the rivers was flooding at that moment, the Paraná River or the Salado River. Sometimes they actually flooded simultaneously. The Westside on the banks of the

---

[257] Indeed, the problem of flooding in the city has increasingly involved also pluvial inundations. This is paradoxically due to the building of fluvial flood embankments, but also to the deficient maintenance of rain drainage systems. Hence, on occasions of heavy rain, lowland neighbourhoods are flooded and disasters produced. The last serious disaster caused by heavy rain occurred in March 2007.

[258] As accounted for in Chapter Five, in 1914 the railway bridge collapsed, as did the highway bridge in 1973, both due to the flooding of the Salado River. In 1966, the National Highway 168 that runs between the cities of Santa Fe and Paraná, crossing the marshlands of the Paraná River, was dynamited in several places. Also this year, the popular recreation park, Parque Oroño, was seriously damaged. In 1983, the 20th century landmark of Santa Fe City, the suspension bridge, collapsed due to the flood of the Paraná River.

Salado River was more often than not flooded also by the Paraná River, as the flooding waters from the latter prevent the waters of the Salado River from flowing out.

While the stories told in the newspapers can be read chronologically as a historiography of the recurrence of disastrous flooding in Santa Fe City, they can also be read as a cyclical narrative, in which the records of past, present and future disasters are collapsed into a history of urban vulnerability. What follows is a selection of headlines in local newspapers from the past hundred years, which can be read in both these ways:

[Among] Flood Victims And Hustlers (*Santa Fe* 1914)
The Poor Neighbourhoods Of Lower Areas Of City Completely Flooded And Inhabitants Evicted (*El Orden* 1929)
Active Rescue Work Carried Out In Flooded Neighbourhoods On Westside And In Barranquitas: Municipality Issued Necessary Measures And Appointed Commissions For Respective Tasks (*Santa Fe* 1931)
Flood Threatening Our Neighbourhoods. Residents In Affected Areas Alarmed: Many Beginning To Leave Homes Before Invasion Of Waters Which Have Already Reached Considerable Level In "Campito Viejo" (*El Orden* 1935)
Once Again Danger Of Flood Has Appeared. Already Families Evicted Due To Waters (*El Orden* 1940)
All Lowland Districts In City Threatened By Increasing Level Of Waters Which Is Slowly Rising. Area Of Salado River Coastline Is Already Flooded. In District Of Centenario Waters Moving In (*El Orden* 1941)
Distressing Situation For Families Affected By Flooding (*El Litoral* 1946)
Rain Aggravates Situation Of Households Established In Lower Parts Of Our City Capital. Relocation Of Families (*El Orden* 1947)
No Imminent Danger For Flooding Of Populated Area Of Centenario [Neighbourhood]: Embankments In This Area Remain Intact. Firefighters Evacuate Many Families In Districts On Westside. River Is Flooding (*El Litoral* 1957)
Large Areas Of City Fringe Invaded By Water: [Safeguarding] Work Carried Out In [Avenue] Blas Parera And Embankment Of Centenario [Neighbourhood] Reinforced *(El Litoral* 1959)
More Than 6,000 People Affected By Flood In [Urban] Neighbourhoods, Coastal Areas And Islands Within Local Jurisdiction (*El Litoral* 1961)
Panorama Of Islands And Other Areas Affected By Flooding Of Paraná River Devastating: Hundreds Of Families Evacuated, Embankments

Broken And Many Houses Damaged In Outcome Of Flood (*El Litoral* 1965)
As Part Of Embankment Of [The District Of] Barranquitas Collapsed Waters Flooded Sectors Of Neighbourhood. 400 Families Affected (*El Litoral* 1966)
True Drama Taking Place On Westside Of City. Road Cut Off. Salado River Cannot Be Contained. 80 Families From [The Neighbourhood Of] Barranquitas Evacuated. Fear For Possibility Of Rain (*Nuevo Diario* 1973)
Residents Threatened By Advance Of Salado River Demanding Urgent Action: Status Of People Evacuated From Clucellas Island (*El Litoral* 1974)
Neighbours From [The Neighbourhood Of] Barranquitas Anticipate The Flooding (*El Litoral* 1977)
Living As Flooded: Common Situation Of Inhabitants Of Santa Rosa De Lima (*El Litoral* 1978)
Alto Verde Battles Against Steady Advance Of Flood (*El Litoral* 1981)
Operation Evacuation Of Alto Verde Under Way (*El Federal* 1983)
Peak Of Flood In Santa Fe Expected Within Next 48 Hours (*El Litoral* 1987)
[The] Flood: Close To Two Hundred Families Evacuated (*El Litoral* 1988)
Dramatic Situation In La Guardia, Colastiné And Rincón: Floodwater Now Covers Most Parts Of Alto Verde (*Noticias* 1990)
Flood Is Second Largest Of Century. Last Night Government Recommended Total Evacuation Of Alto Verde, Considering It "High Risk" Zone…Approximately 30,000 Evacuated (*El Matutino* 1992)
Five Fatalities Due To Flood In Santa Fe (*La Voz Del Interior* 1992)
Floods: Critical Situation In Colastiné And Other Sectors Of Riverside (*El Litoral* 1998)
Flooding Of Salado River Already Affected More Than 50,000 [On The Westside] (*El Litoral* 2003)

Forgetting flooding?

While the topic of *la Inundación* was on everybody's lips in Santa Fe during my fieldwork, and a few other floods were remembered, the many past floods affecting the city's outskirts were rarely mentioned. Rather, these events seemed to dwell in public oblivion even if flooding was recognised as an integral part of local history. When I began to carry out participant observation and to do interviews in the Westside outskirts and the suburban Coastside, I expected to find some kind of "counter memories" to this public forgetfulness (Foucault 1977;

Fabian 2007). Yet I was at first puzzled to find so little social life focused on the subject of past floods or the problem of flooding in general. During my fieldwork in these districts I did not participate in or overhear any everyday conversation in which flooding was the subject matter. I found no hidden scripts (Scott 1992), nor any performative rituals of remembering (cf. Cole 2001; Shaw 2002; Argenti 2007). Only when prompting could I elicit stories, especially in interviews with elderly people, but these were not very long or detailed narratives. Similar to Anna Bohlin in her fieldwork in a South African fishing village (2001), I was much more easily able to learn the residents' own flood memories in these neighbourhoods and this was through informal conversations, rather than by observing commemorative rituals of particular floods or listening to myths about flooding in general. In contrast, most people I talked to in Santa Rosa de Lima, Villa del Parque, Barranquitas Oeste, La Tablada, Alto Verde, La Boca or La Vuelta del Paraguayo, were not very interested in talking about such past experiences. When, despite their disinterest, I did manage to steer the conversation to the topic of flooding, the 2003 disaster immediately came to the fore and, in particular, the issue of economic compensation from the provincial government. This issue was rendering hope to many of the flooded families on the impoverished Westside of the city.

At the same time, this issue was provoking bitterness and envy among inhabitants on the Coastside, who had not been affected by the 2003 flood and thus would not benefit from any economic compensation. On these occasions, interlocutors in Alto Verde reminded me that they too had been flooded many times but never been recompensed for their losses. Nevertheless, compared to the intense memory-work of *la Inundación* carried out by the *inundados/victims* and *inundados/activists*, it seemed to me that they had incorporated the structural amnesia (Barnes 2006) surrounding the disasters they themselves had suffered. With time I understood that their forms of remembering past flooding formed part of their daily life, which was not as easily observable as the memory-work around *la Inundación*.

How can we understand these less visible ways of remembering? Nora (1989) uses his concept *lieux de mémoire* in binary opposition with that of *milieux de mémoire*. He argues that the latter, translated as "real environments of memory," in contrast to the first, is authentic and real because it is "[a] quintessential repository of collective memory" (ibid.: 7). Unfortunately the analytical usefulness of the concept *milieux de mémoire* is reduced, not only by the fact that Nora by this reasoning essentialises certain cultural forms of remembering, but more importantly, because he neglects to operationalize the concept. Connerton's (2009b) concept "locus" (in pair with the concept "memorial") is more clearly defined in this sense. He exemplifies locus with a house and the street, that is, social spaces in which memories are embedded. He argues that remembering as locus operates inexplicitly and culturally because "…relationships to places are not lived exclusively or even mainly in contemplative moments of social isolation, but most often in the company of other people and in the process of doing something with them" (ibid.: 33). The locus is a taken for granted topography, in which memories are inscribed and that we experience without really being aware about it. Cole has a similar discussion about the house as a space of memory of Betsimaraka ancestors (Cole 2001:113-16). I consider Connerton's and Cole's ideas about remembering as something embedded in everyday life to be useful for thinking about how remembering and forgetting disastrous floods take place in the Santafesinian outskirts and suburbs, which are seemingly forgotten at a discursive level, both when it comes to the larger urban scale and within these suburban districts. Yet, instead of the locus concept, which focuses mostly on the unconscious forms of remembering the spatiality of memory, I shall use the concept "embedded remembrance" to encompass how the commemorative, the reminiscent and the evocative modes of remembering form part of daily practices and places. In the urban outskirts, the latter two modes were more salient even if there were some flood commemorative practices and artefacts too. The point I want to make by using this concept is that in this setting, all modes of remembering were intrinsically embedded. What seemed to be social oblivion of past floods in these districts was memory albeit less observable at first glance.

Disaster memories in the everyday suburban economy

That day in 2005, when Luis and I walked to the flood embankment on the Westside (see Chapter Three), was the first time I met Adriana. After having walked on the top of the embankment, we crossed the ring road to walk back through the Santa Rosa neighbourhood to our own Barrio Roma. We came to a path on what seemed like an overgrown hill. Luis told me that the hill was in fact the remains of the old Irigoyen Embankment. Suddenly, seemingly from nowhere in the overgrown shrubbery, a slender woman with a bike and a teen girl with a baby girl on her arm appeared on the path. The woman was Adriana. We greeted each other and she asked where we were heading. Luis replied that we had been exploring the embankments because I was a Swedish woman about to write a book about *la Inundación*. While I felt slightly uncomfortable with Luis's presentation of me, it made Adriana cry out: "Ah, but then you must come with us now and visit my parents! They are still living on the top of the embankment." She pointed towards the northern end of the new flood embankment, in the opposite direction from where Luis and I had walked, and invited us to join them over there. Luis looked a bit hesitant about the invitation, but I was enthusiastic about the opportunity to meet people who, two years after the 2003 disaster, still lived as evacuees. Luis later confessed to me that he had been reluctant to go to an area of the Westside, where neither people nor cars circulated. He had only decided to go when I accepted the invitation, in order to protect me, he said.

As we turned around and walked back towards the embankment, we introduced ourselves. Adriana was in her thirties like me. At the time, I had not yet had my second child, while she was already the mother of six. With her on that first encounter was her eldest daughter Lorena, then aged 15, and her youngest daughter, Catalina, only one and a half years. Adriana had two more daughters and two sons, of which one was her foster son, a *hijo de crianza* whose biological father was a friend of the family. Later I got to know Adriana's entire family and they became key interlocutors for me. Adriana lived with her husband Marcelo and their children in a four room brick house with a big fenced backyard in the outskirts of the district of Santa Rosa. Both Adriana and Marcelo had been born and raised in the *barrio* of Santa Rosa. Their respective parents, in contrast, had arrived in Santa Fe from the northern rural parts of the country in the 1970s looking for job opportunities. Doña Elena, the mother of Adriana, was born in the Province of Chaco but as a girl she had moved with her family to the town of Villa Ocampo in the north of the Province of Santa Fe, where her father began to work in the local forest industry. Here she had Adriana as a single mother. A couple of years later, Elena met with Joaquín, who adopted Adriana as his own daughter when he married Elena. Don Joaquín also grew up in the shadows of the forest company La Forestal.[259] After military service he enrolled in the Marine, hoping to sail around the world. After four years he signed off, because he was engaged to Elena and she did not want him to leave. They moved to Santa Fe City in 1970 where Joaquín got a job in the wholesale market while Elena worked as a maid. They settled on the Westside and soon had two more children, Ana and Miguel. With time, they were able to build a small brick house in the outskirts of the Santa Rosa de Lima district. In the 1980s, they got the title deed for the land lot.

On the top of the flood embankment

During most of my fieldwork, Doña Elena and Don Joaquín lived in a *rancho* in the outskirts of the Westside. However, on the day I met them through Adriana, they were living on the top of the flood embankment behind the neighbourhoods Santa Rosa de Lima and Villa del Parque. They had evacuated to the embankment in *la Inundación* together with their daughters and their respective families. Hundreds of other families from these neighbourhoods had also escaped the flood by seeking refuge there. Doña Elena said that at first they had stayed under a shelter that they made out of tarpaulins. Once the flood was over, they built a *rancho* and stayed on the top of the embankment until the municipality drove them off.

The *rancho* stood on the exterior side of the embankment facing the Salado River. It was made with tin plates, but even if they were all rusty, the dwelling seemed properly built with a wooden door entrance, a window and drain-pipes. The interior was divided into two separate rooms, a dine-in kitchen and a bedroom. The entrance had a curtain as a door. On the outside wall hung a

---

[259] The *quebracho colorado* tree was exploited in this region from the beginning of the 20th century until the 1960s close to the point of extinction. The English company The Forestal Land, Timber and Railways Company Ltd, colloquially called La Forestal, was the principal company in this region. The tree is hardwood and extremely heavy, which made it extensively used to make railway sleepers. It also contains high levels of tannin used for the tanning of leather. For a historical account of the *quebracho* industry see Gori (1965).

bird cage with a *cardenal* songbird, which made it look homelike. Don Joaquín brought chairs out from the *rancho* and invited us to sit, while Doña Elena prepared the *mate*. She put the pan with hot water on the *brasero* (charcoal heater) on the ground next to her and started serving the *mate*. Meanwhile she lamented loudly that had she known we were coming she could have at least prepared some *torta frita* pastries. As we sat there, drinking and engaging in the small talk, I asked them how it was to live in this place.

Don Joaquín explained that it was much better here than down in the *barrio*. Here they had plenty of space and had been able to expand their pig breeding. He pointed towards a heap of tin plates some 25 metres from where we were sitting. I suddenly realised that it was in fact a pigsty. He told us that he had bred pigs for a long time, although on a smaller scale than now. He used to work at the wholesale market for a merchant and could bring home bad vegetables to feed the pigs. They used to keep a few pigs in a small pigsty on the field behind the railway embankment, but that was not a good place because it was too far from the house and they could not watch out for it. Thus, they had suffered numerous break-ins and losses of piglets. Don Joaquín had lost his market job in the wake of *la Inundación* because his employer, a small family company that traded vegetables, had been flooded and had therefore not been able to keep their employees. Don Joaquín had then engaged in *cirujeo*. He began to take his horse cart to the city every day to collect all kinds of tradable trash but above all discarded fruit and vegetables from the local vegetable stores, to feed the pigs with. For these purposes, the present place on the embankment was much better than the former one in the *barrio*. The two horses could graze on the slopes of the embankment, while they could keep them and the pigsty within safe sight. Their business had grown in these two years, as people got back on their feet again after the disaster and began asking for pork to barbecue around festivities and holidays. Don Joaquín did not even consider to go back to work for the vegetable trader (who was also back in business). He said proudly that they had even become renowned in the city for selling piglets of good quality. "Well, every cloud has a silver lining,"[260] he added, referring to the 2003 flood. As he said that, Doña Elena cried out "Oh, that flood!" She shook her head as if she could not believe it and chuckled:

> I sometimes sit up here and watch the [Salado] river and I recall that the water level [during the flood] was almost up to the top [of the embankment]. Never in all my years in [the city of] Santa Fe had I seen that high a water level. Normally it only reaches up to here.

She lifted her hand a meter or so over the ground to indicate the normal level of a flood. When I asked if they had experienced other floods, Doña Elena replied that flooding from the Paraná River was always a problem for the inhabitants and the farmers when she grew up in Villa Ocampo. In Santa Fe city she had also suffered many floods, in the 1970s, 1980s and 1990s. She couldn't even recall them

---

[260] "*No hay mal que por bien no venga*" is the Spanish proverb.

all, she said as she continued to remember: "Ah, it was a hassle every time!" She explained that even when the old Irigoyen Embankment had been in place, the men in the neighbourhood had to reinforce it with sand bags in times of flooding. Despite this, there was always some water, half a metre or so, inside the house. The furniture and the tin roof dwelling were ruined by the dampness left by the floodwater, no matter if she placed the things she could not take with her on the top of cabinets and cupboards, or sometimes even on the roof. Even when they had a brick house, it was affected by the floodwater. She said:

> The mark from the water is there, even if you try to paint it over, because of the dampness in the walls. We could never afford to repair them, so those wall marks were always a reminder…Now we're hoping to get the disaster benefit from the government for this [2003] flood. We could really use that money, you know.

Between *trámites* and *planes*

Doña Elena turned to her daughter and asked her, in passing, how the *trámite* was going, referring to the application paperwork for the economic compensation. Adriana replied that she was still waiting for their names to be published in the lists of beneficiaries and that she was fed up with going to the office of the Unit to check those lists. Suddenly Adriana's daughter Lorena, who had been sitting there quietly all along, spoke up, saying to her grandmother in a slightly annoyed tone: "You know, *abuela*, it's just like the *plan*!" When I asked what she meant by this, her mother explained that the bureaucratic procedures involved in the economic compensation for *la Inundación* were basically the same as any of the ordinary social welfare programmes they were enrolled in. They had to visit the office of the agency involved and get a queue number or sometimes come back at another day because there were no more turns for the day. They had to sit there and wait, and when they were finally attended to they had to answer all kinds of questions regarding the family situation by filling in forms and presenting certificates from different realms. Being the eldest daughter, Adriana had sent Lorena many times, both to the Municipality and to the Unit to carry out *trámites* on her behalf, such as to get a queue number or to deliver certificates, among other things. It was clear to me from Lorena's expression that she loathed the task.

What was commonly referred to as the "*plan*" during my fieldwork in Santa Fe, was not the kind of contingency plan of policy documents referred to in Chapter Five. The *plan* in the urban peripheries referred instead to social welfare programmes and consisted of an intricate web of many different governmental and non-governmental actions aimed at alleviating long term social and economic structural problems such as unemployment, poverty, poor health, precarious housing and lack of education. In spite of being one of the wealthiest provinces in the country, Metropolitan Santa Fe[261] has historically had a high rate of poverty. The governmental social allowance programmes were schemes designed at national or provincial levels but there were also municipal programmes.

---

[261] Gran Santa Fe includes Santa Fe City with all suburbs

Some of these programmes were internationally funded,[262] while others were sustained by national or provincial funding. Some were administered in the offices of the municipality or the provincial government, while others were managed by contact persons, who themselves lived in the neighbourhood. The latter are generally labelled *punteros*, a well-known category of actors in Argentinian political and social life,[263] and analysed within the social sciences (see for example Auyero 2001; Frederic 2004; Balbi 2007; DuBois 2008; Quirós 2011). The *puntero*, literally a pointer, is generally defined as a political broker who embodies political clientelism. The *puntero* is an informal representative in a district of a political party, or a faction and a particular leader within a party. By helping residents with different favours and resources the *puntero* expects that the residents will vote for his/her candidate in the elections. In addition to the governmental institutions and programmes, a vast number of NGOs (both church organisations and secular ones) were working in the vulnerable districts of Santa Fe City. Overall, the actions of both governmental organisations and NGOs were oriented to alleviate poverty. Their tasks ranged from providing employments and schooling through subsidies, to ensuring the provision of housing, clothing and food to the needy. The *punteros* had multiple engagements such as managing people in projects to build their own house; supporting local FM radio stations; or running day-care centres or canteens, where poor children could have their lunch and afternoon snack (cf. Faya 2004).

During my fieldwork in this realm, two things struck me. One was that the NGOs were keen on separating themselves from the governmental institutions that were viewed as politicised agencies. This aversion between non-governmental and governmental staff has been identified as a longstanding and mutual one (Faya ibid.: 40-41). The other noticeable aspect was that while people being assisted by these organisations would know very well which organisation was running which *plan*, to me it was very difficult to keep track of which programme and which organisation they were engaged with. People often bunched them all together: organisations, people, programmes and projects. This was particularly striking in contrast to those people working in the organisations who were keen on establishing a distance from one another. Besides the intrinsic complexity of this social field, the tendency to label the agents in the same way made it even harder for me to navigate it. One such example was the *plan* that Adriana and her family was preoccupied with. In that conversation at her grandparents' *rancho*, Lorena specifically referred to the Heads of Households Plan,[264] in which Adriana was enrolled. I later learned that her husband Marcelo was

---

[262] For example, the World Bank or the Interamerican Development Bank (Banco Interamericano de Desarrollo 2002; Bazzan 2010).
[263] In 2011 it even reached the sphere of Argentinian popular culture, as the soap opera (*telenovela*) *El Puntero* was broadcasted in a one of the mayor television networks (Canal 13), casted with many of the Argentinian actors in vogue.
[264] The *Plan Jefas y Jefes del Hogar* was an extensive national social programme implemented by the then provisory president Eduardo Duhalde and designed to alleviate the high rates of unemployment and social exclusion.

enrolled in another, namely the Work Plan.[265] In 2009 and onwards, they received the Universal Child Benefit for their three youngest children.[266] Doña Elena was also enrolled in a *plan*, although I never managed to find out which one it was and whether it was within a governmental or a non-governmental regime. The common denominator for all of them was the reciprocity involved. The beneficiary had to return the "gift" (Mauss 1954) of the assistance in a specific manner. Adriana had to send her school age children to school and have them inoculated at the health centre in order to comply with the National Programme of Immunisations. Marcelo had to work as a painter (which was indeed his profession) for a certain number of hours per day in the public works built by the provincial government in return for his money. Doña Elena was required to assist literacy classes two evenings a week in return for hers. The reciprocal actions show that the *plan* were not of pure charity but inscribed in relations of "contractual exchange" (Dahl 2001), in which moral concerns about responsibility were central.

The extraordinary repair of *la Inundación*

The so-called extraordinary repair granted by the provincial government to the victims of the 2003 flood was not a *plan* of social assistance, like the ones mentioned above. Indeed, judging from official documents and statements, it was to be understood as an exceptional measure to handle a singular disaster. Doña Elena, Adriana and all the other people in the western outskirts flooded in 2003 saw it as an extraordinary measure. So did my interlocutors on the Coastside, who had been flooded many times before in prior disasters, but had never been granted any compensation. In fact, everybody I asked agreed that never before had the government of the province of Santa Fe granted this kind of economic repair to any flood victims. While the public officials would frame this as an occasion of great generosity, the residents in the flood-prone outskirts and suburbs rather interpreted it as a turning point – finally, the government had paid notice to their recurrent losses. Yet, many people in Santa Fe who had not been flooded, interpreted this as a *derecho adquirido*, that is, a benefit that the *inundados/victims* from the 2003 disaster had acquired but were not really entitled to. Many, albeit not all, of my middle-class interlocutors considered that the claims of further compensation put forward by the *inundados* protest movement were asking too much and that this would set precedence for coming floods. The people on the Coastside thought the compensations were unfair to them. During one of my boat trips over to Alto Verde, a man in his fifties, angry with both the government and the *inundados/victims*, replied to my question about the extraordinary repair:

---

[265] The *Plan Trabajar* was a federal programme funded by the World Bank which was implemented during the second government of Carlos Menem (1995-99) and consisted of an unemployment allowance in exchange for the accomplishment of different tasks, mainly in the public works, such as in the construction sector but also in the sanitary, the educational and the health sectors. This federal programme was, to my understanding, administered at the local level by the municipalities.
[266] This benefit, *Asignación Universal por Hijo,* was another poverty alleviation policy implemented by the government of Cristina Fernández in 2009.

> Yes, did you hear about this [the repair]?! Recall all the times we have been flooded here in Alto Verde. **We** never claimed anything [from the government] but we **too** suffered losses. People and livestock drowned occasionally, and we always had to build up our *ranchos* from scratch, [we had to] get new animals and without help from anybody. Once we were out of [the public] sight [as evacuated refugees in the city centre] and back in Alto Verde, we were forgotten [by the public].

This view can be compared to one from the Westside. Susana, who had lived in the *barrio* of Barranquitas Oeste since she was a girl in the early 1960s, said this to me:

> This is the first time of all the floods we have had here [in this neighbourhood] that the government is helping us to come back. Ok, it was the worst flood of them all – at other times only half the house was filled with water, but still, nobody cared then. This time it was different. This [money] will be of big help to us.

Hence, on the one hand this unusual regime of economic repair evoked memories from the experiences of past floods in the city. The issue of entitlement or no entitlement of compensation became in itself a locus of remembering past flooding, as it resounded of inequality and of oblivion to many residents on the Eastside. To many of my Westside interlocutors, however, the repair signified an economic opportunity as much as a final recognition of them as vulnerable subjects.

The bureaucratic procedures required to achieve the compensation were analogous to – and clearly reminiscent of – other such practices, such as the *plan* mentioned by Lorena. These involved having to attend the Unit's morning office hours, queuing, waiting, filling in forms and making and bringing photocopies. It meant answering questions about family relations and economy, not being able to certify property or tenure because deeds and contracts were lost in the disaster, paying a notary public to issue certificates and spending days on end in checking "if the paperwork [for the subsidy] had gone through."[267] The list of cases that were finished and entitled to receive the compensation was published in the local newspaper or hanging in the display windows of the Unit's office. The repair scheme was not the same as the *plan*, yet the procedures were more or less the same. The stakes were also similar, given that some kind of reciprocity was required. In this case, the law that enabled people to start over proscribed any legal action against the State:

> The payment of extraordinary assistance established in this law will imply for the beneficiary, to waive any possible claim against the State for compensation for the damages resulting from flooding and,

---

[267] The Argentinian expression is "*Si el trámite salió.*"

where applicable, to waive any claims or legal actions for compensation initiated [before the implementation of the present law] (*Régimen de Reparación Excepcional Por El Desborde Del Río Salado* §7 2003).

This clause was disputed and claimed to be unconstitutional by the *inundados* movement and in the court cases of the *Causa Inundación*. Yet to the people in the urban periphery, this was rather business as usual. At least this was how Adriana and her family in Santa Rosa de Lima, Susana in Barranquitas Oeste, Lorena and José in La Nueva Tablada and many other residents in the western districts talked about it. They made no distinction between the "ordinary" *plan* and the "extraordinary" one. The capacity of poor people to comply with endless and arbitrary bureaucratic practices is what turns them into "patients of the state" (Auyero 2012). The politics of waiting, so pervasive of the relation between poor citizens and the State in many countries and certainly in Argentina, is not merely the expression of an inefficient public administration. It is an exercise of power that shapes the subjects of the state, providing them with critical insights into political subordination. Poor citizens, in the words of Auyero, "know through repeated encounters that if they are to obtain the much needed 'aid' . . . they have to show that they are worthy of it by dutifully waiting" (2012:9).

Trading memories at the *Trueque*

The Parque Garay was an enormous park with lush trees, green lawns and small lakes. I visited it quite frequently, both because it was close to where I lived and I enjoyed the environment, but also because fieldwork took me to this place. This was close to where Juan had taken me and Maria to see one of the sites of memory of *la Inundación*; one of the monuments of the *inundados/victims* was placed here. Adriana used to bring her small children to the park to play, and finally this was also the place of the Barter Market, the *Feria del Trueque*, colloquially called the *Trueque*.

    Barter is a widespread economic practice, yet as an anthropological object of analysis it has received relatively small attention in comparison to predominant debates on "the gift" and "the commodity" (Ferraro 2011:170). This form of exchange boomed in Argentina in the context of the economic crisis in 2001-2002. Barter markets first appeared in the province of Buenos Aires the mid-1990s as nodes,[268] forming social networks of solidarity and an economical alternative to conventional markets. The number of nodes increased quickly[269] all over Argentina as a means for the middle and working classes to cope with the acute devaluation of the legal tender (Hintze 2003). All kinds of goods and services were traded without regular money, either using a system of direct exchange or a fictional currency and *vales* (vouchers), attaching differentiated val-

---

[268] *Nodo* (node) is the local term to describe one single barter market, referring to it being a point of connection in a network.
[269] The number went from 400 nodes in the year 2000, to around 5,000 in 2002 (Ovalles 2002).

ues to the things and services traded. As the economy stabilised in the following years, most of these markets vanished. During my fieldwork, I was told that there had been other barter markets in Santa Fe City in those years, but I only saw for myself the one in the Parque Garay.

As I passed by the stands, made by blankets laid out on the ground, I observed the vendors, many of them entire families, standing or sitting behind their stands, drinking *mate* and eating, watching people pass by and making small talk with the vendors next to them. Potential clients passed slowly, eyeing the goods for sale. Children ran around and played football on the lawn. A steady flow of people went between the market and the neighbourhoods behind the railway embankment, that was, Villa del Parque and Santa Rosa de Lima, giving me the impression that most vendors and buyers came from that side of the railway embankment. All kinds of items were displayed on the blankets: pirate copies of CDs, food in cans and boxes, freshly baked bread, cleaning products, lamps and objects of decoration; even water for the *mate* was heated up and sold. Most abundant were clothes and shoes in all types, colours and sizes. I never observed many exchanges actually taking place and the practice of pure barter seemed to have been abandoned. The barter is generally thought of as the exchange of goods for goods. It has recently been suggested that it can be defined as the exchange of goods for goods or cash for goods or both (Ferraro 2011). This seemed true for the Garay Park market. Many goods had prices in pesos labelled on them. Despite rather low prices, ranging between USD 0,50-2,50 at the time, not much business seemed to be going on.

I returned to the *Trueque* a couple of times during my fieldwork in 2005, in company of Margarita, a woman in her fifties from the Westside, who used to sell stuff there. She explained to me that much of the goods at sale in the market came from the donations in the wake of *la Inundación*.

Figure 31 | Trading at the Barter Market in Parque Garay (Photo by author 2005)

Margarita confirmed what so many other people of the Westside had told me already; that this had been the worst flood of all. Her family's house had been completely flooded. They had evacuated to a school on the other side of Lopez y Planes Avenue. During the evacuation and afterwards, they had received loads of clothes and shoes, as had most evacuated families. Representatives of NGOs such as Caritas and the local Red Cross had told me about the enormous amount of donated clothing that had arrived from the rest of the country in Santa Fe as a response to the 2003 disaster. Much of it was never rendered useful in the end, because either there were too many clothes, or they were not usable.

This mismatch is a phenomenon well known from many disaster relief situations (Taylor 1979; Lasalandra 2008). In Santa Fe, the above mentioned NGOs and numerous others had first received the loads of clothes in order to sort them, so that they could be distributed properly to the flood evacuees. Eventually, some of the garments that Margarita and all the other evacuees received, fit their sizes and needs, but much of the stuff did not. These useless garments were thus exchanged or sold at the Barter Market, in addition to the remaining dry and canned food that they had also received during the evacuation. Clearly, two years after the disaster, cash was required to sustain livelihoods in Santa Fe City. Disaster relief donations had become part of the capital of those *inundados/victims* who had a hard time remaking their lives in poverty. The goods traded at the market not only provided them with this opportunity, but also materialised the memories from this recent disaster within their suburban everyday economy.

Yet, this opportunity, vital to the subsistence to many people in the urban outskirts, was threatened in 2005. The municipal government had announced that the *Trueque* was no longer permitted in the Parque Garay. It came to my knowledge that neighbours in the middle-class neighbourhood at the eastern end of the park had complained about noise and garbage. This upset the people who attended the market. In front of the market-place there was a long wall painted with graffiti, demanding that the mayor arrange for a new place to hold the market because "more than 1,500 families want solutions [to their livelihood situations]." The graffiti was signed "*Los inundados* from Villa del Parque."

Short- and long-term conflicts over space are common in post-disaster contexts. Displacement of disaster victims in terms of temporal evacuation or permanent relocation challenges existing notions of the use of space (cf. M. Gupta 2011; Weber and Peek 2012). A disaster in itself and the immediate recovery constitutes something of a liminal phase in which the altruistic community of sufferers is created and withheld. Yet with time, a kind of "disaster fatigue" (Peek 2012) generally sets in, as things are expected to return to normal. So is the use of particular spaces. In Santa Fe during *la Inundación*, this was the case with the schools where people were evacuated. After some weeks, the families who were not flooded began to claim that schools should be de-evacuated because their children needed to go back to school. The Barter Market in the Parque Garay had been a way of coping with recurrent crises. The economic breakdown of 2001-2002 and *la Inundación* in 2003 affected both the middle classes and the poor sectors on the Westside. In those years, the Barter Market constituted a livelihood for all people living around the park. As time went by and middle-income *inundados/victims* recovered, the barter exchange became redundant to many of them. The market activities furthermore brought painful memories about loss and havoc. Hence, from the perspective of the middle classes living next door, the market in the Parque Garay eventually seemed out of place. But to the people living in the poor neighbourhoods on the other side, the Barter Market continued to be vital in order to make a living. Scarcity, need, barter and participating in the informal economy were not extraordinary to them but, on the contrary, part of daily life.

On my return to Santa Fe in 2008, this *Trueque* had indeed disappeared. It had been moved by the municipality several times, first to the yard of the Mitre Railway Station on the Southeast Side and then to a cycling field in the neighbourhood Don Bosco up north. In 2009, the market was moved again further north (Municipalidad de la Ciudad de Santa Fe 2009). Flood memories were embedded elsewhere in the suburban economy.

Notions of the economy of solidarity

Villa del Parque was a *barrio* on the Westside, located between the Mitre and the Belgrano railways. Both railway lines used to be highly trafficked but since the 1990s only cargo trains passed occasionally. In this *barrio* too, children used to run after the trains, begging the passengers for a dime (see Chapter Six). At that time, the name of the *barrio* was El Triángulo. It was later renamed by Father Catena, a legendary Catholic priest who lived and worked in the *barrio* between the 1950s and 1974, when he had to leave the city due to the violent political climate of the time. I was told that he had died in the town of Tandil in the province of Buenos Aires. Osvaldo Catena had belonged to the Movement of Priests for the Third World, inspired by liberation theology.[270] In Argentina, as elsewhere in Latin America, the priests engaged in this movement were largely active in the country's shantytowns and working-class neighbourhoods (Burdick 1995). Ramón, who I met in one of the *asambleas* of the *inundados/activists* in 2005, lived in Villa del Parque for many years. He had never met Father Catena himself, having moved in after the priest had left, but he emphasised the "spirit of Father Catena" that used to reign in the neighbourhood. By this he referred to a strong sense of identity with this *barrio* and solidarity among its neighbours. Ramón used to be active in the *vecinal* of Villa del Parque in the 1980s. According to him, the neighbourhood association had achieved a lot of development due to this particular spirit, such as electricity and pavement of certain streets:

> There used to be a strong sense of community in Villa del Parque in those days, not like nowadays when the *vecinal* is co-opted by the

---

[270] Liberation theology is a Christian movement in political theology that began as a movement within the Roman Catholic church in Latin America in the 1950s–1960s, arising principally as a moral reaction to the poverty caused by social injustice in that region.

punteros and the 2003 flood. More than uniting us, this has only divided us further.

Ramón's statement echoed the voice of many Santafesinos that I talked to, especially in the low-income districts. Community relations were said to have deteriorated during the last decades, but in particular in the years that followed upon the economic crisis and *la Inundación*. These changes were described in terms of community fragmentation, politicisation and alienation between neighbours. When the post-disaster compensation procedures started in 2004-2005 and the damages were calculated, envy and distrust rose towards government and authorities. The resentment between neighbours and kin was reinforced because of the differences in how much the families received. Pablo, a young man, born and raised in the Westside neighbourhood of Barranquitas, put it this way in an interview in 2005:

There are a lot of people that they [the government] have paid [the compensation] already ... a lot of people on the other side of the Lopez y Planes [Avenue] have received compensation, where the floodwater did not even reach [the level of] the sidewalk. Well, what can you do about this – there's always somebody to take advantage of the disgrace of others.

What Ramón, Pablo and many others wanted to say was that while the reimbursement contributed to material reconstruction, it also reinforced the already conflict-ridden social relations in the *barrio*. This is similar to what Erikson observed in his study on the Buffalo Creek flood (1976), where the disaster only exacerbated already existing conditions of social vulnerability.

Such notions of urban conditions of solidarity and conflict are subject to memories situated in time and space. Ramón was convinced that the deterioration of social relations was due to an increasing extent of poverty during the last decades, in particular after *la Inundación*. He gave me an example by which he compared the past and the present. Close to the southern vertex of the *barrio*, next to the railway embankment was the one block-long Solidarity Street. The branches of a high willow standing in the corner almost covered the characteristic dark blue street sign nailed to a power pole. According to one source, the street got its name "in honour of the action of all the neighbours of the district of Villa del Parque who, in the 1972 flood worked incessantly and in a coordinated manner to contain the waters of the Salado [River], threatening to flood the entire place" (Cello 1997:125). Ramón passed the street every day on his way to work. In his view, the name of the street recalled, not the particular disaster, but rather the solidarity and sense of *communitas* that he too remembered from past life in the *barrio*.

Figure 32 | Solidarity Street in Villa del Parque (Photo by author 2011)

In 2011, I asked some of the residents in the street why it had this name. They replied that they had no idea. One lady in her sixties, working in her small garden added that: "It must have been the idea of Father Catena, surely!" This could be true, according to Ramón, because it was during the years when the priest lived in the *barrio* that the streets were named. Among them was the alley named after the neighbourhood association, the Vecinal Alley; the Cristo Obrero Street commemorating the primary school founded by Father Catena; the Work Alley commemorating a protest for the rights to work as *cirujas* that the residents carried out against the military government in the early 1970s; and the Liberation Street, commemorating when the residents in Villa del Parque managed to get the imprisoned Father Catena set free in 1971. As these examples of place memory illustrate, the past in the *barrio* included important events in terms of community self-reliance and entitlement. In contrast to the communitarian spirit that all these street names referred to, young Pablo however considered that community relations had always been equally bad:

> As far as I can remember, I have lived here [in Barranquitas] with my family. My folks built this house. The butcher's store at the front [of the house] was [built by] my grandfather, but instead of leaving it to my dad, he sold it and left [my family] all enclosed in this god damn place!

I don't like it [here] because nobody helps you with anything. I think this [had nothing to do with *la Inundación*, but] was always the case . . . This place doesn't help you to make progress, on the contrary, it draws you down, because they [the people in the *barrio*] put you in the same crap, in which they are [living] themselves. I want to get the hell out of here, I just haven't been able to yet. You know, since these people live in poverty, they learn many tricks and they want to put you in the same sack. I also always have problems with the police – since I live here [in Barranquitas] they always have the perfect excuse to take me [to the police station] every time. They [the police] encounter me in the street and they ask where I'm from, and when I say Barranquitas, they immediately order me to get into the car. To be honest, there are people who want to progress [in life] but then, the government won't let you.

Both Ramón and Pablo had experienced social life in the poverty-stricken Westside district for most of their lives, yet they had different memories of the past. This difference reflected the twenty something years of difference of age in between them. As Borgström underscores: "[W]e have to base notions of history current among people, not only at the level of intellect, but also on the passing of years experienced by an individual in all his and her capacities…[a]ffect, habit, comprehension, all aspects must be understood as playing a part, both for the appreciation of, and the ability to communicate in a sensible and competent way about, the past" (1997:36). Ramón had not lived in Villa del Parque at the time of Father Catena, but he was contemporaneous with the priest and his works in Santa Fe. That was why he could remember this spirit. Pablo's memories, in contrast, were that social vulnerability in terms of conflict and lack of communion had always been the sign of poverty and marginalisation on the Westside. As evident from these examples, flooding was only one of many crises that people in Villa del Parque and other poverty-stricken neighbourhoods of Santa Fe, had faced. Memories of such past events are embedded in the present experience of conditions of vulnerability and relate to expected future losses. This is similar to the illegal squatters in the Ganges delta living in socially and environmentally vulnerable conditions whose "remembered pasts are constructed with recourse either to normalised destitution or to worsening disastrous processes" (Harms 2012:119).

Landscape, task and small talk on the Coastside

There used to be two ways to travel from Santa Fe City to the suburban neighbourhood of Alto Verde. You could either go by bus, crossing the Palito Bridge, or by rowboats crossing the Santa Fe Creek between Puerto Piojo downtown and jetty number 4 in Alto Verde. In 2005, the means of transport to Alto Verde were changing. Municipal funding made possible the purchase of motor boats to replace the old rowboats. By the time I returned to Santa Fe in 2008, most boats were motorised. This reduced the travel time from fifteen to five minutes, which was a benefit for the local commuters. Yet, in contrast to the rowboats, the short trip and the noise made by the motorboats made small talk with other passengers difficult. In 2005, when I travelled regularly to Alto Verde, the conversations I had with the *boteros* (rowers) and the passengers, and the ones I overheard, were a major source of information about current and past events in Alto Verde. I was all ears about the topic of flooding during these occasions, yet this was rarely a matter of conversation unless I asked about it. The answers I got were shorthanded and rarely led anywhere: "Oh yes, we have had many floods here, but who in Santa Fe ever cared?!" or "Yes, the problem here [in Alto Verde] is the water, you see."

Eventually, I was invited to the home of one of the *boteros*. José was a man in his late sixties, born in a fisherman family on an island close to Rosario. He had lived in Alto Verde since the 1960s, working in the harbour and as a fisherman. His scarce pension from the harbour forced him to continue working, and thus he worked as a *botero*. I visited him and his wife Ester several times in their small lime-painted house in one of the winding alleys behind the embankment. Ester did not say much but José told me about the life on the island where he grew up and about the hard work loading and unloading shipping grains in the harbour. He had a son and a daughter from an earlier marriage, who lived in Recreo and Santa Fe City respectively. In passing, José once said: "Can you imagine, my daughter who lives in the Centenario [neighbourhood] had to be evacuated to stay with us in Alto Verde, when the Salado flooded [in 2003]." His remark referred to the many times he and the inhabitants of Alto Verde had evacuated from the island to the city. He therefore considered the 2003 flood to be rather the exception to this rule of flooding in Santa Fe.

The rowabout

During one of my visits in the winter of 2005, José took me on a short boat trip around the surrounding area. It turned out to be a "rowabout" (cf. Riaño-Alcalá 2006) in the landscape of flood memories of the Coastside.

We started out from the jetty of the *boteros*, located below the embankment around the 4th Block where the small wooden houses stand one next to the other under large lush trees. The suburban neighbourhood of Alto Verde had been settled on an embankment in the beginning of the 20th century. Throughout the years, the embankment has been subject to numerous reinforcements, not least in the 1990s, when the flood defence system was reinforced (see Chapter Five). The boat traffic and recurrent flooding were constant eroding forces that forged this landscape. The embankment, built with sand and soil, was about ten metres high and up to five metres wide. A concrete cast staircase led down from the top of the embankment to the beach where numerous rowing boats in different colours were docked, one next to each other. José explained:

> That boat you see there is a wooden canoe, one piece, like the old ones. Nowadays they are laminated on top, to last longer. This one is really old. Nowadays there are canoes entirely made of plastic, but you can't

compare the plastic with the wood. The plastic is too light a material. It's not firm in the water. Tiny winds, like these, grab the plastic canoe and push it anywhere. In contrast, the wood doesn't float away, it is firm. It resists the tide and the strong currents in times of flooding. Also to put the fish in [the wood boat] is better because if you put the fish [in the plastic boat] when it is hot the temperature is so high that the fish dies immediately. The plastic is not natural, like wood.

The jetty itself consisted of two planks laying half in the water and half on the beach, on which the passengers could step to get in or out of the rowboat. A dirt road wriggled out on the top of the embankment. On the waterside, the embankment was covered with grass and trees, but also with a lot of scattered garbage. Plastic bags and plastic bottles, old car tires, rusty cans and worn out household appliances lay strewn on the beach reminding me that the otherwise rural, riverine and leafy landscape was in fact a suburban environment.

Figure 33 | Setting out from the jetty of Alto Verde (Photo by author 2005)

Despite his age, José rowed energetically. We were soon quite far down the river. We headed southwards through the Canal de Derivación channel, passing by the harbour of Santa Fe with the Lake Sur on the starboard side and Alto Verde on our port side. A fisherman in his rowboat approached us. It was one of José's neighbours. The man, slightly younger than José, stopped in front of our boat.

They exchanged a few words about some neighbours, the weather and the river. They had both noticed that the tide was low that day. After this short conversation we continued down the canal. The encounter with the fisherman seemed to have prompted José to tell me about fishing in these waters:

> When I used to fish with my father...back in [the years] '52, '53, the amount of fish was amazing: the *surubí*, the *patí*, the *sábalo*, the *manduvé*, all large fish, good fish: 30 kilos, 25 kilos. The size of the fish has decreased since then. What most damaged these fishing waters were the [hydroelectric] dams [upstream], they have affected the behaviour of the fish. The fish which are beyond the dam stay there, on the other side, and do not come here. The fish don't pass through the dam gates. The dams also alter the behaviour of nature. Before, we knew when the river was flooding, which was at the time when the fish came to spawn. Nowadays, the number of fish decreases. There are fewer fish also when there is low tide because if there is little water they have nowhere to spawn. Yet when the river is flooding, there are other plagues: the molars fish, the *mojarrines* [fish] and the crab come from upstream and eat the fish eggs.

José suddenly stopped rowing and looked at me:

> Nowadays the river is unpredictable. It doesn't stay still. Before, the [water level of the] river didn't move for six months, well, one centimetre more, one centimetre less, but nowadays the flood suddenly raises water levels by three metres in fifteen days and two weeks later it is flooding again.

This latter remark made clear that, from José's perspective, the river environment had deteriorated over the last decades, changes that he associated with the hydroelectric dams upstream. His everyday experience living by and working in the river made his judgment authoritative. His memories about the Paraná River's past were constituted through a lifetime of practice in the environment, constituting what has been called a "taskscape" (Ingold and Bradley 1993).

As we continued the rowabout towards the area of La Boca, we passed a couple of small *ranchos* on the shores. I asked José if people were living there but he said that most of these sheds were for fishing and hunting purposes. He used to have a *rancho* himself that he used when he was out fishing, to cook, to clean the fish and sometimes to stay overnight. He had built it on an island further south, with the permission of the property owner, who was a wealthy man in Santa Fe City. I asked what his *rancho* had looked like. He explained that it had been similar to all the others, namely built with planks of wood and a tin roof. He had been forced to rebuild it several times in different places due to landslides caused by constant erosion and flooding. José provided me with a brief history:

Before, there used to be many more *ranchos* like these, many people used to live here on the islands. At the time of the [Second] World War, many people from other countries came to live here [on the islands] too. I was a young boy. The *gringos* built their *ranchos* too. They stayed for one year, sometimes two years, and then they left. There were Italians, Galicians and Poles who had a really hard time! They had nothing, not even canoes, and could not fish or hunt. Instead they had to day-work as *changarines* on the ships or in the sandpits for two or three pesos a month. The rascals here took advantage of their situation; poor *gringos*! Anyway, you should have seen the islands when I grew up, it was like a town with all the people breeding animals [such as] goats, pigs and chickens. There used to be two schools, but the big floods took everything. Then they moved the schools to Alto Verde and many people went to live there instead.

On our way back through the canal, arriving at the southern end of Alto Verde, we passed a place called Corte Grande (Big Cut). I observed that the land was lower here. José explained that, as far as he could remember, this place was always flooded, cutting off the dirt road between Alto Verde and La Boca. To prevent the latter settlement to be isolated in times of flooding, a 300 metres long bridge had recently been built over the cut. This was only to use in times of flooding and had to be crossed by foot and by one vehicle at a time. I had not heard of Corte Grande before this rowabout in June 2005. Only later, as I met with interlocutors from La Boca and asked them about past flooding, was this place mentioned. José's mentioning of it and the problem of flooding as we passed by it that day, illustrate the evocative power of places that embed our memories (cf. Feld and Basso 1996; Riaño-Alcalá 2006).

Absent places

In a different yet similar vein, places that no longer exist can also evoke memories. This has been called the "paradox of the presence of absence" (Bille, Hastrup, and Sørensen 2010:4). Close to the jetty where José had his rowboat, he pointed to a place in the embankment:

> There used to be another jetty right there. We who worked in the harbour used to go with the *boteros* from there. The flood in '83, I think it was, took it though. That [jetty] of the 4th Block was the only one left.

Since the embankment was the highest point of the Alto Verde Island, the houses had always been built almost on top of it or just behind it. Another of my interlocutors in Alto Verde, Doña Maria, lived in a house just behind the flood embankment. She was born there in the 1920s and had lived there her entire life, except for a short period in Buenos Aires in her youth. When I interviewed Doña Maria in September 2005 in her backyard, she told me why she had stayed put in Alto Verde all these years "in spite of the hardship that it means to live here." When she married, she and her husband moved to Córdoba, where her husband worked harvesting wheat and maize. Her parents did not approve that they had settled elsewhere, so the couple eventually returned to Alto Verde. They built themselves a small *rancho* on the plot where her parents lived. Doña Maria indicated a corner of the backyard to show me, where her first home had stood:

> And then another one right there because the flood, well, you know here [in Alto Verde] the treacherous thing is the water. My father built five *ranchos* in his lifetime! The last one was the one you see there, where my son lives. The [flood] water would collapse the brink and the *rancho*, and my father would build a new one. And so did we [Doña Maria and her husband].

I tried to locate the many long-gone dwellings and asked her again to indicate their location. She pointed to a place beyond the embankment. When I remarked that this was a place that no longer existed, she just smiled and shrugged her shoulders.

Another example of the evocative power of absent places was when Martín, another interlocutor and resident of Alto Verde, shared his spatialised flood memories with me during a walk in 2005. As we were approaching the neighbourhood, he pointed to a piece of land next to the scattered houses in the 1st Block:

> There used to be people living there too, but the flood took their homes. That's why they [the municipality] decided to build the new houses in El Arenal and move the people.

The new houses Martín referred to were located at the entrance of Alto Verde, east of the main street, in a place called El Arenal because it used to be a sandpit. The concrete houses were built by the provincial government after the 1998 flood to relocate the families who lived across the street in houses that collapsed. The remaining houses built in wood, adobe or concrete blocks were to be demolished by the authorities because of the risk of more house collapses. According to Martín, the demolition never took place. That was why the houses in the 1st Block were still standing there. He said: "The families who relocated to the new public housing sold their old houses to other people to settle in Alto Verde." He added as he shook his head discouragingly: "And nobody [from the government] said a word [about this omission]." The loss of one's home can be traumatic because the dwelling as a place as much as an object expresses identity, values and memory over generations (Herzfeld 1991). Disasters actualise notions of place attachment (Oliver-Smith and Hoffman 2002:10). The unexpected loss of home and belongings can be not only a material detriment, but deprive people of their experiential familiarity with a place (Hastrup 2011:43). As the examples here illustrate, spatial or material absences of things that once existed can work as mnemonic cues instead of producing forgetting (Küchler 2001). In terms of remembering, both the newly built block of houses and the place where the collapsed houses had been standing, constituted the embedded remembrance spatially and materially, reminding inhabitants about past floods as much as of future risks.

Intergenerational place-making through conversation

There were two primary schools (one public and one private) and two public secondary schools in Alto Verde, one with an agro-technical profile and the other a sailor school. Students were mainly from the Coastside, but some of the children crossed the creek from Santa Fe every day to attend these schools. The agro-technical school was located in the small suburban neighbourhood of La Boca. In 2005, I had the chance to accompany two of the coordinators of a local NGO to this school, where they were scheduled for a meeting that day. Their NGO was co-financing a social programme in this particular school. The programme was called Everybody to School[271] and basically consisted of granting 100 pesos a month to some of the neediest families of the secondary students, in order to enable them to pay for school supplies, shoes and school transport. The programme aimed to motivate these families to send their children to school, since secondary school dropouts were a serious problem in the district. At this meeting, I seized the opportunity to talk to the head of the school and with one of the teachers about my research. They became interested and invited me to come back on another occasion to visit the school. So I did several times in the spring of 2005.

    I joined in the classes of the 8th grade. There were about 20 students in this grade, of which two thirds were boys. They all lived nearby in Alto Verde or in La Boca. I took part in their practical agriculture classes in the field and shared meals with them at school. On these occasions I tried to ask them questions about their own past and the history of La Boca and Alto Verde. They were not very keen on engaging in such conversations with me however. When I commented to the male teacher that it was really difficult for me to have them talk to me, he had them sit down in a circle and he asked them straightforwardly (on my behalf) what they remembered about past flooding on the island. This direct pedagogy was not very successful either. Only after the teacher had insisted, one boy mentioned that he recalled the [Paraná River] flood in 1998. He had been a small boy at the time but he remembered having crossed the Corte Grande in a rowboat. He had overheard his parents discussing whether the embankments would resist the flood or not. As I listened to this boy narrating his experience I watched the expressions of the other students. Not all seemed to listen to him, but several of those who did, nodded their heads affirmatively, as if they too recalled this event in this manner. When he was finished, the teacher let them go, since nobody else wanted to talk. The initial testimony by one of the boys, instead of propelling comments and other stories, produced silence. While I sensed that it

---

[271] In Spanish: *Todos a estudiar*

was my presence that made them go silent, the teacher reassured me that these students were never very keen on talking in public. Their reluctance reminded me of my co-passengers on the short rowboat journeys between Santa Fe and Alto Verde, when nobody ever talked much or extended answers to my questions. I had a new chance to approach these young people, however, when the teacher asked if I wanted to join the group for a field excursion around the island. I was hopeful that moving outside the school walls could provide a more relaxed setting for small talk and engaging in their past.

We set out from the school on a warm and sunny spring afternoon. Not all of the students were present on this day, only five boys and two girls participated. We walked through the bush at a fairly quick pace. The boys, and in particular one boy called Lucho, took the lead, clearly very knowledgeable about the environment and the way to go. As we walked, the youngsters talked and laughed between themselves. Suddenly the girls seemed keen on making friends with me. The boys were still timid at the beginning of the walk, yet after a while they began teasing me with ironic comments and pulling my leg. When we arrived in a small meadow in the forest, the two girls, who were obviously friends, took me by the arm to show me a small hut made by branches and reed. They told me that ever since they were small girls, they had used to come to this place to play. When I asked what they used to play, they replied giggling that when they were small, they used to play house. One of the girls said to the other, laughing: "Remember that you always wanted to have so many children!?" The other girl agreed smilingly: "Yes, and do you remember that we used to collect the snail shells right there on the riverside for our 'babies'?!" She then turned to me and explained that, on the islands, babies had water in water snail shells to drink from. She could not really tell me why mothers carried out this practice, but she assumed it was for them to "grow properly." She added that empty shells were found everywhere at the water's edge, where the snails lived. "Speaking of snails," the other girl suddenly interjected. She had come to think of something important to share with me:

> You know, they lay their small eggs on the straws of the reed and when the flooding is due, they put them higher or further up towards the top of the straw. My grandfather who was a fisherman always said that the flood was coming when he had seen the snail eggs higher than usual.

The girls seemed satisfied to have provided me with information regarding flooding. I considered her comment on how to foresee a recurrent hazard very telling of this context of social remembering. By sharing her knowledge of the past with me, remembrance of flooding was embedded in conversation. In the words of Borgström: "[F]acts and chains of facts were spelled out and defined in an authoritative manner for the benefit of an audience who was ignorant of those very facts and circumstances" (1997:58).

The walkabout with the students continued along a path parallel to the Canal de Acceso channel. One of the boys spotted a poisonous *yarará* snake. The teacher, who had brought a machete knife with him, killed it by cutting it in two. After a while we sat down for a rest in the shade of the trees on the shores watching small fishing boats and a couple of bigger ships pass by. Despite the brownish colour of the river water, the idea of taking a swim nevertheless appealed to me after having walked for a long while in the warm weather. My statement prompted different responses. The girls said that they never swam in the river, because of the abundance of the *palometa* fish[272] and the fear of getting attacked. Some of the boys, on the other hand, stated that they shared my wish and immediately started to discuss which places along the channel and the creeks were the best for swimming. They explained to me that the *palometa* fish could bite swimmers if the fish came close to shallow waters. Another problem was the currents that could be treacherous in certain parts of the river and pull swimmers under the surface. Finally, one should avoid swimming close to where there were clusters of *camalote* water lilies, because the latter could carry poisonous snakes and other dangerous animals. The teacher explained to me and the students, that while there were always *camalotes* in the rivers of Santa Fe, huge clusters of them were released in times of flooding. The danger with the *camalote* clusters was that they were the preferred place for the *yacaré* caiman to lay eggs.

Figure 34 | Excursion with students in the surroundings of La Boca (Photo by author 2005)

---

[272] The *palometa* is a carnivorous fish related to the more well-known piraya, and both are piranha species.

The above is not only an example of intergenerational transmission of memory (Argenti and Schramm 2012), but also another example of how memory is mediated through the landscape and by way of the practice of conversation. We recognise from our daily lives that the past may appear in any kind of conversation. Borgström in his Swedish study (1997) explored social memory through everyday conversation from the position of being an "insider-outsider" anthropologist doing fieldwork "at home" (cf. Narayan 1993). In my case, this was not an everyday conversation that the students and their teacher had. They were very much aware of who I was and why I was there. Despite my relative "insiderness," to them I represented more of "outsiderness." This was why these explanations came about. Nevertheless, the situation created a setting of social remembering, for me as much as for them.

Safety buildings, risk reminders

As we have seen in Chapter Five, the flooding in the last decades of the 20th century prompted several risk-reducing actions on the part of the Santafesinian government. Besides building flood embankments and installing water pumps on the Westside and the Coastside, the municipal and provincial governments implemented a couple of other projects such as the relocation of residents from flood-prone areas and the building of evacuation centres to be used instead of schools and the like. According to my interlocutors, relocation was only a relative success, because the residents were relocated by force and other people soon settled in the places that had been evicted. As for the evacuation centres, the buildings were only half-finished and virtually abandoned by the authorities, bringing instead looting and destruction. Another failed project was the lake dwellings built in the neighbourhood of La Vuelta del Paraguayo. In a regional context, such dwellings exist in the Río de la Plata Delta at the outlet of the Paraná River (Rosato 1988; Boivin, Rosato, and Balbi 2012), but perhaps somewhat surprisingly, never existed on the shores of Santa Fe, according to local architects. In passing, an interlocutor from the *barrio* Centenario on the Southwest Side told me that she had been informed by her mother that there used to be such lake dwellings on the southern shores of the city in the early 20th century. Yet nobody else that I asked subscribed to this memory. To the knowledge of urban historians at the local university, this building style had never existed in the Santa Fe area.[273] Be this as it may, the lake dwellings in La Vuelta del Paraguayo were of a much later date, built by the government in the 1980s, presumably after the 1982-83 floods. They were made in concrete and erected on concrete pile-supported platforms, materialising modernist ambitions of endurance in hazardous environments (cf. Harvey 2010). On a sunny spring morning in September 2005, Martín, one of my interlocutors in Alto Verde, took me there on one of his week-

---

[273] Thanks to Adriana Collado at the National University of the Littoral for this information (e-mail communication 2009-04-16).

ly visits. He worked as communitarian worker for the municipality in this neighbourhood and in Alto Verde.

All six houses were inhabited except for one, which appeared to be used more as a utility room. Small children were playing in the sun and in the dirt road passing the houses that stood one next to each other. Martín explained to me as we walked, that poor families were living here and that they all had many children. I estimated the houses to be around 40 square metres, which seemed to be far too small for such big families. Yet the scarcity of space explained why at least two of the houses had been enlarged by building a ground floor below the platform, turning it into a two storey building. This enlargement subverted the original architectonical concept of lake dwelling for the purposes of flood mitigation, since the ground was meant to remain empty. Under current living conditions, however, the addition was clearly more functional for these families however. As many other development projects implemented top down, the people who are subject to the projects are rarely consulted about usefulness or functionality. For example, for the lake dwelling to work properly, the families needed rowboats or canoes to be able to fetch supplies and go to work and school in the case of flooding. But the dwellers of these houses did not, in 2005, possess any boats or canoes, given that they were not fishermen families. Acquiring a boat for the purposes of a possible flood was an insurmountable investment for these poor families. Hence, while the original purpose of the lake dwellings was to offer mitigation and safety to the inhabitants in times of flooding, the dwellers did not comply with these expectations. To municipal clerks working with flood protection, like Rolando and the Venezuelan mentioned earlier, the inhabitants in the lake dwellings were considered unruly "savages" (Harvey ibid.: 35) who embodied the "culture of risk" discussed in the municipal contingency plan. To the inhabitants themselves, objects of this policy, living in the lake dwellings did not generate a sense of safety. Rather, living in a locus (Connerton 2009) they were constantly reminded that they lived in a place of utmost risk.

Figure 35 | Lake dwellings in Vuelta del Paraguayo (Photo by author 2005)

Commemoration in Alto Verde: Foundation, *fiesta* and flooding

Just as the foundation of Santa Fe City was commemorated, so was that of the neighbourhood Alto Verde. I attended this celebration on September 11th, 2005. It was a crowded and cheerful event, and a display of suburban institutional life. The venue had been set up in the middle of the neighbourhood, which was somewhere in the middle of the long main street that ran through it. A podium had been built just outside the *vecinal's* building and Mayor Balbarrey held a speech there. So did the nationally famous folklore musician Horacio Guarany, a man in his eighties who had been raised in Alto Verde. He was something of a local hero and his speech was cheered by all people present. He was really there to present his recently published book (Guarany, 2005), written as a fictional memoir of his upbringing in Alto Verde. The title of the book was *La Creciente (Alto Verde Querido)*.[274] *Creciente* in Spanish means rising waters as in the tidewater. In river areas of Argentina it also refers to flooding, albeit not necessarily of a catastrophic magnitude.[275] The *creciente* Guarany referred to had nothing to do with the 2003 flood but was really a story of all floods in the outskirts of Santa Fe and about *inundados,* a story told from the vantage point of living with flooding as a constant risk. Guarany's tale had nothing to do with other narratives in Santa Fe about being flooded. It was neither a picaresque novella like that by Mateo Booz, nor a political satire like the film by Fernando Birri, nor was it a "testimonial" like the many books and documentaries about *la Inundación* of 2003. Guarany's book was rather a fictional social biography, depicting life in vulnerable conditions. Instead of a story of disaster trauma, it was a narrative about social suffering (Kleinman, Das and Lock 1997; Das 2001).

The commemoration of the foundation of Alto Verde continued with a typical Argentinian military civic street parade in which all local institutions were represented. They all carried the Argentinian and the Santafesinian flags. People stood along the road and applauded as the parade marched to the rhythm of a military band and the voice of an announcer announcing each and every institution represented in the parade. First out were the schools. Students dressed in school uniforms marched in a row led by an *abanderado* (standard-bearer) and a couple of *escoltas* (escorts). Following the students were the NGOs: members of the communitarian sewing atelier La Tranquerita dressed in folk costumes; the tropical *cumbia* orchestra Isla Tropical; the *murga* troupe El Picaflor; and the rowing men's cooperative Cooperativa Boteros Alto Verde. Next were the local police officers, the fire corps, guards from the Argentinian Naval Prefecture and the National Gendarmerie, as well as soldiers from the Argentinian Armed Forces. A delegation of local war veterans was also present. Finally, the many *gaucho* (cowboy) associations were represented by boys and girls, women and men, all dressed in typical *gaucho* garments and riding on their horses.

---

[274] In English: The Flood (Dear Alto Verde)
[275] Another word for flooding is *crecida*, often used to denote flash flooding.

After the parade, people passed to watch the unveiling of the two marble plaques placed on the wall of the *vecinal's* headquarters commemorating the 95th anniversary of Alto Verde. Inside the hall, a dozen plaques in marble and bronze hung on the wall, commemorating prior anniversaries. There was also an exhibition displaying all kinds of images and objects. Local artisans sold crafts and school students exhibited their assignments. On the walls were posted old posters, children's drawings, newspaper clippings, maps, school photographs and written short stories about the past in Alto Verde. All together, these objects, images and stories configured the embedded remembrance of the neighbourhood's past, highlighting the economic life such as fishing and cattle raising as modes of subsistence, but above all the role of the harbour. Similar to Santa Fe City, Alto Verde had its own foundation story which said the island was settled in 1905 by harbour construction workers and fishermen at the time when the Santa Fe harbour was built. The very island of Alto Verde was said to consist largely of the bottom sediments from the dredging of the river.

On display in the exhibition were also images and stories representing local institutions and past social events and milestones. For example, there were presentations of the *vecinal* association, the dispensary and the only telephone booth called La Central. The Jesús Resucitado parish, established by missionaries in 1916, had been an important institution, where the first communions were held. The parish's patron saint, the Sacred Heart of Jesus, was celebrated annually through a rowboat parade. Wedding and funeral ceremonies were also carried out in boats. Another important event in the neighbourhood was, as in the rest of Santa Fe City, the annual carnival. An old *murga* troupe, the Payasos de Alto Verde, was legendary in Santa Fe City. Popular dancing halls in the neighbourhood had been Don Benites, Marino and the Police Support Association.[276]

Besides all the images, objects and texts recalling past people, events and places, numerous family pictures had been put up on the walls of the hall. Most of these depicted family members having fun in public festivities or in private parties, working, or simply posing smilingly in particular places. Next to these were photos that depicted past floods. One black and white photocopy of a photograph depicted four men standing on the top of the embankment filling sand bags to reinforce the levee. This photograph was titled "Flood year 1992." Another group of photos were posted behind the desk where students and teachers from the agricultural school in La Boca were exhibiting their school work. These photos depicted the 1998 flood in particular places such as the dirt road to La Boca in Corte Grande and the school in La Boca. One picture in black and white with no date was taken from the river showing the flood completely covering the embankment and flooding the houses on top.

---

[276] In Spanish: *Cooperadora Policial*

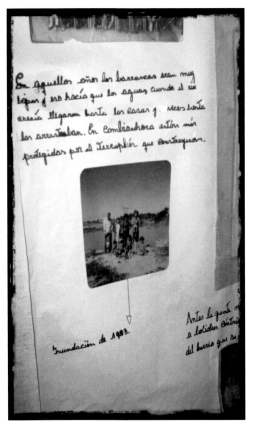

Figure 36 | Family picture in the Alto Verde 95th anniversary exhibition (Photo by author 2005)

There was one photo that was particularly striking. It was a colour photo taken with a Polaroid camera depicting what was presumably a family. The picture must have been taken at noon because there were almost no shadows and it must have been warm because all family members were all lightly dressed. In the background, there is water and a high-voltage line crossing the landscape. What struck me was the absence of drama in the picture as much as in the caption which was simply a chronological statement: "Flood of 1983." One can imagine, with the help of the caption, that the family in the picture was being evacuated at the time, yet in the picture there is nothing of a "disaster mood" transmitted. Above this photo it was handwritten: "In those years, the gullies were very low . . . [T]his made the flood reach [the top of] the houses and sometimes even wash them down. In contrast nowadays [the houses] are more protected thanks to the embankment that they built."

Contrary to the exhibition of the 1905 flood in the Municipal Cultural Centre (see Chapter Six), the objects and images of the local past that were on display in the Alto Verde *vecinal* hall were haphazardly placed. The memory-work here did not achieve any particular order of time or space, nor any particular ranking of past events. The people visiting the exhibition seemed familiar with the images and stories displayed. In front of some of the family photographs, neighbours gathered and talked about the people, the places and the situations depicted, adding personal memories to the past at display. The photographs of the floods, which were all family pictures, did not call any particular attention to the flooding issue itself, as far as I could observe. Taken together, this indicated the existence of a local community of memory which was not an "accidental" one such as that of the *inundados/victims*, but intrinsically configured through social life in this place. Hence, major events, such as the many disastrous floods that had harshly affected Alto Verde since the time of its foundation, were not singled out as the most striking memories but were rather embedded within other memories and at the same time embedding others.

Figure 37 | Reminiscence through photos in the Alto Verde 95th anniversary (Photo by author 2005)

The commemorative celebration of the foundation of Alto Verde ended with a *jineteada* (rodeo) that lasted until late hours. This was held on a large grass field only a few blocks from the main street. I immediately felt as if I had stepped into rural Argentina. The bush landscape that extended towards the river forged this feeling, but also the horses and the horse carts; the horsemen dressed *gaucho* style; the people dressed in more rural outfits; the women in the street kitchens frying and selling *empanada* pasties, sweet fried *torta frita* pastries and candy-floss; and the men cooking the *asado* barbecue of beef and sausages grilled on open fire on the ground. All this, to the sound of a folk band playing the typical *chamamé* folk music on top of a flatbed truck, made me feel far from the urban life across the river. As we have seen, the 95th anniversary of the foundation of Alto Verde was an ensemble of commemorating practices, narratives and objects. Flooding was recalled and some particular floods even commemorated, yet these memories entangled fluidly with others in the remembering of the suburban past.

On embedded remembrance

This chapter has addressed how past flooding were remembered in the urban and suburban outskirts of Santa Fe City where the people most vulnerable to this hazard lived. Their evocative, reminiscent and commemorative modes of remembering were intrinsically embedded in everyday social practices and places, and present also in de-materialisations or absences of formerly existing buildings and sites. I have shown that, what to the ethnographer's first glance might seem to represent the social oblivion of past floods in these districts, actually also constitute forms of memory – albeit less observable ones, precisely because of their embeddedness.

Connerton argues that what differentiates commemorative modes from evocative modes of remembering, or the memorial from the locus, is their respective relation to forgetting (2009:27). The locus is, in contrast to the memorial, a taken for granted topography in which memories are inscribed and that we experience "*inattentively*, in a state of distraction . . . as something which is inconspicuously familiar to us" (ibid.: 34. Italics in original). Therefore, the locus is not subject to oblivion. Cole has reasoned along these lines saying that "many traces of the past may be incorporated in the sociocultural environment so that they are not consciously remembered" (Cole 2001:2). In a similar manner, Argenti (2007) has argued that the discursive silence in the Cameroon Grassfields about violent memories from slavery is due to the contemporary reinstatement of new violence. In his view, the slavery memories are not forgotten, but remembered through embodied and material practices. They are "belated memories" because the collective experience of violence has been constant throughout history in the Grassfields (ibid.: xx). The belatedness of the experience of violence is precisely what produces apparent oblivion, for the past is always in the making of the future. For the *flood-prone/inundados* in Santa Fe, the risk of disastrous flooding is part of living in the poor outskirts. Theirs is a history of recurrent flooding and loss and they are well aware that this can also be their future. Flood embankments have been destroyed many times and cannot be fully trusted. The flooded past is not forgotten to them, but present and future in their lives through daily practices, objects and places.

Chapter 8 | Conclusion

Watermarks

I have called this study "Watermarks" as a multiple metaphor for the phenomenon it deals with: flood memories. In the context of memory studies, different metaphors have been used to convey what social memory is. In the introductory chapter, I mentioned that "landscape" is often used in this regard. Guber (1996, 1999a) uses the idea of "layers" from the earth sciences when she analyses how cataclysmic events forge the "social layers of memory" in Argentina. Borgström argues that remembering is a constant process of unpredictable becoming and likens the process of social remembering with "a day's movement of clouds across the sky, compressed into a few minutes on film" (1997:2). Perhaps the most widely used metaphor to describe the dynamic nature of social remembering however is the "palimpsest" (Huyssen 2003; Shaw 2002; Basu 2007). This is a parchment that has been written upon twice or more, having the first writing erased to make place for the second and later inscriptions. My contribution to this array of tropes is the "watermark." This refers generally to two things. Firstly, in common talk the watermark refers to a mark or a line indicating the former level or passage of water on a particular occasion. Watermarks can thus be seen as mnemonic cues of past floods (cf. Langumier 2008), which is indeed what this study is about. Secondly, the word watermark refers to the image impressed on paper during manufacture, which is only visible when the paper is held to the light. This illustrates nicely how the Santafesinian flood memoryscape is configured, by multiple and interrelated individual and social memories, of which some are more conspicuous than some others that appear only in a faded way when held into the light. In this sense, the watermark is also a methodological metaphor. By way of translocal and transtemporal fieldwork, this ethnography has aimed at exploring and illuminating both conspicuous and faded spaces of the Santafesinian flood memoryscape in order to understand how it was configured at the turn of the 21st century.

The Santafesinian flood memoryscape

The study has revealed that a memoryscape is best approached as a multifaceted and dynamic social phenomenon made through many different modes and forms of remembering. Throughout this study, I have conveyed how the memoryscape is made. Many ethnographies of memory focus on one way of remembering. In contrast, this study has aimed at revealing the multiple forms, modes and temporalities of remembering (and forgetting) that configure a memoryscape, focusing on how they articulate and interact with each other. Rather than contrasting memory in terms of individual versus social memory, un-reflected evocation versus reflective reminiscence and purposeful commemoration, memory versus history, remembering versus forgetting, narrative and embodied remembering versus material and spatial memory, this study has analysed how all these ways co-exist, intersect and conflict and thereby configuring this particular flood memoryscape.

The chapters in Part One focused mainly on how *la Inundación* was remembered in Santa Fe during my fieldwork. This was extraordinary memory-work taking place in many different forms, in different settings and at various scales of this urban community, from intimate evocation to everyday reminiscence and public commemoration. My interlocutors in the low- and middle-income neighbourhoods on the Westside told me how they were continuously reminded of this disaster through different evocative cues such as rainy and humid weather, particular places in the city and old and new photographs taken of the family and the neighbourhood. People who had perished in the disaster or moved elsewhere and belongings that had been ruined by the floodwater and discarded, became evocative reminders by sheer absence in people's everyday lives. Small talk with neighbours, discussions with the public servants at the Reconstruction Unit and interviews with the ethnographer were moments and venues of reminiscence by recounting narratives about the tragedy. While this evocative and reminiscent process is a feature of most post-disaster processes, what was really extraordinary in Santa Fe was the commemoration around *la Inundación*. This was carried out through an array of objects, narratives, practices, and places by Santafesinos directly or indirectly affected by the flood. In the study I have distinguished the people participating in this process as the *inundados/victims* and *inundados/activists*. The first category of people created an "accidental community of memory" that enabled them to make sense of the tragedy and of being *inundados*. The second category of people produced what I have called a "polity of remembering" driven by *ressentiment* and the quest for accountability of political decision makers whom they held responsible for the disaster. In both categories it was largely people from the working and middle classes who were driving this memory-work; people who had never before been flooded.

Taken together, these processes illustrate in particular that individual and social remembering are indeed interactive processes of making meaning out of past disasters, processes in which emotions play a significant role. They also shed light on a less discussed aspect of meaning-making in the wake of disaster, namely moral notions. Past actions (and non-actions), mediated through memory are socially judged as good or bad, acceptable or despicable, as shown in the discussion around the polity of remembering. The intense memory-work undertaken and sustained by the *inundados/activists* throughout the years also illustrates how memory and morality are intertwined when values are at stake. To the public authorities, the issue of governmental responsibility in *la Inundación* in particular and in flooding in general was discursively reframed by blaming the climate crisis and by omitting selected information about the past. To this, the *inundados/victims* and the *inundados/activists* accused the decision makers of *lavarse las manos*, meaning that they washed their hands of the responsibility for the disaster. Another example of the moral aspects of memory was that the governmental authorities disqualified the moral entitlement to aid of the *inundados* by depicting them as cunning and by intentionally neglecting to commemorate their disgrace. When the municipality, after many years, finally engaged in the memory-work around *la Inundación*, they did so to celebrate the moral virtues of stoic resilience and social cohesion of the urban community in the wake of this disaster. To the *inundados/activists*, this was a major offense as they claimed to be the only legitimate carriers of this disaster memory. They accused the political establishment of merely exploiting the memory for political purposes and charged them with promoting public oblivion about the government's responsibility. Overall, the activists' quest for recognition as victims and as political subjects was a moral endeavour to assert their worthiness of compensation and their right to protest. Therefore, in the context of the *inundados* movement, to make memory and to recall a particular past became something of a duty or a moral obligation among the activists.

Did their memory-work have any effect? While it is difficult to prove, it is impossible to ignore that the protests carried out by the *inundados/activists* have entailed a public pressure on the municipal and provincial governments to enhance disaster preparedness in Santa Fe City. Even the municipal policy of commemorating the 10th anniversary of the disaster in 2013, can be seen as a political effort to counter the persistent memory-work of the *inundados* movement of *la Inundación* as a political fraud. In this sense, the 2003 disaster indeed constituted a "critical event" (Das 1996). Yet even so, it is clear from this study that the public expression of *ressentiment*, claims for accountability and memory-work are largely the only means for ordinary citizens to influence policies around disaster risk reduction. Argentina is formally a democracy, yet ordinary people seldom exercise any autonomy of choice to which they are legally entitled.

If moral understandings were central in the emergence of the *inundados/activists* and their use of memory for the purposes of protest, we want to understand how this was the case. I have argued that two other interrelated social and political forces in Argentina contributed to the forming of the polity of remembering. One was a genealogy of social mobilisations in Argentina, the most recent in the field of human rights. The other was the "politics of regret" set in motion, first after the return of democracy in 1983 and resumed with the Kirchner couple in power. In Santa Fe, the official meaning-making of *la Inundación* was characterised precisely by a lack of regret and responsibility for the deficient disaster preparedness. As described in Chapter Five, it took several years and two new governments before the issue of responsibility was publicly addressed in the political realm. Meanwhile, in contrast to the intense memory-work undertaken by the *inundados/victims* and *inundados/activists*, both the municipal and the provincial public administrations practiced oblivion of *la Inundación*. Many examples in this chapter illustrate the process of selective remembering and forgetting that imbue political life, what I have characterised as the "logic of omission." This can be seen as inherent to the Argentinian political world shaped by clientelist relations and a politicised bureaucracy, and to the ways existing legislation is selectively complied with, as well as to how political decisions and actions are made, communicated and documented. The chapters in Part One illustrate clearly that local memoryscapes are forged in larger and situated spheres of remembering and forgetting. In this case, Argentinian political life, forged by path dependent processes as much as by contemporary preoccupations of the politics of regret, shaped the accidental community of memory, the polity of remembering and the logic of omission of the Santafesinian memoryscape. Taken together, the interrelated processes of remembering and forgetting placed *la Inundación* at the centre stage of the Santafesinian memoryscape, casting shadows over memories of most other past floods in the city with only a few exceptions.

In Part Two, I have tried to illuminate some of those shaded memories. In Chapter Six I analyse the "mythico-history" of urban flooding, referring to the entwined processes of memory and history that present flooding as a problem of the city since the time of its foundation. Myths, historiography and fiction narrated in various forms have shaped local, regional and even national memories about flooding in the area. Flooding was over all not framed as tragic disasters, however, but rather as a recurrent risk. The mythico-history also created the social category of the *inundado*, the flooded subject. The *inundados* were depicted as poor, yet resistant if not cunning, people who would take advantage of the relief operations in times of flooding as a coping strategy to deal with poverty. The category of *inundado* was well established in Santa Fe through the mythico-history and operated especially in times of flooding. Yet to the people of the Santafesinian upper and middle classes, it articulated semantically with the social categories they used in everyday talk about the poor people living in the outskirts: *criollos, morochos* and *negros*. In Chapter Seven I describe how the people living in the impoverished lowland districts in the urban and suburban peripheries have indeed been flooded many times throughout history. Hence, for ethnographic purposes I have called them the *flood-prone/inundados*. In this chapter I have described how they themselves remembered the floods as disasters and times of loss, quite far from the supposed windows of opportunity that were produced through the mythico-history of flooding. In contrast to the memory-work around *la Inundación*, memories of most past floods were embedded in more mundane rather than ritual practices and places. When evoked or recalled, disastrous floods were remembered as extraordinary events of the past, bound to happen again in the future.

The case of Santa Fe has not only shed light on the complexity and dynamic of the urban disaster memoryscape, but also on its heterogeneity. Processes of meaning-making around urban disasters are by and large shaped by the diversity inherent in city life. In a milieu where people cannot possibly share personal or collective experiences with everyone else, the memoryscape becomes diverse and multifaceted. Yet, as this study has illustrated, all memories are not equally remembered. The Santafesinian flood memoryscape was at the time of my fieldwork dominated by memories of *la Inundación* on all levels, from the private to the public. In line with Cole, I have argued that this is a matter of the remembering subjects being positioned in a particular position in the social space at a given point in time. By way of comparing the process of remembering *la Inundación* to that of other past floods in Santa Fe City, it becomes clear that the degree, the scale and, to some extent, the mode of remembering flooding depended largely on who and which areas of the city had been affected, and thereby who undertook the memory-work. Past floods like *la Inundación* in 2003 and the Great Flood in 1905 affected not only the people who were normally flooded in the low-income neighbourhoods but also residents in the middle-income districts. To the latter, being flooded and being an *inundado*, was unexpected if not unthinkable. They considered flooding to be a recurrent problem of other places in the city and to affect other people. I have argued that the different temporalities at play in the memoryscape, the "path-dependent" and the "presentist," enabled the semantic differentiation between *inundados/victims* and *inundados/activists* from *flood-prone/inundados*. *La Inundación* was understood as an extraordinary and unthinkable disaster in Santa Fe, prompting equally extraordinary memory-work by those affected and other Santafesinos, most notably through commemorative practices. In contrast, most other floods were remembered as rather ordinary disasters, and the *inundados* as ordinary flood victims. One could perhaps interpret this through the lenses of Ulrich Beck, as a result of risk society. Yet by referring in principle to the work of Pierre Nora and Paul Connerton, I have argued here that we need to handle such temporal dichotomies carefully when ethnography displays a far more complex and nuanced relation between people and environment over time. On the basis of this study, which is both an ethnography of remembering and a social history of flooding in Santa Fe, I argue that urban disaster memory has been shaped by social relations stemming from colonial times as much as of the contemporary politics of regret. The effect of such ways of remembering the Santafesinian flooding past has been a cultural and institutional normalisation of flooding as belonging to certain parts of the city and to certain sectors of the population. Eventually, I argue, it was this normalisation of flooding that made *la Inundación* possible.

Normalisation of disaster: Adaptation or vulnerability?

The notion of normalisation integrates the multidisciplinary research fields of risk, disaster and crisis. In this context, there are two meanings of the word. Normalisation refers mostly to the process of recovery and reconstruction in the wake of a disaster, that is, the return to the social order that was in existence before the disruptive event – in other words, going back to normal. From the vantage point of the victims of a disaster and disaster managers alike, the wish for the crisis to end is a comprehensible reaction. As I have stated in the introductory chapter, however, from the conceptual perspective of disaster risk reduction, the "return-to-normal" paradigm is problematic for ignoring that it was precisely those normal societal conditions that produced vulnerability and enabled a disaster to occur in the first place.

Normalisation also refers to the process that turns a particular extraordinary condition into a regular accepted fact of the ordinary state of things. Normalisation is here inherent in the concept of adaptability or adaptation to hazard, related both to the objective and to the subjective side of things. According to some scholars, accidents become inevitable in certain technological systems, because of their sheer complexity and interdependence (Perrow 1984), but also because of the gradual acceptance of certain risks in organisations due to "history, competition, scarcity, bureaucratic procedures, power, rules and norms, hierarchy, culture, and patterns of information" (Vaughan 1997). Bankoff has argued that such normalisation of threat creates "cultures of disaster," referring to societies that "have come to terms with hazard in such a way that disasters are not regarded as abnormal situations but as quite the reverse, as a constant feature of life" (Bankoff 2002:153). My study of flood memory in Santa Fe City has shown that cultural processes are indeed at the heart of disaster preparedness, in ways that problematise notions of resilience and adaptability to hazards.

In Santa Fe, recurrent flooding became normalised in both these ways. On the one hand, processes of migration, urbanisation, impoverishment, and political omissions increased risk for flooding throughout the 20th century. As the number of inhabitants grew, so did the demand for inhabitable land, which increased land values and prompted real estate exploitation. The surrounding Paraná and Salado rivers had hitherto constituted geographical limits for settlement. In the 20th century however, the demand for land expanded over the urban limits into flood-prone land. The risk was spatialised and socially stratified, as it was the poor inhabitants who were relegated to live in the urban outskirts where flooding was recurrent. Public works of infrastructure, such as embankments, flood pumps and flood safe buildings, were undertaken as mitigative efforts. Yet they were insufficient actions when political and economic processes at local, provincial and national levels worked in detriment, increasing instead conditions of social vulnerability in these areas. Hence, flooding was normalised because it became a recurrent problem and because after every flood, things largely returned to the normal state of vulnerability.

On the other hand, disastrous flooding was normalised in Santa Fe through processes of meaning-making regarding the people and places in the city that were repeatedly affected. Poor people living in the urban outskirts were considered to embody the social category of *inundados* and were largely held responsible for their own disgrace, akin to the blame-the-victim stance of the "culture of poverty" paradigm. Here we find another instance of moral connotations at play in the process of remembering, which was that the *flood-prone/inundados* were not really considered entitled to or worthy of assistance. Similar moral notions imbue the discourses of social policy and international aid (Midré 1990; Dahl 2001). Hence, the cultural normalisation of disaster was in this case very much an integral part of the historical processes of Santa Fe. It profoundly influenced local politics and the urban social order, yet instead of reducing risk and creating resilience to flooding in the city, it contributed to the reproduction of vulnerable conditions for the inhabitants in the flood-prone outskirts. While most people in the outskirts themselves recalled past floods as embedded in the harsh conditions of their life in poverty, they nevertheless remembered them as extraordinary disasters that had caused them all kinds of losses and distress. While they had knowledge about the risk and had coped with flooding throughout history by way of evacuation and with the relative support of structural mitigative devices, this had not really reduced their risk for being flooded. In this sense it is quite possible to see coping in terms of individual or collective human agency without taking a stand on the "adaptability" of society in relation to the environment. Resilience as coping and as adaptability actualises quite different time horizons. The first is concerned with disaster recovery and the latter with the evolutionary span over generations. This study makes clear that most, albeit not all, people in Santa Fe have coped with and survived recurrent flooding, which can be taken as a form of societal adaptability in a long-term perspective. Yet it makes little sense to speak about "adaptation" to disastrous flooding when, in a short- to medium-term perspective, the *flood-prone/inundados* were really rather trapped in a vicious circle of recurrently coping with disasters (cf. Segnestam 2009).

This result has certain implications relevant to the field of disaster studies. It sheds light on the need to further develop our conceptual tools to better understand the causes and effects of disasters. By this I do not refer to the often-made call for common definitions of key concepts, but rather to more fine-grained theoretical tools that allow us to analyse the contradictions of heterogeneous and unequal social worlds. A couple of decades ago, the new understanding of disasters as the outcome of hazard and social vulnerability called for a shift in focus from disaster response to disaster prevention and mitigation. Recognising in this setting that disasters disrupt development, and also that social vulnerability is constitutive of disasters, made disaster risk reduction a key strategy in the multilateral cooperation for a safer world. The resilience concept has had the benefit of bringing human agency and local capacities into the larger understanding of how people survive and cope with strain and loss (Scheper-Hughes 2008; Gren 2009; Wisner, Gaillard, and Kelman 2011a). The problem arises when resilience is presumed to be a property of communities and furthermore one equally distributed within them. Not only should we not see vulnerability as a property of social groups, because it stigmatises and victimises particular people, but also we should not see resilience as a trait of communities, because it romanticises and tempts to overrate capabilities. Rather, both vulnerability and resilience need to be seen as dynamic and produced in social relations. This enables us to identify and analyse how such conditions and capacities are produced, reproduced or transformed in a given community over time.

Urban communities are characterised by heterogeneity. This study has illustrated that when communities are stratified and fraught with social, economic and political inequalities, this contributes to differentiated vulnerable conditions. Resilience of one sector of the community can be upheld at the expense of the vulnerability of another. In Santa Fe, the extraordinary memory-work around *la Inundación* contributed to the public forgetting of prior floods. Hence, the experiences of the *inundados/victims* and the *inundados/activists* were largely recalled at the expense of those of the *flood-prone/inundados*.

Another aspect that has been highlighted through this study is the need to differentiate between the institutional and the social in a given community. Policies for risk reduction in local communities, as much as at regional and national scales, are often institutional matters more than an all-encompassing participatory endeavour. As Beckman revealed in her study on Vietnam (2006), societal institutions can be resilient to disasters while citizens are vulnerable to them. In the case of Santa Fe, the political efforts made to enhance preparedness, in particular from 2008 and onwards, have earned the municipality international acknowledgement in the United Nations. Yet, this has not really empowered people to engage in processes of risk reduction. Despite the explicit intentions of implementing a community participatory approach in the planning process, participation has been largely limited to the engagement of specific NGOs. As clear from the ethnography at hand, Santafesinos did not acknowledge all local civil society organisations as representative. Many, but not all, neighbourhood associations were seen as politically co-opted and corrupt institutions. Some *vecinales* and other types of NGOs, of which several integrated the *inundados* movement, actively counteracted the efforts made by the municipal and provincial governments in achieving societal engagement due to the conflict with the government. While certain other NGOs were well established in the city and acknowledged by the inhabitants, this case illustrates that it cannot be taken for granted that because local communities are involved in processes of risk reduction planning everybody within the community is able or entitled to engage. As Hilhorst et al. (2010) convincingly demonstrate, focusing on local communities is important in the area of humanitarian and development action, yet current efforts by international donors, NGOs and national governments alike are fraught with problems and idealistic untested assumptions. Hence, I agree with them that contemporary policies aiming at "reconstruction from below," is "shooting from the hip" rather than being the "magic bullet" (ibid.: 1120).

In line with Nadasdy (2007), I hold that when the advocates for resilient communities cherish resilience, they valorise a particular social order of that community. This is the order of things that has been disrupted by disaster and that it is desirable to return to, in the wake of crisis. The larger social, political and economic processes that put certain people at risk in the first place are not addressed. The stakes are set high to achieve sustainable development. Environmental degradation, poverty and social exclusion are identified as central problems that need to be addressed by the international community as much as by national and local governments. While such problems can be understood from different ideological angles, they are nevertheless pretty large political and economic issues for any government to deal with. In effect, they have been identified as the least well achieved goal of all the actions set out in the Hyogo Framework for Action to reduce disaster risk (United Nations International Strategy for Disaster Reduction 2011b). The lack of development in this regard is "…hardly surprising, given that the underlying risk factors include some of the biggest challenges facing the world today: poverty, rapid urbanisation and climate change" (p.27). Such a statement reveals the depoliticised nature of contemporary disaster risk reduction policies. Similar to the global politics of development, they constitute what Ferguson has called an "anti-politics machine" (1990). While social vulnerability is recognised as constitutive of disaster risk, responsibilities are not located with and actions are not aimed at those economic and political processes that can be said to produce vulnerability to disasters in the first place. Economic and social inequalities are rarely addressed, nor are the ecological processes that exacerbate the crises. Rather, policies have shifted to focus on the community in general and on the vulnerable subjects themselves in particular, presumably a more doable project for governments. Discourses of resilient communities are more often than not framed as a form of local empowerment, yet in practice they often serve the purposes of maintaining the established social order at the local level through normalisation. Hence, returning to the point made above, it seems to make little sense to understand this as adaptation or adaptability, because as is clear from the Santafesinian case, this would be adapting to vulnerability. As Sharma (2012) has pointed out when discussing the situation of the low caste Dalit in relation to contemporary environmentalism in India, people living in vulnerable conditions want transformation, not normalisation, of oppressing social structures, because only this can empower them in order to improve their livelihoods.

In sum

To sum up, this study can be seen as an anthropological contribution to dealing with disaster in society (cf. Kimura 2012). In this sense, it is an inquiry **of** memory as much as **for** memory. By demonstrating ethnographically that there is no straightforward relation between experience, memory and action, the study engages in discussions about societal vulnerability and resilience to disasters. The memoryscape, in which experiences of the past are mediated, is featured by heterogeneity, dynamics and unequal relations. Remembering and forgetting are therefore shaped not only by experience and social interaction but also by moral understandings, social relations and political interests, stemming from the past as well as shaped in the present. Hereby a crucial insight is confirmed, namely that the way an environmental disaster unfolds and is handled has more to do with society and societal relations than with nature and the hazard involved. This insight is valid for the field of environmental studies as a whole and points to the need to further explore the relations between social, cultural, economic and political processes in pursuing answers to pressing planetary problems. The study has disclosed the temporal and spatial dynamic and situatedness of how disaster memory is made. This has both methodological and analytical implications. Reasoning counterfactually I cannot help asking myself how the Santafesinian flood memoryscape would have been configured if *la Inundación* had not occurred. It is reasonable to think that, would I have undertaken fieldwork in past decades, I would have shared much of the memories (and the oblivion) around past flooding as I did during fieldwork in the 2000s. Yet the particular conjuncture, place, mode and form of the memory-work in Santa Fe (and in Argentina) would have been different. There would most probably have been fewer documents, fewer photographs, fewer films and less politics of regret for me to share. The idea that context in time and space matters for the meaning-making of the world may sound like a truism to the ears of anthropologists, yet it deserves to be repeated for multidisciplinary and policy purposes. If the past is to guide us through the challenges of the present and the uncertainties of the future, we need to understand it properly. Only from there can attempts to change the course of things make a difference.

Sammanfattning på svenska

Vattenmärken
Urbana översvämningar och minnesskap i Argentina

Inom det tvärvetenskapliga forskningsområdet katastrofstudier betraktas sambandet mellan erfarenhet och handling i samband med återkommande katastrofer ofta i termer av anpassning. Denna studie problematiserar detta teoretiska antagande ur ett antropologiskt perspektiv genom att undersöka de processer som förmedlar erfarenheter; minne. I studien analyseras kollektivt minne och glömska som sociala processer vilka förmedlar tidigare erfarenheter av katastrofer. Staden Santa Fe i nordöstra Argentina ligger mellan två stora floder. Här har katastrofala översvämningar inträffat regelbundet sedan kolonialtiden. Under det senaste århundradet har effekterna emellertid blivit allvarligare på grund av ökad social, ekonomisk och miljömässig sårbarhet. Den senaste översvämningen, som var en av de värsta någonsin, drabbade staden i april 2003.

Studien är baserad på translokalt och transtemporalt fältarbete i Santa Fe under åren 2004-2011 och undersöker hur tidigare översvämningar är ihågkomna – eller bortglömda – i den heterogena staden. Olika perspektiv på det förflutna analyseras: de översvämningsdrabbade i olika medel- och låginkomstkvarter, tjänstemän i den lokala byråkratin och aktivisterna i den proteströrelse som uppstod i kölvattnet av 2003-katastrofen. I fokus är hur tidigare översvämningar beskrivs i den lokala historieskrivningen och i myter, hur de representeras i samtida medier och hur de bevaras i minnet i offentliga monument och ritualer, men också hur människor minns sådana erfarenheter i vardagslivet. Minnen skapas på olika sätt: genom frammaning (när olika saker påminner oss om någonting), erinring (när man aktivt drar sig till minnes någonting) och åminnelse (när man aktivt och regelbundet hedrar något eller någon i det förflutna) sätt. Att minnas tar sig uttryck i berättelser, objekt, platser och olika sociala praktiker. Dessa former innefattar exempelvis myter, monument och ritualer, men också vardagliga praktiker, byråkratiska dokument, landskap och infrastruktur för att nämna några. Sammantaget konfigurerar dessa sätt och former ett minnesskap i vilket vissa katastrofer är mer framträdande än andra.

Det studerade katastrofminnesskapet återskapas i lokala historiska relationer men är också inbäddat i en större argentinsk kontext som präglats av politisk turbulens, ekonomiska kriser och minnespolitik. Sammantaget formar detta föreställningar om skuld och ansvar när det handlar om katastrofer. Studien analyserar, med hjälp av antropologiska och sociologiska teorier, relationen mellan minne, moral, politik och social ojämlikhet, och dess konsekvenser för frågor om sårbarhet, resiliens och anpassning. Studien visar att socialt minne är en dynamisk, heterogen och situerad process som inte nödvändigtvis förmedlar alla erfarenheter från det förflutna. Minnet är selektivt, intimt förknippat med glömska och skapas i relation till olika kulturella föreställningar. I det studerade fallet har sådana föreställningar lett till att de katastrofala översvämningar som drabbat de mest sårbara delarna av befolkningen har normaliserats och kommit att betraktas som oundvikliga problem, en slags anpassning. De riskreducerande åtgärder som vidtagits har fokuserat på tekniska lösningar emedan frågor om social sårbarhet, som är centrala i det riskreducerande arbetet, har trängts undan. Slutsatsen är att sambandet mellan erfarenhet och handling inte är entydigt eftersom minnesskapet kan skapa en anpassning som snarare leder till sårbarhet mer än resiliens.

Reference list

Acuña, Carlos. 1994. "Politics and Economics in the Argentina of the Nineties (or Why the Future No Longer Is What It Used to Be)". In *Democracy, Markets, and Structural Reform in Latin America: Argentina, Bolivia, Brazil, Chile, and Mexico*, edited by William C. Smith, Carlos H. Acuña, and Eduardo Gamarra, 30–73. London: Transaction Publishers.

Acuña, Lidia Graciela. 2005. "Aportes Del Cine Documental a La Construcción de La Memoria y El Pasado Reciente". Ponencia presentada en X Congreso Interclaustros de Historia en la Facultad de Humanidades de la Universidad Nacional de Rosario.

Agamben, Giorgio. 2005. *State of Exception*. Chicago: University of Chicago Press.

Akiko, Naono. 2002. "Embracing the Dead in the Bomb's Shadow: Journey Through the Hiroshima Memoryscape". Doctoral thesis, mimeo, Santa Cruz (CA): University of California at Santa Cruz, Department of Sociology.

Alabarces, Pablo. 2006. "Tropicalismos y Europeísmos En El Fútbol. La Narración de La Diferencia Entre Brasil y Argentina". *Revista Internacional de Sociología* LXIV (45): 67–82.

Aldao, Jorge Reynoso. 1999. "Los Infundios, La Polémica y Los Amigos de Santa Fe La Vieja". *Revista América* (15): 3–37.

Aldrich, Daniel P. 2012. *Building Resilience: Social Capital in Post-Disaster Recovery*. Chicago: University of Chicago Press.

Allatson, Paul. 2002. *Latino Dreams: Transcultural Traffic and the U.S. National Imaginary*. Amsterdam: Rodopi.

Allen, Barton. 1969. *Communities in Disaster: A Sociological Analysis of Collective Stress Situations*. Garden City, New York: Doubleday.

Alonso, Luciano, Araceli Boumerá, and Julieta Citroni. 2007. "Confrontaciones en Torno del Espacio Urbano: Dictadura, Gobierno Constitucional y Movimiento de Derechos Humanos en Santa Fe (Argentina)". *Historia Regional* (25): 11–32.

Alvarez Rivera, Fermín. 2009. *Huellas y Memoria de Jorge Prelorán*. Documentary-Ethnobiograhy. http://www.huellasdepreloran.com.ar/.

Amit, Vered, ed. 1999. *Constructing the Field: Ethnographic Fieldwork in the Contemporary World*. London: Routledge.

———. 2002. "Reconceptualizing Community". In *Realizing Community: Concepts, Social Relationships and Sentiments*, edited by Vered Amit, 1–20. London: Routledge.

———. 2012. "Community as 'Good to Think With': The Productiveness of Strategic Ambiguities". In *Community, Cosmopolitanism and the Problem of Human Commonality*, edited by Nigel Rapport. 357-63 London: Pluto Press.

Anderson, Benedict. 1991. *Imagined Communities: Reflections on the Origin and Spread of Nationalism*. Brooklyn, New York: Verso Books.

Anderson, Mary B. 1994. "Understanding the Disaster-Development Continuum". *Gender & Development* 2 (1) (February): 7–10. UK: Oxfam and Taylor & Francis.

Andreis, Andrés Alejandro. 2003. *El Ferrocarril. Lo Que el Tiempo no Borró*. Santa Fe, Argentina: Ediciones Universidad Nacional del Litoral.

Antze, Paul, and Michael Lambek, eds. 1996. *Tense Past: Cultural Essays in Trauma and Memory*. London: Routledge.

Appadurai, Arjun. 1981. "The Past as a Scarce Resource". *Man* 16 (2). New Series (June 1): 201–219.

———. 1986. "Center and Periphery in Anthropological Theory". *Comparative Studies in Society and History* 28 (2): 356–361.

———. 1988. *The Social Life of Things: Commodities in Cultural Perspective*. Cambridge, UK: Cambridge University Press.

———. 1991. "Global Ethnoscapes: Notes and Queries for a Transnational Anthropology". In *Interventions: Anthropologies of the Present*, edited by R. G. Fox, 191–210. Santa Fe, New Mexico: School of American Research.

———. 1996. *Modernity at Large. Cultural Dimensions of Globalization*. Minneapolis: University of Minnesota Press.

Archetti, Eduardo. 1988. "Ideología y Organización Sindical. Las Ligas Agrarias Del Norte de Santa Fe." *Desarrollo Económico. Revista de Ciencias Sociales* 28 (111): 447–461.

———. 1994. *Exploring the Written: Anthropology and the Multiplicity of Writing*. Oslo: Scandinavian University Press.

———. 1999. *Masculinities: Football, Polo and the Tango in Argentina*. Oxford, UK: Berg Publishers.

Archetti, Eduardo, and Kristi-Anne Stølen. 1974. "Tipos de Economia, Obstaculos al Desarrollo Capitalista y Orientaciones Generales de Los Colonos Del Norte de Santa Fe". *Desarrollo Económico. Revista de Ciencias Sociales* 14 (53): 151–179.

———. 1976. *Explotación Familiar y Acumulación de Capital En El Campo Argentino*. Buenos Aires: Siglo Veintiuno Editores.

Areces, Nidia, ed. 1999. *Poder y Sociedad. Santa Fe La Vieja, 1573-1660*. Colección Universos Históricos 1. Rosario, Argentina: Manuel Suarez Editor and Prohistoria. Escuela de Historia Universidad Nacional de Rosario.

Areces, Nidia, Cristina De Bernardi, and Griselda Tarragó. 1999. "Blancos e Indios En El Corredor Fluvial Paranense". In *Poder y Sociedad. Santa Fe La Vieja, 1573-1660*, edited by Nidia Areces, 13–37. Colección Univer-

sos Históricos. Rosario, Argentina: Manuel Suarez Editor and Prohistoria.
Areces, Nidia, and Griselda Tarragó. 1999. "Encomiendas y Vecinos: Estrategias y Transgresiones". In *Poder y Sociedad. Santa Fe La Vieja, 1573-1660*, edited by Nidia Areces, 61–87. Colección Universos Históricos. Rosario, Argentina: Manuel Suarez Editor and Prohistoria. Escuela de Historia, Universidad Nacional de Rosario.
Argenti, Nicolas. 2001. "Ephemeral Monuments". In *The Art of Forgetting*, edited by Adrian Forty and Susanne Küchler, 21–52. Oxford, UK: Berg Publishers.
———. 2007. *The Intestines of the State. Youth, Violence and the Belated Histories in the Cameroon Grassfields*. Chicago: University of Chicago Press.
Argenti, Nicolas, and Ute Röschenthaler. 2007. "Introduction: Between Cameroon and Cuba: Youth, Slave Trades and Translocal Memoryscapes". *Social Anthropology* 14 (1) (January 19): 33–47.
Argenti, Nicolas, and Katharina Schramm, eds. 2012. *Remembering Violence: Anthropological Perspectives on Intergenerational Transmission*. Oxford, UK: Berghahn Books.
Arias, Arturo. 2001. *The Rigoberta Menchú Controversy*. Minneapolis: University of Minnesota Press.
Arrillaga, Hugo, María Lucila Grand, and Gabriela Busso. 2009. "Vulnerabilidad, Riesgo y Desastres. Sus Relaciones de Causalidad Con La Exclusión Social En El Territorio Urbano Santafesino". In *La Construcción Social del Riesgo y el Desastre en el Aglomerado Santa Fe*, edited by Hilda Herzer and Hugo Arrillaga, 59–104. Santa Fe, Argentina: Ediciones Universidad Nacional del Litoral.
Asad, Talal. 1973. *Anthropology & the Colonial Encounter*. New York: Humanities Press.
Assmann, Jan. 2011a. "From Moses the Egyptian: The Memory of Egypt in Western Monotheism". In *The Collective Memory Reader*, edited by Jeffrey K. Olick, Vered Vinitzky-Seroussi, and Daniel Levy. 209-15 Oxford, UK: Oxford University Press.
———. 2011b. *Cultural Memory and Early Civilization: Writing, Remembrance, and Political Imagination*. Cambridge, UK: Cambridge University Press.
Augé, Marc. 2004. *Oblivion*. Minneapolis: University of Minnesota Press.
Auyero, Javier. 2001. *Poor People's Politics, Peronist Networks and the Legacy of Evita*. Durham, North Carolina: Duke University Press.
———. 2003. *Contentious Lives. Two Argentine Women, Two Protests, and the Quest for Recognition*. Durham, North Carolina: Duke University Press.
———. 2007. *La Zona Gris: Violencia Colectiva y Política Partidaria en la Argentina Contemporánea*. Sociología y Política. Buenos Aires: Siglo Veintiuno Editores.
———. 2012. *Patients of the State: The Politics of Waiting in Argentina*. Durham, North Carolina: Duke University Press.
Bacchiega, J.D., J.C. Bertoni, and J.A. Maza. 2005a. –"Informe Pericial Correspondiente a La Pericia Hidráulica Encomendada Por El Juzgado de In-

strucción Penal de La 7ma. Nominación Del Poder Judicial de La Provincia de Santa Fe En El Marco Del Expediente N° 1341/2003 "Fiscal N° 2 S/ Req. de Instrucción En Relación Denuncia de Zanutigh Ana Isabel y Otros". Expert Inquiry for Court Case. Santa Fe, Argentina: Poder Judicial de la Provincia de Santa Fe.

———. 2005b. "Anexo II: Obras de Infraestructura Existentes En El Valle Del Río Salado. Pericia Hidráulica Correspondiente Al Expediente N° 1341/2003: Poder Judicial de La Provincia de Santa Fe". Expert Inquiry for Court Case. Santa Fe, Argentina: Poder Judicial de la Provincia de Santa Fe.

———. 2005c. "Anexo III: Antecedentes Sobre Plan de Contingencia. Pericia Hidráulica Correspondiente Al Expediente N° 1341/2003: Poder Judicial de La Provincia de Santa Fe". Expert Inquiry for Court Case. Santa Fe, Argentina: Poder Judicial de la Provincia de Santa Fe.

Balbi, Fernando. 2007. *De Leales, Desleales y Traidores: Valor Moral y Concepción de Política en el Peronismo*. Serie Antropología Política y Económica edited by M. Boivin. Buenos Aires: Editorial Antropofagia.

Bankoff, Greg. 2002. *Cultures of Disaster ociety and Natural Hazards in the Philippines*. Richmond, Surrey: Curzon Press.

Bankoff, Greg, Georg Frerks, and Dorothea Hilhorst, eds. 2004. *Mapping Vulnerability: Disasters, Development, and People*. London: Earthscan Publications.

Bankoff, Greg, and Dorothea Hilhorst. 2004. "Introduction". In *Mapping Vulnerability: Disasters, Development, and People* edited by Greg Bankoff, Georg Frerks and Dorothea Hilhorst. 1-9. London: Earthscan Publications.

Barnes, John. 2006. *Models and Interpretations: Selected Essays*. Cambridge, UK: Cambridge University Press.

Barreira, D. G. 2006. *Conquista y Colonización Hispánica. Santa Fe La Vieja (1573-1660)*. Edited by D. G. Barriera. Serie Nueva Historia de Santa Fe: 2. Rosario, Argentina: Prohistoria and La Capital.

Barrenechea, Julieta, and Claudia Natenzon. 1997. "Direccion Nacional de Defensa Civil y Segunda Reforma Del Estado: Modificación Del Encuadre Institucional". Ponencia presentada en el XI Encuentro de Geógrafos de América Latina - Territorios en Redefinición. Lugar y Mundo en América Latina. Buenos Aires: Universidad de Buenos Aires.

Barrios, Roberto E. 2005. "Flying Rooftops and Matchbox Houses: Politics of Knowledge, Performative Realities, and the Materialization of Crisis in the Reconstruction of Southern Honduras After Hurricane Mitch". Doctoral thesis, mimeo. Gainesville, Florida: University of Florida.

Barsky, Lauren, Joseph Trainor, and Manuel Torres. 2006. "Disaster Realities in the Aftermath of Hurricane Katrina: Revisiting the Looting Myth". DRC Miscellaneous Reports. Newark: Disaster Research Centre, University of Delaware.

Barthel, Stephan, Carl Folke, and Johan Colding. 2010. "Social–ecological Memory in Urban gardens—Retaining the Capacity for Management of Ecosystem Services". *Global Environmental Change* 20 (2): 255–265.

Barthel, Stephan, Sverker Sörlin, and John Ljungqvist. 2010. "Innovative Memory and Resilient Cities: Echoes from Ancient Constantinople". In *The Urban Mind: Cultural and Environmental Dynamics*, edited by Paul J. J. Sinclair, Gullög Nordquist, Frands Herschend, Christian Isendahl, and Laura Wrang, 391–405. Uppsala: Department of Archaeology and Ancient History, Uppsala University.

Barthes, Roland. 1982. *Camera Lucida: Reflections on Photography*. New York: Farrar, Straus and Giroux.

Bartholdson, Örjan, Malin Beckman, Linda Engström, Klara Jacobson, Kristina Marquardt, and Lennart Salomonsson. 2012. "Does Paying Pay Off? Paying for Ecosystem Services and Exploring Alternative Possibilities". *Reports – Department of Urban and Rural Development 1.* Uppsala: Department of Urban and Rural Development, Swedish Agricultural University.

Bartolomé, Leopoldo J. 1990. *The Colonos of Apóstoles: Adaptive Strategy and Ethnicity in a Polish-Ukrainian Settlement in Northeast Argentina*. New York: AMS Press.

Basso, Keith. 1996. *Wisdom Sits in Places: Landscape and Language Among the Western Apache*. Albuquerque: University of New Mexico Press.

Basu, Paul. 2007. "Palimpsest Memoryscapes: Materializing and Mediating War and Peace in Sierra Leone". In *Reclaiming Heritage: Alternative Imaginaries of Memory in West Africa*, edited by Michael Rowlands and Ferdinand de Jong, 231–260. Walnut Creek: Left Coast Press.

Bauman, Richard. 1986. *Story, Performance, and Event: Contextual Studies of Oral Narrative*. Cambridge, UK: Cambridge University Press.

Bauman, Zygmunt. 2005. *Liquid Life*. Cambridge, UK: Polity.

Beck, Ulrich. 1992. *Risk Society: Towards a New Modernity*. London: Sage Publications.

Beckman, Malin. 2006. "Resilient Society, Vulnerable People". Doctoral thesis. Uppsala: Department of Urban and Rural Development, Swedish Agricultural University.

Beito, David T. 2000. *From Mutual Aid to the Welfare State: Fraternal Societies and Social Services, 1890-1967.* Chapel Hill, NC: Univ of North Carolina Press.

Benadusi, Mara, Chiara Brambilla, and Bruno Riccio, eds. 2011. *Disasters, Development and Humanitarian Aid: New Challenges for Anthropology.* Rimini, Italy: Guaraldi.

Berger, Gregory, and Ben Wisner. 2011. "Hazards and Disasters Represented in Film". In *The Routledge Handbook of Hazards and Disaster Risk Reduction* edited by Ben Wisner, JC Gaillard and Ilan Kelman, 121–130. London: Routledge.

Berkes, Fikret, Johan Colding, and Carl Folke. 2002. *Navigating Social-Ecological Systems: Building Resilience for Complexity and Change*. Cambridge, UK: Cambridge University Press.

Berkes, Fikret, and Carl Folke. 2000. *Linking Social and Ecological Systems: Management Practices and Social Mechanisms for Building Resilience*. Cambridge, UK: Cambridge University Press.

Beverley, John. 2004. *Testimonio: On the Politics of Truth*. Minneapolis: University of Minnesota Press.

Bille, Mikkel, Frida Hastrup, and Tim Sørensen. 2010. *An Anthropology of Absence: Materializations of Transcendence and Loss*. New York Springer.

Birkland, Thomas. 2010. "Federal Disaster Policy. Learning, Priorities, and Prospects for Resilience". In *Designing Resilience: Preparing for Extreme Events*, edited by Louise Comfort, Arjen Boin, and Chris Demchak, 106–128. Pittsburgh: University of Pittsburgh Press.

Birri, Fernando. 1987. *Pionero y Peregrino*. Buenos Aires: Editorial Contrapu to.

———. 2008. Second edition. *La escuela documental de Santa Fe*. Rosario, Argentina: Prohistoria Ediciones.

Björklund-Larsen, Lotta. 2010. *Illegal yet Licit: Justifying Informal Purchases of Work in Contemporary Sweden*. Stockholm Studies in Social Anthropology. New Series 2. Stockholm: Acta Universitatis Stockholmiensis.

Björklund, Ulf. 2001. "Att Studera En Diaspora. Den Armeniska Förskingringen Som Fält". In *Flera Fält i Ett - Socialantropologer om Translokala Fältstudier*, edited by Ulf Hannerz. Stockholm: Carlssons.

Boas, Franz, and Henry W. Tate. 1916. *Tsimshian Mythology*. In *Thirty-First Annual Report of the Bureau of American Ethnology to the Secretary of the Smithsonian Institution*. Washington: Government Printing Office. Not in copyright but available at the US Library of Congress.

Bodnar, John. 1992. *Remaking America: Public Memory, Commemoration, and Patriotism in the Twentieth Century*. Princeton, New Jersey: Princeton University Press.

Bohannan, Paul, and Laura Bohannan. 1968. *Tiv Economy*. London: Longmans.

Bohlin, Anna. 2001. *In the Eyes of the Sea: Memories of Place and Displacement in a South African Fishing Town*. Doctoral thesis. Gothenburg: School of Global Studies, University of Gothenburg.

Boholm, Åsa. 1997. "Reinvented Histories: Medieval Rome as Memorial Landscape". *Cultural Geographies* 4 (3) (July 1): 247–272.

Boin, Arjen, and Paul 't Hart. 2007. "The Crisis Approach". In *Handbook of Disaster Research*, edited by Havidán Rodríguez, Enrico Quarantelli, and Russell R. Dynes, 42–54. Handbooks of Sociology and Social Research. New York: Springer.

Boin, Arjen, Paul 't Hart, Eric Stern, and Bengt Sundelius. 2005. *The Politics of Crisis Management: Public Leadership Under Pressure*. Cambridge, UK: Cambridge University Press.

Boin, Arjen, Allan McConnell, and Paul 't Hart. 2008. *Governing After Crisis: The Politics of Investigation, Accountability and Learning*. Cambridge, UK: Cambridge University Press.

Boivin, Mauricio, Ana M. Rosato, and Fernando Balbi, eds. 2012. *Calando La Vida*. Buenos Aires: Editorial Antropofagia.

Booz, Mateo. 1944. *Santa Fe, mi pais*. Santa Fe, Argentina: Talleres Gráficos El Litoral.

———. 1999a. "Foreword". In *Cuentos Completos*. Santa Fe, Argentina: Ediciones Universidad Nacional del Litoral.

———. 1999b. "Los Inundados". In *Cuentos Completos*. Santa Fe, Argentina: Ediciones Universidad Nacional del Litoral.

Borgström, Bengt-Erik. 1997. *Cherished Moments: Engaging with the Past in a Swedish Parish*. Stockholm Studies in Social Anthropology 40. Stockholm: Almqvist & Wiksell.

Boström, Magnus, and Christina Garsten, eds. 2008. *Organizing Transnational Accountability*. Cheltenham, UK: Edward Elgar Publishing.

Bourdieu, Pierre. 1990. *The Logic of Practice*. Stanford: Stanford University Press.

———. 1996. *Photography: A Middle-Brow Art*. Palo Alto, California: Stanford University Press.

Bourgois, Phillippe. 2001. "Culture of Poverty." In *International Encyclopedia of the Social and Behavioral Sciences*, edited by Neil J Smelser and Paul B Baltes, 11904–11907. Amsterdam: Elsevier.

Bravi, Carolina. 2010. "Cine, Política y Clases Populares En Los Inundados de Fernando Birri". *Revista Imagofagia (on line)* 2. http://www.asaeca.org/imagofagia/sitio/index.php?option=com_content&view=article&id=100%3Acine-politica-y-clases-populares-en-los-inundados-de-fernando-birri&catid=35&Itemid=66.

Brint, Steven. 2001. "Gemeinschaft Revisited: A Critique and Reconstruction of the Community Concept". *Sociological Theory* 19 (1): 1–23.

Briones, Claudia, ed. 2005. *Cartografías Argentinas: Políticas Indigenistas y Formaciones Provinciales de Alteridad*. Buenos Aires: Editorial Antropofagia.

Briones, Claudia, and Rosana Guber. 2008. "Argentina: Contagious Marginalities". In *A Companion to Latin American Anthropology*, edited by Deborah Poole, 11–31. Blackwell Companions to Anthropology. Oxford: Blackwell Publishing.

Bronstein, P., R.E. Henning, H.J. Hopwood, and G.F. Vernet. 2003. "Aspectos Hidrológicos e Hidráulicos de La Crecida Del Río Salado de Abril de 2003. Informe Final". DOC: SSF-IF-01-0. Santa Fe, Argentina: Unidad Ejecutora de Recuperación de la Emergencia Hídrica y Pluvial - Gobierno de la Provincia de Santa Fe.

Brower, Ralph S., Sang O. Choi, Hong-Sang Jeong, and Janet Dilling. 2009. "Forms of Inter-Organizational Learning in Emergency Management Networks". On line. *Journal of Homeland Security and Emergency Management* 6 (1).

Brown, Steve D., and David Middleton. 2005. *The Social Psychology of Experience: Studies in Remembering and Forgetting*. London: Sage Publications.

De Bruijne, Mark, Arjen Boin, and Michel van Eeten. 2010. "Resilience: Exploring the Concept and Its Meanings". In *Designing Resilience: Preparing for Extreme Events*, edited by Louise Comfort, Arjen Boin, and Chris Demchak, 13–32. Pittsburgh: University of Pittsburgh Press.

Brändström, Annika, and Sanneke Kuipers. 2003. "From 'Normal Incidents' to Political Crises: Understanding the Selective Politicization of Policy Failures". *Government and Opposition* 38 (3) (July 1): 279–305.

Burchell, Graham, Colin Gordon, and Peter Miller, eds. 1991. *The Foucault Effect: Studies in Governmentality: with Two Lectures by and an Interview with Michel Foucault*. Chicago: University of Chicago Press.

Burdick, Michael. 1995. *For God and Fatherland: Religion and Politics in Argentina*. Albany, New York: State University of New York Press.

Butler, Toby. 2007. "Memoryscape: How Audio Walks Can Deepen Our Sense of Place by Integrating Art, Oral History and Cultural Geography". *Geography Compass* 1 (3): 360–372.

Button, Gregory. 1993. "Social Conflict and the Formation of Emergent Groups in a Technological Disaster: the Exxon Valdez Oil Spill and the Response of Residents in the Area of Homer, Alaska". Doctoral thesis, mimeo. Brandeis University.

———. 2010. *Disaster Culture. Knowledge and Uncertainty in the Wake of Human and Environmental Catastrophe*. Walnut Creek: Left Coast Press.

Caldeira, Teresa P. R. 2012. "Imprinting and Moving Around: New Visibilities and Configurations of Public Space in São Paulo". *Public Culture* 24 (2 67) (March 20): 385–419.

Calvo, Luis María. 1992. "La Fundacion de Santa Fe: Ocupación Del Territorio y Contacto Hispano-indígena". *Revista América* (11). 41-60.

———. 2006. *La construcción de una ciudad hispanoamericana: Santa Fe la Vieja entre 1573-1660*. Santa Fe, Argentina: Ediciones Universidad Nacional del Litoral.

Camargo da Silva, Telma. 2009. *Radiation Narratives and Illness: The Politics of Memory on the Goiânia Disaster*. Saarbr ck en, Germany: VDM Verlag Dr. M ller.

Cancionero Popular Argentino. 2000. Buenos Aires: Centro Editor de la Cultura Argentina.

Canessa, Andrew. 2008. "The Past Is Not Another Country: Exploring Indigenous Histories in Bolivia". *History and Anthropology* 19 (4): 353–369.

Carey-Webb, Allen, and Stephen Connely Benz. 1996. *Teaching and Testimony: Rigoberta Menchú and the North American Classroom*. New York: SUNY Press.

Castro, Jorge. 2011. *Verdades Locas Contra Impunes Mentiras. Fábula Política Inundada Bajo El Reino de Los Fangos*. Santa Fe, Argentina.

Catela Da Silva, Ludmila. 2004. "Nos vemos en el piquete...'. Protestas, violencia y memoria en el Noroeste Argentino". In *La cultura en las crisis lati-

noamericanas, edited by Alejandro Grimson and Ana María Ochoa Gautier, 123–43. Buenos Aires: Consejo Latinoamericano de Ciencias Sociales (CLACSO) Argentina.

Catela da Silva, Ludmila, and Elizabeth Jelin. 2002. *Los archivos de la represión*. Buenos Aires: Siglo Veintiuno de Argentina Editores and Social Science Research Council.

Celis, Alejandra, and Hilda Herzer. 2003. "Conocer es Poder Anticipar: Inundaciones en Santa Fe 2003". Working paper. Buenos Aires: Centro Estudios Sociales y Ambientales.

Celis, Alejandra, Fernando Ostuni, Graciela Kisilevsky, Enrique Schwartz, Soledad Fernández Bouto, and Leticia Lopresti. 2009. "Documento País: Riesgos de Desastres En Argentina". Buenos Aires: Cruz Roja Argentina and Centro Estudios Sociales y Ambientales.

Cello, Miguel. 1997. *Calles de Santa Fe: ¿Por Qué? ¿Por Quién*. Santa Fe, Argentina: Ediciones de la Cortada and Universidad Nacional del Litoral.

Cervera, Manuel. 1979. *Historia de La Ciudad y Provincia de Santa Fe. Contribución a La Historia de La República Argentina (1573-1853)*. 3 vols. Santa Fe, Argentina: Ediciones Universidad Nacional del Litoral.

Cerwonka, Allaine, and Liisa Malkki. 2007. *Improvising Theory: Process and Temporality in Ethnographic Fieldwork*. Chicago: University of Chicago Press.

Chandra, Anita. 2011. *Building Community Resilience to Disasters: A Way Forward to Enhance National Health Security*. Santa Monica, California: Rand Corporation.

Chatterjee, Partha. 2006. *The Politics of the Governed: Reflections on Popular Politics in Most of the World*. New York: Columbia University Press.

Christianson, Sven-Åke, and Elisabeth Engelberg. 1999. "Memory and Emotional Consistency: The MS Estonia Ferry Disaster". *Memory* 7 (4) (July 1): 471–482.

Christoplos, Ian, Tomás Rodríguez, E. Lisa F. Schipper, Eddy Alberto Narvaez, Karla Maria Bayres Mejia, Rolando Buitrago, Ligia Gómez, and Francisco J. Pérez. 2010. "Learning from Recovery After Hurricane Mitch". *Disasters* 34: 202–219.

Civantos, Christina. 2006. *Between Argentines And Arabs: Argentine Orientalism, Arab Immigrants, And The Writing Of Identity*. New York: SUNY Press.

Claret, Maria, Adriana Falchini, Edgardo Gómez, Jimena González, Martín Morales, Gabriela Redero, and Alan Valsangiácomo. 2005. *Memorias y Olvidos de La Gente Del Oeste*. Santa Fe, Argentina: Memoria Urgente and Movimiento Ecuménico por los Derechos Humanos.

Clarke, Lee Ben. 1999. *Mission Improbable: Using Fantasy Documents to Tame Disaster*. Chicago: University of Chicago Press.

Clarke, Matthew, Ismet Fanany, and Sue Kenny. 2012. *Post-Disaster Reconstruction: Lessons from Aceh*. Boca Raton, Florida: CRC Press.

Cleary, Heather. 2012. "The Geometry of Dissent: On the Novels of Juan José Saer". *Quarterly Conversation* (27) (March 5). On line.

        http://quarterlyconversation.com/the-geometry-of-dissent-on-the-novels-of-juan-jose-saer

Clifford, James, and George Marcus, eds. 1986. *Writing Culture: the Poetics and Politics of Ethnography*. Berkeley, California: University of California Press.

Climo, Jacob, and Maria G. Cattell. 2002. *Social Memory and History: Anthropological Perspectives*. Lanham, Maryland: Rowman Altamira.

Coetzee, Christo. 2009. "The Development, Implementation and Transformation of the Disaster Management Cycle". Master's thesis. Potchefstroom, South Africa: North-West University.

Colabella, Laura. 2012. *Los Negros Del Congreso. Nombre, Filiación y Honor en El Reclutamiento a La Burocracia Del Estado Argentino*. Buenos Aires: Editorial Antropofagia.

Cole, Jennifer. 2001. *Forget Colonialism? Sacrifice and the Art of Memory in Madagascar*. Berkeley, California: University of California Press.

Collado, Adriana. 2007. "Modernización Urbana En Ciudades Provincianas de Argentina. Teorías, Modelos y Prácticas, 1887-1944". Sevilla: Universidad Pablo de Olavide, Departamento de Humanidades.

Colombres, Adolfo. 2001. *Seres Mitológicos Argentinos*. Buenos Aires: Emecé Editores.

Comfort, Louise. 1994. "Risk and Resilience: Inter-organizational Learning Following the Northridge Earthquake of 17 January 1994". *Journal of Contingencies and Crisis Management* 2 (3): 157–170.

———. 1999. *Shared Risk: Complex Systems in Seismic Response*. Oxford, UK: Pergamon.

Comfort, Louise, Arjen Boin, and Chris Demchak. 2010. *Designing Resilience: Preparing for Extreme Events*. Pennsylvania: University of Pittsburgh Press.

Connerton, Paul. 1989. *How Societies Remember*. Cambridge, UK: Cambridge University Press.

———. 2008. "Seven Types of Forgetting". *Memory Studies* 1 (1) (January 1): 59–71.

———. 2009. *How Modernity Forgets*. Cambridge, UK: Cambridge University Press.

Crenzel, Emilio. 2011a. "Present Pasts: Memory(ies) of State Terrorism in the Southern Cone of Latin America". In *The Memory of State Terrorism in the Southern Cone: Argentina, Chile, and Uruguay*, 1–13. New York: Palgrave Macmillan.

———. 2011b. *The Memory of the Argentina Disappearances: The Political History of Nunca Mas*. London: Routledge.

Cundill, Georgina. 2010. "Monitoring Social Learning Processes in Adaptive Comanagement: Three Case Studies from South Africa". *Ecology and Society* 15 (3). On line: http://www.ibcperu.org/doc/isis/12880.pdf http://www.ecologyandsociety.org/vol15/iss3/art28/

Dahl, Gudrun. 2001. *Responsibility and Partnership in Swedish Aid Discourse: Discussion Paper 9*. Uppsala: Nordic Africa Institute.

———. 2009. "Sociology and Beyond: Agency, Victimisation and the Ethics of Writing". *Asian Journal of Social Science* 37 (3): 391–407.
Das, Veena. 1996. *Critical Events: An Anthropological Perspective on Contemporary India*. Oxford, UK: Oxford University Press.
———. 2001. *Remaking a World: Violence, Social Suffering, and Recovery*. Berkeley, California: University of California Press.
David, Bruno, and Meredith Wilson. 2002. *Inscribed Landscapes: Marking and Making Place*. Honolulu: University of Hawaii Press.
Dery, David. 1998. "'Papereality' and Learning in Bureaucratic Organizations". *Administration & Society* 29 (6) (January 1): 677–689.
DuBois, Lindsay. 2008. *The Politics of the Past in an Argentine Working-Class Neighbourhood*. Toronto: University of Toronto Press.
Durkheim, Émile. 2001 [1912]. *The Elementary Forms of Religious Life*. Oxford, UK: Oxford University Press.
———. 1984. *The Division of Labor in Society*. Edited by W. D. Halls. New York: Free Press.
Ebron, Paulla A. 1999. "Tourists as Pilgrims: Commercial Fashioning of Transatlantic Politics". *American Ethnologist* 26 (4): 910–932.
Edensor, Tim. 1997. "National Identity and the Politics of Memory: Remembering Bruce and Wallace in Symbolic Space". *Environment and Planning D: Society and Space* 15 (2): 175-194.
Elias, Norbert. 1978. *The Civilizing Process*. New York: Urizen Books.
Enander, Ann. 2006. "Recalling Chernobyl: Reflections Among Swedish Farmers". *International Journal of Mass Emergencies and Disasters* 24 (2): 251–269.
Erikson, Kai. 1976. *Everything in Its Path: Destruction of Community in the Buffalo Creek Flood*. London: Simon & Schuster.
Escobar, Arturo. 1994. *Encountering Development: The Making and Unmaking of the Third World*. Princeton, New Jersey: Princeton University Press.
Escuela nro 1298 Monseñor Vicente Zazpe. 2006. *Entre Todos Escribimos, Dibujamos, Cantamos*. Edited by Claudia Marcela Franco and Sergio Moreyra. Santa Fe, Argentina: Ediciones Universidad Nacional del Litoral.
Evans-Pritchard, Edward. 1956. *Nuer Religion*. Oxford, UK: Clarendon Press.
Fabian, Johannes. 2007. *Memory Against Culture. Arguments and Reminders*. Durham, North Carolina: Duke University Press.
Facciuto, Alejandra. 2003. "El Surgimiento de La Política Social En Argentina". *Revista de Humanidades: Tecnológico de Monterrey* (14): 165–206.
Fassin, Didier, and Mariella Pandolfi. 2010. "Introduction: Military and Humanitarian Government in the Age of Intervention". In *Contemporary States of Emergency: The Politics of Military and Humanitarian Interventions*, edited by Didier Fassin and Mariella Pandolfi, 9–25. New York: Zone Books.
Fassin, Didier, and Paula Vasquez. 2005. "Humanitarian Exception as the Rule: The Political Theology of the 1999 Tragedia in Venezuela". *American Ethnologist* 32 (3): 389–405.

Faya, Alfonsina. 2004. "Les Mères de San Pantaleon: Patriarcat Et Identité." Undergraduate thesis. Tolouse, France: Université de Tolouse Mirail, Département de Sociologie.

Feld, Steven, and Keith H. Basso. 1996. *Senses of Place*. Santa Fe, New Mexico: School of American Research Press.

Fentress, James, and Chris Wickham, eds. 1992. *Social Memory: New Perspectives on the Past*. 1st ed. Hoboken, New Jersey: Wiley-Blackwell.

Ferguson, James. 1990. *The Anti-Politics Machine: "Development," Depoliticization, and Bureaucratic Power in Lesotho*. Minneapolis: University of Minnesota Press.

Ferguson, James, and Akhil Gupta. 2002. "Spatializing States: Toward an Ethnography of Neoliberal Governmentality". *American Ethnologist* 29 (4) (November): 981–1002.

Ferme, Marianne. 2001. *The Underneath of Things: Violence, History, and the Everyday in Sierra Leone*. Berkeley, California: University of California Press.

Fernández, Ana María. 2008. *Política y Subjetividad: Asambleas Barriales y Fábricas Recuperadas*. Buenos Aires: Editorial Biblos.

Fernández, Sandra. 2006. "Las Figuras Institucionalizadas de Asociación". In *Sociabilidad, Corporaciones, Instituciones (1860-1930)*, edited by Sandra Fernández, 27–44. Serie Nueva Historia de Santa Fe. Rosario, Argentina: Prohistoria Ediciones and Diario La Capital.

Fernández, Sandra, and Gisela Galassi. 2006. "En Unión y Fraternidad". In *Sociabilidad, Corporaciones, Instituciones (1860-1930)*, edited by Sandra Fernández, 45–66. Nueva Historia de Santa Fe. Rosario, Argentina: Prohistoria Ediciones & Diario La Capital.

Ferraro, Emilia. 2011. "Trueque: An Ethnographic Account of Barter, Trade and Money in Andean Ecuador". *The Journal of Latin American and Caribbean Anthropology* 16 (1) (April 7): 168–184.

Finnström, Sverker. 2008. *Living with Bad Surroundings: War, History, and Everyday Moments in Northern Uganda*. Durham, North Carolina: Duke University Press.

Firth, Raymond. 1936. *We, the Tikopia: a Sociological Study of Kinship in Primitive Polynesia*. Woodstock, Georgia: American Book Company.

Folke, Carl. 2010. "On Resilience". *Seedmagazine.com*, December 13. http://seedmagazine.com/content/article/on_resilience/.

Folke, Carl, Thomas Hahn, Per Olsson, and Jon Norberg. 2005. "Adaptive Governance of Social-Ecological Systems". *Annual Review of Environment and Resources* 30 (1): 441–473.

Fortes, Meyer, and E. E Evans-Pritchard, eds. 1940. *African Political Systems*. Oxford, UK: Oxford University Press.

Fortun, Kim. 2001. *Advocacy After Bhopal: Environmentalism, Disaster, New Global Orders*. Chicago: University of Chicago Press.

Forty, Adrian. 2001. "Introduction". In *The Art of Forgetting*, edited by Susanne Küchler and Adrian Forty, 1–18. Oxford, UK: Berg Publishers.

Forty, Adrian, and Susanne Küchler. 2001. *The Art of Forgetting*. Oxford, UK: Berg Publishers.
Foucault, Michel. 1977. *Language, Counter-memory, Practice: Selected Essays and Interviews*. Edited by Donald Bouchard. Ithaca, New York: Cornell University Press.
Frade del, Carlos, Julieta Haidar, and Miguel Cello. Forthcoming. *Lo Que El Salado Sigue Gritando: Diez Años Después*. Santa Fe, Argentina.
Frederic, Sabina. 2004. *Buenos Vecinos, Malos Políticos: Moralidad y Política En El Gran Buenos Aires*. Buenos Aires: Prometeo Libros.
———. 2005. "Región etnográfica y microanálisis. A propósito de la política como problema moral en una ciudad bonaerense". In *Cultura y política en etnografías sobre la Argentina*, edited by Sabina Frederic and Germán Soprano, 315–341. Quilmes, Argentina: Universidad Nacional de Quilmes.
Freidenberg, Judith. 2009. *The Invention of the Jewish Gaucho: Villa Clara and the Construction of Argentine Identity*. Austin, Texas: University of Texas Press.
Frenkel, Roberto, and Martín Rapetti. 2008. "Five Years of Competitive and Stable Real Exchange Rate in Argentina, 2002–2007". *International Review of Applied Economics* 22 (2) (March): 215–226.
Friedländer, Saul. 1993. *Memory, History, and the Extermination of the Jews of Europe*. Bloomington, Indiana: Indiana University Press.
Fritz, Charles. 1961. "Disasters". In *Contemporary Social Problems: An Introduction to the Sociology of Deviant Behavior and Social Disorganization*, edited by Robert Merton and Robert Nisbet, 651–94. San Diego, California: Harcourt.
Gallasi, Gisela. 2006. "Asociacionismo e Identidad". In *Sociabilidad, Corporaciones, Instituciones (1860-1930)*, edited by Sandra Fernández, 67–78. Nueva Historia de Santa Fe. Rosario, Argentina: Prohistoria Ediciones and Diario La Capital.
Gallo, Ezequiel. 1976. "Farmers in Revolt: the Revolutions of 1893 in the Province of Santa Fe, Argentina." Oxford, UK: University of Oxford Press.
———. 1984. *La Pampa Gringa: La Colonización Agrícola En Santa Fe (1870-1895)*. Buenos Aires: Editorial Sudamericana.
Garbulsky, Edgardo, and Diana Vicuña Martínez. 2006. "Los Pueblos Orginarios Hoy". In *Los Pueblos Originarios*, edited by Juan Nobile, 147–76. Nueva Historia de Santa Fe: 1. Rosario, Argentina: Prohistoria Ediciones and Diario La Capital.
Garsten, Christina. 2010. "Ethnography at the Interface: "Corporate Social Responsibility" as an Anthropological Field of Enquiry". In *Ethnographic Practice in the Present*, edited by Marit Melhuus, Jon P. Mitchell, and Helena Wulff, 56–68. Oxford, UK: Berghahn Books.
Geertz, Clifford. 1973. *The Interpretation of Cultures: Selected Essays*. New York: Basic Books.
Gentile, Elvira. 1994. "El Niño No Tiene La Culpa: Vulnerabilidad En El Noreste Argentino". *Desastres y Sociedad* (3): 87–106.

Gerlak, A. K., and T. Heikkila. 2011. "Building a Theory of Learning in Collaboratives: Evidence from the Everglades Restoration Program". *Journal of Public Administration Research and Theory Journal of Public Administration Research and Theory* 21 (4): 619–644.

Giarracca, Norma, and Miguel Teubal, eds. 2010. *Del Paro Grario a Las Elecciones de 2009: Tramas, Reflexiones y Debates*. Buenos Aires: Editorial Antropofagia.

Giddens, Anthony. 2003. "Risk and Responsibility". *The Modern Law Review* 62 (1) (February 17): 1–10.

Gilligan, Chris. 2003. "Constant Crisis/permanent Process: Diminished Agency and Weak Structures in the Northern Ireland Peace Process". *Global Review of Ethnopolitics* 3 (1): 22–37.

Giorgis, Marta. 2004. *La Virgen Prestamista: La Fiesta de La Virgen de Urkupiña En El Boliviano Gran Córdoba*. Buenos Aires: Editorial Antropofagia.

Giusti, Alejandro, and Gladis Massé. 2001. "Informe Definitivo: Evaluación de La Información Ocupacional Del Censo 2001. Análisis Del Nivel de Desocupación". Censo Nacional de Población, Hogares y Viviendas 2001. Buenos Aires: Instituto Nacional de Estadísticas y Censos. http://www.indec.gov.ar/censo2001s2_2/ampliada_index.asp?mode=82.

Gonzalez, G. 2008. *Santa Fe. Ciencias Sociales*. Buenos Aires: Puerto de Palos.

Gordillo, Gastón. 2004. *Landscapes of Devils. Tensions of Place and Memory in the Argentinean Chaco*. Durham, North Carolina: Duke University Press.

———. 2005. *Nosotros Vamos A Estar Acá Para Siempre: Historias Tobas*. Buenos Aires: Editorial Biblos.

Gorenstein, Alejandro. 2012. *Vidas Que Enseñan*. Resiliencia. Buenos Aires: Del Nuevo Extremo.

Gori, Gastón. 1965. *La Forestal: la tragedia del quebracho colorado*. Buenos Aires: Editoriales Platina/Stilcograf.

Gow, Peter. 2001. *An Amazonian Myth and Its History*. Oxford, UK: Oxford University Press.

Grandin, Greg. 2011. *Who Is Rigoberta Menchu?* Brooklyn, New York: Verso Books.

Grau, H.R., and M. Aide. 2008. "Globalization and Land-Use Transitions in Latin America". *Ecology and Society* 13 (2). On line: http://www.ecologyandsociety.org/vol13/iss2/art16/

Gravano, Ariel. 2003. *Antropología De Lo Barrial: Estudios Sobre Producción Simbólica De La Vida Urbana*. Buenos Aires: Espacio Editorial.

Greenhouse, Carol J. 2005. "Hegemony and Hidden Transcripts: The Discursive Arts of Neoliberal Legitimation". *American Anthropologist* 107 (3): 356–368.

Gren, Nina. 2009. "Each Day Another Disaster: Politics and Everyday Life in a Palestinian Refugee Camp in the West Bank". Doctoral thesis. Gothenburg, Sweden: University of Gothenburg.

Grimson, Alejandro. 2012. *Mitomanías Argentinas*. Buenos Aires: Siglo XXI Editores.

Guala, Pilar. 2005. "Inundados: Identidad Que Emerge Con El Agua". Undergratuate thesis, mimeo, Paraná, Argentina: Universidad Nacional de Entre Ríos.

Guarany, Horacio. 2005. *La Creciente (Alto Verde uerido)*. Santa Fe, Argentina: Ediciones Universidad Nacional del Litoral.

Guber, Rosana. 1996. "Las Manos de La Memoria". *Desarrollo Económico* 36 (141): 423.

———. 1999a. "From Chicos to Veteranos: Argentine Uses of Memory and the Nation in the Making of Mavinas Postwar Identities". Doctoral thesis, mimeo. Baltimore, Maryland: John Hopkins University, Department of Anthropology.

———. 1999b. ""El Cabecita Negra" o Las Categorías de La Investigación Etnográfica En La Argentina". *Revista de Investigaciones Folclóricas* 14: 108–20.

Gugelberger, Georg M. 1996. *The Real Thing: Testimonial Discourse and Latin America*. Durham, North Carolina: Duke University Press.

Gupta, Akhil, and James Ferguson, eds. 1997. *Anthropological Locations: Boundaries and Grounds of a Field Science*. Berkeley, California: University of California Press.

Gupta, Manu. 2011. "Settlement and Shelter Reconstruction". In *Handbook of Hazards and Disaster Risk Reduction*, edited by Ben Wisner, JC Gaillard, and Ilan Kelman, 553–65. Routledge Handbooks. London: Routledge.

Gusterson, Hugh. 1997. "Studying up Revisited". *Political and Legal Anthropology Review* 20 (1): 114–19.

———. 1998. *Nuclear Rites: A Weapons Laboratory at the End of the Cold War*. Berkeley, California: University of California Press.

Hacking, Ian. 1996. "Memory Sciences, Memory Politics". In *Tense Past: Cultural Essays in Trauma and Memory*, edited by Michael Lambek and Paul Antze. 67-867. London: Routledge.

Halbwachs, Maurice. 1941. *On Collective Memory*. Chicago: University of Chicago Press.

———. 1980. *The Collective Memory*. New York: Harper & Row.

Hammer, Juliane. 2001. "Homeland Palestine: Lost in the Catastrophe of 1948 and Recreated in Memories and Art". In *Crisis and Memory in Islamic Societies, Proceedings of the Third Summer Academy of the Working Group on Modernity and Islam at the Wissenschaftskolleg zu Berlin*, edited by Angelika Neuwirth and Andreas Pflitsch, 453–81. Beirut: Orient Institute of the German Oriental Society in Beirut.

Handmer, John W., and Stephen R. Dovers. 1996. "A Typology of Resilience: Rethinking Institutions for Sustainable Development". *Organization & Environment* 9 (4) (January 12): 482–511.

Hannerz, Ulf. 1992. *Cultural Complexity: Studies in the Social Organization of Meaning*. New York: Columbia University Press.

———. ed. 2001. *Flera fält i ett: socialantropologer om translokala fältstudier*. Stockholm: Carlssons Bokförlag.

———. 2003a. "Several Sites in One". In *Globalisation: Studies in Anthropology*, edited by Thomas Hylland Eriksen, 18–38. London: Pluto Press.

———. 2003b. "Being There...and There...and There! Reflections on Multi-site Ethnography". *Ethnography* 4 (2): 201–16.

Hardoy, Jorgelina, Gustavo Pandiella, and Luz Stella Velásquez Barrero. 2011. "Local Disaster Risk Reduction in Latin American Urban Areas". *Environment and Urbanization* 23 (2) (October 1): 401–413.

Harlow, Barbara. 1987. *Resistance Literature*. London: Routledge.

Harms, Arne. 2012. "Squatters on a Shrinking Coast". In *Negotiating Disasters: Politics, Representation, Meanings*, edited by Ute Luig, 105–128. Bern, Switzerland: Peter Lang Publishing Company.

Harris, Christian. 2013. "Investigation Discovers "Deleted" Data Still Recoverable From Hard Disks | BCW". *Business Computing World*. January 14. http://www.businesscomputingworld.co.uk/investigation-discovers-deleted-data-still-recoverable-from-hard-disks/.

Harris, Marvin. 1979. *Cultural Materialism: The Struggle for a Science of Culture*. Lanham, Maryland: Rowman Altamira.

Hartley, Leslie Poles. 1953. *The Go-between*. London: H. Hamilton.

Harvey, Penelope. 1995. "Nations on Display: Technology and Culture in Expo '92 1". *Science as Culture* 5 (1) (January 1): 85–105.

———. 2010. "Cementing Relations: The Materiality of Roads and Public Spaces In Provincial Peru". *Social Analysis* 54 (2) (August 30): 28–46.

Hastrup, Frida. 2009. "A Sense of Direction: Responsibility and the Span of Disaster in a Tamil Coastal Village". In *The Question of Resilience: Social Responses to Climate Change*, edited by Kirsten Hastrup. 114-31. Copenhagen: Royal Danish Academy of Sciences and Letters.

———. 2011. *Weathering the World: Recovery in the Wake of the Tsunami in a Tamil Fishing Village*. Vol. 16. Studies in Environmental Anthropology and Ethnobiology. Oxford, UK: Berghahn Books.

Hastrup, Kirsten, and Peter Hervik. 1994. *Social Experience and Anthropological Knowledge*. London: Routledge.

Hayden, Dolores. 1997. *The Power of Place: Urban Landscapes as Public History*. Cambridge, Massachusetts: The MIT Press.

Hechim, María Angélica, and Adriana Falchini. 2005. *Contar la inundación*. Santa Fe, Argentina: Ediciones Universidad Nacional del Litoral.

Heijmans, Annelies. 2004. "From Vulnerability to Empowerment". In *Mapping Vulnerability: "Disasters, Development and People"*, edited by Greg Bankoff, Georg Frerks, and Thea Hilhorst. 115-27. London: Routledge.

Helmus, Andrea M. 2009. *Grassroots Democracy and Environmental Citizenship in Tigre, Argentina*. Master's thesis, mimeo. Tucson, Arizona: University of Arizona, Department of Latin American Studies.

Henning, Annette. 2001. ""Det finns ingen sol i Sverige": Nätverk kring solenergin". In *Flera fält i ett: socialantropologer om translokala fältstudier*, edited by Ulf Hannerz, 134–162. Stockholm: Carlssons Bokförlag.

Herzer, Hilda, and Hugo Arrillaga, eds. 2009. *La Construcción Social Del Riesgo y El Desastre En El Aglomerado Santa Fe*. Santa Fe, Argentina: Ediciones Universidad Nacional del Litoral.

Herzer, Hilda, Graciela Caputo, Alejandra Celis, Hernán Petit, Mara Bartolomé, Raquel Gurevich, and Carla Rodriguez. 2000. "Grandes Inundaciones En La Ciudad de Pergamino: Extraordinarias, Pero Recurrentes …Análisis de Un Proceso de Vulnerabilidad Progresiva". *Revista Realidad Económica Buenos Aires* (175).

Herzer, Hilda, Carla Rodriguez, Alejandra Celis, Mara Bartolomé, and Graciela Caputo. 2002. "Convivir Con El Riesgo o La Gestion Del Riesgo". Buenos Aires: Centro Estudios Sociales y Ambientales.

Herzfeld, Michael. 1991. *A Place in History: Social and Monumental Time in a Cretan Town*. Princeton, New Jersey: Princeton University Press.

———. 2004. *Cultural Intimacy: Social Poetics in the Nation-State*. London: Routledge.

Hewitt, Kenneth. 1983. *Interpretations of Calamity: From the Viewpoint of Human Ecology*. London: Unwin Hyman.

———. 1998. "Excluded Perspectives of the Social Construction of Disaster". In *What Is A Disaster?: Perspectives on the Question*, edited by Enrico Quarantelli, 71–90. London: Routledge.

Hilhorst, Dorothea, Ian Christoplos, and Gemma Van Der Harr. 2010. "Reconstruction "From Below": a New Magic Bullet or Shooting from the Hip?" *Third World Quarterly* 31 (7): 1107–1124.

Hinton, Alexander Laban. 2005. *Why Did They Kill?: Cambodia in the Shadow of Genocide*. Berkeley, California: University of California Press.

Hintze, Susana, ed. 2003. *Trueque y Economía Solidaria*. Buenos Aires: Prometeo Libros and Universidad Nacional General Sarmiento.

Hirsch, Marianne. 1997. *Family Frames: Photography, Narrative, and Postmemory*. Harvard, Massachusetts: Harvard University Press.

———. 1999. *The Familial Gaze*. Hanover, New Hampshire: Dartmouth College.

———. 2012. *The Generation of Postmemory: Writing and Visual Culture After the Holocaust*. New York: Columbia University Press.

Hobsbawm, Eric, and Terence Ranger. 1992. *The Invention of Tradition*. Cambridge, UK: Cambridge University Press.

Hodgkin, Katharine, and Susannah Radstone. 2003a. "Regimes of Memory: An Introduction". In *Regimes of Memory*, edited by Susannah Radstone and Katharine Hodgkin, 1–22. London: Routledge.

———. 2003b. *Memory, History, Nation: Contested Pasts*. New Brunswick, New Jersey: Transaction Publishers.

Hoffman, Susanna. 1999. "The Worst of Times; The Best of Times: Toward a Model of Cultural Response to Disaster". In *The Angry Earth: Disaster in Anthropological Perspective,* edited by Anthony Oliver-Smith and Susanna Hoffman, 134–155. London: Routledge.

Hoffman, Susanna, and Anthony Oliver-Smith, eds. 2002. *Catastrophe & Culture: The Anthropology of Disaster*. Santa Fe, New Mexico: School of American Research Press.

Holmes, Douglas, and George E. Marcus. 2010. "Epilogue 2: Prelude to a Refunctioned Ethnography". In *Ethnographic Practice in the Present*, edited by Marit Melhuus, Jon P. Mitchell, and Helena Wulff, 176–84. Oxford, UK: Berghahn Books.

Hornborg, Alf. 2009. "Zero-Sum World Challenges in Conceptualizing Environmental Load Displacement and Ecologically Unequal Exchange in the World-System". *International Journal of Comparative Sociology* 50 (3-4) (January 6): 237–262.

Howell, Signe, and Aud Talle. 2011. *Returns to the Field: Multitemporal Research and Contemporary Anthropology*. Bloomington, Indiana: Indiana University Press.

Humphrey, Caroline, and Stephen Hugh-Jones. 1992. *Barter, Exchange and Value: An Anthropological Approach*. Cambridge, UK: Cambridge University Press.

Huyssen, Andreas. 2003. *Present Pasts: Urban Palimpsests and the Politics of Memory*. Stanford, Berkeley, California: University of California Press.

Höjdestrand, Tova. 2009. *Needed by Nobody: Homelessness and Humanness in Post-Socialist Russia*. Ithaca, New York: Cornell University Press.

Höjer, Louise. 2008. "Concrete Thorught and the Narrative Wall: Graffiti - Monument and Ruin". In *Witness. Memory, representation and the media in question*, edited by Frederik Tygstrup and Ulrik Ekman, 243–49. Copenhagen: Museum Tusculanum Press.

Ingold, Tim, and Richard Bradley. 1993. "The Temporality of the Landscape". *World Archaeology* 25 (2): 152–174.

Ingold, Tim, David Lowenthal, Gillian Feeley-Harnik, Penelope Harvey, and Susanne Küchler. 1996. "The 1992 Debate. The Past Is a Foreign Country". In *Key Debates in Anthropology*, edited by Tim Ingold, 199–248. London: Routledge.

Inter-American Development Bank. 1998. "Inter-American Development Bank Annual Report 1998: The Year in Review". Washington D.C.: Inter-American Development Bank.

Intergovernmental Panel on Climate Change. 2012. "Managing the Risks of Extreme Events and Disasters to Advance Climate Change Adaptation Special Report of the Intergovernmental Panel on Climate Change". New York: Intergovernmental Panel on Climate Change.

Irwin-Zarecka, Iwona. 1994. *Frames of Remembrance: the Dynamics of Collective Memory*. New Brunswick, New Jersey: Transaction Publishers.

Ivarsson, Carolina. 2007. "Webs of Security, Waves of Destruction: Social Recovery and Human Security in Post-tsunami Sri Lanka". Working paper. Gothenburg: University of Gothenburg.

Jacobs, Brian. 2005. "Urban Vulnerability: Public Management in a Changing World". *Journal of Contingencies and Crisis Management* 13 (2): 39–43.

Jelin, Elizabeth. 2002. *Los trabajos de la memoria*. Madrid: Siglo XXI de España Editores and Social Science Research Council.

———. 2007. "Public Memorialization in Perspective: Truth, Justice and Memory of Past Repression in the Southern Cone of South America". *International Journal of Transitional Justice* 1 (1): 138–156.

Jelin, Elizabeth, and Susana G. Kaufman. 2006. *Subjetividad y figuras de la memoria*. Buenos Aires: Siglo XXI Editores.

Johnson, Richard. 2007. *Making Histories: Studies in History-writing and Politics*. London: Routledge.

Jones, Eric C., and Arthur D. Murphy. 2009. *The Political Economy of Hazards and Disasters*. Lanham, Maryland: Rowman Altamira.

Kaiser, Susana. 2002. "Escraches: Demonstrations, Communication and Political Memory in Post-dictatorial Argentina". *Media, Culture & Society* 24 (4) (January 7): 499–516.

Keesing, Felix Maxwell. 1952. *The Papuan Orokaiva Vs. Mt. Lamington: Cultural Shock and Its Aftermath*. Oklahoma City, Oklahoma: Society for Applied Anthropology.

Kendra, James M., and Tricia Wachtendorf. 2003. "Elements of Resilience After the World Trade Center Disaster: Reconstituting New York City's Emergency Operations Centre". *Disasters* 27 (1) (March 19): 37–53.

Ketelaar, Eric. 2007. "The Panoptical Archive". In *Archives, Documentation, and Institutions of Social Memory: Essays from the Sawyer Seminar*, edited by Francis X. Blouin and William G. Rosenberg, 144–50. Ann Arbor, Michigan: University of Michigan Press.

Khosravi, Shahram. 2013. "Graffiti in Tehran". *Anthropology Now* 5 (1): 1–17.

Kimura, Shuhei. 2012. "Lessons from the Great East Japan Earthquake: The Public Use of Anthropological Knowledge". *Asian Anthropology* 12: 65–74.

Kirmayer, Laurence. 1996. "Landscapes of Memory: Trauma, Narrative and Dissociation". In *Tense Past: Cultural Essays in Trauma and Memory*, edited by Paul Antze and Michael Lambek, 173–98. London: Routledge.

Klein, Richard, Robert Nicholls, and Frank Thomalla. 2003. "Resilience to Natural Hazards: How Useful Is This Concept?" *Global Environmental Change Part B: Environmental Hazards* 5 (1–2): 35–45.

Kleinman, Arthur, Veena Das, and Margaret Lock. 1997. *Social Suffering*. Berkeley, California: University of California Press.

Kofman Bos, Celesta, Susann Ullberg, and Paul 't Hart. 2005. "The Long Shadow of Disaster: Memory and Politics in Holland and Sweden". *International Journal of Mass Emergencies and Disasters* 23 (1): 5–26.

Kontopodis, Michalis. 2009. "Editorial: Time. Matter. Multiplicity". *Memory Studies* 2 (1) (January 1): 5–10.

Kundera, Milan. 1999. *The Book of Laughter and Forgetting: A Novel*. London: Harper Collins.

Kupfer, D., and R. Karimanzira. 1990. "Agriculture, Forestry, and Other Human Activities". In *Climate Change: The IPCC Response Strategies*, 75–122. Intergovernmental Panel on Climate Change Working Group III.

Kwint, Marius, Christopher Breward, and Jeremy Aynsley. 1999. *Material Memories: Design and Evocation*. Oxford, UK: Berg Publishers.

Küchler, Susanne. 1993. "Landscape as Memory: The Mapping as Process and Its Representation in a Melanesian Society". In *Landscape: Politics and Perspectives*, edited by Barbara Bender, 85–106. Oxford, UK: Berg Publishers.

———. 2001. "The Place of Memory". In *The Art of Forgetting*, edited by Adrian Forty and Susanne Küchler, 53–72. Oxford, UK: Berg Publishers.

———. 2002. *Malanggan: Art, Memory and Sacrifice*. Oxford, UK: Berg Publishers.

Langumier, Julien. 2008. *Survivre à L'inondation: Pour Une Ethnologie de La Catastrophe*. Lyon, France: ENS Éditions.

Larrechea, Carmen de. 2008. "Análisis de Crecimiento Poblacional: Provincia de Santa Fe". Santa Fe, Argentina: Ministerio de Gobierno y Reforma del Estado, Secretaría de Tecnologías para la Gestión. Gobierno de la Provincia de Santa Fe.

Lewis, C. 1983. *British Railways in Argentina 1857-1914: A Case Study of Foreign Investment*. London: Athlone.

Lewis, Laura. 2001. "Of Ships and Saints: History, Memory, and Place in the Making of Moreno Mexican Identity". *Cultural Anthropology* 16 (1): 62–82.

Lewis, Oscar. 1959. *Five Families: Mexican Case Studies in the Culture of Poverty*. New York: Basic Books.

———. 1966. *La Vida: A Puerto Rican Family in the Culture of poverty – San Juan and New York*. New York: Random House.

Lévi-Strauss, Claude. 1955. "The Structural Study of Myth". *The Journal of American Folklore* 68 (270): 428–444.

Lindqvist, Galina. 1996. "Att Definiera Ett Translokalt Fält: Samtal Mellan Tommy Dahlen, Ulf Hannerz och Galina Lindqvist". *Antropologiska Studier* Temanummer "Om Fältet" (54-55): 3–14.

Litvan, Valentina. 2012. "'A medio borrar' en el origen: de Saer a Saer". *Cuadernos LIRICO (en línea). Revista de la red interuniversitaria de estudios sobre las literaturas rioplatenses contemporáneas en Francia* (6) (June 1). http://lirico.revues.org/219.

Lovell, Anne M. 2011. "Debating Life After Disaster: Charity Hospital Babies and Bioscientific Futures in Post-Katrina New Orleans". *Medical Anthropology Quarterly* 25 (2): 254–277.

Lovell, Anne M., Samuel Bordreuil, and Vincanne Adams. 2010. "Public Policy and Publics in Post-Katrina New Orleans: How Critical Topics Circulate and Shape Recovery Policy. *Kroeber Anthropological Society Papers* 100 (1): 104–28.

Lowenthal, David. 1985. *The Past Is a Foreign Country*. Cambridge, UK: Cambridge University Press.

———. 2001. "Preface". In *The Art of Forgetting*, edited by Adrian Forty and Susanne Küchler, xi–xiii. Oxford, UK: Berg Publishers.

Lundgren, Inger. 2000. *Lost Visions and New Uncertainties: Sandinista Profesionales in Northern Nicaragua.* Doctoral thesis. Stockholm: Almqvist & Wiksell International.

Lynch, Michael. 1999. "Archives in Formation: Privileged Spaces, Popular Archives and Paper Trails". *History of the Human Sciences* 12 (2): 65–87.

Magrin, Graciela, and Carlos Gay García. 2007. "Latin America. Climate Change 2007: Impacts, Adaptation and Vulnerability. Contribution of Working Group II to the Fourth Assessment Report of the Intergovernmental Panel on Climate Change". Cambridge, UK: Cambridge University Press.

Mahoney, James. 2000. "Path Dependence in Historical Sociology". *Theory and Society* 29 (4): 507–548.

Malinowski, Bronislaw. 1926. *Myth in Primitive Psychology.* New York: W.W. Norton & Company.

Malkki, Liisa. 1995. *Purity and Exile: Violence, Memory, and National Cosmology Mong Hutu Refugees in Tanzania.* Chicago: Chicago University Press.

———. 1997. "News and Culture: Transitory Phenomena and the Fieldwork Tradition". In *Anthropological Locations: Boundaries and Grounds of a Field Science.*, edited by Akhil Gupta and James Ferguson, 86–101. Berkeley, California: University of California Press.

De Man, Paul. 1970. "Literary History and Literary Modernity". *Daedalus* 99 (2) (April 1): 384–404.

Manyena, Siambabala Bernard. 2006. "The Concept of Resilience Revisited". *Disasters* 30 (4): 434–450.

March, James G. 2010. *The Ambiguities of Experience.* Ithaca, New York: Cornell University Press.

Marcucci, Hugo M. 2004. "La Catástrofe En Santa Fe: Informe Inundaciones 2003". Santa Fe, Argentina: Cámara de Diputados de la Provincia de Santa Fe.

Marcus, George E, and Michael M. J. Fischer. 1986. *Anthropology as Cultural Critique: an Experimental Moment in the Human Sciences.* Chicago: University of Chicago Press.

Marcus, George E. 1995. "Ethnography In/of the World System: The Emergence of Multi-Sited Ethnography". *Annual Review of Anthropology* 24: 95 117.

———. 1998. *Ethnography Through Thick and Thin.* Princeton, New Jersey: Princeton University Press.

Margalit, Avishai. 2011. "From 'The Ethics of Memory'". In *The Collective Memory Reader*, edited by Jeffrey K. Olick, Vered Vinitzky-Seroussi, and Daniel Levy, 471–72. Oxford, UK: Oxford University Press.

Martínez-Sarasola, Carlos. 1992. *Nuestros Paisanos Los Indios.* Buenos Aires: Emecé Editores.

Maskrey, Andrew. 1989. *Disaster Mitigation: a Community Based Approach.* Oxford, UK: Oxfam.

Mauss, Marcel. 1954. *The Gift: The Form and Reason for Exchange in Archaic Societies.* London: Routledge.

McAllister, Kirsten Emiko. 2010. "Archive and Myth: The Changing Memoryscape of Japanese Canadian Internment Camps". In *Placing Memory and Remembering Place in Canada*, edited by John C. Walsh and James William Opp. 214-46. Vancouver, Canada: UBC Press.

———. 2011. "Memoryscapes of Postwar British Columbia: A Look of Recognition". In *Cultivating Canada: Reconciliation Through the Lens of Cultural Diversity*, edited by Ashok Mathur, Mike DeGagné, and Jonathan Dewar. 419-44. Canada: Aboriginal Healing Foundation.

McEntire, David, Christopher Fuller, Chad Johnston, and Richard Weber. 2002. "A Comparison of Disaster Paradigms: The Search for a Holistic Policy Guide". *Public Administration Review* 62 (3): 267–281.

Menchú, Rigoberta, and Elisabeth Burgos-Debray. 1984. *I, Rigoberta Menchú: An Indian Woman in Guatemala*. Brooklyn, New York: Verso Books.

Le Menestrel, Sara, and Jacques Henry. 2010. "'Sing Us Back Home': Music, Place, and the Production of Locality in Post-Katrina New Orleans". *Popular Music and Society* 33 (2): 179–202.

Mérega, Herminia. 2008. *Ciencias Sociales Santa Fe (4to Año)*. Edited by Maria del Carmen Caeiro, Patricia Jitric, and Cecilia Sagol. Serie Ciencias Sociales Provincias. Buenos Aires: Ediciones Santillana Argentina.

Métraux, Alfred. 1946. *Myths of the Toba and Pilagá Indians of the Gran Chaco*. Columbus, Ohio: American Folklore Society, Ohio State University.

Middleton, David, and Derek Edwards. 1990. *Collective Remembering*. London: Sage Publications.

Midré, Georges. 1990. *Bot, bedring eller brød?: om bedømming og behandling av sosial nød fra reformasjonen til folketrygden*. Oslo, Norway: Rådet for samfunnsvitenskapelig forskning (NAVF) and Universitetsforlaget.

Miller, Daniel. 2009. *Stuff*. Cambridge, UK: Polity.

Miller, Joan B. 1974. *Aberfan: a Disaster and Its Aftermath*. London: Constable & Robinson.

Mino, Luis. 1998. *Para Conocernos*. Vol. 1. Santa Fe, Argentina: Luis Mino Producciones.

Minujin, Alberto, and Gabriel Kessler. 1995. *La nueva pobreza en la Argentina*. Buenos Aires: Editorial Planeta.

Misztal, Barbara A. 2003. *Theories Of Social Remembering*. New York: McGraw-Hill International.

Mitchell, Jon P. 2010. "Introduction". In *Ethnographic Practice in the Present*, edited by Marit Melhuus, Jon P. Mitchell, and Helena Wulff, 1–15. Oxford, UK: Berghahn Books.

Montenegro, Cecilia, María Gabriela Parmuchi, Mabel Strada, Julieta Bono, Eduardo Manghi, and Marcelo Brouver. 2005. "Mapa Forestal: Provincia de Santa Fe. Actualización 2002". Buenos Aires: Secretaría de Ambiente y Desarrollo Sustentable, Dirección de Bosques, Unidad de Manejo del Sistema de Evaluación Forestal.

Moore, Sally Falk. 2007. *Law and Anthropology: a Reader*. Malden, Massachusetts: Blackwell Publishers.

Moro, Luis, Pablo Benito, and Claudia Moreno. 2005. *29-A. 29 de Abril de 2003 / Inundación En Santa Fe*. Santa Fe, Argentina: Tercer Mundo.

Munich Re. 2012. "Natural Catastrophes Worldwide 1980–2011". Focus Analyses. Munich, Germany: Munich Re.

Munn, Nancy D. 1992. "The Cultural Anthropology of Time: A Critical Essay". *Annual Review of Anthropology* 21 (January 1): 93–123.

Nadasdy, Paul. 2007. "Adaptive Co-Management and the Gospel of Resilience". In *Adaptive Co-Management: Collaboration, Learning, and Multi-Level Governance*, edited by Derek Russel Armitage, 208–27. Vancouver, Canada: UBC Press.

Narayan, Kirin. 1993. "How Native Is a "Native" Anthropologist?" *American Anthropologist* 95 (3): 671–686.

Natenzon, Claudia. 1998. "Riesgo, Vulnerabilidad e Incertidumbre. Desastres Por Inundaciones En Argentina". Conference paper. Seminario sobre Problemas Ambientais e Vulnerabilidade. Abordagem Integradoras para o campo da Saude Publica. Rio de Janeiro, Brazil. June 25.

———. 2003. "Inundaciones Catastróficas, Vulnerabilidad Social y Adaptaciones En Un Caso Argentino Actual. Cambio Climático, Elevación Del Nivel Medio Del Mar y Sus Implicancias". Conference paper. Climate Change Impacts and Integrated Assessment EMF (Energy Modeling Forum) Workshop IX. Snowmass, Colorado: Stanford University.

Neal, Dave M. 1984. "Blame Assignment in a Diffuse Disaster Situation: A Case Example of the Role of an Emergent Citizen Group". *International Journal of Mass Emergencies and Disasters* 2: 251–66.

Neil, Claudia, and Sergio Peralta. 2007. "1956-1976. Instituto de Cinematografía de La Universidad Nacional Del Litoral". In *Fotogramas Santafesinos: Instituto de Cinematografía de La UNL 1956/1976*, edited by Claudia Neil, Sergio Peralta, Luis Priamo, and Raúl Becerro, 11–82. Santa Fe, Argentina: Ediciones Universidad Nacional del Litoral, Secretaría de Extensión.

Nora, Pierre. 1989. "Between Memory and History: Les Lieux de Mémoire". *Representations* Special Issue: Memory and Counter-Memory (26): 7–24.

———. 2001. *Rethinking France: Les Lieux de Mémoire, Volume 1: The State*. Chicago: University of Chicago Press.

Norman, Karin. 2001. "Från Dalarna till Kosovo: att följa fältet i hälarna". In *Flera fält i ett: socialantropologer om translokala fältstudier*, edited by Ulf Hannerz. 36-64. Stockholm: Carlssons Bokförlag.

Novick, Marta, Miguel Lengyel, and Marianela Sarabia. 2009. "From Social Protection to Vulnerability: Argentina's Neo-liberal Reforms of the 1990s". *International Labour Review* 148 (3): 235–252.

Numazaki, Ichiro. 2012. "Too Wide, Too Big, Too Complicated to Comprehend". *Asian Anthropology* 11: 27–38.

Nuttall, Mark. 1992. *Arctic Homeland: Kinship, Community and Development in Northwest Greenland*. Toronto: University of Toronto Press.

Nyqvist, Anette. 2008. *Opening the Orange Envelope: Reform and Responsibility in the Remaking of the Swedish National Pension System*. Stockholm Studies in Social Anthropology 64. Stockholm: Almqvist & Wiksell.

Oberlin, Dante. 2005. *La Tragedia Santafesina*. Santa Fe, Argentina: Sindicato de Artes Gráficos de Santa Fe.

Okada, Hiroki. 2012. "An Anthropological Examination of Differences". *Asian Anthropology* 11: 55–63.

Olesen, Thomas. 2012. "Televised Media Performance for HIV/AIDS Sufferers in Africa: Distance Reduction and National Community in Two Danish Fundraising Shows". *Communication, Culture & Critique* 5 (1) (March 1): 99–119.

Olick, Jeffrey K. 2007. *The Politics of Regret: On Collective Memory and Historical Responsibility*. London: Routledge.

Olick, Jeffrey K., Vered Vinitzky-Seroussi, and Daniel Levy. 2011. *The Collective Memory Reader*. Oxford, UK: Oxford University Press.

Oliver-Smith, Anthony. 1977a. "Disaster Rehabilitation and Social Change in Yungay, Peru". *Human Organization* 36 (1): 5–13.

———. 1977b. "Traditional Agriculture, Central Places, and Postdisaster Urban Relocation in Peru". *American Ethnologist* 4 (1): 102–116.

———. 1979a. "Post Disaster Consensus and Conflict in a Traditional Society: The 1970 Avalance of Yungay, Peru". *Mass Emergencies* (4): 39–52.

———. 1979b. "The Yungay Avalanche Of 1970: Anthropological Perspectives On Disaster And Social Change". *Disasters* 3 (1): 95–101.

———. 1986. *The Martyred City: Death and Rebirth in the Andes*. Albuquerque, New Mexico: University of New Mexico Press.

———. 1994. "Peru's Fivehundred Year Earthquake: Vulnerability in Historical Context". In *Disasters, Development and Environment*, edited by Ann Varley. Chichester, New York: J. Wiley.

———. 1996. "Anthropological Research on Hazards and Disasters". *Annual Review of Anthropology* 25: 303–328.

———. 1999. "The Brotherhood of Pain: Theoretical and Applied Perspectives on Post-disaster Solidarity". In *The Angry Earth: Disaster in Anthropological Perspective*, edited by Anthony Oliver-Smith and Susanna Hoffman, 156–172. London: Routledge.

———. 2002. "Theorizing Disasters. Nature, Power and Culture". In *Catastrophe & Culture. The Anthropoogy of Disaster*, edited by S. & A. Oliver-Smith Hoffman. Santa Fe, New Mexico: School of American Research Press.

———. 2009. "Anthropology and the Political Economy of Disasters". In *The Political Economy of Hazards and Disasters*, edited by Eric C. Jones and Arthur D. Murphy, 11–28. Lanham, Maryland: Rowman Altamira.

Oliver-Smith, Anthony, and Susanna Hoffman, eds. 1999. *The Angry Earth: Disaster in Anthropological Perspective*. London: Routledge.

———. 2002. "Introduction: Why Anthropologists Should Study Disasters". In *Catastrophe & Culture. The Anthropology of Disaster*, edited by Susanna Hoffman and Anthony Oliver-Smith, 3–22. Santa Fe, New Mexico: School of American Research Press.

Orta, Andrew. 2002. "Burying the Past: Locality, Lived History, and Death in an Aymara Ritual of Remembrance". *Cultural Anthropology* 17 (4): 471–511.

Ortiz, Ana. 2008. *Río Liberado: Emergentes Culturales En El Sistema Ambiental Paraná Medio*. Serie Antropología Política y Económica. Edited by M. Boivin. Buenos Aires: Editorial Antropofagia.

Osborne, Thomas. 1999. "The Ordinariness of the Archive". *History of the Human Sciences* 12 (2) (May 1): 51–64.

Ovalles, Eduardo. 2002. "Argentina Es El País Del Mundo En El Cual El Fenómeno Del Trueque Tiene Mayor Dimensión Social". *Nueva Mayoría: El Portal Socio Polítoco de Iberoamérica*. May 8. http://www.nuevamayoria.com/invest/sociedad/cso080502.htm.

Pais, Fernando. 2008. *Agua de Nadie: La Historia de Cómo El Salado Inundó Santa Fe*. Santa Fe, Argentina: Ediciones Universidad Nacional del Litoral.

Palser, Barb. 2007. *Hurricane Katrina: Aftermath of Disaster*. Mankato, Minnesota: Capstone Publishers.

Pantaleón, Jorge. 2004. *Entre La Carta y El Formulario: Política y Técnica En El Desarrollo Social*. Serie Etnográfica. Buenos Aires: Editorial Antropofagia.

Paoli, Carlos and Dora Goniadzki. 2003. "La Cuenca Del Río Salado y La Crecida de Abril de 2003". Santa Fe, Argentina: Instituto Nacional del Agua Centro Regional Litoral.

Paoli, Carlos, and Mario Schreider, eds. 2000. *El Río Paraná En Su Tramo Medio: Contribución Al Conocimiento y Prácticas Ingenieriles En Un Gran Río de Llanura*. Tomo 2. Santa Fe, Argentina: Ediciones Universidad Nacional del Litoral.

Passerini, Luisa. 1992. *Memory and Totalitarianism*. London: Transaction Publishers.

Paton, Douglas, and David Moore Johnston. 2006. *Disaster Resilience: An Integrated Approach*. Springfield, Illinois: Charles C Thomas Publisher.

Paxson, Margaret. 2005. *Solovyovo. The Story of Memory in a Russian Village*. Washington D.C.: Woodrow Wilson Center Press.

Peek, Lori A. 2012. "They Call It "Katrina Fatigue": Displaced Families and Discrimination in Chicago". In *Displaced: Life in the Katrina Diaspora*, edited by Lynn Weber and Lori A Peek, 31–46. Austin, Texas: University of Texas Press.

Pelling, Mark. 2003. *The Vulnerability of Cities: Natural Disasters and Social Resilience*. London: Earthscan.

Pels, Peter, and Oscar Salemink. 1994. "Introduction: Five Theses on Ethnography as Colonial Practice 1". *History and Anthropology* 8 (1-4): 1–34.

Perez, Liliana, Maria Lastra, and Juan Carlos Forconi. 2005. "Análisis Organizacional de La Unidad Ejecutora de Recuperación de La Emergencia

  Hídrica y Pluvial (UEREHyP)". Santa Fe, Argentina: Gobierno de la Provincia de Santa Fe.

Perin, Constance. 2004. *Shouldering Risks: The Culture of Control in the Nuclear Power Industry*. Princeton, New Jersey: Princeton University Press.

Perrow, Charles. 1984. *Normal Accidents: Living with High-risk Technologies*. New York: Basic Books.

Perry, Ronald W. 2007. "What Is a Disaster?" In *Handbook of Disaster Research*, edited by Havidán Rodríguez, Enrico Quarantelli, and Russell R. Dynes, 1–15. Handbooks of Sociology and Social Research. New York: Springer.

Petryna, Adriana. 2002. *Life Exposed: Biological Citizens After Chernobyl*. Princeton, New Jersey: Princeton University Press.

Phillips, Brenda. 2009. *Disaster Recovery*. UK: Taylor & Francis.

Phillips, Kendall R., and G. Mitchell Reyes, eds. 2011. *Global Memoryscapes: Contesting Remembrance in a Transnational Age*. Tuscaloosa, Alabama: University of Alabama Press.

Pistone, Catalina. 1989. "El Río En La Historia de La Ciudad de Santa Fe". *Revista de La Junta Provincial de Estudios Históricos de Santa Fe* (54): 57–90. Santa Fe, Argentina: Junta Provincial de Estudios Históricos de Santa Fe.

Pita, Nicolás. 2006. "Afrodescendientes: Una Realidad Que Sale a La Luz". Washington, D.C.: The International Bank for Reconstruction and Development and The World Bank.

Pomian, Krzysztof. 2010. "The Archives: From the Trésor Des Chartes to the CARAN". In *Rethinking France: Les Lieux de Mémoire*, Volume 4: Histories and Memories:27–100. Chicago: University of Chicago Press.

Powers, Nancy. 1995. "The Politics of Poverty in Argentina in the 1990s". *Journal of Interamerican Studies and World Affairs* 37 (4) (December 1): 89–137.

Priamo, Luis. 2007. "Sobre Los Fotodocumentales Del Instituto de Cinematografía de La Universidad Nacional Del Litoral". In *Fotogramas Santafesinos: Instituto de Cinematografía de La UNL 1956/1976*, edited by Claudia Neil, Sergio Peralta, Luis Priamo, and Raúl Becerro, 83–96. Santa Fe, Argentina: Ediciones Universidad Nacional del Litoral - Secretaría de Extensión.

Prince, Samuel Henry. 1920. *Catastrophe and Social Change: Based Upon a Sociological Study of the Halifax Disaster*. New York: Columbia University.

Proust, Marcel. 2006. *Remembrance of Things Past*. Hertfordshire, UK: Wordsworth Editions.

Quarantelli, Enrico. 1998. *What is a Disaster? Perspectives on the Question*. London: Routledge.

Quarantelli, Enrico, and Russell R. Dynes. 1977. "Response to Social Crisis and Disaster". *Annual Review of Sociology* 3: 23–49.

———. 1985. "Community Response To Disasters". Research Paper 179. Newark, Delaware:University of Delaware, Disaster Research Center. Quarantelli, Enrico, Patrick Lagadec, and Arjen Boin. 2007. "A Heuristic Approach to Future Disasters and Crises: New, Old and In-between Types". In *Handbook of Disaster Research*, edited by Havidán Rodríguez, Enrico Quarantelli, and Russell R. Dynes, 16–41. Handbooks of Sociology and Social Research. New York: Springer.

Quirós, Julieta. 2011. *El Porqué de Los Que van: Peronistas y Piqueteros En El Gran Buenos Aires (una Antropología de La Política Vivida)*. Buenos Aires: Editorial Antropofagia.

Radstone, Susannah. 2000. "Working with Memory: An Introduction". In *Memory and Methodology*, edited by Susannah Radstone, 1–22. Oxford, UK: Berg Publishers.

Radstone, Susannah, and Katharine Hodgkin, eds. 2003. *Regimes of Memory*. UK: Taylor & Francis.

Randall, Margaret. 1985. *Testimonios: A Guide to Oral History*. New York: Participatory Research Group - Institute of Development Studies.

Rappaport, Joanne. 1990. *The Politics of Memory: Native Historical Interpretation in the Colombian Andes*. Cambridge, UK: Cambridge University Press.

Rappaport, Roy. 1971. "The Flow of Energy in an Agricultural Society". *Scientific American* 225 (3) (September): 117–122. London: Nature Publishing Group.

———. 1984. *Pigs for the Ancestors: Ritual in the Ecology of a New Guinea People*. Waveland Press.

Rapport, Nigel, and Joanna Overing, eds. 2000. *Social and Cultural Anthropology: The Key Concepts*. London: Routledge.

Ratier, Hugo. 1971a. *El cabecita negra*. Buenos Aires: Centro Editor de América Latina.

———. 1971b. *Villeros y Villas Miserias*. Buenos Aires: Centro Editor de América Latina.

Read, Allen Walker. 1977. *Classic American Graffiti: Lexical Evidence from Folk Epigraphy in Western North America: a Glossarial Study of the Low Element in the English Vocabulary*. Waukesha, Wisconsin: Maledicta.

Reato, Ceferino. 2012. *Disposición Final: La Confesión de Videla Sobre Los Desaparecidos*. Buenos Aires: Editorial Sudamericana.

Regis, Helen A. 2001. "Blackness and the Politics of Memory in the New Orleans Second Line". *American Ethnologist* 28 (4): 752–77.

Revet, Sandrine. 2007. *Anthropologie D'une Catastrophe. Les Coulées de Boue de 1999 Au Venezuela*. Paris: Presses de la Sorbonne Nouvelle.

———. 2011. "Remembering La Tragedia: Commemorations of the 1999 Floods in Venezuela". In *Grassroots Memorials: the Politics of Memorializing Traumatic Death*, edited by Peter Jan Margry and Cristina Sánchez Carretero, 208–28. Oxford, UK: Berghahn Books.

———. 2013. ""A Small World": Ethnography of a Natural Disaster in Lima, Peru". *Social Anthropology* 21 (1): 38–53.

Riaño-Alcalá, Pilar. 2006. *Dwellers of Memory. Youth and Violence in Medellin, Colombia*. New Brunswick: Transaction Publishers.

Ricoeur, Paul. 2004. *Memory, History, Forgetting*. Chicago: University of Chicago Press.

Riera, Gabriel. 2006. *Littoral of the Letter: Saer's Art of Narration*. Lewisburg, Pennsylvania: Bucknell University Press.

Riles, Annelise. 2006. *Document : Artifacts of Modern Knowledge*. Ann Arbor: University of Michigan Press.

Rivkin-Fish, Michele. 2009. "Tracing Landscapes of the Past in Class Subjectivity: Practices of Memory and Distinction in Marketizing Russia". *American Ethnologist* 36 (1): 79–95.

Robben, Antonius. 2005. "How Traumatized Societies Remember: The Aftermath of Argentina's Dirty War". *Cultural Critique* (59): 120–164.

———. 2007. *Political Violence and Trauma in Argentina*. Philadelphia: University of Pennsylvania Press.

Rodriguez, Havidan, Enrico Quarantelli, and Russell Dynes. 2007. *Handbook of Disaster Research*. New York: Springer.

Roldán, Diego. 2006. *La Sociedad En Movimiento. Expresiones Culturales, Sociales y Deportivas (Siglo XX)*. Serie Nueva Historia de Santa Fe. Rosario, Argentina: Prohistoria Ediciones and Diario La Capital.

Ronan, Kevin, and David Johnston. 2005. *Promoting Community Resilience in Disasters: The Role for Schools, Youth, and Families*. New York: Springer.

Rosato, Ana M. 1988. "Ganadería, Pesca y Caza En El Delta Bonaerense". *Desarrollo Económico. Revista de Ciencias Sociales* 27 (108): 607–626.

Rowlands, Michael, and Ferdinand de Jong. 2008. "Reconsidering Heritage and Memory". In *Reclaiming Heritage: Alternative Imaginaries of Memory in West Africa*, edited by Ferdinand de Jong and Michael Rowlands, 13–29. Walnut Creek: Left Coast Press.

Roybal, Karen. 2012. "History, Memory, and Ambivalence: Testimonio as Alternative Archive". *Culture, Theory and Critique* 53 (2) (May 10): 215–232.

Rozema, Ralph. 2011. "Forced Disappearance in an Era of Globalization: Biopolitics, Shadow Networks, and Imagined Worlds". *American Anthropologist* 113 (4) (November 25): 582–593.

Ruano Gomez, Juan de Dios, ed. 2005. *Riesgos colectivos y situaciones de crisis. El desafío de la incertidumbre*. Santiago de Compostela, Spain: Universidade da Coruña.

Röschenthaler, Ute. 2010. "An Ethnography of Associations? Translocal Research in the Cross River Region". In *Ethnographic Practice in the Present*, edited by Marit Melhuus, Jon P Mitchell, and Helena Wulff, 121–34. New York, Oxford, UK: Berghahn Books.

Sa'Di, Ahmad H., and Lila Abu-Lughod. 2007. *Nakba: Palestine, 1948, and the Claims of Memory*. New York: Columbia University Press.

Saer, Juan José. 1976. "A Medio Borrar". In *La Mayor*. Buenos Aires: Editorial Planeta.

———. 1983. *El entenado*. México D.F.: Folios Ediciones.
———. 1997. *Las nubes*. Buenos Aires: Seix Barral.
———. 2000. *Lugar*. Buenos Aires: Seix Barral.
Said, Edward W. 1989. "Representing the Colonized: Anthropology's Interlocutors". *Critical Inquiry* 15 (2): 205–225.
Said, Edward W. 1979. *Orientalism*. New York: Vintage Books.
Sanford, Victoria. 2003. *Buried Secrets: Truth and Human Rights in Guatemala*. Basingstoke, UK: Palgrave Macmillan.
Santino, Jack. 2006. *Spontaneous Shrines and the Public Memorialization of Death*. Basingstoke, UK: Palgrave Macmillan.
Sather-Wagstaff, Joy. 2011. *Heritage That Hurts: Tourists in the Memoryscapes of September 11*. Walnut Creek: Left Coast Press.
Schamber, Pablo. 2008. *De Los Desechos a Las Mercancías. Una Etnografía de Los Cartoneros*. Buenos Aires: SB Editorial.
Scheper-Hughes, Nancy. 1993. *Death Without Weeping: The Violence of Everyday Life in Brazil*. Berkeley, California: University of California Press.
———. 2008. "A Talent for Life: Reflections on Human Vulnerability and Resilience". *Ethnos* 73 (1) (February 28): 25–56.
Schramm, Katharina. 2010. *African Homecoming: Pan-African Ideology and Contested Heritage*. Walnut Creek: Left Coast Press.
Scott, James C. 1992. *Domination and the Arts of Resistance: Hidden Transcripts*. New Haven, Conneticut: Yale University Press.
———. 1999. *Seeing Like a State: How Certain Schemes to Improve the Human Condition Have Failed*. New Haven, Conneticut: Yale University Press.
Segnestam, Lisa. 2009. "Division of Capitals—What Role Does It Play for Gender-Differentiated Vulnerability to Drought in Nicaragua?" *Community Development* 40 (2) (June 12): 154–176.
Serafino, Alicia. 2010. "La Celebración de Una Virgen Migrante, Construcciones Identitarias Entre Bolivianos y Santafesinos en Un Sector de Quintas al Norte de la Ciudad de Santa Fe, Argentina". *Revista Economía y Sociedad* (19): 117–34.
Sharma, Mukul. 2012. "Dalits and Indian Environmental Politics". *Economic and Political Weekly* (June 2012). On line
Shaw, Rajib, and Anshu Sharma. 2011. *Climate and Disaster Resilience in Cities*. Bingley, West Yorkshire, UK: Emerald Group Publishing.
Shaw, Rosalind. 2002. *Memories of the Slave Trade: Ritual and the Historical Imagination in Sierra Leone*. Chicago: University of Chicago Press.
———. 2007. "Memory Frictions: Localizing the Truth and Reconciliation Commission in Sierra Leone". *International Journal of Transitional Justice* 1 (2) (July 1): 183–207.
Shever, Elana. 2012. *Resources for Reform: Oil and Neoliberalism in Argentina*. Palo Alto, California: Stanford University Press.
Shukla, J., C. Nobre, and P. Sellers. 1990. "Amazon Deforestation and Climate Change". *Science* 247 (4948) (March 16): 1322–1325.

Sikkink, Kathryn. 2008. "From Pariah State to Global Protagonist: Argentina and the Struggle for International Human Rights". *Latin American Politics and Society* 50 (1): 1–29.

De Simone, Carla. 2006. "El Desempeño Del Sector Agropecuario y Agroindustrial En El Nuevo Milenio". Buenos Aires, Argentina: Secretaría de Agricultura Ganadería Pesca y Alimentos, Subsecretaría de Agricultura Ganadería y Forestación, Dirección de Economía Agraria.

Sion, Brigitte. 2008. *Absent Bodies, Uncertain Memorials: Performing Memory in Berlin and Buenos Aires.* Doctoral thesis, mimeo. New York: New York University.

Smith, Gavin. 2012. *Planning for Post-Disaster Recovery: A Review of the United States Disaster Assistance Framework.* Washington D.C.: Island Press.

Smith, William. 1991. *Authoritarianism and the Crisis of the Argentine Political Economy.* Palo Alto, California: Stanford University Press.

Sonzogni, Élida. 2006. "Un Mundo En Cambio". In *La Organización Productiva y Política Del Territorio Provincial (1853-1912)*, edited by Marta Bonaudo, 9–30. Serie Nueva Historia de Santa Fe: 6. Rosario, Argentina: Prohistoria Ediciones and Diario La Capital.

Stallings, Robert A., and E. L. Quarantelli. 1985. "Emergent Citizen Groups and Emergency Management". *Public Administration Review* 45 (January 1): 93–100.

Steward, Julian Haynes. 1955. *Theory of Culture Change: The Methodology of Multilinear Evolution.* Campaign, Illinois: University of Illinois Press.

Stoll, David. 1999. *Rigoberta Menchú and the Story of All Poor Guatemalans.* Boulder, Colorado: Westview Press.

Sturken, Marita. 1997. *Tangled Memories. The Vietnam War, The AIDS Epidemic and the Politics of Remembering.* Berkeley, California: University of California Press.

———. 2007. *Tourists of History: Memory, Kitsch, and Consumerism from Oklahoma City to Ground Zero.* Durham, North Carolina: Duke University Press.

Stølen, Kristi-Anne. 2004. *La Decencia de La Desigualdad: Género y Poder En El Campo Argentino.* Buenos Aires: Editorial Antropofagia.

Susman, P., Philip O'Keefe, and Ben Wisner. 1983. "Global Disasters, a Radical Interpretation". In *Interpretations of Calamity: From the Viewpoint of Human Ecology*, edited by Kenneth Hewitt, 262–83. London: Unwin Hyman.

Taylor, Alan J. 1979. "Assessment of Victim Needs". *Disasters* 3 (1): 24–31.

Teubal, Miguel, and Tomás Palmisano. 2010. "El conflicto agrario: características y proyecciones". In *Del paro agrario a las elecciones de 2009: Tramas, reflexiones y debates*, edited by Norma Giarracca and Miguel Teubal, 193–252. Buenos Aires: Editorial Antropofagia.

"The Manizales Declaration". 2004. The Inter-American Conference of Disaster Risk, Nov 17-19, Manizales, Colombia.

http://www.unisdr.org/2005/wcdr/preparatory-process/inputs/Declaration-Manizales-eng.pdf.

Thedvall, Renita. 2006. *Eurocrats at Work: Negotiating Transparency in Postnational Employment Policy*. Stockholm Studies in Social Anthropology 58. Stockholm: Almqvist & Wiksell.

Tidball, Keith G., Marianne E. Krasny, Erika Svendsen, Lindsay Campbell, and Kenneth Helphand. 2010. "Stewardship, Learning, and Memory in Disaster Resilience". *Environmental Education Research* 16 (5-6): 591–609.

Tierney, Kathleen. 2003. "Conceptualizing and Measuring Organizational and Community Resilience: Lessons From The Emergency Response Following The September 11, 2001 Attack on The World Trade Center". DRC Preliminary Papers. Newark, Delaware: Disaster Research Centre, University of Delaware.

Tilly, Charles, and Lesley J. Wood. 2013. *Social Movements, 1768-2012*. Boulder, CO: Paradigm Publishers.

Tommasi, Mariano. 2006. "Fiscal Federalism in Argentina and the Reforms of the 1990s". In *Federalism and Economic Reform: International Perspectives*, edited by Jessica Wallack and T. N. Srinivasan, 25–84. Cambridge, UK: Cambridge University Press.

Torry, William. 1973. *Subsistence Ecology Among the Gabra: Nomads of the Kenya-Ethiopia Frontier*. New York: Columbia University.

———. 1978a. "Natural Disasters, Social Structure and Change in Traditional Societies". *Journal of Asian and African Studies* 13 (3-4): 167–183.

———. 1978b. "Bureaucracy, Community, and Natural Disasters". *Human Organization* 37 (3): 302–308.

Torry, William, William A. Anderson, Donald Bain, Harry J. Otway, Randall Baker, Frances D'Souza, Philip O'Keefe. 1979. "Anthropological Studies in Hazardous Environments: Past Trends and New Horizons [and Comments and Reply]". *Current Anthropology* 20 (3): 517–540.

Townsend, Patricia K. 2009. *Environmental Anthropology: From Pigs to Policies*. Grove, Illinois: Waveland Press.

Travasso, M., G. Magrin, W. Baethgen, and J. Castaño. 2006. "Adaptation Measures for Maize and Soybean in Southeastern South America". *AIACC Working Paper Series* (28) (June). http://www.aiaccproject.org/working_papers/working_papers.html.

Trouillot, Michel-Rolph. 1995. *Silencing the Past: Power and the Production of History*. Boston, Massachusetts: Beacon Press.

———. 2000. "Abortive Rituals: Historical Apologies in the Global Era". *Interventions: The International Journal of Postcolonial Studies* 2 (2) (July): 171–86.

Tsing, Anna Lowenhaupt. 2011. *Friction: An Ethnography of Global Connection*. Princeton, New Jersey: Princeton University Press.

Turner, Terence. 2011. "Forty-five Years with the Kapayo". In *Returns to the Field: Multitemporal Research and Contemporary Anthropology*, edited by Signe Howell and Aud Talle, 25–48. Bloomington, Indiana: Indiana University Press.

Turner, Victor Witter. 1967. *The Forest of Symbols: Aspects of Ndembu Ritual*. Ithaca, New York: Cornell University Press.

———. 1972. *Schism and Continuity in an African Society: A Study of Ndembu Village Life*. Manchester, UK: Manchester University Press.

———. 1975. *Dramas, Fields, and Metaphors: Symbolic Action in Human Society*. Ithaca, New York: Cornell University Press.

———. 1995. *The Ritual Process: Structure and Anti-Structure*. London: Transaction Publishers.

Tönnies, Ferdinand. 1887. *Gemeinschaft Und Gesellschaft*. Darmstadt, Germany: Wissenschaftliche Buchgesellschaft.

Ullberg, Susann. 2001. *Environmental Crisis in Spain: The Boliden Dam Rupture*. Vol. 14. Stockholm: CRISMART, Swedish National Defence College.

———. 2005. *The Buenos Aires Blackout: Argentine Crisis Management Across the Public-private Divide*. Vol. 28. Stockholm: CRISMART, Swedish National Defence College.

United Nations International Strategy for Disaster Reduction. 2005. "Hyogo Framework for Action 2005-2015: Building the Resilience of Nations and Communities to Disasters". Kobe, Japan: United Nations International Strategy for Disaster Reduction.

———. 2011a. "Cities Emerge Top in United Nations-Sasakawa Award Competition on Innovative Disaster Risk Reduction Initiatives - UNISDR". May 12. http://www.unisdr.org/archive/19916.

———. 2011b. "Hyogo Framework for Action 2005-2015. Mid-Term Review 2010-2011". United Nations International Strategy for Disaster Reduction. http://www.unisdr.org/files/18197_midterm.pdf.

———. 2012. "Annual Report 2011: UNISDR Secretariat Work Programme 2010-2011". United Nations International Strategy for Disaster Reduction Secretariat (UNISDR).

———. 2012b. "Crearán El 'Circuito Urbano 29 de Abril' Para Que No Se Olvide La Catástrofe Hídrica". October 18. http://www.unosantafe.com.ar/santafe/Crearan-el-Circuito-Urbano-29-de-Abril-para-que-no-se-olvide-la-catastrofe-hidrica--20121018-0021.html?fb_action_ids=3252585291796&fb_action_types=og.recommends&fb_source=aggregation&fb_aggregation_id=288381481237582.

Vale, Lawrence J., and Thomas J. Campanella. 2005. *The Resilient City: How Modern Cities Recover from Disaster*. Oxford, UK: Oxford University Press.

Vallejos, Celina. 2004. *Raices en El Agua*. Santa Fe, Argentina: Ediciones Universidad Nacional del Litoral.

Vansina, Jan. 1965. *Oral Tradition: a Study in Historical Methodology*. London: Routledge.

Vaughan, Diane. 1997. *The Challenger Launch Decision: Risky Technology, Culture, and Deviance at NASA*. Chicago: University of Chicago Press.

Vayda, Andrew P., and Bonnie J. McCay. 1975. "New Directions in Ecology and Ecological Anthropology". *Annual Review of Anthropology* 4 (January 1): 293–306.

Velásquez, Angélica, ed. 2004. *Las Aguas Subían Turbias*. Santa Fe, Argentina.

Verbitsky, Bernardo. 1957. *Villa Miseria también es América*. Buenos Aires: Paidós.

Vergo, Peter. 1989. "Introduction". In *The New Museology*, edited by Peter Vergo, 1–5. London: Reaktion Books.

Viand, Jesica. 2009. "El Antes Del Desastre. La Construcción Social Del Riesgo En La Ciudad de Santa Fe y La Inundación Del Año 2003". Undergratuate thesis, mimeo. Buenos Aires: Universidad de Buenos Aires, Departameto de Geografía.

Viano, Cristina, and Marisa Armida. 2006. "Rebelión y Nuevo Protagonismo Social". In *El Tiempo Presente*, edited by Gabriela Águila and Oscar Videla, 13–46. Serie Nueva Historia de Santa Fe. Rosario, Argentina: Prohistoria Ediciones y Diario La Capital.

Vigh, Henrik. 2008. "Crisis and Chronicity: Anthropological Perspectives on Continuous Conflict and Decline". *Ethnos* 73 (1): 5–24.

Visacovsky, Sergio. 2002. *El Lanús: memoria y política en la construcción de una tradición psiquiátrica y psicoanalítica argentina*. Alianza Estudio 51. Buenos Aires: Alianza Editorial.

———. ed. 2011. *Estados Críticos: La Experiencia Social de La Calamidad*. La Plata, Argentina: Ediciones Al Margen.

Visacovsky, Sergio, and Enrique Garguin. 2009. *Moralidades, Economías e Identidades de Clase Media: Estudios Históricos y Etnográficos*. Buenos Aires: Editorial Antropofagia.

Volk, Lucia. 2010. *Memorials and Martyrs in Modern Lebanon*. Bloomington, Indiana: Indiana University Press.

Walker, R., J. Browder, E. Arima, C. Simmons, R. Pereira, M. Caldas, R. Shirota, and S.Zen. 2009. "Ranching and the New Global Range: Amazonia in the 21st Century". *Geoforum* 40 (5): 732–745.

Weber, Lynn, and Lori A. Peek, eds. 2012. *Displaced: Life in the Katrina Diaspora*. Austin, Texas: University of Texas Press.

Weichselgartner, Juergen. 2001. "Disaster Mitigation: The Concept of Vulnerability Revisited". *Disaster Prevention and Management* 10 (2) (May 1): 85–95.

Werbner, Richard P. 1998. *Memory and the Postcolony: African Anthropology and the Critique of Power*. London: Zed Books.

Wertsch, James V. 2002. *Voices of Collective Remembering*. Cambridge, UK: Cambridge University Press.

Weszkalnys, Gisa. 2010. *Berlin, Alexanderplatz: Transforming Place in a Unifed Germany*. Oxford, UK: Berghahn Books.

White, Leslie A. 2007. *The Evolution of Culture: The Development of Civilization to the Fall of Rome*. Walnut Creek: Left Coast Press.

Wilches Chaux, Gustavo. 1989. *Herramientas para la crisis: desastres, ecologismo y formación profesional*. Popayán, Colombia: SENA.

Wilson, Richard. 2001. *The Politics of Truth and Reconciliation in South Africa: Legitimizing the Post-apartheid State*. Cambridge, UK: Cambridge University Press.

Wisner, Ben, Piers Blaikie, Terry Cannon, and Ian Davis. 2004. *At Risk: Natural Hazards, People's Vulnerability and Disasters*. Second Edition. London: Routledge.

Wisner, Ben, JC Gaillard, and Ilan Kelman, eds. 2011a. *Handbook of Hazards and Disaster Risk Reduction*. Routledge Handbooks. London: Routledge.

———. 2011b. "Framing Disaster: Theories and Stories Seeking to Undrestand Hazards, Vulnerability and Risk". In *Handbook of Hazards and Disaster Risk Reduction*, edited by Ben Wisner, JC Gaillard, and Ilan Kelman, 18–33. Routledge Handbooks. London: Routledge.

———. 2011c. "Challenging Risk". In *Handbook of Hazards and Disaster Risk Reduction*, edited by Ben Wisner, JC Gaillard, and Ilan Kelman, 1–7. Routledge Handbooks. London: Routledge.

———, ed. 2011d. "Introduction to Part I". In *Handbook of Hazards and Disaster Risk Reduction*, 11–17. Routledge Handbooks. London: Routledge.

World Bank. 1999. "Argentina - Flood Rehabilitation Project (Loan 3521-AR)". Implementation Completion and Results Report 18769. Washington D.C.: World Bank. http://documents.worldbank.org/curated/en/1999/01/728057/argentina-flood-rehabilitation-project.

Wright, Daniel B. 1993. "Recall of the Hillsborough Disaster over Time: Systematic Biases of 'Flashbulb' Memories". *Applied Cognitive Psychology* 7 (2): 129–138.

Wulff, Helena. 1998. *Ballet Across Border : Career and Culture in the World of Dancers*. Oxford, UK: Berg Publishers.

———. 2002. "Yo-yo Fieldwork : Mobility and Time in a Multi-local Study of Dance in Ireland". *Anthropological Journal on European Cultures* 11: 117–36.

———. 2007. *Dancing at the Crossroads: Memory and Mobility in Ireland*. Oxford, UK: Berghahn Books.

———. 2008. "Literary Readings as Performance: On the Career of Contemporary Writers in the New Ireland". *Anthropological Journal of European Cultures* 17 (2): 98–113.

———. 2009. "Ethnografiction: Irish Relations in the Writing of Éilís Ní Dhuibhne". In *Éilís Ní Dhuibhne: Perspectives*, edited by Rebecca Pelan, 245–261. Galway, Ireland: Arlen House.

Wylde, Christopher. 2011. "State, Society and Markets in Argentina: The Political Economy of Neodesarrollismo Under Néstor Kirchner, 2003–2007". *Bulletin of Latin American Research* 30 (4): 436–452.

Yael Ríos, Sabrina. 2006. "El Movimiento Obrero Durante La Última Dictadura Militar, 1976-1983". Research paper, mimeo. Los Polvorines, Argentina: Universidad Nacional de General Sarmiento.

Yoneyama, Lisa. 1999. *Hiroshima Traces: Time, Space, and the Dialectics of Memory*. Berkeley, California: University of California Press.

Zagalsky, Ruth. 2004. "A Cinco Años de La Creacion Del Sistema Federal de Emergencias - SIFEM - Una Evaluacion Critica de Su Desarrollo Institucional". Buenos Aires: Centro de Estudios de Política, Administración y Sociedad (CEPAS).

Zapata Gollán, Agustin. 1990. *Obras Completas*. Santa Fe, Argentina: Ediciones Universidad Nacional del Litoral.

Zenobi, Diego. 2011. "Masacre, Familia y Política: Un Análisis Etnográfico de La Lucha de Los Familiares y Sobrevivientes de Cromañón". Doctoral thesis, mimeo. Buenos Aires: Universidad de Buenos Aires.

Newspapers

Bazzan, Gustavo. 2010. "Más Créditos Del Banco Mundial Para Argentina". *iEco, Clarín.com*, April 26. http://www.ieco.clarin.com/economia/creditos-Banco-Mundial-Argentina_0_250781960.html.

Downes, Patricio. 2005. "Negros En El País: Censan Cuántos Hay y Cómo Viven". *Clarín*, April 2. www.clarin.com/diario/2005/04/02/sociedad/s-04815.htm.

El Federal. 1983. "En Marcha El Operativo Evacuación En Alto Verde", March 2.

El Litoral. 1946. "Afligente Situación de Las Familias Afectadas Por La Inundación". May 18.

———. 1957. "No Es Inminente El Peligro de Que Se Inunde La Zona Poblada Del [Barrio] Centenario: Las Defensas En Esa Zona Se Mantienen Intactas. En Los Barrios Del Oeste Los Bomberos Tuvieron Que Evacuar a Muchas Familias. Crece El Río". October 9.

———. 1959. "Grandes Zonas Marginales de La Ciudad Se Encuentran Invadidas Por Las Aguas: Se Trabaja Apresuradamente En [la Avenida] Blas Parera y El Terraplén Del [Barrio] Centenario Debió Ser Reforzado". March 3.

———. 1961. "Más de 6000 Personas Han Sido Afectadas Por La Inundación En Barrios, Zonas Costeras e Islas En La Juridicción Local". April 9.

. 1965. "Es Desolador El Panorama En Las Islas y Otras Zonas Afectadas Por La Creciente Del Paraná: Cientos de Familias Evacuadas, Terraplenes Rotos y Muchísimas Viviendas Dañadas, Es El Saldo de La Inundación". April 10.

———. 1966. "Al Ceder Parte de Las Defensas de Barranquitas Las Aguas Anegaron Sectores Del Barrio. Hay 400 Familias Afectadas". February 8.

———. 1974. "Vecinos Amenazados Por El Avance Del Río Salado Reclaman Urgentes Medidas: Situación de Los Evacuados de La Isla Clucellas". February 24.

———. 1977. "Previenen Vecinos de Barranquitas Sobre La Crecida". *El Litoral*, January 19.

———. 1978. "Vivir Inundados: Una Situación Frecuente de Los Habitantes de [el Barrio de] Santa Rosa de Lima". January 3.

———. 1981. "Alto Verde Libra Su Batalla Contra El Sostenido Avance de La Creciente". February 22.

———. 1987. "Se Espera Para Las Próximas 48 Horas el Pico de La Creciente en Santa Fe". June 13.

———. 1988. "Inundación: Casi Doscientas Familias Debieron Ser Evacuadas". n.d.

———. 1998. "Inundaciones: Crítica Situación En Colastiné y Otros Sectores de La Ribera". April 20.

———. 2003. "La Inundación Por La Crecida Del Río Salado Ya Afectó a Más de 50.000 Personas [en El Oeste]". April 29.

———. 2003. "Gieco y Heredia Dicen Presente". May 9 http://www.ellitoral.com/accesorios/imprimir.php?id=/diarios/2003/05/09/pantallayescenarios/PAN-01.html.

———. 2006a. "Comenzaron Las Obras En La Isleta Oeste". March 28. http://www.ellitoral.com/index.php/diarios/2006/03/28/metropolitanas/AREA-01.html.

———. 2006b. "Nuevo Referente Urbano En La Unión de Alem y 27 de Febrero". September 22. http://www.ellitoral.com/index.php/diarios/2006/09/22/metropolitanas/AREA-03.html.

———. 2007a. "Vuelven a Pintar El Mural En Santa Rosa". June 14. http://www.ellitoral.com/accesorios/imprimir.php?id=/diarios/2007/06/14/informaciongeneral/INFO-04.html.

———. 2007b. "Radican Denuncia Penal Contra El Jefe de Las Estaciones de Bombeo". July 13. http://www.ellitoral.com/index.php/diarios/2007/07/13/metropolitanas/AREA-03.html.

———. 2012a. "La Circunvalación Es Una Obra Enorme". May 30. http://www.ellitoral.com/index.php/diarios/2012/05/30/metropolitanas/AREA-04.html.

———. 2012b. "Esperan Aval Para El Nuevo Puerto". July 20. http://www.ellitoral.com/index.php/diarios/2012/07/20/politica/POLI-02.html.

El Matutino. 1992. "La Crecida Es La Segunda Del Siglo. El Gobierno Recomendó Anoche La Evacuanción Total Del Alto Verde Al Considerarlo Zona de Alto Riesgo. Hay Alrededor de 30.000 Evacuados". June 19.

El Orden. 1929. "Se Hallan Completamente Inundadas Las Barriadas Humildes de Las Zonas Bajas de La Ciudad y Desalojados Sus Habitantes". February 28.

———. 1935. "La Creciente Amenaza Nuestros Barrios. Vecinos de Las Zonas Afectadas Están Alarmados: Muchos Comienzan a Abandonar Sus Viviendas Ante La Invasión de Las Aguas Que Alcanzan Ya Una Altura Apreciable En "Campito Viejo"". October 23.

———. 1940. "Nuevamente Se Ha Presentado El Peligro de La Creciente. Ya Hay Familias Desalojadas Por Las Aguas". April 24.

———. 1941. "Todos Los Barrios Bajos de La Ciudad Están Amenazados Por La Subida de Las Aguas Que van Creciendo Lentamente. La Zona de La Costa Del Salado Está Ya Inundada. En Barrio Centenario Las Aguas Avanzan". May 9.

———. 1947. "La Lluvia Agrava Aún Más La Situación de Los Hogares Establecidos En Las Zonas Bajas de Nuestra Capital. El Traslado de Familias". April 5.

Giubellino, Gabriel. 2003. "Rock Solidario Para Santa Fe, Ante Una Multitud En Obras". *Clarín*, May 12. http://edant.clarin.com/diario/2003/05/12/s-02901.htm.

Heguy, Silvina. 2005. "El 56% de Los Argentinos Tiene Antepasados Indígenas". *Clarín*, January 16.
http://old.clarin.com/diario/2005/01/16/sociedad/s-03415.htm.

Jastreblansky, Maia. 2010. "Claves y Cronología de Un Complejo Conflicto". *La Nación*. December 10. http://www.lanacion.com.ar/1332425-claves-y-cronologia-de-un-complejo-conflicto.

La Voz del Interior. 1992. "Cinco Muertos Por La Inundación En Santa Fe", June 23.

Libertella, Mauro. 2010. "Los Que Vinieron Después de Borges". *Ñ Revista de Cultura, Clarín*, September 28.
http://www.revistaenie.clarin.com/literatura/vinieron-despues-Borges_0_341965907.html.

Maggi, José. 2008. "Porque No Hay Sentencia Definitiva". *Página/12*, October 1, Rosario/12 edition.
http://www.pagina12.com.ar/diario/suplementos/rosario/10-15435-2008-10-01.html.

La Nación. 2012. "Malvinas: La Argentina Busca Un Apoyo de La OEA". June 4. http://www.lanacion.com.ar/1478914-malvinas-la-argentina-busca-un-apoyo-de-la-oea.

Noticias. 1990. "Drámatica Situación En La Guardia, Colastiné y Rincón: El Agua Ya Cubre Gran Parte de Alto Verde", February 15.

Notife. 2007. "Censura Contra Los Vecinos de Santa Rosa de Lima". June 4. http://www.notife.com/noticia/articulo/911941.html#.UWCfFDfZrCo.

———. 2011a. "Inauguraron Murales En La Plaza de La Memoria 29 de Abril" May 5. http://www.notife.com/noticia/articulo/1029725.html.

———. 2011b. "La Corte Suprema Decidió Que La Causa Inundaciones Siga Adelante". May 24.
http://www.notife.com/noticia/articulo/1031195.html.

———. 2013. "La Ciudad Se Prepara Para Conmemorar Los 10 Años de La Inundación de 2003". February 28.
http://www.notife.com/noticia/articulo/1077506/zona/1/La_ciudad_se_prepara_para_conmemorar_los_10_anos_de_la_inundacion_de_2003.html#.US_P-zdajqJ.

Nueva Época. 1914. "A Propósito de Las Inundaciones". April 21.

Nuevo Diario. 1973. "Un Verdadero Drama Se Vive En El Oeste de La Ciudad. Corte de Ruta. Incontenible Avance Del Salado. Fueron Evacuadas 80 Familias de Barranquitas. Temor Ante La Posibilidad de Lluvia", May 9.

Página/12. 2003. "Discos: Un Seleccionado Solidario". December 17. http://www.pagina12.com.ar/diario/discos/12-29369-2003-12-17.html.

———. 2007. "Un Mural Muy "Peligroso"". May 13, Rosario/12 edition. http://www.pagina12.com.ar/diario/suplementos/rosario/subnotas/8524-1134-2007-05-13.html.

———. 2008. "No Se Sentará En El Banquillo". May 6, Rosario/12 edition. http://www.pagina12.com.ar/diario/suplementos/rosario/10-13412-2008-05-06.html.

———. 2012. "Se Cerró Período de Pruebas". May 12, Rosario/12 edition. http://www.pagina12.com.ar/diario/suplementos/rosario/10-33611-2012-05-03.html.

Phillippis de, Matias. 2012. "Proponen Que La Circunvalación Oeste Se Denomine '29 de Abril'". *Uno Santa Fe*. September 29. http://www.unosantafe.com.ar/santafe/Proponen-que-la-Circunvalacion-Oeste-se-denomine-29-de-Abril-20120929-0012.html.

Román, Valeria. 2013. "Otra Deuda Del Estado: El Plan Nacional Para Enfrentar Desastres Nunca Arrancó". *Clarín*, April 14. http://www.clarin.com/sociedad/plan-nacional-enfrentar-desastres-arranco_0_901109999.html.

Santa Fe. 1914. "Inundados y Vividores". May 27.

———. 1931. "Se Trabaja Activamente En El Salvataje de Los Inundados de Barrios Oeste y Barranquitas: La Municipalidad Ha Dictado Las Medidas Del Caso y Ha Designado Las Comisiones Encargadas de Los Trabajos Respectivos". May 25.

Tizziani, Juan Carlos. 2013. "Para Evitar Más Dilaciones". *Página/12*, April 18, Rosario/12 edition. http://www.pagina12.com.ar/diario/suplementos/rosario/10-38517-2013-04-18.html.

Torres Molina, Ramón. 2008. "Los Archivos de La Dictadura". *Página/12*, September 8. http://www.pagina12.com.ar/diario/elpais/1-111244-2008-09-09.html.

Union Provincial. 1905. "Las Crecientes y Las Inundaciones". June 13.

Uno Santa Fe. 2012a. "En Santa Fe Aún Nos Quedan Por Erradicar 2.500 Ranchos". February 12. http://www.unosantafe.com.ar/santafe/En-Santa-Fe-aun-nos-quedan-por-erradicar-2.500-ranchos-20120212-0018.html#.

Usborne, David. 2012. "Cristina Fernandez Takes Fight for Falklands to UN". *The Independent*. June 11. http://www.independent.co.uk/news/world/americas/cristina-fernandez-takes-fight-for-falklands-to-un-7834932.html.

Internet

"Acta de Fundación de Santa Fe". 2013. *Parque Arqueológico Santa Fe La Vieja*. http://www.santafevieja.ceride.gov.ar/ActaFundacion.htm.

"American Anthropological Association Katrina Resources — SSRC". 2013. http://asci.researchhub.ssrc.org/Members/admin/resource-lists/american-anthropological-association-katrina-resources.

"An STS Forum on Fukushima". 2013. *An STS Forum on Fukushima*. http://fukushimaforum.wordpress.com/.

Argentina.ar. 2012. "Reforma Del Código Civil y Comercial". *Argentina.ar Portal Público de Noticias*. http://www.codigocivil.argentina.ar/.

Banco Interamericano de Desarrollo. 2002. "BID Acelera Desembolsos Por 1.000 Millones de Dólares Para Programas Sociales Prioritarios En Argentina - Banco Interamericano de Desarrollo". *Banco Interamericano de Desarrollo*. January 28. http://www.iadb.org/es/noticias/comunicados-de-prensa/2002-01-28/bid-acelera-desembolsos-por-1000-millones-de-dolares-para-programas-sociales-prioritarios-en-argentina,516.html.

"Conference Statement from the Second International Conference Early Warning II, 16-18 October 2003". 2003. http://www.unisdr.org/2006/ppew/info-resources/docs/ewcii-Conference-Statement.pdf.

Instituto Espacio para la Memoria. 2012. "Otros Sitios de Memoria". http://www.institutomemoria.org.ar/exccd/otros.html.

"Jorge Prelorán Collection at Human Studies Film Archives". 2013. *Smithsonian National Museum of Natural History*. http://anthropology.si.edu/accessinganthropology/preloran/.

Lasalandra, Michael. 2008. "Twelve Myths and Misconceptions in Disaster Response". *Harvard School of Public Health Now: Biweekly Publication of News and Notices from the Harvard School of Public Health*. February 8. http://archive.sph.harvard.edu/now/20080201/twelve-myths-and-misconceptions-in-disaster-response.html.

Memoria Abierta, Acción Coordinada de Organizaciones argentinas de Derechos Humanos. 2012. "La Dictadura En El Cine". *Memoria Abierta*. http://www.memoriaabierta.org.ar/ladictaduraenelcine/index.html.

Radio Universidad - Universidad Nacional de Rosario. 2010. *Entrevista Completa Con María Langhi 2010-04_30*. www.archive.org/download/MariaLanghi/MaraLanghi2010-04-30-lmdaDocumentalSeguirRemando.mp3.

"Understanding Katrina: Perspectives from the Social Sciences". 2013. *Social Science Research Council*. http://understandingkatrina.ssrc.org/.

Videla Habla Sobre Los Desaparecidos 1979. 2012. Video. http://www.youtube.com/watch?v=EQhY06BZy8c&feature=youtube_gdata_player.

Public records

Concejo Municipal de Santa Fe. 2012a. "Emotiva Conmemoración de La Inundación de 2003 En El Oeste de La Ciudad". April 27.

http://www.concejosantafe.gov.ar/noticia_Emotiva-conmemoracion-de-la-inundacion-de-2003-en-el-oeste-de-la-ciudad_880.html.

———. 2012b. "Santa Fe Tiene Su "Plaza de La Memoria"". August 2. http://www.concejosantafe.gov.ar/noticia_Aprobaron-la-nominacion-de-la--Plaza-de-la-Memoria-29-de-abril--_987.html.

Corte Suprema de la Provincia de Santa Fe, and Corte Suprema de la Nación de la República Argentina. 2007. "Sentencias Varias de La Corte Suprema de La Prov de Santa Fe y de La Nación". http://www.santafe.gov.ar/index.php/web/content/download/124092/614261/file/Sentencias%2023.5.07,%2023.4.08%20y%2030.9.08.pdf.

Gobierno de la Ciudad de Santa Fe. 2008a. *Decreto Publicación de Normativa En Internet*. http://www.santafeciudad.gov.ar/informacion_publica/normativa.

———. 2008b. "La Municipalidad Avanza Hacia Un Sistema Integral de Archivos". November 15. http://www.santafeciudad.gov.ar/noticia/municipio_avanza_hacia_sistema_integral_archivos.

———. 2009. "Principales Características de Planes de Contingencias Ante Emergencias Hídricas". Santa Fe, Argentina: Dirección de Gestión de Riesgos.

Gobierno de la Provincia de Santa Fe. 2005. "A Dos Años de La Inundación Extraordinaria Del Rio Salado, Santa Fe Se Recupera Con Inversión y Trabajo". *Portal de Noticias Del Gobierno de La Provincia de Santa Fe*. April 29. http://gobierno.santafe.gov.ar/prensa/mitemplate.php?idnoticia=22382&mostrarmenu=si&include=noticias_prensa/2005/290405s5.htm&ptitulo=Noticia%20del%20viernes%2029%20de%20abril%20de%202005%20(290405s5.htm)&fechanoticia=&volverurl=&pDescDiaMax=Viernes&intvalDiaMax=21&pDescMesMax=setiembre&A%F1oMax=2005&DiaMax=21&MesMax=09&pdia=29&pmes=04&panio=2005.

———. 2006a. "Sistema Provincial de Archivos (SIPAR)". http://www.santafe-conicet.gov.ar/sipar/.

———. 2006b. *Crea En El Ambito de La Secretaria de Derechos Humanos El Archivo Provincial de La Memoria*. http://gobierno.santafe.gov.ar/sin/mitemplate.php?tiponorma=decreto&anio_norma=2006&fecha_norma=23/10/2006&gestion_dec=0&nro_dec=2775.

Gobierno de la Provincia de Santa Fe, Fiscalía de Estado. 2011. "Publicación de Las Causas Judiciales - Inundaciones Del Año 2003". http://www.santafe.gov.ar/index.php/web/content/view/full/125497/%28subtema%29/%20downloaded%202012-05-03.

Honorable Congreso de la Nación Argentina. 2002. *Conmemoraciones Ley 25633: Institúyese El 24 de Marzo Como Día Nacional de La Memoria Por La Verdad y La Justicia*.

http://infoleg.mecon.gov.ar/infolegInternet/verNorma.do;jsessionid=44CF684D82E5FF986093799DDC716BFA?id=77081.
"Hugo Marcucci - Senador Del Departamento La Capital / Santa Fe". 2012. June 11. http://www.hugomarcucci.com.ar/.
"Información Agropecuaria: Comercio Exterior 2005-2009". 2012. *Sistema Integrado de Información Agropecuaria: Ministerio de Agricultura, Ganadería y Pesca*. http://www.siia.gov.ar/index.php/series-por-tema/comercio-exterior.
Instituto Nacional de Estadísticas y Censos. 1869. "Primer Censo de La República Argentina". Bueno Aires: Instituto Nacional de Censos y Estadísticas. http://www.indec.mecon.ar/.
———. 2001. "Censo Nacional de Población, Hogares y Viviendas 2001 - Provincia de Santa Fe: Población Total Por Sexo e Índice de Masculinidad, Según Edad En Años Simples y Grupos Quinquenales de Edad. Departamento La Capital. Provincia de Santa Fe". Buenos Aires: Instituto Nacional de Estadísticas y Censos. http://www.indec.mecon.ar/.
———. 2005a. "Encuestas Agropecuarias, Serie Histórica: Años 1993-2005." Buenos Aires: Instituto Nacional de Estadísticas y Censos. http://www.indec.mecon.ar/.
———. 2005b. "Los Censos de Población En La Argentina". http://www.indec.gov.ar/proyectos/censo2001/historia/historia2a.htm.
———. 2010a. "Censo Nacional de Población, Hogares y Viviendas 2010". Buenos Aires: Instituto Nacional de Estadísticas y Censos.
———. 2010b. "Censo Nacional de Población, Hogares y Viviendas 2010 - Provincia de Santa Fe: Población Total Por Sexo e Índice de Masculinidad, Según Edad En Años Simples y Grupos Quinquenales de Edad. Departamento La Capital. Provincia de Santa Fe". Buenos Aires: Instituto Nacional de Estadísticas y Censos.
———. 2012. "Encuesta Permanente de Hogares: Tasa de Actividad, Empleo, Desocupación y Subocupación Por Regiones y Aglomerados Urbanos. Serie Histórica de 2003 En Adelante". Instituto Nacional de Censos y Estadísticas. http://www.indec.gov.ar/.
Instituto Nacional del Agua. 2012. "SIyAH: Sistemas de Información y Alerta Hidrológico". http://www.ina.gov.ar/alerta/index.php?alerta=27.
Instituto Provincial de Estadísticas y Censos. 2006. "Cuadro 10.3.p Población Asalariada (excluido Servicio Doméstico) Por Rama de Actividad Según Tipo de Sector - Porcentajes - 2do. Semestre 2006 Encuesta Permanente Hogares (EPH) Continua. Aglomerado Gran Santa Fe. Semestral". Santa Fe, Argentina: Instituto Provincial de Estadísticas y Censos, Gobierno de la Provincia de Santa Fe. http://www.santafe.gov.ar/index.php/web/content/download/38876/198345/file/ISabana-2do.semestre2006-GranSantaFe-R-mparr-09-mar-2007-16.pdf.
———. 2012. "Pobreza e Indigencia En Hogares y Personas Según La Encuesta Permanente de Hogares Continua: Provincia de Santa Fe: 2003-2012". Instituto Provincial de Estadísticas y Censos, Gobierno de la Provincia

de Santa Fe. http://www.santafe.gov.ar/index.php/web/Temas-del-IPEC/Condiciones-de-Vida/Pobreza/Pobreza-e-Indigencia-en-Hogares-y-Personas-segun-la-Encuesta-Permanente-de-Hogares-EPH-Continua.

Ley de Defensa Civil. 1977. Nr 8094. Gobierno de la Provincia de Santa Fe, Argentina.

Ley de Ministerios. 2007. Nr 12817. Legislatura de la Provincia de Santa Fe, Argentina.

Ley de Pacificación Nacional. 1983. Nr. 22924. Gobierno de la República Argentina

Ley Orgánica de Las Municipalidades. 1939. Nr. 2756. Legislatura de la Provincia de Santa Fe, Argentina.

Ley Orgánica de Ministerios. 2003. Legislatura de la Provincia de Santa Fe,

Municipalidad de la Ciudad de Santa Fe. 2009. "'La Feria' Ya Funciona En Facundo Zuviría Al 8000". June 19. http://www.santafeciudad.gov.ar/noticia/feria_funciona_facundo_zuviria_8000.

Municipalidad de la Ciudad de Santa Fe de la Vera Cruz, Compañía Industrial Cervecera S.A:, Colegio de Arquitectos de la Provincia de Santa Fe, and Colegio de Arquitectos de Santa Fe. Distrito 1. 2005. "Bases Concurso Distrital de Anteproyectos 'Diseño Urbano y Paisajístico de Las Isletas Centrales' Avda. Alem y 27 de Febrero". http://www.capsf.org.ar/cad1/concurso_isletas/downloads/Bases_Concurso_Isletas_Alem.pdf.

Ordenanza Municipal Sobre Defensa Civil. 1976. Nr. 7204. Municipalidad de la Ciudad de Santa Fe de la Vera Cruz, Argentina.

Ordenanza Municipal: Creación de La Junta Municipal de Defensa Civil. 2000. Nr. 10548. Honorable Concejo Municipal de la Ciudad de Santa Fe de la Vera Cruz, Argentina.

Ordenanza Municipal: Creación Del Sistema de Defensa Civil. 2005. Nr. 11178. Honorable Concejo Municipal de la Ciudad de Santa Fe de la Vera Cruz, Argentina.

Presidencia de la Nación Argentina. 2010a. "¿Que Nos Representa a Los Argentinos? Elegí Los 200 Símbolos Del Bicentenario". *200 Años Bicentenario Argentino*. http://www.bicentenario.argentina.ar/catalogo/.

———. 2010b. "La Agenda Federal. Un País Con Espacio Para Todos". *200 Años Bicentenario Argentino*. http://www.bicentenario.argentina.ar/foros.php.

Régimen de Reparación Excepcional Por El Desborde Del Río Salado. 2003. Law Nr. 12183. Legislatura de la Provincia de Santa Fe, Argentina.

Reparación Por Inundación - Modifica Ley 12.183. 2004. Law Nr. 12.259. Legislatura de la Provincia de Santa Fe, Argentina.

Secretaria de Cultura, Presidencia de la Nación. 2010. "Casa Nacional Del Bicentenario". http://www.casadelbicentenario.gob.ar/.

Servicio Meteorológico Nacional. 2012. "Servicios Climáticos: Tendencias Observadas En Argentina". *Servicio Meteorológico Nacional de La*

República Argentina. June 13. http://www.smn.gov.ar/serviciosclimaticos/?mod=elclima&id=71.

Multimedia

Alarcón, Sebastian, Juan Altamirano, Javier Bonati, Claudio Cortopassi, and Leonardo Davicino. 2004. *El Agua y La Sangre (Memorias de La Inundación)*. Documentary.

Bersuit - "Otra Sudestada" - La Argentinidad Al Palo En Vivo (DVD). 2010. http://www.youtube.com/watch?v=86UajUeR5aI&feature=youtube_gdata_player.

Birri, Fernando. 1961. *Los Inundados*. Motion picture. Argentina.

Cable y Diario. 2004. *La Lección Del Salado*. Documentary. Santa Fe, Argentina.

Langhi, María. 2009. *Seguir Remando: La Tragedia de La Ciudad de Santa Fe*. Documentary. Argentina.

LT10 Radio Universidad Nacional del Litoral. 2003. *la inundación | voces de una tragedia*. CD. Santa Fe, Argentina: Universidad Nacional del Litoral.

Rabaini, Mariana. 2008. *Vanesa*. Documentary-Ethnobiography. Santa Fe, Argentina.

Santa Fe Documenta-Colectivo de Video. 2003. *Inundaciones*. Documentary. Matecosido Producciones. Santa Fe, Argentina.

———. 2005. *Informe a 15 Meses*. Documentary. Matecosido Producciones. Santa Fe, Argentina.

Solanas, Pino. 1990. *El Viaje*. Motion Picture. Drama. Argentina.

Traffano, Darío, and Fernando Pais. 2005. *Agua de Nadie*. Documentary. Nuevos Espacios Periodísticos, Santa Fe, Argentina.

List of figures

1	Location of Santa Fe Province and Santa Fe City in Argentina	42
2	Map of Santa Fe City	47
3	Costanera Oeste in autumn (2005)	48
4	Costanera Este in summer (2005)	48
5	Municipal Female Traffic Brigade in Downtown (2009)	49
6	*Ranchos* on the Westside (2005)	50
7	Fish catch of the day on the shores of Alto Verde (2005)	51
8	Sunday morning in Barrio Roma (2005)	52
9	*Rancho de paja* on the Coastside (2005)	67
10	View of Santa Rosa de Lima from the railway embankment (2005)	85
11	Graffiti in the abandoned water tower (2005)	86
12	Children *murga* troupe on May 25th (2005)	92
13	Wall paintings at Plaza 29 de Abril (2005)	107
14	*Monumento Homenaje al Pueblo Inundado* at Plaza 29 de Abril (2005)	108
15	Wooden crosses in Plaza de Mayo (2005)	125
16	*Inundados/activists'* memory stone in Plaza de Mayo (2005)	125
17	Commemorating *la Inundación* in Plaza de Mayo on April 29th (2005)	126
18	Street propaganda in the 2005 political campaign overwritten (2005)	130
19	Making memory through street graffiti (2005)	131
20	*Asamblea* of the *inundados/activists* in the Plaza de Mayo (2005)	136
21	"Impunity flat out" (2005)	143
22	"The Flood Makers" (2005)	144
23	Monument at the Alem Avenue (2008)	148
24	Torches' March's post on Facebook (2013)	154
25	Fountain in Parque Oroño with the *Puente Colgante* bridge ca. 1960	161
26	Westside flood embankment, the Salado River and the ring road (2005)	165
27	Checking the state of flooding preparedness on the Coastside (2005)	181
28	432nd anniversary of the foundation of Santa Fe City (2005)	188
29	Family portrait on display in the Great Flood century exhibition (2005)	197
30	Film poster of *Los Inundados* advertising its première 1961	206
31	Trading at the Barter Market in Parque Garay (2005)	226
32	Solidarity Street in Villa del Parque (2011)	230
33	Setting out from the jetty of Alto Verde (2005)	233
34	Excursion with students in the surroundings of La Boca (2005)	239
35	Lake dwellings in Vuelta del Paraguayo (2005)	241
36	Family picture in the Alto Verde 95th anniversary exhibition (2005)	244
37	Reminiscence through photos in the Alto Verde 95th anniversary (2005)	245

Index

accidental community of memory 30, 75-110, 115, 119, 211, 248, 250
accountability 28, 30, 113, 116-119, 128, 138, 151, 157, 174, 183, 248-49 *see also* polity of remembering
adaptability 9-10, 251-255
adaptation 1, 9-11, 34, 251-255
agriculture
    in Argentina 38, 43-44, 52, 56
    in Santa Fe 29, 42-44, 56, 59, 70, 180, 189, 204, 237, 243
Alfonsín, Raúl 36, 39, 123, 168
Alto Verde 25, 44, 47, 50, 51, 66-70, 161, 208, 210-18, 223-24, 231-45
Amit, Vered 10-11, 22, 110
amnesia 15-16, 20, 160, 168-69, 171-74, 217
amnesty 20, 35-36, 160, 171-74
anamnesis 16
Appadurai, Arjun 14, 17, 19, 155, 176
Archetti, Eduardo 52, 58, 199, 203
archives as memory *see* memory as archive
    as research sites 27, 149, 202, 214
Argenti, Nicolas 14, 19-21, 88, 93, 196, 240
Argentina 42
    and colonisation 46, 71
    and demography 37

and economy 39-41, 62-65 *see also* agriculture in Argentina
and migration 38, 52, 53, 57-59, 71
and Peronism 40-41, 53, 56, 59, 61-63, 117, 130, 142-43, 154, 156-57, 188, 213
and poverty alleviation 62, 222-23, 225
and social protest 64, 116-17, 145-46
and memory 33-38
and urbanisation 46, 57-61
as a white immigrant nation 38-39, 57-59
Argentinazo 65, 101
asamblea 134-36, 153, 178, 228
Asamblea Permanente de Afectados por la Inundación 111, 115-16, 124, 134
Auyero, Javier 54, 63-65, 117, 145, 222, 225
Bankoff, Greg 6, 8, 10, 71, 252
Barranquitas 26, 213-17, 224-25, 229-31
Barrio Roma 2, 25-26, 49, 51-61, 77, 84-85, 90, 105-06, 112, 115, 218
barter *see trueque*
Barthel, Stephan 9, 11-12
Basu, Paul 14, 17, 212, 247
Beck, Ulrich 4, 7, 167, 176, 251
Beckman, Malin 4, 8, 254
Bersuit Vergarabat 100-01, 142-43

303

Bille, Mikkel 19, 235
Birkland, Tom 164, 180
Birri, Fernando 89, 91, 96, 101, 205-11, 242
Black Tent 113-16, 121, 125, 131, 135-37, 146
blame game 118 *see also* accountability
Bohlin, Anna 18, 81, 217
Boholm, Åsa 17-18
Booz, Mateo 202-08, 210-11, 242
Borgström, Bengt-Erik 18, 231, 238, 240, 247
botero 69, 232-35, 242
cabecita negra 59
cajonear 183
catastrophe *see* disaster as an object of study
Catena, Osvaldo 228, 230-31
Causa Inundación 132, 138, 144, 158-60, 173-74, 176, 178, 225
Centenario 96, 103, 191, 207, 213-15, 232, 240
changa / changarín 63-64, 202, 235
Christoplos, Ian 4, 10, 254
ciruja / cirujeo 50, 63-64, 79, 83, 122, 220, 230
city of comrades 82-83, 211
Cole, Jennifer 14-15, 19, 191, 212, 217-18, 246, 251
communitas 83, 228-30
community
    altruistic 83, 118
    concept of 8, 10-11, 70, 253-54
    enunciatory 119
    of memory *see* accidental community of memory
    of suffering 46, 83
    resilient 9-10, 180, 255
    therapeutic 83

complex adaptive systems 9
Connerton, Paul 13, 16, 18-20, 82, 87, 147, 167, 217-18, 241, 246, 251
contingency plan
    as artefact of modernity 175-76, 221
    as social artefact of memory and oblivion 30, 177-78, 180, 184
    Santafesinian 109, 139, 172-74, 176-83, 241
    shelved 180-83
contractual exchange 223
creciente 242
Crenzel, Emilio 20, 36
criollo 48, 52, 58-59, 70-71, 169, 203, 208, 250 see also *viveza criolla*
crisis *see* disaster as an object of study
critical event 7, 11, 76, 249
Cromañón discotheque disaster 116, 122
cultural intimacy 39, 143
culture of poverty 10
culture of disaster 10, 252
Dahl, Gudrun 10, 116, 212, 223, 252
Das, Veena 6-7, 116, 242, 249
derecho adquirido 233
desaparecidos 35-36, 116, 157
de Man, Paul 20
Dirty War 34-37, 79, 106, 109, 121, 141, 157, 168
disaster
    aid 78, 104, 226-27
    as objects of exchange *see trueque*
    as objects of memory 221-28
    as objects of morality 210-12, 223, 252

as a contemporary development problem 4-5
as an object of study 5-6
concept of 1, 6-7
and normalisation 251-55
disaster risk reduction (DRR) 4, 9-10, 178-80, 249, 251-55
and legislation in Argentina 169-70
and legislation in Santa Fe 170-71, 174
documentos 134, 136-37, 140, 153, 178
documents as social artefacts 175
driveabout 81-84
embedded remembrance 31, 213, 217-246, 250
emergent citizen groups 117-18
enactment of hybridity 28
escrache 117, 127-29, 141
ethnografiction 200, 205
ethnographic fieldwork 21-29
and insider/outsider 28-29
and interlocutor 28-29
and methodological improvisation 25, 27
classical 22-23
multisited 22
multitemporal 23-24
translocal 1, 23
transtemporal 1, 24
yoyo 24
Executive Unit for the Repair from the Hydrological and Pluvial Emergency 79-80, 128-29, 131, 154, 210, 221, 224
explosion of memory 36
Fabian, Johannes 14, 18-19, 76, 212, 217
familial gaze 103-05

farmers-government conflict 43, 129
Fentress, James 12-13, 16-18, 76, 187
Ferguson, James 4, 22-23, 180, 255
Feria del Trueque see *trueque*
Fernández Cristina 34, 40-41, 43, 117
flood embankments 48, 57, 69, 81-82, 84-88, 122-24, 139, 141, 144, 154, 160, 164-68, 172, 214, 218-221, 240, 246
Flooded Mothers 106, 108-10, 131-32, 152
flood-prone/inundados 29-30, 214, 246, 250-54
Folke, Carl 9, 11-12
forgetting *see* oblivion
Forty, Adrian 21, 24, 196
Foucault, Michel 14, 216
Gaillard, JC 4, 6, 10, 70-71, 253
Gordillo, Gastón 18, 81, 192
Guber, Rosana 34, 37, 39, 59, 148, 156, 169, 183, 247
H.I.J.O.S. 35
habitus 19
Halbwachs, Maurice 12-13, 17-18, 25, 81
Hannerz, Ulf 22-23, 25, 118
Harms, Arne 6, 11-12, 231
Harvey, Penelope 167, 182, 196, 240-41
Hastrup, Frida 6, 10-12, 19, 105, 235, 237
Herzfeld, Michael 39, 143, 236
Hilhorst, Thea 6, 8, 10, 71, 254
Hirsch, Marianne 14, 93, 103
Hodgkin, Katharine 13, 17
Hoffman, Susanna 5-7, 236
House of Human Rights in Santa Fe 116, 135-36, 138, 140, 160

Howell, Signe 23-24
human rights
   in Argentina 33-37, 94, 109, 117, 249
   in Santa Fe 90, 92, 127, 136, 145, 156-57
Hyogo Framework for Action 10, 254
Ingold, Tim 3, 13, 14, 18, 194, 234
intergenerational remembering *see* memory, intergenerational
inundados
   as a social category 3, 30, 84, 103-04, 116, 188, 201-202, 211-12, 252
inundados/activists
   as an ethnographic category 29-30, 111
inundados/victims
   as an ethnographic category 30, 75
isleños / isleros 68-69
Kelman, Ilan 4, 6, 10, 70-71, 253
Kirchner, Néstor 34-35, 40-41, 129
Küchler, Susanne 14, 18-19, 21, 196, 237
La Boca 47, 50, 66, 68, 213-14, 217, 234-35, 237-39, 243
La Tablada and La Nueva Tablada 26, 47, 63-64, 98, 213, 217, 225
lake dwellings 240-41
lieux de mémoire 16, 19, 217
locus
   concept of 18, 217-18, 224, 241
   and memory 246
logic of omission 30, 147, 151-52, 156, 158, 160, 168-69, 180, 183-84, 250
Los Inundados
   the film 89, 101, 205-09, 210-11

   the novella 202-05, 210-11
   the song 209-11
Malkki, Liisa 18, 25, 27, 30, 75, 77-78, 110, 187, 212
March of the Torches, *see* Torches' March
memorial 36-37, 105-06
   absent 195-96, 212
   concept of 16, 18, 82, 87, 217, 246
   ephemeral 21, 196
   of governance 167
   of *la Inundación* 110, 123, 131, 141, 144, 147-151, 152-53
memory
   commemorative, concept of 16
   evocative, concept of 16
   intergenerational 93, 237-40
   presentist model of 17, 169, 251
   reminiscent, concept of 16
   social-ecological model of 11
   and absence 19, 21, 30, 77, 103, 178, 183, 196, 213, 235, 237, 246, 248
   and body 11, 19-20, 34, 87, 102, 146, 246, 248
   and conversation 18, 26, 76-77, 110, 167, 202, 217, 232, 237-240
   and documents *see documentos*; *see* contingency plan
   and documentary film 96-102
   and historicity 12, 187, 192
   and history 17-18
   and methodology 25-28
   and morality 119-20, 248-49
   and music 27, 92-95, 141-42, 209-10
   and museum *see* memory and exhibition
   and photography

family 102-105, 199, 243-45
professional 89-90, 102, 196-99
and place 16, 18-19, 81-88, 105-10, 122-27, 150-51, 180, 184, 192-94, 196, 200-01, 210-12, 217-18, 230-46, 250-51
and social media 111, 123-24, 153-54, 167
and visualisation 18, 30, 87, 96-105, 129, 142-44, 178, 196-99, 205-09
and weather 76-77, 246
as archive 12, 16, 19, 27, 149, 156-160, 177, 180, 183, 197, 199, 207
as artefacts 15, 18-19, 27, 94, 127, 131-37, 154, 160, 175-76, 195-96, 218
as exhibition 37-38, 102, 114, 153, 196-99, 243-45
as graffiti 86-88, 127-31
as hidden and public transcript 151
as infrastructure 160-68
as landscape 14-15, 18, 81, 122-23, 167, 231-37, 247
as law 36, 168-69
as literature 88-91, 133-34, 137, 188, 190-92, 199-205
as narrative 3, 15, 18, 23, 28, 76-83, 88, 91, 94-97, 101-02, 112-16, 118, 126, 148, 156, 184, 187, 192-194, 201-02, 207-12, 214-17, 242, 248
and oblivion, relation between 19-21
as palimpsest 247
as performance 89-95, 101, 187, 210

as testimonial 88-93, 97-102
Memory Archive 157-60
Memory Museum of *la Inundación* 114-15
memoryscape 1, 3, 16-17, 19, 24, 27, 29-30, 33, 37, 42, 70-71, 76, 81, 87, 95, 102, 122, 146, 151, 154, 167, 174, 181, 184, 188, 194, 197, 199, 201, 211-12, 247-51, 255
definition of concept 1, 13-15, 21
memory-work
definition of concept 3, 14
Midré, Georg 212, 252
milieux de mémoire 217
mneme 16
mnemonic resistance 120
monument *see* memorial
morality 155, 203, 211
and entitlement 153, 224, 230, 249
and memory *see* memory and morality
and negative agency 212
and *ressentiment* 119-20, 145-46
morocho, social category of 59, 211, 250
Mothers of the Plaza de Mayo 34, 109, 116, 134, 138, 145
murga 60-61, 91-93, 125, 208, 242
museum *see* memory and exhibition
mythico-history 18, 30, 101, 187-88, 202, 210-12, 250
Nadasdy, Paul 9, 254
Narayan, Kirin 28, 201, 240
narrative
canonised 77-83, 95, 112-16, 118, 126
panels 77
negro as a social category 59, 66, 205, 211, 250

New Argentinian Cinema 206
NGOs 25-26, 30, 34, 41, 60, 62-63, 98, 111, 115, 136, 140, 171, 180, 195, 198, 222, 227, 242, 254
Nora, Pierre 16, 19-20, 34, 217, 251
normalisation of disaster 251-255
Norman, Karin 23
oblivion
    and bureaucratic cycles of exclusion 154-56
    and computer technology 158
    and law 169, 174
    and logic of omission 147
    and memory, *see* memory and oblivion, relation between
    and modernity 20
    and shelved artefacts 183
    as abandonment 149
    as hidden transcript 151
    as repressive erasure 20
    as structural amnesia 20, 217
    of risk 161, 167, 184
    public 216, 218, 246, 249, 253
Olick, Jeffrey 13, 33, 37, 119-20
Oliver-Smith, Anthony 1, 4-6, 8, 21, 33, 71, 75, 83, 118, 211, 236
pampa gringa 58
paradox of the presence of absence 19, 235
Paraná River 1, 42, 44, 47, 50, 68-69, 123, 161-65, 170, 176, 189-93, 200-201, 204, 209, 214-15, 220, 234, 237, 240, 252
Parque Garay 47, 105, 164, 225, 226-28
path dependence 17-18, 250-51
patients of the state 225
Paxson, Margaret 14-15, 18, 81
Peronism *see* Argentina and Peronism

piquetero 63-64, 124
plan 64-65, 221-25
Plaza 29 de Abril 106-10, 131-32
Plaza de Mayo as the scene of protest
    in Buenos Aires 35-37, 116, 126-27
    in Santa Fe City 90, 97, 100, 109, 113, 124-27, 129, 132, 134, 135-37, 141, 153, 196, 213
Plaza España 195-96
political clientelism 54, 145, 155-56
politics of regret 33-38, 71, 151-52, 168, 174, 249, 251, 256
polity of remembering 25, 30, 111-121, 132, 142, 145-46, 174, 201, 213, 248, 250
post-disaster context 11, 21, 111, 154, 157, 176, 180, 192-94, 227, 248
    and compensation 79-80, 104, 116, 119, 126, 128, 132, 137-38, 155, 210, 217, 221, 223-25, 229, 249
    and conflicts over space 227-28
    and social mobilisation 117-20, 122, 145
    and victimisation 116, 119, 145
    defintion of concept 75-76
poverty alleviation *see* Argentina and poverty; Santa Fe City and poverty alleviation
Proceso de Reorganización Nacional (*PRN*) 34-35
process mitigation 180
project mitigation 164
puntero 222, 229
Radstone, Susannah 13, 17
Ramírez, Ariel 209-10

rancho 49-50, 60, 63, 66-68, 85-86, 98, 202-05, 207, 209-10, 219-22, 234-36

Reconstruction Unit *see* Executive Unit for the Repair from the Hydrological and Pluvial Emergency

remembering *see also* memory
- and temporality 16-18
- as memory-work 3, 14
- as social process 7, 11, 14-16
- forms of 18-19
- selective 15, 20, 30, 147, 156, 183, 187, 249

resilience 1, 31, 212, 252-55
- definition of 8-9, 11
- and community *see* community, resilient
- and disaster 8-10
- and vulnerability 8-10
- and memory 11-12, 110, 249
- as policy field 9, 180

ressentiment see morality and *ressentiment*

Reutemann, Carlos 43, 78, 96, 112-13, 121-22, 127, 129, 138, 142-44, 159, 168, 172-74

Revet, Sandrine 6, 10, 12, 118, 180, 182

Riano-Alcalá, Pilar 18, 26, 81, 232, 235

Riles, Annelies 168, 175, 177-78

risk society 176, 251

Robben, Antonius 20, 36, 117

rowabout 26, 232-35

sabalero as a social category 61, 211

Saer, Juan José 200-01

Salado River 1-2, 44, 47, 60, 68, 78, 81, 85, 95, 97-98, 106, 115, 122-23, 132-34, 139, 141, 150, 162-65, 170, 172, 178, 193, 202-04, 207, 214-16, 219-20, 229, 232, 252

Santa Fe City 1
- *Ciudad Cordial* 45-46, 82-83, 211
- and cultural notions of spatial boundaries 59, 65-66, 70-71, 84
- and demography 45
- and economy 45, 54-57, 67
  - informal 63-65
- and flooding 1, 33, 69, 214
- and geography 42, 44, 47
- and immigration 46, 51-52, 57-58
- and poverty alleviation 62-63
- and religion 53
- and spatial stratification 48-51, 59-60
- and unemployment 51
- and urbanisation 57
- and vulnerability 8, 44, 51, 63-65, 70-71

Santa Fe Province 42
- and economic history 42-44, 52-53
- and geography 42, 47
- and poverty alleviation 52

Santa Rosa de Lima 25, 59, 65, 85-87, 90-93, 107-10, 152, 165, 207-08, 213-14, 216-19, 225-26

Sather-Wagstaff, Joy 6, 12, 14, 19, 87, 105

Schramm, Katharina 14, 19, 93, 240

Scott, James 151, 175, 217

Segnestam, Lisa 4, 253

Shaw, Rosalind 14, 18, 19, 20, 169, 217, 247

social protest *see* Argentina and social protest; *see* post-disaster

and social mobilisation
Sørensen, Tim 19, 235
Stølen, Kristi-Anne 52, 58
structural amnesia *see* oblivion as structural amnesia
Talle, Aud 23-24
taskscape 234
testimony 88-91, 97-98, 101-02, 154, 238, *see also* memory as testimonial
Torches' March 115-16, 122-29, 132, 135-37, 141, 153-54, 159, 213
trámite 221, 224
trueque 225-28
Turner, Victor 5, 83
Unit *see* Executive Unit for the Repair from the Hydrological and Pluvial Emergency
Van Der Harr, Gemma 10, 254
vecinal 53-54, 61-63, 66, 112, 180, 207, 228, 242-44, 254
victimisation *see* post-disaster and victimisation

Villa del Parque 25, 47, 82-84, 96, 103, 105, 164-65, 213-14, 217, 219, 226-31
villero as a social category 59
Visacovsky, Sergio 6, 39, 46, 58, 77
viveza criolla 202, 208, 211
Vuelta del Paraguayo 47, 50, 66, 68, 213-14, 217, 240-41
vulnerability 1, 4, 6-7, 9-10, 31, 33, 198, 229, 251-55
    as a policy field 178-80, 184
    concepts of 8
    in Santa Fe City *see* Santa Fe City and vulnerability
walkabout 239
watermark as a metaphor for memory 247
Weszkalnys, Gisa 18, 81, 175, 177
Wickham, Chris 12-13, 16-18, 76, 187
Wisner, Ben 4, 6, 8, 10, 70-71, 206, 208, 253
Wulff, Helena 17, 19, 20, 24, 91, 200-01

Stockholm Studies in Social Anthropology

1. Caymanian Politics: Structure and Style in a Changing Island Society. Ulf Hannerz. 1974.
2. Having Herds: Pastoral Herd Growth and Household Economy. Gudrun Dahl och Anders Hjort. 1976.
3. The Patron and the Panca: Village Values and Pancayat Democracy in Nepal. Bengt-Erik Borgström. 1976.
4. Ethnicity and Mobilization in Sami Politics. Tom Svensson. 1976.
5. Market, Mosque and Mafraj: Social Inequality in a Yemeni Town. Tomas Gerholm. 1977.
6. The Community Apart: A Case Study of a Canadian Indian Reserve Community. Yngve G. Lithman. 1978.
7. Savanna Town: Rural Ties and Urban Opportunities in Northern Kenya. Anders Hjort. 1979.
8. Suffering Grass: Subsistence and Society of Waso Borana. Gudrun Dahl. 1979.
9. North to Another Country: The Formation of a Suryoyo Community in Sweden. Ulf Björklund. 1981.
10. Catching the Tourist: Women Handicraft Traders in the Gambia. Ulla Wagner. 1982.
11. The Practice of Underdevelopment: Economic Development Projects in a Canadian Indian Reserve Community. Yngve G. Lithman. 1983.
12. Evil Eye or Bacteria: Turkish Migrant Women and Swedish Health Care. Lisbeth Sachs. 1983.
13. Women of the Barrio: Class and Gender in a Colombian City. Kristina Bohman. 1984.
14. Conflict and Compliance: Class Consciousness among Swedish Workers. Mona Rosendahl. 1985.
15. Change on the Euphrates: Villagers, Townsmen and Employees in Northeast Syria. Annika Rabo. 1986.
16. Morally United and Politically Divided: The Chinese Community of Penang. Claes Hallgren. 1987.
17. In the Stockholm Art World. Deborah Ericson. 1988.
18. Shepherds, Workers, Intellectuals: Culture and Centre-Periphery Relationships in a Sardinian Village. Peter Schweizer. 1988.
19. Women at a Loss: Changes in Maasai Pastoralism and their Effects on Gender Relations. Aud Talle. 1988.
20. "First we are People...": The Koris of Kanpur between Caste and Class. Stefan Molund. 1988.
21. Twenty Girls: Growing Up, Ethnicity and Excitement in a South London Microculture. Helena Wulff. 1988.
22. Left Hand Left Behind: The Changing Gender System of a Barrio in Valencia, Spain. Britt-Marie Thurén. 1988.
23. Central Planning and Local Reality: The Case of a Producers Cooperative in Ethiopia. Eva Poluha. 1989.
24. A Sound Family Makes a Sound State: Ideology and Upbringing in a German Village. Karin Norman. 1991.
25. Community, Carnival and Campaign: Expressions of Belonging in a Swedish Region. Ann-Kristin Ekman. 1991.

26. Women in a Borderland: Managing Muslim Identity where Morocco meets Spain. Eva Evers Rosander. 1991.
27. Responsible Man: The Atmaan Beja of North-Eastern Sudan. Anders Hjort of Ornäs och Gudrun Dahl. 1991.
28. Peasant Differentiation and Development: The Case of a Mexican Ejido. Lasse Krantz. 1991.
29. Kam-Ap or Take-off: Local Notions of Development. Gudrun Dahl och Annika Rabo (Eds.). 1992.
30. More Blessed to Give: A Pentecostal Mission to Bolivia in Anthropological Perspective. Göran Johansson. 1992.
31. Green Arguments and Local Subsistence. Gudrun Dahl (Ed.). 1993.
32. Veils and Videos: Female Youth Culture on the Kenyan Coast. Minou Fuglesang. 1994.
33. Apple World: Core and Periphery in a Transnational Organizational Culture. Christina Garsten. 1994.
34. Land is Coming Up: The Burunge of Central Tanzania and their Environments. Wilhelm Östberg. 1995.
35. Persistent Peasants: Smallholders, State Agencies and Involuntary Migration in Western Venezuela. Miguel Montoya Diaz. 1996.
36. Progress, Hunger and Envy: Commercial Agriculture, Marketing and Social Transformation in the Venezuelan Andes. Monica Lindh de Montoya. 1996.
37. Shunters at Work: Creating a World in a Railway Yard. Birgitta Edelman. 1997.
38. Among the Interculturalists: An Emergent Profession and its Packaging of Knowledge. Tommy Dahlén. 1997.
39. Shamanic Performances on the Urban Scene: Neo-Shamanism in Contemporary Sweden. Galina Lindquist. 1997.
40. Cherished Moments: Engaging with the Past in a Swedish Parish. Bengt-Erik Borgström. 1997.
41. Forests, Farmers and the State: Environmentalism and Resistance in Northeastern Thailand. Amare Tegbaru. 1998.
42. Pacific Passages: World Culture and Local Politics in Guam. Ronald Stade. 1998.
43. Under One Roof: On Becoming a Turk in Sweden. Judith Narrowe. 1998.
44. Ambiguous Artifacts: Solar Collectors in Swedish Contexts: On Processes of Cultural Modification. Annette Henning. 2000.
45. "The Hospital is a Uterus": Western Discourses of Childbirth in Late Modernity – A Case Study from Northern Italy. Tove Holmqvist. 2000.
46. "Tired of Weeping": Child death and mourning among Papel mothers in Guinea-Bissau. Jónína Einarsdóttir. 2000.
47. Feminine Matters: Women's Religious Practices in a Portuguese Town. Lena Gemzöe. 2000.
48. Lost Visions and New Uncertainties: Sandinista Profesionales in Northern Nicaragua. Inger Lundgren. 2000.
49. Transnational.Dynamics@Development.Net. Internet, Modernization and Globalization. Paula Uimonen. 2001.
50. "Gold is Illusion": The Garimpeiros of Tapajos Valley in the Brazilian Amazonia. Enrique Rodriguez Laretta. 2002.
51. Lucknow Daily: How a Hindi Newspaper Constructs Society. Per Ståhlberg. 2002.
52. Only For You! Brazilians and the Telenovela Flow. Thaïs Machado Borges. 2003.
53. "They Call For Us": Strategies for Securing Autonomy among the Paliyans, Hunter-Gatherers in the Palni Hills, South India. Christer Norström. 2003.

54. "Our Fury is Burning": Local Practice and Global Connections in the Dalit Movement. Eva-Maria Hardtmann. 2003.
55. Species Aid: Organizational Sensemaking in a Preservation Project in Albania. Peter Green. 2004.
56. India Dreams: Cultural Identity Among Young Middle Class Men in New Delhi. Paolo Favero. 2005.
57. Irish Scene and Sound: Identity, Authenticity and Transnationality Among Young Musicians. Virva Basegmez. 2005.
58. Eurocrats at Work: Negotiating Transparency in Postnational Employment Policy. Renita Thedvall. 2006.
59. The Un/selfish Leader: Changing Notions in a Tamil Nadu Village. Björn Alm. 2006.
60. "When Women Unite!" The Making of the Anti-Liquor Movement in Andhra Pradesh, India. Marie Larsson. 2006.
61. Med facit i hand: Normalitet, elevskap och vänlig maktutövning i två svenska skolor. Åsa Bartholdsson. 2007.
62. From Slaves to princes: The role of NGOs in the contemporary construction of race and ethnicity in Salvador, Brazil. Örjan Bartholdson. 2007.
63. Exercising Peace: Conflict Preventionism, Neoliberalism, and the New Military. Mattias Viktorin. 2008.
64. Opening the Orange Envelope: Reform and Responsibility in the Remaking of the Swedish National Pension System. Anette Nyqvist. 2008.

Stockholm Studies in Social Anthropology. New Series.
Published by Stockholm University
Editors: Gudrun Dahl and Christina Garsten

1. Christina Hedblom. "The Body is Made to Move": Gym and Fitness Culture in Sweden. Stockholm 2009.
2. Lotta Björklund Larsen. Illegal yet Licit. Justifying Informal Purchases of Work in Contemporary Sweden. Stockholm 2010.
3. Urban Larssen. Call for Protection: Situating Journalists in Post-Cold War Romania in a Global Media Development Discourse. Stockholm 2010.
4. Katja Sarajeva. Lesbian Lives: Sexuality, Space and Subculture in Moscow. Stockholm 2011.
5. Raoul Galli. Varumärkenas fält. Produktion av erkännande i Stockholms reklamvärld. Stockholm 2012.
6. Gudrun Dahl, Örjan Bartholdson, Paolo Favero and Sharam Khosravi. Modernities on the Move. Stockholm 2012.
7. Erik Nilsson. Conserving the American Dream: Faith and Politics in the U.S. Heartland. Stockholm 2012.
8. Susann Ullberg. Watermarks: Urban Flooding and Memoryscape in Argentina. Stockholm 2013.

ACTA UNIVERSITATIS STOCKHOLMIENSIS

Corpus Troporum
Romanica Stockholmiensia
Stockholm Cinema Studies
Stockholm Economic Studies Pamphlet Series
Stockholm Oriental Studies
Stockholm Slavic Studies
Stockholm Studies in Baltic Languages
Stockholm Studies in Classical Archaeology
Stockholm Studies in Comparative Religion
Stockholm Studies in Economic History
Stockholm Studies in Educational Psychology
Stockholm Studies in English
Stockholm Studies in Ethnology
Stockholm Studies in Film History
Stockholm Studies in History
Stockholm Studies in History of Art
Stockholm Studies in History of Ideas
Stockholm Studies in History of Literature
Stockholm Studies in Human Geography
Stockholm Studies in Linguistics
Stockholm Studies in Modern Philology N.S.
Stockholm Studies in Musicology
Stockholm Studies in Philosophy
Stockholm Studies in Psychology
Stockholm Studies in Russian Literature
Stockholm Studies in Scandinavian Philology N.S.
Stockholm Studies in Social Anthropology N.S.
Stockholm Studies in Sociology N.S.
Stockholm Studies in Statistics
Stockholm Theatre Studies
Stockholmer Germanistische Forschungen
Studia Fennica Stockholmiensia
Studia Graeca Stockholmiensia. Series Graeca
Studia Graeca Stockholmiensia Series Neohellenica
Studia Juridica Stockholmiensia
Studia Latina Stockholmiensia
Studies in North-European Archaeology

Isbn   9789187235269
Tryck Exakta Print AB, Malmö 2020
Stockholm University